S.E.C.R.E.T.S. of the First Ladies, VOLUME II

ALSO BY PASTOR SHIRLEY

S.E.C.R.E.T.S. of the First Ladies, Volume I
(Available at fine booksellers nationwide)

S.E.C.R.E.T.S. of the First Ladies, VOLUME II

By:

Pastor Shirley

"We are <u>PRAYING</u> because our husbands are <u>PREYING</u>"
Bizarre true stories of First Ladies in the church!

Red Pig Media, LLC

S.E.C.R.E.T.S. OF THE FIRST LADIES, VOLUME II. Copyright © 2011 by Pastor Shirley. All rights reserved. Printed in the United States of America. No part of this book may be reproduced or transmitted in any form or by any means, electronic or mechanical, including photocopying, recording, or by any information storage and retrieval system, without written permission from the author or publisher, except for the inclusion of brief quotations in a review. For more information contact Red Pig Media LLC, 926 Haddonfield Road, Suite E131, Cherry Hill, NJ 08002 or at www.redpigmedia.com.

Bible quotations are taken from the King James Version (KJV), the New International Version (NIV), or the Today's New International Version (TNIV) of the Bible. Scripture taken from the HOLY BIBLE, NEW INTERNATIONAL VERSION. Copyright 1973, 1978, 1984, Biblica. Used by permission of Zondervan. All rights reserved. Scripture taken from the HOLY BIBLE, TODAY'S NEW INTERNATIONAL VERSION. Copyright 2001, 2005, by Biblica. Used by permissions of Biblica. All rights reserved worldwide.

Disclaimer
This book is intended as a reference volume for adults only. It is not intended for children. The information contained herein is for informational purposes only. It is not intended as a substitute for treatment prescribed by a doctor or therapist. Neither the author nor the publisher has any liability regarding damage, loss, or injury suffered directly or indirectly as a result of the information contained in this book.

Mention of specific companies, organizations, or authorities in this book does not imply endorsement by the author or publisher, nor does mention of specific companies, organizations, or authorities imply that they endorse this book, its author, or the publisher. Internet addresses and telephone numbers given in this book were accurate at the time of printing. All story content is true and based on actual interviews. Everything else has been changed to protect the identities of the courageous First Ladies who so graciously shared their stories. Names, businesses, organizations, places, events, and incidents are used fictitiously.

As in Volume I, all poems are original works created by my youngest daughter, Gaylene Gordon. All illustrations are original works created by Barbara T. Any resemblance to actual persons, either living or dead, is entirely coincidental. Cover design by Odd Ball Dsgn, Inc.

© 2011 Pastor Shirley

First published by Red Pig Media, LLC
926 Haddonfield Road, Suite E131
Cherry Hill, NJ 08002
www.redpigmedia.com
ISBN 978-1-93-697400-9

Cataloging Data
   Shirley, Pastor
      S.E.C.R.E.T.S. of the First Ladies, Volume II / by
      Pastor Shirley - 1st. ed.
      p. cm.
   Summary: Part two of the highly anticipated follow-up to the blockbuster sensation, S.E.C.R.E.T.S. of the First Ladies, Volume I – Provided by publisher.

ISBN 978-1-93-697400-9
1. Abuse in the church. 2. Man-woman relationships. 3. Signs of abuse. 4. Therapist selection.

This book is dedicated to the memory of my beloved mother,

Addie Kelley

who went on to be with the Lord shortly before this book was published. My mother was my friend, confidante, advice-giver, prayer partner, and one of my most enthusiastic cheerleaders.

She was a blessed and anointed woman of prayer. She taught me the power of divine favor and uncensored praise no matter my situation or perceived adversity. She was an inspiration in my life in myriad ways, which I could never enumerate.

She taught me to always put God first, to never become complacent and to reach for the stars. She taught me to be a praying wife and an interceding mother. She taught me to stand up and be a sanctified role model, even when I would rather sit down and cry. Above all, my mother allowed me to be human.

Mother, I will always keep you in my thoughts and in my heart. I will keep you alive through the memories you and I forged together. I am a highly favored, extremely blessed and totally awesome woman, because I had the most amazing mentor: MY MOTHER!

Mother, I love you dearly and I miss you so very much.

TABLE OF CONTENTS

SECTION ONE

Author Acknowledgements 4
People Are Talking 6
The Meaning Of S.E.C.R.E.T.S. . . . 9
Series Availability 10
Introduction 11
God's Divine Mandate For Me 18
Why I Wrote This Book 23
Why You Should Read It 27
Headlines In The News 33
To The Amazing First Ladies 34

SECTION TWO - CHARACTER ACCOUNTS

Opening Poetic Summation 36

Summer Hamilton,
    Librarian's Assistant 39

Viola Lucas & Sharon Baker-Lucas,
    Housewife & Attorney 49

Maggie Mason,
    Elementary School Teacher . . . 97

Sara Wells,
    Sales Associate, Furniture Store . . 125

Frances Murdock-Washington,
    Vice President of Sales and Marketing . 149

Nettie Proctor,
    Customer Service Manager . . . 159

TABLE OF CONTENTS

Janet Davis & Mary Waters,
  Housewife & Housewife . . . 185
Leta Byron & Mei Li Byron,
  Hair Stylist & Student 227
Rita Morgan,
  Bank Teller 251
Evelyn Norton,
  Domestic 293
Apostle Gina Miller,
  Pastor/Ministry Leader 311
Ending Poetic Summation 337

SECTION THREE - REFERENCE

Forgiveness 345
Verbal & Emotional Abuse 359
Pornography 371
Selecting A Therapist 379
Incest 387
Duties Of A Wife 398
Duties Of A Husband 399
Duties Of A Bishop, Pastor, Elder, Preacher,
  Apostle, & Deacon . 401
Bibliography 403

SECTION FOUR - BOOK CLUB

Book Club Discussion Guide 415

SECTION FIVE - CONTACT

Contact Information 424

Author Acknowledgements

Thank You!

To God Be The Glory For All He Has Done! I thank God, my Heavenly Father, and my Lord and Savior Jesus Christ for divine inspiration in leading me to write the S.E.C.R.E.T.S. Series. To my family, I say thank you for the love, support, and patience that you exhibited during this tedious journey..

- *To my husband, Elder Kenneth J. Gordon Sr.: Thank you for being my greatest supporter, my friend, and my confidant. Because you are secure in who you are, you have allowed me to spread my wings and fly. "So shalt thou find favor and good understanding in the sight of God and man" (Proverbs 3:4, King James Version, KJV). "The just man walketh in his integrity: his children are blessed after him" (Proverbs 20:7, KJV).*

- *To Von Alise, my eldest daughter: Thank you for your commitment, dedication, and unwavering faith in this project. Thank you for the long hours, the sleepless nights, and for your sweet spirit, which you have exhibited over the years as you worked by my side. "Give her of the fruit of her hands; and let her own works praise her in the gates" (Proverbs 31:31, KJV).*

- *To my only son, Ken Jr.: You have been an inspiration and a blessing to this project. Your perception, insight, and ideas have been paramount. "A man's gift maketh room for him, and bringeth him before great men" (Proverbs 18:16, KJV).*

- *To my baby daughter, Gaylene: Your enthusiasm, joy, and contribution to this project have been a blessing sent to me from above. I believe that the unique and in-depth way in which you wrote the poems for the First Ladies stories were truly divinely inspired. God has given you such an awesome and blessed gift of writing. "It is God that girdeth me with strength and maketh my way perfect" (Psalms 18:32, KJV).*

- *To my awesome grandchildren, Valeree, VeNeis, Kenneth III (KT), and Cidnee (who was born on my birthday): You inspire me daily. You illuminate my life and bring a smile to my lips. I thank God every day for the wonderful relationship I have with each of you. "But the mercy of the LORD is from everlasting to everlasting upon them that fear him, and his righteousness unto children's children" (Psalms 103:17, KJV).*

- *To the independent bookstores, radio disc jockeys, and the establishments that have stood behind the S.E.C.R.E.T.S. series, thank you from the depths of my heart. You understood the need to get the word out and the call for voices to be found and heard. Your kindness, cooperation, and belief in this project do not go unnoticed by me or my team as we bring these testimonies to light, and they definitely do not go unnoticed by God. Your effort is not in vain and you will continue to be blessed. "Give, and it will be given to you. A good measure, pressed down, shaken together and running over, will be poured into your lap. For with the measure you use, it will be measured to you"(Luke 6:38, KJV).*

- *Last, but not least, I would like to thank you, the readers, for your interest, time, support, prayers, and for encouraging others to purchase and read these books ☺. Meeting so many of you during book signings, as well as those who sent emails and made phone calls, sharing your testimony and tears and giving your encouragement not only touched my heart but blessed my soul. It has been a delightful experience and I look forward to continuing this journey with you! God is with us all and I pray you continue to allow God to break yokes in your life and for you to take flight and soar. "For I know the plans I have for you," declares the LORD, "plans to prosper you and not to harm you, plans to give you hope and a future" (Jeremiah 29:11, New International Version, NIV).*

People Are Talking

Both men and women should read this book.
--New Jersey

Thank you so much for the gift of your book. My prayer is that your willingness to speak on a subject that has been behind closed doors will set a nation free.
--Florida

It took courage, commitment, and dedication to God to have penned this literary masterpiece. Keep writing for God. Ain't nobody mad but the devil.--Missouri

Whew! What an emotional journey S.E.C.R.E.T.S. has taken me on! From the very first character's story to the last.
--Canada

I visited your website this evening and all I could say is WOW! What an awesome anointing God has poured out upon your life. On behalf of all women, thank you for exposing the S.E.C.R.E.T.S. of being a first lady or just simply a WOG - (Woman of God). May the Father continue to pour out His power upon the works of your heart and hands. This is truly a work that is not in most areas and is greatly needed everywhere.

--Florida

I have found S.E.C.R.E.T.S. to be hard-hitting, riveting, insightful, realistic, raw, and refreshingly (yet brutally) honest. The characters were exceptionally well developed, which made them very relatable and made me experience their emotions in a way that is usually quite unusual for readers to do. You have done an excellent job of addressing the taboo issues that people are usually very uncomfortable discussing and this, in my view, is the first step to change. I also found it extremely commendable that the lessons in the stories were applicable to all societies and cultures. Finally, you have not only addressed these important issues; you have also guided your readers in the direction of help if they so need it.   --Caribbean

What an extraordinary body of work. My eyes remained riveted to each word, each sentence, each paragraph. Once I started reading, I could not put the book down. It was 1:33 am when I finally said light's out for the night. You have skillfully woven an exceptional tapestry of S.E.C.R.E.T.S. revealed. A timely topic. A breakthrough for many, I am sure, and an assurance that these voices are to be heard. I cannot wait for the next volumes to be released. I see this book published in foreign languages. The problems uncovered cross miles and continents, and cultures. This work should be in every library in the country and required reading on college campuses. Thank you for sharing such a wonderful gift.

--Indiana

I am a First Lady living with S.E.C.R.E.T.S. After reading the book I took a long look at my situation and I did not like what I saw. I praise God for revealing the truth to me through the pages of your book. --Texas

I just couldn't put the book down. I was literally reading it at stoplights as I drove to work!
 --California

It is high time someone took a stand for right. This book does not depict the church in a bad way it only confirms God is not pleased with the hypocrisy of the church leaders.
--Pennsylvania

Very eye-opening.
--North Carolina

I've never read anything like this book.
         --Hawaii

Absolutely amazing.
--New York

I believe that many readers may not even realize that they are in abusive relationships until they are able to put themselves on the outside and read the emotional stories in your book. In a nutshell, these stories will be very eye-opening for such persons and may literally save lives. --Jamaica

I'M STILL IN SHOCK! If you are going through your own silent hell with your spouse or significant other and have told yourself that you will not make it through, you are wrong! Purchase this book, grab some tissue and start reading. It will take you from a fantastic Forward, to poems of laughter then onto unbelievable stories of survival   --Maryland

The Meaning of S.E.C.R.E.T.S.

S. ilence
E. ncourages
C. ruelty and
R. eality
E. ventually
T. hreatens your
S. anity

Silence Encourages Cruelty and Reality
Eventually Threatens your Sanity

Don't allow silence to ruin your life.

SILENCE?
NO!

FIND YOUR VOICE!

voice

Series Availability

S.E.C.R.E.T.S.
VOLUME I
2010

Stories 1-10

S.E.C.R.E.T.S.
VOLUME II
2011

Stories 11-21

S.E.C.R.E.T.S.
TRILOGY
2012
Conclusion
of all Stories

Introduction

As a child, I had this romantic fantasy regarding how married people were supposed to act; especially Christian married people. As a result, I often observed the relationship between my parents, as well as those of other married couples in the church, and I paid close attention to the way in which husbands and wives interacted.

When I was 10 years old, I was traumatized by an event I witnessed. At the time, I had no idea of the profound effect that it would have on my life; nor did I realize that the event would send me reeling and in search of the meaning of fidelity and truth.

The pastor of our church, Bishop Burke Robbins, was an outstanding preacher and a great man of God. I was truly mesmerized by him. He was married to First Lady Mae Ellis Robbins and they appeared to be very happy.

Bishop Robbins was the keynote revival speaker at another church in our district, and he requested that the junior choir accompany him. We were to represent our church on the program with a musical selection. Prior to his sermon, Bishop Robbins announced that First Lady Mae Ellis Robbins was ill and could not attend. He asked all the saints who knew the power of prayer to pray for his wife that God would heal her body. He then proceeded to deliver an anointed, power-filled message that had everyone out of their seats shouting and dancing to the glory and honor of God.

We had a good service that night and I was looking forward to returning the following night. I was young, but I loved going to church, especially revivals. My siblings got very upset with me because I always asked my mother to attend church with her. They were afraid that if I were allowed to go, they would also be required to attend. Unlike me, they tried to find reasons not to attend church. The most popular excuse was having a large amount of homework due the following day. Sometimes this excuse worked. Other times, it didn't.
During those days, there were no vehicular laws regarding seat belt usage. For this reason, there were usually three people in the front seat (in this

case, Bishop Robbins, who drove, and two ladies from the church, Sister Lettie and Sister Mary) and as many people as you could fit into the back; in this instance, there were seven children tightly wedged into the back seat. We were returning home after the service when Bishop Robbins said that he was hungry. Because Black people were not permitted to obtain service in the front of eating establishments, we pulled into the back of a restaurant to get a few hamburgers and sodas. The slowing down of the vehicle awakened me, though it wasn't apparent as I kept my eyes closed. For some unknown reason, I did not move nor did I speak. I just lay quietly. However, all of the other children were asleep.

As Sister Mary got out to get the food, Bishop Robbins peered into the back seat. He studied each child intently to ensure we were sleeping. Concluding that we were, he turned back around and proceeded to put his arm around Sister Lettie's shoulder, pull her closer, and kiss her passionately. She objected at first saying that they had to be careful and that the kids in the back might see or hear something. He assured her that he had already checked the children and they were all asleep. However, I was listening and now watching them through mere slits in my eyelids. I was able to open my eyes a tiny bit because my face was partially hidden by the darkness of the night and Sarah Willow's head on my shoulder. Her hair was long and bushy and shielded some of my face, allowing me to easily watch them from my vantage point.

I watched in absolute shock as Bishop Robbins kissed Sister Lettie passionately over and over again, stroked her hair, and aggressively fondled her breasts. He told her he'd enjoyed spending the afternoon with her while her husband had been at work. He then went on to describe some of the highlights of their afternoon tryst, using expletives and vulgar words.

I was absolutely horrified and sick to my stomach! My 10-year-old sheltered mind could not believe the language my pastor was using. I literally had to pinch myself to keep from shouting "Ooowee, the bishop is using bad words!" Sister Lettie did not deny his account of the afternoon, break away, or slap his face; so I surmised that Bishop Robbins was telling the truth.

The kissing and fondling went on for a few more minutes, then Sister Lettie loudly whispered, "Stop! Stop! Scoot over! Here comes Sister Mary!" To disguise what they'd been doing, Bishop Robbins put his hands back on the steering wheel while Sister Lettie hurriedly adjusted her blouse and quickly finger-combed her hair to tame any stray locks. Just as Sister Mary came fully into view, they began talking about the church service.

Sister Mary got back into the car with the food while talking a mile a minute about the revival service. She was completely oblivious to the sexual tension between Bishop Robbins and Sister Lettie. Sister Mary told the pastor how much she'd enjoyed his sermon and that she was so blessed that he was her pastor. She also told him that she was looking forward to returning the following night. Bishop Robbins chuckled and glanced from Sister Lettie to Sister Mary. He then replied, "Praise the Lord, Sister. Kingdom work sure does take a lot out of you." Changing the subject, he said, "Pass me one of those burgers. I'm hungry as a bear."

Approximately 15 minutes later, we arrived at my home and Sister Lettie said, "Wake up; it's time for the Crawford Girls to get out." I got out of the car rubbing my eyes and yawning as if I was just waking up. I took my little sister by the hand, waved good night, and walked into the house. My legs were so wobbly that they felt like jelly, making it difficult for me to walk. As I prepared for bed, there were so many images and thoughts bombarding my mind; I couldn't comprehend them all. I felt faint, almost like I was in a daze, and I felt nauseated. I was so confused. I felt as if I was caught up in a horrible nightmare, except I wasn't sleeping—I was fully awake!

More than anything else, I felt a deep sense of hurt and disappointment. There was so much pain in my little heart that it felt as if it would break into a million pieces. I had never experienced anything like it and it hurt so very much! My young spirit was crushed and wounded. Even my dreams of being saved were now shattered because I was shaken to my very core.

At 10 years old, I didn't understand *why* I was hurting. I didn't understand that the deep pain stemmed from the way in which I'd been raised. My seven siblings and I grew up in a very, very strict Pentecostal household. We were "PKs"—preacher's kids. My father was a minister and my mother was an evangelist/missionary and a highly anointed woman of God. We all attended Bishop Robbins' church.

Bishop Robbins was a *very strict* teacher and interpreter of the Bible. Per his teachings, we were not permitted to wear pants, shorts, makeup, wigs, go to the movies, listen to secular music, or even play ball, among a plethora of other things. All of these things were considered sinful and we were certainly going to hell if we engaged in any of them. It seemed to me that everything that was fun or just plain interesting was wrong. Our entire life revolved around what the church deemed we could and could not do. We went to school, church, and back home.

My mother even had to speak to our principal to explain why her daughters would not be participating in gym class. Because of the physical activities, the school required all students to dress in shorts and a t-shirt for gym class. My parents felt that it was wrong for females to wear shorts, so we were not permitted to wear the gym uniform. As a result, my sisters and I received an "F" in gym every year. Thank God our other grades were good enough to balance out the gym grade.

Being unable to wear pants, shorts, or makeup made us peculiar and distinctively different. Regardless of the weather—sunshine or snow—we were only permitted to wear skirts and dresses. We stood out from everyone else and were subjected to a great deal of whispering behind our backs and cruel comments from other students. Oh, how we longed to be what we called "normal"! We wanted to dress normally, like everyone else, and go to dances and to the movies.

As I prepared for bed and crawled under my blankets trying to find a comfortable position in which to fall asleep, I continued to think about what I had seen. Then I became extremely angry. *How dare he?! How double dog dare he?! How could Bishop Robbins preach about wearing pants and makeup and he was committing adultery?!* In fact, he seemed to come up with new things *we* couldn't do weekly! The burdens were so heavy that his loyal members could barely carry them. Because of *his* rules and *his* interpretation of the Bible, his poor congregation was burdened, restricted, and separated from the rest of the world. But he obviously didn't apply all those rules to his personal behavior. It was apparent that he was picking and choosing the rules that he obeyed. *"Thou shalt not commit adultery"* was undoubtedly a rule that he was blatantly ignoring.

Bishop Robbins was a married man and he never failed to remind us that he was saved, sanctified, Holy-Ghost filled, and fire baptized, and he spoke in tongues as the Spirit of the Lord gave him utterance. He was a preacher of the gospel and he was well known and respected as a holy man of God. Yet, he was romancing Sister Lettie, who just happened to be his wife's best friend and right-hand woman.

Though only a child, I was wise and intuitive beyond my years. I knew that what I'd witnessed was wrong; and it was wrong in a very big way. This experience rocked the very core of what I had been taught and, therefore, what I believed. I knew that adultery was wrong. Before this incident, it had never occurred to me to question any of the church rules or teachings. Now I had questions zooming in and out of my head at warp speed. Were there different rules for preachers? Did God give preachers of the gospel special privileges? Could they commit adultery and keep on preaching as if they had done nothing wrong? What about the heaven and hell that Bishop Robbins preached so much about? Could someone commit adultery and still preach the gospel?

I wanted to tell someone about what I had seen and heard. As I racked my brain, I couldn't think of one person I could tell in safety. Times were different then and kids were seen and not heard. No one would take the word of a 10-year-old girl over the word of a renowned preacher. If I told someone and it got back to Bishop Robbins, what type of repercussions would I suffer as a result? Or worse, what if it got back to my parents? Would they believe me? Would they be mad at me for not telling them first? Would they be negatively affected in some way?
Questions. Sleepless nights. More questions. More sleepless nights. This burden was just too heavy for me; after all, I was only 10 years old. Many nights I thought about what my pastor had done and I wished I had been asleep like all the other kids.

This conundrum began to affect my performance at school because I found it increasingly difficult to concentrate on anything other than what I had witnessed. During class, I rarely listened to my teacher but watched the video of my pastor in my head; it seemed to run on a continuous loop, over and over. Instead of interacting with my friends or siblings, I often just went off by myself to ponder the relationship between what I'd seen and what I'd been taught. Time after time, the two didn't match up, which left me even more frustrated. I finally had to face the facts that there was no one I could tell. This was not something kids discussed. Kids just didn't talk about grown-up issues in those days.

The next Sunday, our pastor and his wife were invited to our house for dinner. I watched Bishop Robbins closely and stealthily to see if he showed any outward signs of sinning. I was so young and naive that I really believed there would be some outward sign to indicate that he had been committing adultery. His nose hadn't grown since I'd last seen him. There was no mark on his forehead. His eyes didn't even twitch. Realizing there was absolutely no difference in my pastor's outward appearance, I lost interest in him and switched my thorough examination to the First Lady.

My thoughts were running rampant, causing me to stare openly at Sister Robbins. Did she know that her husband was carrying on a torrid affair with her best friend? Maybe she did know but was putting on a happy face for other people? My little heart ached for her. Poor, poor Sister Robbins. I wanted the pain in my heart to stop and I wondered, if I told her, would the pain end? I wanted to shout what I'd witnessed from the rooftop, letting the words tumble from my mouth in fast succession. I wanted to tell her while looking my pastor in the eye. I wanted to see his shock…then his denial. I wanted to see my First Lady slap his face repeatedly for humiliating her, disappointing God, and causing me so much confusion and pain.

However, this was merely wishful thinking. I dared not utter one single word for fear that my life would end that day. My parents would have been mortified had I blurted out my story, and I had no wish to anger or embarrass them.

I turned my attention back to my pastor. I wondered how he could sit there scarfing down my mother's fabulous food, laughing and talking about God as if he were living according to the rules he advocated for his members; as if he had not committed adultery. (For all I knew he was probably still committing it.) How could he act so normal when he was no longer saved? At least I didn't think he was. In light of his normalcy,

I was even more confused. I'm not sure what I expected, but it certainly wasn't this normal acting, laughing, eating man and his normal acting wife.

In my later years, I would understand the scriptures, *"man looks on the outward appearance, but God looks on the heart"(I Samuel 16:7)* and *"let the wheat and tares grow together" (St. Matthew 13:30).*

About a year later, my father started pasturing his own church about 40 miles from our home. I was elated because I no longer had to see Bishop Robbins, listen to him preach, or see his girlfriend, Sister Lettie, jump up and down shouting "Preach Bishop! Preach the Word!"

The knowledge of my pastor committing adultery with Sister Lettie stirred something within me, sending me on a mission of truth and accountability. I am compelled to stand up for righteousness! I am compelled to cry loudly and spare not! Sin must be exposed wherever it is found regardless of the title or position of the perpetrators!

First Ladies everywhere, regardless of race, color, or creed, know that you are not alone. Know that God can and will heal your hurt.

God's Divine Mandate for Me

Some years ago while attending a summer camp meeting, the Lord impressed upon me to write a book—but not just any book. This book would be used to expose the devil, and help thousands of women in the church who were abused, victimized, and trapped by their circumstances. God then revealed the name of the book to me.

It was **S.E.C.R.E.T.S. OF THE FIRST LADIES.** I subsequently shared this new revelation with my family. As I sat in awe and amazement, I thought of the many First Ladies with whom I was personally acquainted or with whom I had counseled over the years:

Women who love the Lord. Women who were suffering and keeping dreadful secrets. Women who were in need of an intervention and inner spiritual healing.

As I sat and contemplated the gargantuan task before me, I realized that there were also people in the Bible who stopped to deliberate when faced with a situation that seemed insurmountable.

When the angel of the Lord told Mary that she would give birth to our Lord and Savior, Jesus Christ, she tried to figure out how this could possibly occur since she had never known a man. Mary became confused as she desperately tried to envision the **"HOW."**

When God told Abraham that Sarah would have a baby in her old age, he, too, became confused as he tried to envision the **"HOW"** because Sarah was well past the childbearing age.

When God told Moses to lead the children of Israel out of Egypt, Moses said that he could not possibly undertake this most important task because he had a speech impediment. Moses struggled with the **"HOW"** as he struggled with his limited vocal abilities.

Now I, too, was confused as I tried to envision the "**HOW."**

How was I going to write a book? I didn't know the first thing about writing a book and I had no idea where to even begin. However, I knew in my heart that I had to follow the leading of the Holy Spirit. I could not disobey God, nor did I want to disappoint Him. He had been too merciful and faithful to me. I thought about God's word in Acts 5:29 KJV, which reads, *"We ought to obey God rather than men."*

As I thought about the book and its subject matter, I felt a spirit of foreboding and apprehension settle upon my shoulders because of the ramifications that were sure to accompany the book's release. Some church members were sure to brand me a traitor for exposing the ugliness in the church. Others would certainly accuse me of 'man-bashing.' Still others might insist that I had made everything up. Did I really want to be the focus of this type of scrutiny? Did I really want to be the topic of Sunday morning sermons? Did I really want to deal with all the controversy that would surely surround the release of the book?

As these thoughts raced through my mind, I decided to encourage myself through the word of God. II Timothy 1:7, reads,

For God hath not given us the spirit of fear, but of **power**, *and of* **love**, *and of a* **sound mind**.
2 Timothy 1:7

Joshua 1:9, reads, *"Be strong and of good courage; be not afraid, neither be thou dismayed: for the Lord thy God is with thee whithersoever thou goest" (KJV).*
Isaiah 58:1, reads, *"Cry aloud, spare not, lift up thy voice like a trumpet and show my people their transgression and the house of Jacob their sins" (KJV).*

WOW! What a revelation! I realized that although God did not promise us that the journey would be easy, He did promise to accompany us every step of the way. My answer now was "YES!" "Yes, Lord I will obey your word."

YES Lord!

As I deliberated further, I realized that I had observed my first lesson on infidelity in the church at the tender age of 10 years old. This experience caused me to question everything I knew about right and wrong.

As my search for First Ladies began, I soon realized that I did not have to look very far. I already had a captive audience. These women are not on street corners or in seedy motels. They are not in back rooms or in the shadows of crack houses. They are not raggedy, uneducated, or deprived. Though these women come from varied and diverse backgrounds, they can be found right in our churches, temples, mosques, synagogues, and state houses. They can be found in our cathedrals, chapels, parishes, tabernacles, and sanctuaries. They are the wives of bishops, apostles, reverends, and evangelists. They are the wives of prophets, pastors, rabbis, and deacons. They are the wives of presidents, governors, senators, and mayors. They are community activists. They associate with foreign dignitaries. They teach our children. They care for our elderly. Regardless of their background, they all have several things in common.

- THEY ARE HIDING TERRIBLE SECRETS
- They are experts in the art of disguise.
- They are highly skilled at bruise concealment.
- They live a life of pretense and fabrication.
- Their lives are shrouded in hypocrisy.
- They live by a code of silence.
- They often smile on the outside while crying on the inside.

These women have carried the guilt and accepted the blame for the predatory acts of their spouses. The sad thing is that many people know that these things are occurring in the church, but for misguided reasons, these **S.E.C.R.E.T.S.** have remained hidden behind closed doors as the First Ladies emerge wearing big, crystal-encrusted hats, elaborate gem-adorned designer suits, and false, painted-on smiles.

Well, the jig is up! The covers are being yanked off! Sin is being exposed! These valiant women are tired of the pretense and hypocrisy. They are tired of the lies and deceit. They are tired of standing by while men and women masquerading as church leaders bamboozle innocent churchgoers. First Ladies are suffering all over the country and are in need of inner healing. This nationwide suffering-in-silence phenomenon has resulted in the publishing of the divinely inspired **S.E.C.R.E.T.S.** series.
After years of interviews, travel, research, and burning the midnight oil, I am ecstatic to announce the completion and publication of

S.E.C.R.E.T.S. OF THE FIRST LADIES, VOLUME I AND S.E.C.R.E.T.S. OF THE FIRST LADIES, VOLUME II.

To God Be the Glory! Some of the stories were extremely painful to hear and even more so to pen, as the First Ladies' heartbreak, pain, tears, and yes, even fear, were sometimes overwhelming. But in spite of this, these women persevered and shared their stories. Again, to God be the Glory!

S.E.C.R.E.T.S. OF THE FIRST LADIES, VOLUMES I AND II are part of a three-part, tell-all series that chronicles 21 First Ladies and the mental, physical, and psychological abuse they have endured. The **S.E.C.R.E.T.S.** series is a therapeutic reference volume for First Ladies, their spouses, their congregations, their families, and their friends. The graphic nature of some of the stories does not glorify the misdeeds of those who are preying on the very people whom they are meant to serve, nor does it "man-bash." Rather, it challenges real men and women everywhere to stand up and renounce the behavior of these abusers, who have used their power and influence to prey on the trusting members of their congregation for personal and immoral gain.

Take a
STAND!

Finally, **S.E.C.R.E.T.S. OF THE FIRST LADIES, TRILOGY,** the third installment of the series, contains the conclusions of the stories from Volumes I and II. **TRILOGY** chronicles the journey, starting where the First Ladies began and ending where they are now.

This highly anticipated final edition of the series will be available in 2012.

<u>Why I Wrote This Book</u>

I wrote this book for all the women who are or have been silent victims of abuse, whether emotional, physical, sexual, verbal, or mental! Abuse in any form negatively impacts the victim's life for many years, and often for an entire lifetime. As a result, women who feel trapped in relationships are left with gaping emotional scars. The cover-up begins, and usually before they even realize it, they are held captive by the code of silence for the rest of their lives.

I wrote this book to expose the devil and to encourage First Ladies everywhere to break the code of silence! You are in denial! **WRONG IS WRONG!** This is true whether you physically engage in abuse or allow it to happen by remaining silent! Your silence will not make it right. But rest assured, it will make *you* wrong! In the pages of this book, you will find that you are not alone. Your situation is not an isolated case and there are many others who can relate to what you are going through. More importantly, you will find that there is help for you.

The devil is using the house of God as his safe haven while perpetrating holiness and openly engaging in atrocious acts. Silence is the devil's best friend. It lies at the core and very existence of First Ladies everywhere, regardless of ethnicity or religious affiliation. Under the umbrella of the church, the Silent Giant has given consent and birth to deception, infidelity, homosexuality, drunkenness, incest, pedophilia, pornography, physical abuse, mental and emotional cruelty, among many others. These scandalous deeds are detailed in the Bible in Galatians and are referred to as works of the flesh:

> [19] *Now the works of the flesh are manifest, which are these; adultery, fornication, uncleanness, lasciviousness,*
> [20] *Idolatry, witchcraft, hatred, variance, emulations, wrath, strife, seditions, heresies,*
> [21] *Envyings, murders, drunkenness, revellings, and such like: of the which I tell you before, as I have also told you in time past, that they which do such things shall not inherit the kingdom of God (Galatians 5:19-21, KJV).*

Please understand that the graphic nature of several of the stories is *not* intended to entice the reader but to accurately describe the horror that these First Ladies encounter on a daily basis. Unfortunately, their experiences cannot always be sugar coated or packaged into a neat little box in order to protect the "delicate ears" of the Christian world. Because I have chronicled the stories as they were told to me, leaving out *none* of the explicit details, the Christian world did not want this book to be published and is consequently in an uproar! Be that as it may, the truth of the matter is that these women are hurting, their world is sometimes ugly, and their experiences are all too often bizarre, graphic, and may sometimes even seem inconceivable.

This book is about saved, sanctified, spirit-filled women who love the Lord and who are suffering greatly in silence. In most cases, the spouses of the First Ladies have perpetrated the horrifying actions described. Yes, you read correctly—their husbands! Men who are community leaders and public officials or who hold titles such as preacher, pastor, bishop, apostle, deacon, lay member, minister of music, etc.

One of the reasons the First Ladies' suffering is so great is because **NO ONE SPEAKS OPENLY ABOUT OR EVEN ACKNOWLEDGES THE EXISTENCE OF THESE TYPES OF PROBLEMS WITHIN THE REALM OF THE CHURCH!** The subject has always been and remains taboo. These women feel that they have no one to turn to for help. They wear masks of happiness to hide the guilt, humiliation, and shame that they experience daily. They smile on the outside while crying on the inside. They shout "Amen" at the appropriate times and clap their hands on cue. They often hide behind big, elaborate hats and glittering suits. The hat is a part of their disguise and makes it easier to keep their masks in place. These women have become great pretenders and masters of lying, deceit, and disguise. They have played the happy, supportive wife for so long that some have chosen to block out the unpleasant parts of their life and instead live in a fantasy world. Unfortunately, this action only compounds their misery like interest accruing on an investment. However, in this sad case, the only dividends paid are low self-esteem and one or more forms of abuse.

THE MASK MUST BE REMOVED!
THE YOKE MUST BE DESTROYED!

The enemy is counting on your silence, which he has destined for your spiritual demise. While you remain silent, some of our most prominent leaders have gone astray and fallen victim to the enemy's attack. The truth is that silence gives consent. You have been silent for far too long! **WAKE UP!** The Bible declares in Romans 13: 11-12, 14 (KJV), *"And that, knowing the time, that now it is high time to awake out of sleep: for now is our salvation nearer than when we believed."*

Some First Ladies declined to share their stories, believing that by the simple act of verbalizing the appalling, and often violent, details of their private lives, they would in some way be committing a sin against God and their spouses. Instead, they have decided to do and say nothing. They've chosen to continue living by the code of silence, which not only controls their entire lives but also smothers them in its ever-consuming need for additional lies and deceit.

I will never forget some years ago when my older children were in junior high school, my family and I attended a church that was also attended by a petite woman whom we called Sister Jessica. She was a really pretty woman who was also on fire for the Lord. She was married to a large, unsaved man who thought it was his right to beat her on a regular basis. She came to church Sunday after Sunday with bruises all over her face and arms and sometimes one of her eyes was swollen shut. Each Sunday, she cried to the pastor and asked for direction saying that she was afraid for her personal safety and didn't know how much more she could take. The pastor and his wife told her that she could not be saved if she left her husband and that she had to stay, pray, and wait for God to deliver her. Sister Jessica's beatings got increasingly worse as evidenced by the numerous bruises crisscrossing the parts of her body that could be seen. She eventually became so angry and bitter that she backslid and left the church. After several more vicious beatings, she finally left her husband. She was angry with God and blamed Him for not caring enough about her to deliver her in her time of need.

Sister Jessica's situation is a graphic illustration of the skewed teachings that many women have received in their churches. **FIRST LADIES, YOU DO NOT HAVE TO ENDURE HORRIFIC SITUATIONS AND BRUTAL ACTS OF VIOLENCE IN ORDER TO BE A CHRISTIAN!** To garner respect from others, you must first love and respect yourself! This simply means you must take care of you! After all, there is only one you. God does not want you to be mentally and physically abused. He does not want you to be humiliated and betrayed. You are not an old dishrag to be used and carelessly tossed aside. You are precious in the eyesight of God.

Stop waiting for a sign! If you're waiting for a voice to come to you in a dream, WAKE UP! Too many of us are looking for some outward revelation to give us permission to leave a bad situation. Stop thinking that God is trying to teach you something.

IT'S TIME FOR YOU TO RELEASE YOURSELF!

Know this! God loves you. He sees your pain! He sees your tears! He sees behind your big hats! He sees behind your practiced mask of happiness and support! He sees behind your expensive suits. He sees behind your false, pasted-on smiles. In I Samuel 16:7, *The Bible states that man looks on the outward appearance, but God looks on the heart.* God is Jehovah El Roi, *"The God who sees me."* There is no circumstance of which God is unaware. He's just waiting on you to find the voice He gave you!

Why You Should Read It

*Y*ou should read this book because it could save both your natural and spiritual life. It will assist you in recognizing where to draw the line and bolster your courage when setting personal boundaries. Additionally, it is my hope that this book will be a revelation and even a new beginning for you.

WE NEED MORE FIRST LADIES LIKE ABIGAIL IN THE BIBLE! Abigail's story can be found in I Samuel 25:1-42. Abigail was an intelligent and very beautiful First Lady who took a stand against the wrong perpetuated by her husband, Nabal. Had Abigail remained silent and simply followed Nabal's lead, she would have been instrumental in the death of her entire household.

Abigail's story begins some months earlier when David and his men were in the wilderness of Maon hiding from Saul. They came upon Nabal's shepherds tending thousands of sheep and goats. David took it upon himself to protect the shepherds and flocks from thieves and instructed his men to form a wall of protection around them both day and night. During the entire time that Nabal's shepherds were in the wilderness, they were not attacked or mistreated, nor were their possessions stolen.

Several months had passed when David heard that Nabal was shearing his sheep in Carmel. Since it was customary during sheep-shearing season to share meat with family, friends, neighbors, and strangers, David called ten of his men and instructed them to go to Carmel and speak to Nabal on his behalf. He was very specific in his instructions to his men, telling them to greet Nabal with respect, good tidings, and to remind him that it was David's men who had protected his shepherds and flocks in the wilderness. Realizing that it was possible that Nabal had not heard of him, he also instructed his men to tell Nabal to confirm his good deeds with his shepherds who had been assigned to watch his sheep in the wilderness. After this, David told his men to ask Nabal for whatever food he could spare for himself and his men.

Nabal's response was not as expected. Instead of providing David and his men with food, which he clearly had in great abundance, Nabal staunchly refused, saying that he was not going to give food that he had prepared for his family, friends, and neighbors to someone whom he had never even heard of.

David's men returned and conveyed all that Nabal had said. David became angry because his good deeds were being repaid with selfishness and stinginess. He told his men to arm themselves for war. Taking 400 men with him, and leaving 200 men behind to guard his possessions, he set out to kill every man in Nabal's household.

As soon as David's men left Nabal's hall empty-handed, Abigail's trusted servant hurried to her chamber to report all that he had just witnessed. He also told her how David's men had protected their flocks for months in the wilderness.

Abigail knew that her husband was being unreasonable, petty, and that he was making a huge mistake. Because of his wealth and position, he thought he was above Jewish customs, established laws, and common courtesy. She knew that her husband was wrong and she could not sit in silence and do nothing. This man, David, had protected their flocks, both day and night, and all he asked for in return was a little food. He wasn't even asking to be paid for his service. Though it would be easier to do nothing and let the chips fall where they may, Abigail chose to take a stand for righteousness. She jumped up and quickly instructed her servants to prepare food to be sent to David and his men. Abigail had 200 loaves of bread, two bottles (whole skins) of wine, five sheep, which had been butchered and dressed for cooking, five measures of parched corn, 100 clusters of raisins, and 200 cakes of figs loaded on donkeys. She told her servants to go on before her, but that she would surely follow.

As she made preparations to follow on her own donkey, she decided not to inform Nabal of her actions, knowing that he would surely forbid her to do it as he was so caught up in his own supposed position of importance. She decided that she would tell him upon her return when the food had already reached its destination. She knew that her decision would make her a target for Nabal's considerable anger, but she could not just sit back and do nothing. Taking no action to rectify a situation after being informed of the circumstances is agreeing and giving silent consent. The Bible says *"To him that knoweth to do and doeth it not, to him it is a sin."* She couldn't do that! She would not assist her husband in this travesty of justice against a man who had shown them only tremendous kindness.

As Abigail traveled to meet David, she saw him coming toward her with a large number of men. Upon reaching him, Abigail jumped down off her donkey and bowed low to the ground.

Master, may I have permission to speak?

She asked for permission to speak to David and then told him that she'd had no knowledge of her husband's actions, but that after being apprised of the situation by her servant, she'd made haste to bring food for him and his army. Abigail then began to prophesy to David. She told him not to avenge himself on Nabal. She told him that God would keep him safe because he was going to be the King of Israel and his enemies would be cast out like stones from a sling.

David received her word, acknowledging that God had surely sent her to him. He told Abigail to go in peace as he would not attack her household. Upon returning to her home, Abigail found Nabal partying and quite drunk. Knowing that he would make no sense of her words in his current state, she decided to wait until the morning, when he would be sober, to tell him of her actions and how she had saved their household from certain death. When morning came, she told her husband about the food she had given to David and his men. Upon hearing this, Nabal's heart immediately stopped and he became paralyzed. The Lord struck Nabal dead 10 days later.

What if she had done nothing even though she knew that her husband was wrong and was making a big mistake? What if Abigail had maintained her silence and not allowed the Lord to use her? She would have been just as guilty as her husband, though she was not the one who had denied David's request. She would also have shared in his punishment. But Abigail chose to take an aggressive stance. She stepped from behind her husband and obeyed the voice of God. She did what she knew was right.

Some of our leaders are wrongly exploiting God's people and hiding behind the veil of the church. Per Jeremiah 23: 1-4 (Today's New International Version, TNIV):

> [1] *"Woe to the shepherds who are destroying and scattering the sheep of my pasture!" Declares the Lord.*
>
> [2] *Therefore this is what the Lord the God of Israel, says to the shepherds who tend my people: "Because you have scattered my flock and driven them away and have not bestowed care on them, I will bestow punishment on you for the evil you have done," declares the Lord.*
>
> [3] *"I myself will gather the remnant of my flock out of all the countries where I have driven them and will bring them back to their pasture, where they will be fruitful and increase in number.*
>
> [4] *I will place shepherds over them who will tend them, and they will no longer be afraid or terrified, nor will any be missing," declares the Lord."*

Some of our leaders' only focus is the money they can get from their members. But, the Bible says in St. John 10:11-13 (TNIV) that Jesus is the good shepherd who truly cares for the sheep, unlike the hireling (preacher, pastor, bishop, apostle, deacon, lay member, rabbi, minister of music, etc.) who cares nothing for the safety and wellbeing of the sheep but only for the amount of money he can get from the sheep.

> *^{11} "I am the good shepherd. The good shepherd lays down his life for the sheep.*
> *^{12} The hired hand is not the shepherd and does not own the sheep. So when he sees the wolf coming, he abandons the sheep and runs away. Then the wolf attacks the flock and scatters it.*
> *^{13} The man runs away because he is a hired hand and cares nothing for the sheep.*

In Isaiah 56:10-12 (TNIV), the Bible describes how the leaders lack understanding, are lazy, and lay around sleeping and indulging in activities in an attempt to sate their appetites.

> *^{10} Israel's watchmen are blind, they all lack knowledge; they are all mute dogs, they cannot bark; they lie around and dream, they love to sleep.*
> *^{11} They are dogs with mighty appetites; they never have enough. They are shepherds who lack understanding; they all turn to their own way, they seek their own gain.*
> *^{12} "Come" each one cries, "let me get wine! Let us drink our fill of beer! And tomorrow will be like today, or even far better."*

The Bible states in Genesis that the wife is the helper of her husband.

> *^{18} And the Lord God said, It is not good that the man should be alone; I will make him an help meet for him" (Genesis 2:18, KJV).*

First ladies, you are his helpmeet. Help your spouse watch and pray. Warn him when you see danger on the horizon. Please understand that this book does not suggest, nor is it intended to in any way, that you should usurp your husband's authority. God made your husband the head and he is your covering. Since you are his helpmeet, you must do your job. However, if he refuses to heed your warning and advice, do not accompany him on the ride over the cliff! SAVE YOURSELF!

FIRST LADIES, ARE YOU AWARE THAT:

- You might be a partner, co-conspirator, or accomplice in crime?
- By remaining silent about wrongdoing, you are giving your consent and approval?
- God will hold you accountable for your actions *and* your silence?
- Your silence might be hurting others who are following and believing in your ministry?
- God is calling you to take a stand against sin regardless of the identity or title of the perpetrator?
- It is wrong to exploit God's people or any other people?

FIRST LADIES, DO YOU REALIZE:

- How strong, beautiful, and intelligent you are?
- That *nothing* and *no one* is worth the loss of your self-esteem, your self-respect, your self-worth, or your soul?
- That a physical push, a verbal put-down, and even the use of foul language directed at you are all forms of abuse?
- That "to love, honor, and obey" does *not* include abuse in any form?
- That God loves you dearly and wants to put an end to your suffering?

Please understand, the stories shared by the 21 courageous women do not constitute the content of the entire book. The remainder of the book deals with scripture and God's desire to restore and heal these women from their pain, and it provides information that enables understanding of their problems, where to go for help, how to select a therapist if needed, and even step-by-step instructions on forgiving the most heinous offenses and offenders.

Headlines in the News

Preachers Gone Wild!
Immorality in the Pulpit!

- *Pastors of mega churches caught in homosexual scandal.*
- *Bishop beats wife. . . police summoned.*
- *Pornography ring discovered in church basement.*
- *Pastor commits adultery resulting in children outside of marriage.*
- *Renowned pastor exposed himself to teenage girls.*
- *More priests admit to sexually abusing young boys.*
- *Pastor commits incest with daughters and granddaughters.*
- *Etc, etc, etc.*

Headlines such as these graphically illustrate just how relevant this book is. Someone must take a stand against the wrong being perpetrated under the veil and perceived safety of the church. Someone must take a stand against Christians who are leaders in the church and community who hold such titles as bishop, apostle, pastor, elder, reverend, minister, and deacon.

Sadly, these are not isolated cases. This type of ungodly behavior has permeated our churches for years. No one, and I mean NO ONE, is talking about it. Instead, the church world has chosen to deal with this crisis by embracing the "ostrich mentality" -- sticking it's head in the sand and hoping this ugliness will just go away.

SIN MUST BE EXPOSED AND CONFRONTED!

Someone's silence is allowing other women to be victimized.

Where? Who? When? Who knew?
First Ladies. That's Who.

To the Amazing First Ladies,

Please pray with me that God will bless the courageous women who selflessly shared their incredible stories and that He will bless the thousands of women who will read the **S.E.C.R.E.T.S.** series. I pray that God will minister through this work He has laid on my heart and through this powerful series, these things will be accomplished.

- Sin will be confronted and denounced
- Church members will stop supporting preying leaders
- Yokes will be broken
- Repentance will prevail
- Marriages will be mended
- Courage will be embraced
- Boundaries will be established
- Inner healing will commence and
- A NATION WILL BE SET FREE!

II Chronicles 7:14, KJV will be the beacon by which a new nation shall live. *"If my people which are called by my name shall humble themselves, and pray, and seek my face, and turn from their wicked ways; then will I hear from heaven, and will forgive their sins, and will heal their land."*
It is only then that we can say, as Jesus said in St. Luke 13:12, *"Woman thou art loosed."*

Section 2

Character Accounts

Chapter 10

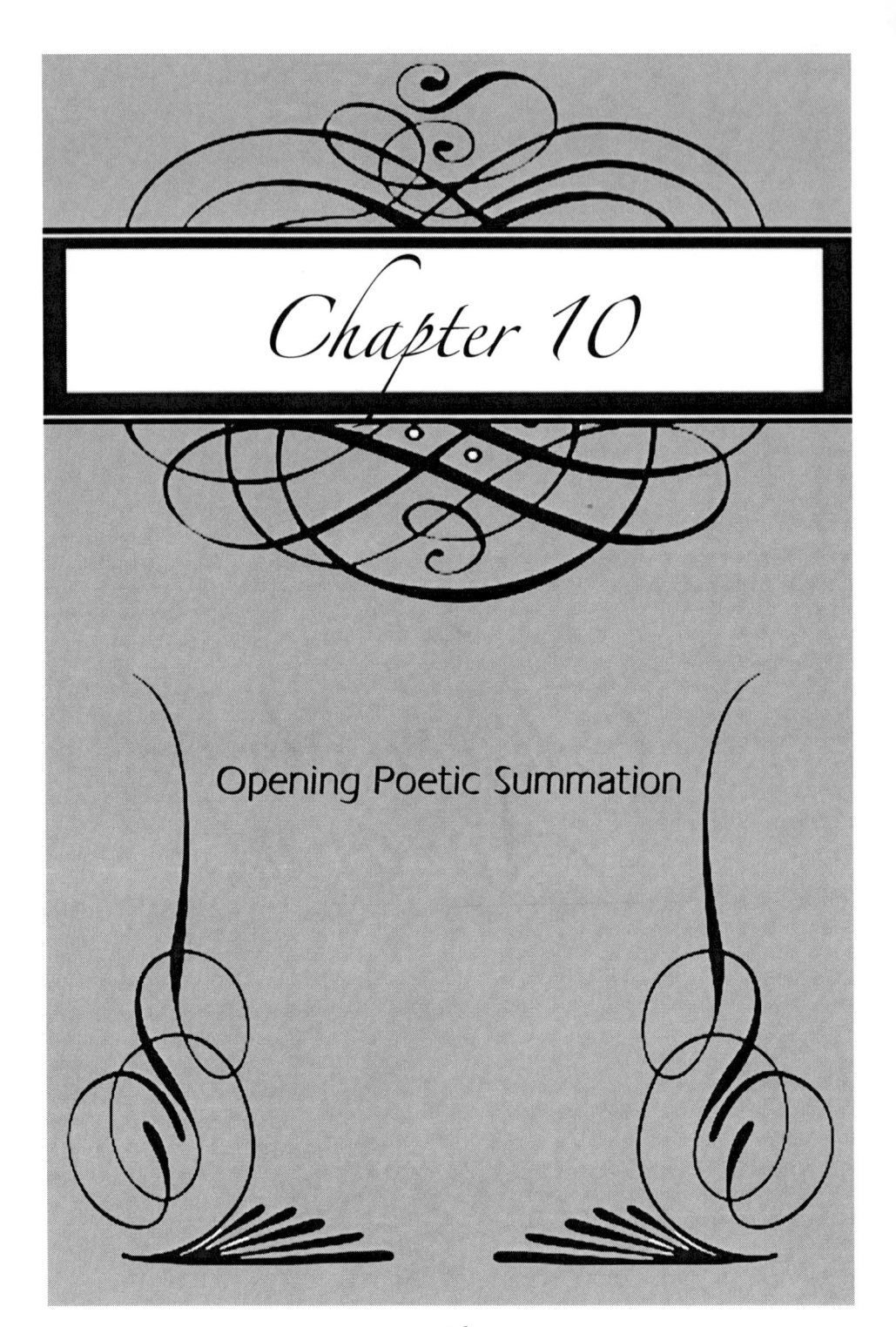

Opening Poetic Summation

Opening Poetic Summation

Come,
Sit down
and I will tell you a tale
Of love, trust, shattered innocence
and tragic betrayal

Love is a strange
 and powerful thing
It comes, it goes,
and it can very well sting!

It is wonderful to celebrate
and can make you rejoice
Or harden your heart
and make you regret your choice
It can melt your emotions
Like sunshine's warm rays
Or cast you into long,
Dark, depressing days.

For a First Lady,
Life is a stage
In which she shows no pain
She is a consummate actress
Never cracking
Under the force of the strain
Her smile is pasted,
But it never appears false
She practices iron-willed self-control
No matter the cost

Inside a fire rages,
Burning hot and bright
She will not allow her secrets
To come to light
No matter what the situation
Or the case
She exudes kindness,
peace, and grace.

You turn the pages,
and read their plight
What emotions
Do their experiences ignite?
Please allow me to
Introduce to you,
The amazing First Ladies
of S.E.C.R.E.T.S. Volume II

Chapter 11

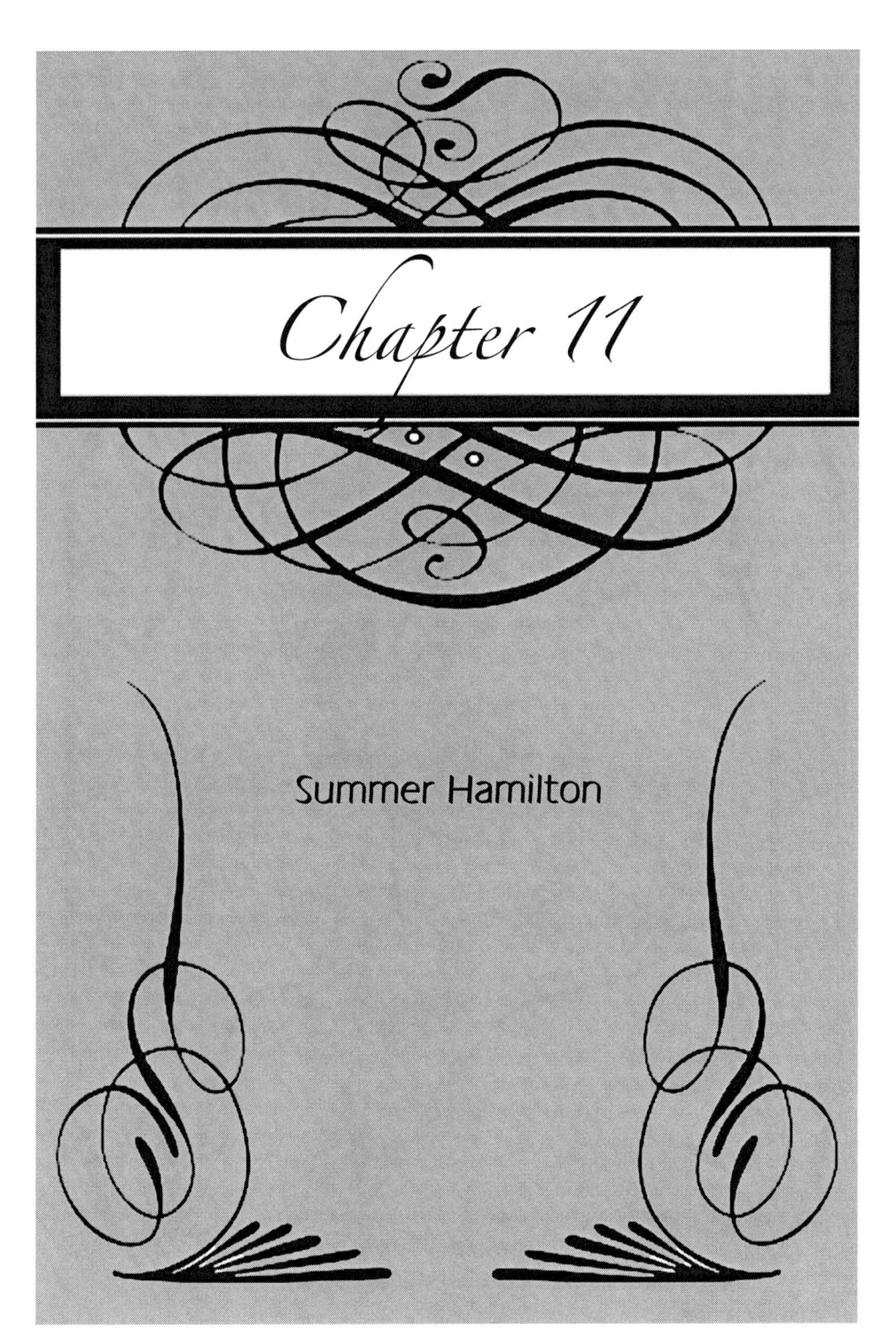

Summer Hamilton

S.E.C.R.E.T.S. VOLUME II by: *Pastor Shirley*

Summer Hamilton
26 Sandstone Court

Summer Hamilton

Summer…

Is silence really golden?
When you keep it,
to whom are you beholden?

Does a face really resemble a mask?
Maintaining a smile
Being its most difficult task?

And when does anger
begin its slow simmer?
Is the result an EXPLOSION
or a glimmer?

As shots rang out
In the soft blue afternoon
You realize the sky is not blue
But shaded gray with gloom…
And doom

S.E.C.R.E.T.S. VOLUME II by: *Pastor Shirley*

*S*ummer Hamilton is a mousy, passive woman who loved God, her family, and her children.

She is employed as a librarian's assistant and the job is perfect for her docile personality. When not helping patrons, she enjoyed immersing herself in the wonderful world of books. She taught her children to read at a young age, and they, too, loved to read.

Summer was a great worker in the church and she could always be found cooking, selling candy, or having car washes with her five children in order to help to generate funds for the church treasuries. On holidays and special occasions, she staged elaborate programs and plays, complete with detailed costumes, which she sewed for the participants. The children were also required to learn speeches commemorating the occasion. It was always a huge success.

Summer's old, beat-up white station wagon was always filled with kids. Her five children, plus as many as she could fit, would pile out of the car on Sunday mornings in time for Sunday school. She was never too busy to pick up a child needing a ride to church. She often went from house to house in her neighborhood asking parents who did not go to church to allow their children to attend church with her. In addition to all of this, Summer and her children cleaned the sanctuary, bathrooms, kitchen, and offices. She also ensured that the pastor's office had fresh water and towels on Sundays. She was always smiling, never seemed to have any problems, and praised God at church as if it were her last chance to do so.

Summer was married to Minister Mark Hamilton. He was a man of average height, build, and looks; neither attractive nor unattractive. He was neither a riveting preacher nor a passive one. He was just an average preacher and was also average in every other way.

Though at church he appeared to be a family man, he wasn't as involved with the children as Summer would have liked. Invariably, the kids rode with Summer in the old beat-up station wagon, while he was alone in his shiny black truck.

Summer Hamilton

Summer was an intensely private person. As a result, it was months before anyone even knew that Minister Hamilton had left her for another much younger woman with no kids and that they'd moved in together. Both of them kept coming to church as if nothing had changed. It wasn't until Deacon Jason had seen Minister Hamilton out with his girlfriend and told his wife that the word got out.

The old saying "tel-a-phone, tel-a-graph, and tel-a-woman" was certainly true in this case. The news spread throughout the church in a matter of hours. The pastor of the church, Elder Carson, hadn't even been aware of Minister Hamilton's new living arrangements until the church gossip mill had begun to churn. Pastor Carson immediately scheduled a meeting with Minister Hamilton. After confirming that the gossip was indeed true, he informed Minister Hamilton that he would not be preaching for a while because he needed to get his family life together and get right with God. To Pastor Carson's supreme astonishment, Summer never said one word to him. She must have told God, because she didn't utter a single word about it to anyone else. She just kept hauling the kids around, cooking dinners, and praising God in church.

Summer had not seen Minister Hamilton in over a year, during which time he had not sent one penny in child support for his five children. Initially, Summer was afraid that she would not be able to support her large family by herself. However, she kept paying her tithes and God miraculously stretched her meager salary. Though she didn't have a great deal left over, her bills were paid and the children were clothed and fed.

One sweltering day in August, Minister Hamilton showed up out of the blue to talk to Summer. She was in the kitchen with two other church members, Sister Beckett and Sister Cruz, frying chicken and fish for the dinners that they were selling to raise money for the church building fund. Minister Hamilton asked Summer to step out into the hall so that he could speak to her privately. She turned and asked Sister Beckett to watch the food, and then she followed him out to the hall. Once outside, Minister Hamilton said, "Summer, I made a mistake and I'm ready to come home now." Though his opening statement lacked sincerity, Summer continued to listen anyway. "Everybody makes mistakes. Surely you are not going

S.E.C.R.E.T.S. VOLUME II by: *Pastor Shirley*

to punish me for one mistake?"

"What about Linda?" Seeing the look of surprise on her husband's face, Summer continued. "Yeah, I know her name. You even have a baby with her. You left me and your children without so much as a backward glance and moved in with her. You have been gone for over a year and during that entire time you haven't sent one penny to support your five children. What about that, Mark? How can we possibly talk about getting back together when we haven't dealt with what split us up to begin with?" Despite the humiliation that Summer had endured in silence, there was no anger or resentment in her voice as she spoke to her husband.

"I can't make you any promises about Linda and the baby," he answered noncommittally.

His nonchalant answer hurt her, but she refused to let him see it. "If you aren't sure you're going to stay with me and the kids, I think it's better you stay where you are. When you come home, you have to be sure that it's me and your five kids you really want. I don't want you to disrupt the kids' lives by coming home and then leaving again. When you're sure you want your family, we'll be ready to take you back."

Minister Hamilton got extremely angry and his facial features took on a crazed look. "If I want to come back now, I WILL!"

Summer had been married to Minister Hamilton for over 10 years and knew first hand that he was prone to violent physical outbursts. Realizing that he was working himself into a fit of anger, Summer calmly said, "Look, I'm not going to stand in the church and argue with you. I have more cooking to do in order to be ready to sell the dinners by 5pm. I'll continue to pray for you." She then turned and walked back into the kitchen to help to get the dinners ready by the deadline.

About 20 minutes later, unbeknownst to Summer, Minister Hamilton quietly reentered the kitchen. He stood for a moment in the doorway glaring at Summer. She actually seemed happy as she cooked and chatted with the other ladies. The longer he stood there observing her happiness, the angrier he became; the angrier he became, the more irrational he became. When he began pacing back and forth in front of the doorway, his movement got the attention of the women in the kitchen. They immediately stopped talking and began watching him in stunned silence. He was mumbling incoherently as if holding a conversation with some invisible person, and his voice was getting louder and louder. He began gesturing wildly and the volume of his voice escalated into screaming. His eyes rolled to the back of his head. Then his head rolled back, remaining there for a few tension-filled seconds. When he raised his head again, the look in his eyes could only be described as deranged and maniacal—or even demon possessed.

To the ladies' utter shock, Minister Hamilton took out a gun and began waving it wildly. Even Summer had never seen her husband like this before. She knew that he was prone to violence, but this was something altogether different. As she watched his increasingly psychotic behavior, she felt the icy tongue of terror lick up her spine and clutch her heart in a stranglehold. Breathing became increasingly difficult as she tried to keep her fear in check and focus on finding a peaceful solution. With Mark waving a gun and acting like a certified lunatic, moving even one inch seemed like a death wish. The other women must have felt the same way as evidenced by their immobility and terrorized expressions. They didn't even move to turn off the stove when the chicken began burning and the smoke detector began screeching its alarm throughout the kitchen.

Sister Joy pulled into the parking lot and entered the sanctuary through the back entrance. She was always late and hoped that the other women were not angry with her and still needed help with the dinners. But she just had to catch that JC Penney shoe sale and she'd found just the right pair to wear with her dress on Sunday. As she hurriedly walked down the hall in the direction of the kitchen, she smelled something burning and she heard someone yelling. She could also hear the smoke detector incessantly bleating its shrill alarm. Oh my goodness! Sister Joy thought. I hope the church kitchen ain't on fire! And what is all that yelling about?

She rushed around the corner and stopped dead in her tracks. Minister

S.E.C.R.E.T.S. VOLUME II by: *Pastor Shirley*

Hamilton was waving a gun and the three women in the kitchen were obviously scared to death. Summer was facing the kitchen door and instantly noticed Joy's arrival. With a barely perceptible shake of her head, she informed Joy not to enter the kitchen. Joy was in shock, but not to the degree that she couldn't move. She slowly backed around the corner and stood still, afraid to even breathe. Since Mark's focus and ranting was on Summer, he noticed her slight movement and bellowed, "Who's there?" as he whirled around to face the door. Seeing no one, he faced his wife again. "Whatchu lookin' at Summer? Huh?"

Summer replied in a quivering voice, "I wasn't looking at nothing." Summer had been praying from the moment she saw Mark pacing in the doorway. Now she prayed for Joy's safety and that her deranged husband hadn't seen her. She desperately hoped that she would be able to get help, and that it would arrive before something awful happened to her or one of the other women in the kitchen.

Mark walked to Summer and peered into her face. "What do you mean 'nothing'? So now I'm nothing?? Well, I've got news for you! I AM SOMEBODY! Don't you dare call me nothing. You best keep your eyes on me," he said pointing to his chest. "I am the head of this family, even if I was gone for 20 years. ME! Not you! Didja got that?"

Summer was so terrified that she no longer trusted her voice and merely nodded. She wanted to tell him that she hadn't been referring to him, but dared not try to explain. The pot containing the chicken now had black smoke billowing over the top and the acrid smell of burning food permeated the air. Mark seemed not to notice and not one of the women dared open her mouth to bring it to his attention.

Joy ran all the way to her car and, once there, locked herself inside and called the police on her cell phone. She waited in her car for them to arrive. Though she wanted to be of more help, she dared not reenter the church without the police. She hoped and prayed that they would arrive before something terrible happened. She heard the siren and the screeching of the tires as the police car made its way through the city toward the church. Hurry! She thought. Please hurry!

Then she heard them. The gunshots pierced the calm of the afternoon. Pandemonium erupted inside the church and screams pierced the air. Oh my God! Please…NO!!! Don't let anybody be hurt! Sister Joy thought. By now, black smoke was billowing out of the windows at the back of the church and the air filled with the smell of burning food and grease. Sister Joy saw the police car pull into the church parking lot and she jumped out of her car and waved the police officer down. She told him that she'd heard gunshots from inside the church. The police officer threw the car into park, and called for backup, a fire truck, and an ambulance. He then jumped out of his car and ran into the church with his gun raised.

To find out what happened to Summer and Minister Hamilton, be sure to read S.E.C.R.E.T.S. of the First Ladies, Trilogy. Available soon in a bookstore near you.

Chapter 12

Viola Lucas
Sharon Baker-Lucas

S.E.C.R.E.T.S. VOLUME II by: *Pastor Shirley*

Viola Lucas
215 Sussex Street

Viola Lucas

50

Viola Lucas and Sharon Baker Lucas

Sharon Baker-Lucas
1762 Somerset Circle

S.E.C.R.E.T.S. of the First Ladies by: *Pastor Shirley*

Viola...

Never would have thought
To comprehend or to detect
That one so quiet
Was the one to watch or suspect.

The rumblings of greediness
Niggle at your brain

As you weigh the cons
Against what you can gain.

Sharon and Viola...

Can you scoff, laugh,
Or even cackle?
Can you imagine
The harsh feel of this shackle?

Oh yes...
What a tangled web we weave
When we nurture power
From another's emotional need...

Viola Lucas and Sharon Baker-Lucas

Senior Pastor Richard Lucas is an extremely good-looking man. He is approximately six feet tall with skin the color of caramel, and has a youthful, trim build. He has what many Black people refer to as "good hair" and he is always immaculately dressed. In addition to his good looks, he is quite the charmer. People are naturally drawn to him not only because of his looks, but also due to his boyish grin and outgoing personality.

He is also a con man and a skilled manipulator who has no problem getting people to do whatever he wants. His reputation for bouncing checks precedes him. Merchants in town no longer accept his personal or church checks and they never extend credit to him. Because of his poor money management skills, he constantly drains all of the church treasuries, thereby subjecting the members to "marathon offering raising sessions" every Sunday. One member reported that they were made to endure over three hours of collecting the offering until Pastor Lucas got exactly the amount he wanted. Pastor Lucas referred to it as his "special offering."

Sister Viola Lucas is the polar opposite of her husband in every way. He is outgoing and extremely good looking; and she is quiet, homely, and positively ugly. He is a flamboyant, stylish dresser; while she has absolutely no fashion sense whatsoever and her clothes never seem to fit properly. Pastor Lucas' eye wear is trendy and fashionable; Viola's glasses sport ridiculously thick coke-bottle lenses, and oversized, unattractive frames that would be much better suited to a man than a woman.

Viola always walks two steps behind Pastor Lucas and usually with her head bowed demurely. She acts as if she is happy just to be allowed in his presence. Her husband is in complete control of everything and neither her children nor the church members ask her opinion on or permission for anything. It's almost as if she doesn't exist. Everyone bypasses her and goes directly to Pastor Lucas because his word is law.

People always whispered behind their backs as to why in the world he married her. How they managed to stay together all these years was also a great mystery. However, they both chose to get married and stay married because it suited them to do so. Certainly not because they were in love.

S.E.C.R.E.T.S. VOLUME II by: *Pastor Shirley*

You see, Pastor Lucas purposefully chose Viola because she was ugly and completely uninspiring. He had never encountered anyone as unattractive or as passive as she. Viola was perfect for what he envisioned and he wasted no time dating her and asking her to marry him. He knew that he was extremely good looking and that any number of women would have jumped at the chance to become his wife. But he decided that he needed a wife who would be so happy to be with him that she would do anything he asked of her. This included management of the household, discipline of the numerous children he knew he would one day have, and, most importantly, turning a blind eye to what he referred to as his "extracurricular activities." He knew that he would one day pastor a church and he wanted lots of sons so that they would follow in his footsteps.

From the beginning of his marriage, he had no intention of confining himself to his quiet, homely wife—and he never did. He often patted himself on the back for choosing Viola as his wife. Not once in all their years of marriage did she ever mention his infidelity. So as a reward for being a good wife, he allowed her to be seen in public with him and he slept with her regularly. He had to admit though that he'd sometimes thought about making her put a bag over her head during sex. Sex with her was for breeding purposes only. He knew that he would have handsome sons because he had been told that he had the more dominant genes. He had been mostly successful. Of their 12 children, sadly, only two looked just like her. The others either looked like him or they only had traces of Viola—luckily for them. Now that her childbearing years were behind her, he made it a point to have sex with her only twice a year—Christmas and her birthday.

Viola was indeed happy to be with Pastor Lucas. To this day, she could not believe he had chosen her. Viola's other three sisters—Claudia Joy, Rebecca, and Tracy—were all pretty girls. She couldn't understand why she wasn't pretty like them. Viola often heard her mother and father refer to her as "Viola the smart one" or "Viola the quiet one." They never referred to her as the pretty one. As a result, she came to grips with her unappealing appearance at a very early age.

When Richard Lucas and his family visited her church, she thought he was the best looking man she had ever seen in her entire life. She knew that he was single and a preacher. What she would give to be Mrs. Richard Lucas! But she knew that someone as good looking as he would never even glance in her direction. Viola reined in her fantasy and kept these thoughts to herself for fear of being laughed at by her sisters. When Richard asked Viola out to dinner a few days later, Claudia Joy, the most beautiful of her sisters, jumped in front of her and said, "You musta got our names mixed up. I'm sure you thought *my* name was Viola, but it's not. It's Claudia Joy. I'm sure it was me you wanted to ask out." Viola just dropped her head and said nothing. She expected Claudia Joy's insensitive remarks to be true. But Richard surprised everyone when he replied, "No. I didn't get the names mixed up. I want to take Viola out to dinner." He looked past Claudia Joy and directly into Viola's eyes. She felt dizzy and thought for sure that she was going to faint dead away.

After a whirlwind courtship, they were married. Viola pinched herself often just to keep her hold on reality. Whenever people saw them together, she knew that they wondered why he had married her. But, she didn't care. *She* was Mrs. Richard Lucas and that was all that mattered. *She* was the mother of his children. Though she had no say in the raising of the children, the management of the church, or anything else for that matter, she was married to the most handsome man alive and she was the First Lady of the church. She would do anything to protect the ministry and her First Lady status.

****

Pastor Lucas had been pastoring for over 35 years, and he and his wife had a very large and talented family. They had seven sons and five daughters, all of who attended his church. As far as Pastor Lucas was concerned, there were only two vocations worthy of his precious sons; they could either become preachers, or they could become musicians, or better yet, they could become both! The ongoing joke among the church world was that if God didn't call one of his sons to preach, PASTOR LUCAS WOULD!

Pastor Lucas had gotten older and though he wouldn't readily admit it, he

S.E.C.R.E.T.S. VOLUME II by: _Pastor Shirley_

was definitely beginning to feel his age. All that tomcatting around over the years had taken its toll on his stamina. Pastor Lucas was grooming his eldest son, Richard Jr., to take over the ministry when he was ready.

Over the years, members came and went on a regular basis. With the exception of his own family members, rarely did a family come to Pastor Lucas' church and remain for a year or more. Pastor Lucas didn't really care about that because his large family did a great job of inviting visitors to the church and participating in weekly fundraising programs. He also kept a steady flow of evangelists who ran revivals on a regular basis.

****

If all the members who had once attended Pastor Lucas' church could be located and surveyed, their stories would all be surprisingly similar. If they gave freely in the offerings and paid their tithes regularly, everything was fine. In fact, Pastor Lucas treated them royally, taking them to dinner and bestowing sought-after committee titles upon them. However, if they reduced the amount of their offerings or stopped paying tithes, the dinners were brought to a screeching halt and they were stripped of their titles. The royal treatment was reserved for generous givers of offerings and payers of tithes only!

He *required* his members to furnish the previous years' w-2 forms to the finance officer, one of his sons, to ensure that they were paying the correct amount of tithes. He also *required* them to pay 15% tithes on the gross amount and advised them to go to personnel at work and have that amount direct deposited into the church account, which Pastor Lucas then promptly withdrew. He explained that the extra 5% was to be given to the glory and honor of God and that they should be happy to do it. Pastor Lucas made it clear that he expected them to be generous in their giving.

When Brother Atkins questioned the 15% tithes requirement during a church business meeting, 50 pairs of eyes were immediately trained on him in blatant disbelief because no one openly questioned Pastor Lucas. He declared that the Bible stated 10% as the amount of tithes and that he felt that it was only fair to pay on the net amount because that was what he actually brought home. Pastor Lucas got very upset, and when he responded his voice was dripping with anger and sarcasm. He told Brother Atkins that after the meeting, he would deal with his questions in his office. But once in his office, Pastor Lucas asked Brother Atkins and his family to leave the church. Pastor Lucas said that if he didn't trust his leadership, he should go to another church, and that he wouldn't allow anyone to undermine his authority and directives, especially in front of the other church members. After that meeting, Brother Atkins and his family were never seen in church again.

Pastor Lucas also borrowed money from his members and never repaid it, saying that it was the members' duty to support their pastor. He conveniently forgot that he had promised to repay it when he initially asked to borrow it. When Pastor Lucas had an accident and totaled his family vehicle, he persuaded one of the church members to sign over his car to him. Pastor Lucas told the member that the Lord would bless him and make a way for his family to get another vehicle. When the member and his family left nine months later, they still did not have a car.

Pastor Lucas *required* some of his members to clean his house, purchase groceries for his family with their own money, cook for his family, wash his vehicles daily, and mow his lawn weekly. He also *required* them to provide him a valet, a personal driver, and a secretary. When he had gotten all he could from one family, he was through with them and moved on to the next conquest.

One ex-church member had a particularly harrowing experience. Sister Hightower was a single, overweight woman in her mid-thirties. She had settled a lawsuit and was awarded $75,000. Upon learning of the large amount, Pastor Lucas told her that most of that money should go to the building of the Lord's kingdom.

Pastor Lucas then took an immediate interest in Sister Hightower. He kept her very close to him and his family. She felt so loved and she viewed the Lucas clan as the large family she'd always wanted. Pastor Lucas knew that Sister Hightower was single and desperately wanted to get married. He even hinted that she would make a good wife for one of

S.E.C.R.E.T.S. VOLUME II by: *Pastor Shirley*

his sons. Sister Hightower was ecstatic because all of Pastor Lucas' sons were extremely good-looking and very talented. However, Pastor Lucas secretly felt that Sister Hightower was too fat and not pretty enough to grace the arms of one of his precious sons. Additionally, having asked them directly, he knew that none of his sons was remotely interested in Sister Hightower romantically. However, he kept all of this information to himself.

Sister Hightower was regularly invited out to dinner with the entire Lucas clan and she usually picked up the tab. She sent Pastor Lucas and his wife on a first-class vacation to Hawaii. She even bought them new clothes and luggage for the trip, and gave them each $2,000 in spending money. During offerings, Pastor Lucas would state that the church needed large sums of money for things like a new roof, a new furnace, etc. While explaining this, he would look directly at Sister Hightower. She would feel guilty and immediately take out her checkbook. However, she never saw a new roof, a new furnace, or a new anything for that matter.

With these large expenditures, it didn't take long for Pastor Lucas to assist Sister Hightower to spend all of her money, and six months later, the settlement was completely gone. Once this happened, she was immediately excommunicated from the Lucas clan. She was thrust aside like an old, used rag. The entire family stopped taking her calls. In church, they acted as if they didn't know her. When she told another member what had happened to her, she was informed that Pastor Lucas had told the church that Sister Hightower was possessed by a demon and that he was going to ask her to leave the church. Sister Hightower couldn't believe this so she tried to call the pastor to talk to him about the apparent misunderstanding. Though she left numerous messages with the church secretaries, the pastor never returned her calls.

Shortly thereafter, Pastor Lucas put a restraining order on Sister Hightower, claiming that she had threatened him. He told the police that she was emotionally unstable and was stalking him and his family. She was forbidden to come within 100 feet of Pastor Lucas or anyone in his family. Therefore, she could not attend church without being arrested.

****

Pastor Lucas never even missed a beat. He just kept replacing old members with new gullible ones and kept fundraising activities going on at the church seven days a week.

This is how Evangelist Meadows came to be at Pastor Lucas' church. Evangelist Meadows was a young, married, powerful preacher whose reputation as an anointed man of God preceded him. His evangelistic schedule was packed solid for the next 18 months. He adored his wife and children and often referenced his family during his sermons. It was originally agreed that Evangelist Meadows would run a one-week revival. But because of his reputation and his ability to preach, people began attending from far and wide. The church was packed every night with many standing both inside and outside the sanctuary to hear the prophet of God. Seeing this, Pastor Lucas extended the revival for an additional week.

Because of the large number of people attending the revival, Head Deacon Henderson decided to clean the sanctuary during the day and to replenish the water and juice in Pastor Lucas' and Richard Jr.'s offices. He arrived at the church and went to the pastor's office first. After completing his maintenance tasks, he went down the hall to Richard Jr.'s office. When he opened the door, he was horrified at the sight before him. Evangelist Meadows and Richard Jr. were both completely nude and in the middle of a particularly spirited bout of gay sex. Richard Jr. was moaning and Evangelist Meadows was murmuring vulgarly. They were so caught up in the throes of their torrid tryst that they didn't even notice Deacon Henderson standing in the doorway.

Unfortunately, he was so shocked that he couldn't move. His feet felt as if they'd been glued to the floor. He was so horrified and embarrassed that he simply wanted the earth to open up and swallow him whole. Though his mind recognized the need to make a quick and hasty retreat, his feet doggedly refused to listen to him. He simply couldn't move.

When Richard Jr. noticed Deacon Henderson in the doorway, he broke

S.E.C.R.E.T.S. VOLUME II by: *Pastor Shirley*

away from Evangelist Meadows yelling, "I thought you said you locked the door!" He anxiously looked over Deacon Henderson's head to see if anyone else had witnessed his indiscretion. "I thought I did" Evangelist Meadows said breathlessly scrambling for his clothes, which had been strewn haphazardly all over the floor.

Finally, Deacon Henderson regained his mobility and his voice. He was so angry at the blatant violation of the sanctuary that he was shaking visibly when he thundered, "This is GOD'S HOUSE! How could you do such a vile thing in GOD'S HOUSE?"

Dressing quickly, Richard Jr. buttoned his shirt and stuffed it into his pants. The whir of his zipper was loud in the quiet that had descended upon his office. While buckling his belt, Richard Jr. raised his head and locked his gaze with Deacon Henderson's furious eyes. The firm timbre of his voice successfully hid his fear at being discovered. "I know whose house it is, Deacon Henderson. It's the LUCAS HOUSE, and I don't need you to tell me anything. Who do you think you are?" After stuffing his feet into his loafers, he leaned nonchalantly against the corner of his massive desk keeping Evangelist Meadows in his sight line. Richard Jr.'s eyes threw daggers at the deacon as he became angrier. "You come bustin' in my office without so much as a knock and you have the nerve to try and get all righteous on me? I don't think so." He pushed off from his desk and began slowly approaching Deacon Henderson where he still stood in the doorway.

"First you need to check yourself and remember who the assistant pastor is and who is just a lowly deacon. Second, you need to keep your mouth shut about anything that may have transpired in my office. Third, if you do decide to go running off at the mouth, you will NOT like the consequences. And last, DON'T. YOU. EVER. enter my office again without knocking. This is my domain, and you WILL RESPECT THAT!" Upon finishing his tirade, Richard Jr. now stood directly in front of Deacon Henderson. He gave the deacon his most intimidating glare and slammed the door in his face.

Richard Jr. turned from the door, assertively strode to the executive chair behind his desk, and began shuffling through papers. Evangelist Meadows wearily dropped into the chair in front of Richard Jr.'s desk and asked, "Do you think it'll work?"

Richard Jr. stopped shuffling and lifted his eyes to Evangelist Meadows. "Will what work?" He replied nonchalantly.

Evangelist Meadows raked a hand through his hair as he replied with anguish, "Do you think the deacon will tell anyone what he saw? Stuff like this cannot get back to my wife." *Well, we both agree on that!* Richard Jr. thought wryly as his beautiful, headstrong wife briefly entered his thoughts. He leaned back in his chair and stared a moment at Evangelist Meadows. The man was practically shaking in fear. *Didn't he know the first rule of all men?* He thought. *Deny, deny, deny!* Well they couldn't very well deny anything with any amount of believability if he didn't pull himself together. Quickly. Weak men totally disgusted Richard Jr.

"Look, the first thing you need to do is pull yourself together. You look like you've just seen a ghost. Go back to your hotel and relax until the evening service. If anything jumps off, I'll call you." He sounded way more confident than he felt. Evangelist Meadows nodded and walked to the door. He opened it and hesitantly stuck his head out looking wildly from one end of the hall to the other. Pure disgust consumed Richard Jr. as he yelled, "Give me break! Will you stop acting like terror-stricken prey being led to the slaughter! And get that scared look off your face! Man up and grow a spine! Pull.. yourself… together… NOW! Just hold your head up and walk casually to your car as if nothing happened!"

Evangelist Meadows left closing the door softly behind him. Richard Jr. shook his head and immediately put Evangelist Meadows out of his mind. He had more important things to ponder like what he was going to say to his father. Pastor Lucas and the deacon were longtime friends and he had no doubt that the deacon had run to the nearest phone to tell him what he'd witnessed. His father was what he'd describe as a "man's man"; no weaknesses of any visible kind, always in control, and completely against homosexuality in any form. He would be forced to fall back on his old standby. Deny everything. Period. It had worked for him all these years,

S.E.C.R.E.T.S. VOLUME II by: *Pastor Shirley*

why change now?

As Richard Jr. predicted, Deacon Henderson went directly to the administrative offices and called Pastor Lucas. He told the Pastor in graphic detail what he'd just seen. Pastor Lucas instructed him to stay there and not to call anyone else. He said that he would be there in 20 minutes. When he arrived, he ushered Deacon Henderson into his office and asked him to tell him again what he'd witnessed. Deacon Henderson repeated his previous story verbatim except now he was so upset that his voice shook and tears streamed down his face.

About five minutes after he'd finished his emotional, detailed account, Richard Jr. sauntered confidently into Pastor Lucas' spacious office. He glared at Deacon Henderson as he passed him and stood by the window. Facing the deacon, he said, "My father called and told me what you said. You're a bold-faced liar! I am not gay and I am not interested in sex with men. The very thought is disgusting to me. I don't know why you felt it necessary to come up with this horrible lie, but you need to leave this church and never come back. We do not need members like you running around telling lies about the pastor's family. If you repeat this vicious lie to anyone else, you WILL be sorry!"

Deacon Henderson couldn't believe his ears! He knew what he'd seen. He hadn't imagined it nor was he making it up. Richard Jr. was obviously gay. Surely Pastor Lucas could see beyond his façade to the heart of the matter.

He turned to Pastor Lucas. He was shocked by the look of solidarity on his face. Pastor Lucas didn't believe him; he believed Richard Jr.! Deacon Henderson waited for Pastor Lucas to countermand Richard Jr.'s edict to leave the church. He didn't. Deacon Henderson was extremely hurt by the Pastor's silence. He was being punished for telling the truth. He laid the keys to the church on Pastor Lucas' desk. He looked at the pastor, who dropped his head. Pastor Lucas couldn't bear to see the look of hurt in the eyes of a man he truly respected. But it had to be done to protect the ministry and the family name. Deacon Henderson looked at Richard Jr. who was smiling triumphantly when he said; "Surely, you didn't expect my father to believe you over me?"

"SHUT UP RICHARD JR.!" Pastor Lucas barked in a loud, booming voice. He wasn't going to allow Richard Jr. to belittle Deacon Henderson. It was bad enough that he was being forced to leave the church. Deacon Henderson walked from the pastor's office directly to his car. Pastor Lucas stood and walked to the window of his office overlooking the parking lot. He watched Deacon Henderson get into his car and pull out of the parking lot. His heart was heavy over what he had just allowed to happen.

He'd always suspected Richard Jr. might be gay though he was not effeminate nor had he ever done anything overtly. It was just a feeling he'd always had. There were a few times that Richard Jr.'s gaze lingered a touch too long on men when he thought no one was watching, though the looks had never been long enough for Pastor Lucas to be certain about his son's sexuality.

He'd never admitted his suspicions to anyone because the very thought both disturbed and disgusted him. How could *his* son prefer the touch of man to the touch of a woman? If he lived to be 100 years old, he would never understand this and he had no intention of trying. He turned to his son angrily. "Richard Jr. how could you possibly be so stupid?" Richard Jr. looked shocked. Did his father know his secret? Since his father didn't see him, he would do what came naturally to him. He would lie. "What are you talking about, Dad? Surely you didn't believe the lies Deacon Henderson made up?"

Pastor Lucas left the window and returned to his desk. He sat down and rubbed his eyes wearily. "Shut up and sit down, Richard Jr." He held his hand up to stop his son from speaking further. "Be quiet and listen to me. I didn't see what Deacon Henderson witnessed and thank God I didn't. But I know he was telling the truth about you. I have always known but I hoped it was a phase you were going through and that you would get over it. Obviously, you didn't." He rose from the desk and walked back to the window. He stared out with unseeing eyes and a heavy heart. He had hoped that he would never have to have this conversation with his son.

S.E.C.R.E.T.S. VOLUME II by: *Pastor Shirley*

"I don't understand your sexual preference and frankly, it makes me sick to my stomach to think of you locked in an intimate embrace with another man. I didn't raise you to be no sissy." Richard Jr. flinched at the word sissy. "I don't know where you got that mess from but you certainly didn't get it from me."

He turned to face his son. "You are a grown man now and I am through raising you. But, I won't let you destroy this ministry. I have worked too hard over the years to keep it going and to build it up to where it is today. You are the son I've been grooming to take over the ministry. However, if you are unfit to do so, I will choose and train one of your brothers. You are NOT a definite choice."

Pastor Lucas saw the panic in Richard Jr.'s eyes. From the time Richard Jr. was an adolescent, he'd dreamed of pastoring his father's church. He hadn't bothered to learn how to do anything else because he had been so sure of succeeding his father. How was he going to support his family if he was no longer a part of the ministry?

Taking note of his panic, Pastor Lucas said, "When I have had my say, you can explain yourself. Or at least try to."

"Anyway…you are to NEVER, EVER have sex with anyone, including your wife, in the church or on church property. Do I make myself clear?! I have done many things in my time, but I have never defiled the house of God, which is exactly what you did. Because of you, I've had to banish one of the few men in this church that I respect and called a friend and I don't take that lightly."

"After today, I never want to discuss your sissy lifestyle and I don't want to hear about it again. If I ever hear rumors or we have to discuss this again, you will no longer be a part of this church. Whatever you do from here on out, you had better cover your tracks and cover them well! Now what do you have to say for yourself?"

Richard Jr. didn't know where to begin. He was horrified at the thought of discussing what he referred to as his "curse" with his father. Homosexuality and bisexuality were taboo topics in African-American homes.

He decided to continue to deny everything. "Dad, I don't know why you insist—"

"STOP LYING, RICHARD JR.! NOW!" Pastor Lucas exploded cutting his son off mid-sentence. "If we cannot have an honest conversation and come to an understanding, you can leave the church right now! Today!"

Richard Jr. heard the hard edge and note of finality in his father's voice. He had hoped that he'd never have to explain this, of all things, to his rigid father. He knew that his father was serious so he quickly reviewed his options. He had to say something to mollify his father. Anything. He decided to play on his father's sympathy and take the I-don't-know-why-I'm-like-this route. He schooled his facial expression to one of supreme sincerity. "Dad, do you think I chose to be this way? I didn't. I wanted to be normal like everyone else. But I realized from an early age that I was attracted to both men and women. I tried to deny the urges, but I just couldn't." His father's stern look began to waiver. *Oh my God, it's beginning to work,* Richard Jr. thought excitedly. He added tears, knowing that they would be effective because he had never cried in front of his father before. "I tried, Dad. I really did. I knew it would break your heart for you to find out something like this about me. The son you had personally groomed to take over the ministry. The son who looks like a younger version of you. The son who never wanted to hurt you or embarrass you. Ever." When the look on his father's face softened, Richard Jr. thought, *Almost got him. Put the blame on Evangelist Meadows; say this was my first time,* Richard Jr. thought. "I had no intention of sleeping with Evangelist Meadows or any other man for that matter. Some boys in the neighborhood tried to get me to try it when I was a teenager, but I refused. Evangelist Meadows called me and asked if we could meet today in my office to discuss his payment. I thought it was odd, because you handled that and he had already agreed to your terms. But, since he was packing out the church every night, I thought I'd better at least meet with him to ensure he wasn't trying to end the revival early. When I got to my office he was waiting for me completely nude. I had no idea he was gay and I was so shocked I didn't even realize he'd moved from the corner of my desk and was unbuckling my pants. The next thing I knew I felt a warm

S.E.C.R.E.T.S. VOLUME II by: Pastor Shirley

mouth on me." Richard Jr. was sobbing so loudly now that Pastor Lucas feared someone else might overhear this sordid story.

"Calm down, Richard Jr., and lower your voice. I don't want anyone else to hear what we're talking about." Pastor Lucas said, his voice a model of comfort and support.

Apologize, say I hated it and it will never happen again and BINGO, CHECK MATE! STICK A FORK IN HIM BECAUSE HE WILL BE DONE! Richard Jr. thought triumphantly, though none of it showed on his tear-streaked face. "Dad, I HATED it! Had Deacon Henderson come in a minute later, he would have found me pushing Evangelist Meadows off me, but instead he walked in when I was still in shock. I'm sorry. I won't allow my emotions to overrule my head again. Dad I'm really sorry… about everything."

Richard Jr. leaned over and rested his head in his hands. He had no idea how his father was going to react, but keeping his head down added to his stellar performance and made him look that much more humble. He waited silently for his father to respond.

Pastor Lucas sat in his chair, stunned. He couldn't believe what his son had just admitted to him. He had to acknowledge that it took a lot of courage to tell the truth, which is what he *thought* he wanted. However, he now realized that he hadn't quite wanted *all* of the truth. But since Richard Jr. had come clean, he would give him another chance to redeem himself and try to put this entire detestable incident behind them.

"Richard Jr., I accept your apology. I'm glad to hear you hated the experience. That makes me feel a lot better to know you ain't no sissy. Let's try to put this incident behind us as quickly as possible. I am closing the revival immediately and telling the congregation that Evangelist Meadows' wife took ill and he had to leave suddenly. Now, get up, go into my bathroom, and clean yourself up. I don't want anyone seeing you like this. This incident is officially squashed."

Richard Jr. rose slowly to his feet and went into his father's private bathroom closing the door softly behind him. *I DID IT!* Richard Jr. thought as he looked into the mirror over the sink. He'd saved his reputation and his place within the ministry. He was so overjoyed that he began doing a touchdown victory dance. Afterward, as he began to clean himself up, he had to agree with his father; he did look a hot mess, as his wife Sharon would say. Tears and snot did have a tendency to do that to a person. He finished making himself presentable, erasing all signs of the meeting he'd just had with his father, and went home to his beautiful wife.

True to his word, Pastor Lucas ended the revival in the manner he had described to Richard Jr., and church went on as usual.

However, the scandal still inched its way around the church until it surfaced. When it broke, it rushed through the church community like a tornado. Richard Jr., the son who Pastor Lucas was grooming to take over the ministry, was gay. Seeing that this could destroy the ministry, Viola stepped from behind her husband to defend her son's reputation. She claimed it was just the devil trying to destroy her son and the ministry. She said that Richard Jr. was happily married with children and had no interest in cheating on his wife with anyone and certainly not with a man. Surprised by Viola's unprecedented, outspoken action, the talk quickly died down. Pastor Lucas was so shocked and overjoyed by Viola's sudden acquisition of a voice that he made a mental note to have sex with her that night as a reward.

Two years had passed since the incident at the church involving Richard Jr. and Evangelist Meadows. Since Pastor Lucas hadn't heard anything else about Richard Jr., he was extremely hopeful that it was a one-time incident and that nothing of that nature would ever occur again.

****

Sharon Baker-Lucas, Richard Jr.'s wife of six years, was an attorney at a prestigious law firm located on prime real estate in the heart of downtown. She loved her job and was an aggressive attorney with an exemplary winning record. She had a reputation for having a sense of humor and being an absolute professional. She was an exceptionally beautiful woman who took pride in her appearance. Because of her commitment to

S.E.C.R.E.T.S. VOLUME II by: _Pastor Shirley_

exercise, her 5'7" body was fit and trim. After the birth of her children, Sharon worked hard to regain her pre-pregnancy figure and gave herself one year to lose the baby weight. However, she usually reached her goal about four months after the birth of her babies. Regular visits to the salon ensured that her hair, nails, and feet were always in the best of shape, and she was always dressed in the height of fashion. She was the epitome of poise and grace. However, she hadn't always been that way. She had worked hard over the years to refine her speech and movements to allow her to interact with those on a higher level. She had been born and raised in the ghetto with five brothers and four sisters. She had learned how to fight at an early age and as a teenager had also taken up Karate. She had continued with her Karate training after she got married because it provided a great source of exercise and toned her body beautifully.

On a cold winter morning, she woke up not feeling her best. Though she had a splitting headache and felt as if she was going to vomit at any moment, she went into the office anyway, hoping to feel better as the day went on. When that didn't happen, she informed her secretary that she was taking the day off and left. As she drove home, she felt increasingly worse. She idly wondered if she could be pregnant again and tried to remember the last time she'd had her period. When she turned into the cul-de-sac known as Somerset Circle, Sharon hit the wireless automatic garage door opener in her car. She passed an unfamiliar car as she turned into her driveway. As the garage door opened, she saw Richard Jr.'s BMW inside. She didn't think much of this because he worked in the ministry and sometimes worked from home. She was glad that he was home today because he could look after her and pick up the children from school.

Sharon loved her husband dearly. She had never been treated as well by anyone as she'd been by Richard Jr. He was intelligent, *extremely* attractive, and in excellent physical shape. Though he was second in command in the ministry, and highly involved, he was an excellent father. Richard Jr. always made time for the kids and for her. Sharon considered Richard Jr. to be her best friend and she felt that she could talk to him about anything. He often asked her opinion on church matters and he told her on a regular basis that he valued her input. Richard Jr. was the most romantic man she had ever met. He sent her flowers and cards for no reason except to say "I love you." He gladly helped with the upkeep of the house as well as with the children. He never had a problem changing a diaper, washing dishes, cooking dinner, or doing the laundry. He always told her that they were partners in every way. His romantic gestures and loving actions touched and excited her on a deeply emotional level.

Their sex life could only be described as amazing! Richard Jr. was a wonderful, considerate lover, and he taught her everything she knew about making love. None of her girlfriends experienced the same type of fulfillment in this area of their marriage. They were always complaining about their lack of fulfillment an their husbands' lack of creativity, gentleness, and skill. Sharon felt blessed to have a good husband, marriage, and family life.

Sharon walked into the house and straight to the kitchen. She grabbed a glass of orange juice and headed to her bedroom. As she walked down the hall, she heard moaning. Sharon stopped dead in her tracks. This could not be happening to her! Surely Richard Jr. wasn't having sex in her bed with some hoochie! Any woman with the guts to have sex in her house was about to get a beat-down because she had to know that Richard Jr. was married, just by the numerous family photos openly displayed throughout the house. Her sickness forgotten, Sharon switched to fighting mode; she removed her shoes and earrings, and set her glass of juice and purse on the hallway table. When she flung the door open, she stopped, unable to believe the sight before her. Richard Jr. *was* having sex. But not with a woman. To her utter amazement and horror, he was having sex with a *man!* A man whom she didn't recognize. And Richard Jr. seemed to be enjoying it way more than he had ever enjoyed sex with her.

"Oh God!" Sharon yelled. Time stood still for her as she watched Richard Jr. extract himself from the man beneath him and stand before her completely nude.

Richard Jr. wanted to say something. Anything. But he had no idea what to say. He was caught in the act. How in the world do you deny that?!

S.E.C.R.E.T.S. VOLUME II by: *Pastor Shirley*

Sharon was livid and became totally irrational. Her ghetto girl background merged with her Karate training to form one powerful force. Before Sharon even realized she had moved, she dropped into a fighting stance and kicked Richard Jr. with a solid roundhouse kick that caught him squarely in the jaw. The force of Sharon's unexpected kick sent Richard Jr. sprawling to the floor where he stared up at her in open-mouthed shock. He clutched his jaw, which had now begun to throb.

"You slimy, gay pervert! Why did you marry me knowing all you wanted to do was plow men on the down low? Oh My God! That's what you are. A down-low brother and I never saw any of the signs!"

During the entire verbal exchange between husband and wife, Richard Jr.'s sex partner, Alton, had scrambled from the bed and dressed himself hastily. When he had agreed to spend some time with the handsome man whom he had met only three hours before at the bank, he had *not* agreed to spend time with his violent, psychotic wife as well. She was crazy and trying to kill her husband, and all he wanted to do now was get out of the house. Unfortunately, the raging lunatic was blocking the door. Alton had seen her drop kick her husband and had no desire to be next on her list. After all, the man had approached him, not the other way around. He now stood undecided about his next course of action. He glanced at Richard Jr., who had regained his footing and was trying in vain to calm his wife down.

Fortunately for Alton, Sharon gave him the chance he needed to escape as she flung herself at Richard Jr. kicking, scratching, punching, screaming, and shouting obscenities. As the couple landed on the bed, propelled by the force of Sharon's lunge, Alton flew past the tussling couple glancing nervously at them as he dashed out of the house. He ran to his car as fast as his legs would carry him, cranked the engine of his car, and sped out of the cul-de-sac.

Richard Jr. was a tall, physically fit man, and though the throbbing in his jaw was *excruciating*, he had no problem subduing his screeching, irate wife. But, before he could do so, she had landed several well-placed punches to his face, stomach, and genitals. As a result, he was now aching all over in addition to his jaw. However, he knew that he deserved her violent outburst and then some. He had never hit a woman in his life and had no intention of doing so now. Though he held her firmly against his body, her arms trapped by her sides, she continued to spew obscenities at the top of her lungs as she kicked violently. Her eyes were glazed over, her face was a mask of rage, and she was yelling like a mad woman. Richard Jr. threw his leg over Sharon's flailing limbs, effectively putting an end to her kicking.

Ignoring his wife's screaming and his own aches and pain, he tried to think of something that he could possibly say to her to save their marriage. Just what that was, he had absolutely no idea. He had vehemently denied the incident with Evangelist Meadows two years ago. He had been extremely careful since then. He hadn't wanted to take money from his household to spend on hotels so he'd started having sex at home. Once a month, he brought some nameless man to his home, had unprotected sex, and never saw him again. He couldn't buy condoms because he would then have to admit to himself that he was regularly having sex with men. He would have to admit that he was gay. Which he wasn't! He just entertained male friends at his home occasionally, and if they ended up having sex during their visit, oh well. At least he wasn't pre-planning the interludes by purchasing condoms. Besides, how would he explain them to Sharon should she ever find them? And, he was careful in his selection. He only chose men who looked clean and disease free.

In all the time that they had been married, Sharon had never come home early. If she had arrived just one hour later, Alton would have been gone. What was he going to do now? He loved Sharon dearly and didn't want to lose her or his kids. He wasn't happy about his monthly sexual liaisons, but he didn't know what to do about them either. If he could ever get the screaming banshee in his arms to calm down enough so they could talk, he would figure out a course of action.

Sharon suddenly stopped screaming. One minute she was screaming and struggling and the next minute she stopped. Just like that. She lay there, trapped by Richard Jr., in shock. She couldn't even cry. She wanted to cry, but she couldn't. Why had she not believed the rumors about him

S.E.C.R.E.T.S. VOLUME II by: Pastor Shirley

and Evangelist Meadows? She knew why. She loved Richard Jr. and she hadn't wanted to believe something so terrible about him. There had been no signs to indicate that he'd been having sex outside their marriage. He didn't work late, he wasn't interested in his appearance any more than usual, his sexual appetite hadn't changed, and he hadn't treated her any differently. If anything, he was more loving, supportive, and understanding. Richard Jr. didn't look gay, if there was such a thing, and he did not act feminine or have feminine gestures. Under the circumstances, how was she supposed to know and, more importantly, what was she going to do now? *And oh my God!* She thought, *Did his father know? Did Viola know?*

She, Sharon Marie Baker-Lucas, was not going to allow Richard Jr. to mistreat or disrespect her. She wasn't Viola! If you looked up the word doormat in the dictionary, surely there would be a full-page color photograph of her mother-in-law. She had never met anyone as sweet as she was, but she allowed her husband and family to completely walk all over her and disregard her feelings. Sharon was aware that Pastor Lucas cheated regularly. Everyone in the church was aware of it, as he didn't appear to put much thought or time into trying to hide it. She had no idea why Viola suffered his indiscretions in silence, but she had absolutely no intention of doing the same.

Sharon just didn't understand Richard Jr.'s desire to have sex with men. Why wasn't she enough for him? Why had he pursued her so relentlessly and married her if he was gay? Had he been having unprotected sex? She could feel his bare penis against her stomach now, but the condom could have come off in his hasty disentanglement. Was she now going to contract some awful disease? Would she die because she had loved and trusted her husband? She made a mental note to schedule a full physical with a complete blood work-up ASAP. For now, angry tears filled her eyes.

Sharon shook her head to focus her thoughts. She was beautiful, successful, and educated. So what if she had three children whom she loved dearly? She also had a trim figure, outgoing personality, and a successful career. Any man would be lucky to have her! Unlike Viola, she didn't define herself by her association with the ministry. She could make a good life, both financially and emotionally, for herself and her kids with or without Richard Jr.

In an attempt to free herself from her husband's vice-like grasp, Sharon shook herself vigorously and told him to unhand her immediately. He released her slowly, remaining on guard for any additional physical outbursts. Sharon went into the bathroom and when she returned, Richard Jr. was fully dressed and sitting in a chair by the recently made-up bed. The TV was on but it was apparent that he wasn't paying any attention to it. Sharon took a seat in the chair opposite him. She saw him clutching his injured jaw and felt an overwhelming sense of satisfaction. Never one to beat around the bush, she plunged right in. "How long have you been gay, Richard?"

Not taking his eyes from the TV, Richard Jr. replied, "I'm not gay."

"OK, since you want to play word games, how long have you been having sex with men?"

"I don't have sex with men."

"Just what do you call that little scene I just witnessed with my own eyes?"

He turned from the TV and looked Sharon directly in the eyes. "I'm not sure what you think you saw. Are you going to believe, me, your loving husband of six years, or are you going to believe your lying eyes?"

Sharon burst into hysterical laughter. Richard Jr.'s dime-store psychology didn't work on her and she was furious that he would even try such a lame opening statement. She wasn't spineless like his mother, she wasn't a doormat, and she wasn't crazy. She shot out of her chair and stood in front of Richard Jr.'s chair. "MY LYING EYES?!" She screamed. "MY… LYING… EYES?" She spat out the words between clenched teeth and punctuated each word with an agitated slash in the air. "WHAT DO YOU MEAN MY LYING EYES?! DON'T INSULT MY INTELLIGENCE BY USING SUCH A PLAYED-OUT LINE! You been watching too much Eddie Murphy if you thought that mess would work. I KNOW

S.E.C.R.E.T.S. VOLUME II by: *Pastor Shirley*

WHAT I SAW, RICHARD! I'm not happy about it and I won't even try to pretend that I understand it. I won't allow you or anyone else to disrespect me, whether it's with a woman or a man. If you insist on lying, I'll leave you today and take the kids with me. But before we go, I'll make a pit stop at your parents' house and tell them why I'm leaving because I don't want them to think I mistreated you in some way. This is the last time I'm going to ask you. How long have you been having sex with men and are you having unprotected sex?"

Sharon could no longer contain her pain at being betrayed. She was angry and disenchanted by a fate not of her own making. She began to wail loudly. Her sobs shook her entire body and she could see nothing through her tears. Richard Jr. stood and reached out to console her, but she angrily shook him off, not wanting him to touch her. Sharon's sobs were breaking his heart. When he embraced her, she struggled wildly, flailing at him with her fists, hitting him blindly in an effort to lessen her pain. He managed to grab her wrists and pull her against his body. He cradled her head against his broad chest. He murmured over and over again, "I'm so sorry Sharon. I love you. We'll work this out. It will be all right." Sharon began to cry in earnest now. She sobbed until he thought his heart would surely break because he knew that he was the cause of her anguish. He had never before heard such sounds of grief from her, or anyone else for that matter. As her sobs quickly escalated into inconsolable wails, he felt at a complete loss. He simply held her until she quieted.

Before Sharon had broken down and begun to cry, Richard Jr. had listened with what he'd hoped appeared to be a nonchalant attitude. The truth was that he was ashamed and scared to death! Ashamed that he had once again succumbed to his urges, and scared that if he was honest with Sharon, she would think that he was weak and some kind of a freak. He didn't want her or anyone else to think of him as a gay man, because he WASN'T!

He also knew that Sharon wasn't going to blindly ignore his infidelity like his mother had repeatedly done through the years with his father. Sharon was beautiful, intelligent, and she had a backbone. He had no doubt that she would leave him and that he would be put out of the church should

Pastor Lucas find out about today's liaison. Complete honesty would only result in Sharon leaving him and the end of his church career, so that was definitely not an option. He would say whatever he had to say in order to keep her from leaving and taking the kids with her. After his marriage was out of hot water, he would figure out a way to continue his monthly liaisons.

Richard Jr. helped Sharon back into the chair and took his seat opposite her. He handed her the tissue box and in a voice laced with sincerity and genuine sadness, he began his tale and desperately hoped that it would be enough to satisfy her. "First of all, I am NOT gay, Sharon." Since she looked completely unconvinced, he said it again in a firmer, though not louder, tone. "I AM NOT GAY! This is the first time I've tried it. Really. Most women wonder about having sex with another woman and many try it. Does that make them gay? No, it doesn't. I tried it, and it doesn't do anything for me. It's not something I will ever repeat." When Richard Jr. looked at Sharon, there were tears in his eyes.

"Sharon, I'm not proud of what you saw. The look on your face will haunt me for the rest of my life. But I swear to you that I have never done it before and I will never do it again." Richard Jr. was crying openly now.

"I'm sorry about doing it in our bed. I could've gotten a hotel but I didn't want to take money from our household. I want my family to have the best life possible and that requires my entire salary. That is no excuse; I'm just explaining my reason for doing what I did in our home."

He knew that the previous incident with Evangelist Meadows had to be going through her head and thought he'd better address it before she did. "That incident with Evangelist Meadows a couple years ago was not true. I did not sleep with him but he wanted to sleep with me. He tried his best to get me to try what he referred to as 'Alpha Love,' and he accosted me on several occasions. I was so ashamed that he was pursuing me; I didn't know what to do. I had never had that happen to me before. I finally went to my father and told him what was going on. He called an immediate meeting with Evangelist Meadows. Afterwards, he ended the revival. I did not sleep with him or any other person, man or woman, for that mat-

S.E.C.R.E.T.S. VOLUME II by: *Pastor Shirley*

ter."

Richard Jr. got on his knees in front of Sharon's chair. "Until today, I have never cheated on you. We have been married over six years and I have never cheated on you. How many of your girlfriends can say that about their husbands with certainty? I love you, Sharon, and I can't make it without you and the kids. I am so sorry. So sorry. Please tell me that you won't leave me. Don't end our marriage over one mistake. We can get through this. I know our love is stronger than one mistake."

Sharon wiped her eyes and blew her nose loudly as she digested the large amount of information she'd just heard. She didn't know what to believe now. Could it be true that this was the first time he had ever cheated on her? They did have a good marriage and he had been an excellent father and husband in the past. She had to give him credit for that. But could she trust him again? She couldn't live her life in "007 mode"—hiding behind bushes, following him everywhere he went, and investigating everything he told her. She had to trust and respect the man she was with. But did she still respect him? That was the million-dollar question. She had to admit that a part of her was repulsed by the fact that he had allowed another man to touch him in an intimate way.

Sharon cleared her throat and began to speak. "It is true that you have been a good father and husband in the past. But I don't know if I can get past this, Richard Jr. I don't know if I can trust you again and I won't live my life wondering if you are with another man if you're five minutes late for dinner." Richard Jr. flinched. She continued. "I don't know if I can regain the respect I lost for you. Even if I wanted to get past this, and I'm not sure I do, I don't know how. I do know this—I will never sleep in that bed again. I'm not sure I can stand for you to touch me and we certainly can't have a strong, healthy relationship without making love. And how am I supposed to hold my head up at church after this?"

Richard Jr.'s head immediately snapped up. "What does the church have to do with any of this?" His tone was edgier than he'd intended, alarm was clearly evident on his face.

"Aren't you going to ask the church for forgiveness?" Sharon asked.

Richard Jr. got off his knees and resumed his seat in the chair he'd vacated. "Sharon, I can't stand before the church and tell them what I've done. The ministry is thriving. An announcement like that would affect its growth negatively. I can't do that to Dad. I can't do that to you and the kids."

Sharon narrowed her eyes, and spat. "Please give me some credit for having a modicum of intelligence. Don't try to act like you can't ask the church for forgiveness because you want to spare the kids and me. The real reason you don't want to stand before the church and ask for forgiveness is because you don't want your father or the church to know you've been gleefully having sex with men," Sharon replied shrewdly.

Richard Jr.'s gut clenched at Sharon's accurate assessment. As humbly as he could manage, he countered, "One man Sharon. Not men."

"Man or men! Whatever! You had sex with a member of the same sex. Period. The Bible is real clear when it comes to homosexuality. God considers it an abomination. What is wrong with you? Do you not believe in God or the Bible anymore? If you don't take your relationship with God seriously, then how can I trust that you'll take our marriage seriously? I don't care about your feelings right now. You didn't care about mine when you decided it was OK to sleep with a man in our bed. You weren't thinking of anyone's feelings but your own… Have you been having unprotected sex?"

"Sharon, I told you that I have only cheated on you this one time. And no, it wasn't unprotected."

"I don't remember seeing a condom. Since you say you were wearing one, you won't mind submitting to a complete physical exam with tests for all sexually transmitted diseases, will you? I'm scheduling one for myself today. Before we can even discuss going further in our marriage, we first need to get the results back. *If* they're negative, then and only then, will we discuss the next steps in trying to put our marriage back together. I don't know what those steps are right now, but I do know we'll

S.E.C.R.E.T.S. VOLUME II by: *Pastor Shirley*

need help in figuring them out so we'll have to go to counseling. And just so you know, we won't be having sex until I feel comfortable again, however long that takes."

"I would never put you at risk by doing something like that in an unprotected state. Yes, I was definitely wearing a condom. I have nothing to hide, Sharon. I love you and I want us to get past this. I know we can work this out. Yes, I'll take any test you want me to take and I have no problem waiting. You can have all the time you need. And we can buy another bed today."

Sharon still wanted to scream and yell. But how could she do that when Richard Jr. was being honest and agreeable? For the moment, she would give him the benefit of the doubt. At least until the tests came back. However, she intended to make him sweat it out for a while.

"OK Richard," Sharon said, "This is the deal. We'll have the tests. *If* they are negative, we'll discuss our marriage. In the meantime, I'll be staying with my sister. You will stand before the church to ask for forgiveness. You don't have to tell them what you've done but you do have to say you've sinned and ask for their forgiveness. I will also be talking to your parents. In the event we split up, they need to know the truth."

Richard Jr. began to protest. Sharon held her hand up, halting his response. "I'm sorry, did I give you the impression any of these terms were negotiable?" She asked sarcastically. "Don't get it twisted. They're not." Her face was a cold mask as she got up from the chair.

Richard Jr. nodded and said "No problem, baby." He pushed his hand impatiently through his wavy black hair as he walked to the kitchen to get an ice pack. Boy, did he have a mess on his hands. He knew he needed to call his mother and tell her what had just transpired. But he just couldn't bear to relive this humiliating experience just yet. He would call her after he got back from the emergency room at the hospital. His jaw was swollen, throbbing tremendously, and he was certain that it would need professional medical attention. He knew that his mother would be able to tell him what to do to fix this situation. She always knew exactly what to do.

At the hospital, the doctor on duty told him that his jaw was not broken but that he had suffered a minor fracture; luckily, it would not require surgery. Richard Jr. received a shot for pain, and to ensure proper alignment and to temporarily mobilize his jaw, it was bandaged around the top of his head. He received a prescription for analgesics for pain, as well as a list detailing a recommended modified soft diet. He was also told to keep his talking to a minimum. As if he needed to be told that! His jaw screamed in agony at the slightest movement.

When Richard Jr. returned from the hospital, his children were so engrossed in "The Proud Family" on the Cartoon Network that they didn't even notice his arrival. He walked into his bedroom and lay down across the bed. He thought about calling his mother to discuss the incident, but decided to wait a little longer. Besides, talking was painful. Really painful.

Sharon walked into the bedroom from the bathroom carrying a handful of toiletries and hair care items. She was packing and she'd hoped to be gone before Richard Jr. returned, but no such luck. She had already packed the kids' suitcases and put them into the car. She just had to finish packing hers.

Under normal circumstances, she would have accompanied her husband to the hospital. Since the circumstances weren't normal, she'd had no intention of accompanying him or asking about the extent of his injuries. Richard Jr. was very intuitive and she knew that her refusal to inquire about his injured jaw wouldn't be lost on him. She also doubted whether his pride would allow him to tell her unsolicited. When she entered the bedroom, she noticed a stack of papers on her dresser. Since they weren't there before, it was obvious that he had put them there for her to see. She picked them up and quickly scanned the contents to learn the extent of his injuries. Quickly extrapolating that his jaw wasn't seriously injured and that he would live, albeit with some pain, she flung the papers to the floor and continued packing.

Sharon glanced at Richard Jr. on the bed with his bandaged head and decided that he looked like Bugs Bunny on crack. She began to laugh at

S.E.C.R.E.T.S. VOLUME II by: *Pastor Shirley*

the thought. Richard Jr. silently watched Sharon laughing and packing. He noticed that she hadn't asked about his jaw and had flung the hospital papers to the floor as if the information they contained was not important. That hurt. He knew that he'd messed up badly and had hurt her in the process, but there was no need to be callous and uncivil toward one another. After all, they'd had a good relationship and a solid marriage. He picked up a pad and pen from the bedside table and wrote, "Where are you going?" He then remembered that she'd been laughing and added, "What's so funny?"

He held the pad up for her to see. The fact that he was writing instead of talking tickled her even more and she chuckled as she momentarily stopped packing and read his quickly scribbled note. She felt that he no longer had the right to question her about anything. She began packing again, ignoring Richard Jr. for the moment. As she turned around to place additional items in her suitcase, she stopped and leveled a hard stare at her husband. She replied, "I can't stay in this…this…this…" Sharon's brow furrowed and her arms were gesturing wildly as she frantically searched for the right word to describe how she now viewed her home, "this den of homosexual sin another minute. I'm going to a place where I'm loved and respected. A place where I can relax. A place where people aren't having lewd sexual encounters on the bed in which I'm supposed to sleep. After what I saw you doing today, I won't find any of those things in this house" she finished pointedly. She thought Richard Jr. winced, but it was hard to be sure with all those bandages on his face and head. Richard Jr. just nodded his head and closed his eyes.

She ignored his question about why she was laughing. She certainly didn't owe him any explanation. Without another word, she finished packing and on her way to the car, instructed the kids to turn off the TV and say goodbye to their daddy. Oblivious to the tension between their parents, the kids scampered off to bid him goodbye. Upon returning, they had a note from Richard Jr. that they happily gave to her. Sharon stuffed the note, unread, into her purse, made sure the kids were buckled in, and buckled her seat belt. She slid her Prada sunglasses over her puffy eyes, started her Mercedes, and backed out of the garage.

After mumbling goodbye to his kids, he lay back down in severe pain and contemplated the day's events. *At least she didn't say she was leaving me,* Richard Jr. thought as relief flooded through him. He assumed that she was going to one of her sisters' homes. Since she needed some time to cool off a bit, tomorrow would be soon enough to track her exact whereabouts.

****

The next day, Sharon pulled up to the Lucas family home on Sussex Street. She got out of her car and walked confidently to the front door. Sharon had called before arriving so Viola was expecting her. She opened the door on the first knock and ushered her daughter-in-law into the living room where she had coffee and strawberry cheesecake waiting for them.

After fixing her coffee and exchanging pleasantries, Sharon dove right in. "Look Viola. I know what I'm about to tell you will come as a shock. But I have too much respect for you to be untruthful. Yesterday, when I came home early from work, I found Richard Jr. in bed with another man. I was so angry, the next thing I knew, I fell into a Karate stance and kicked him in the jaw." Viola looked at her askance, horror clearly evident on her face. Holding up her hands, palms out, Sharon said, "He's ok, Viola. Really, he is. He suffered a mild fracture. He has to keep his head bandaged for a few days and take aspirin for the pain. Talking is probably a little painful, but he will heal as good as new."

"I love you, Viola, and excuse me if you feel my next statement is crossing the line or disrespectful; that is not my intention. But I cannot sit idly by and allow my husband to repeatedly cheat on me."

Viola interrupted her. "You mean the way I have tolerated Pastor Lucas' indiscretions?" She asked knowingly, her dark eyes piercing Sharon's.

S.E.C.R.E.T.S. VOLUME II by: *Pastor Shirley*

Sharon was a little shocked by Viola's straight talk. "Frankly, yes. That's exactly what I mean. I don't know how you—"

"Sharon, I'm glad you came here today and I'm glad you told me what happened yesterday. Honey, God don't want your marriage to end. You and Richard Jr. was put together and condoned by God. You have three beautiful little kids who would be devastated if their parents split up. What about you? I know you love Richard Jr. and I know he loves you. I'm sure this is the first time he has cheated on you. He loves you too much. Richard Jr. and I have a good relationship and he talks to me. He talks to me about you all the time and how happy he is that you married him. Don't let one mistake ruin a good marriage."

After taking a sip of her coffee, Viola changed the subject. "About my marriage to Pastor Lucas. Few women would have stayed married to him. But what you don't see, what no one else sees is how he treats me behind closed doors. He treats me like a queen." Sharon looked at Viola skeptically. She'd never seen Pastor Lucas show Viola the slightest bit of attention or respect, so she found it really hard to believe that he ever treated her like a queen.

Seeing the skepticism on Sharon's face, Viola explained. "I'm going to tell you something that I have never told anyone else," she continued in her calm, soothing voice. "I have a problem with sex and it is extremely painful for me. I endured it as long as he wanted to have children. Since that is no longer an issue, he doesn't require me to perform in that area of our marriage. Pastor Lucas loved me in spite of my inability to enjoy sex without excruciating pain. So, he takes his pleasures elsewhere. It doesn't bother me because I know he loves me and he treats me well when we are together."

"But that wasn't always the case. There was a time when it did bother me and I had many sleepless nights and I cried a lot. I should have been an actress because as the First Lady, I have given numerous performances at church that would have won me an Oscar. As Pastor Lucas stood in the pulpit shouting and preaching, and the congregation was going forth and speaking in tongues, I was wondering whose bed he'd just crawled out of because I knew it wasn't mine. But as I stood and shouted "Preach! Preach! Hallelujah!" No one knew I was in so much pain. I hid it, praised God, and protected the ministry at all costs by holding my peace. I suffered in silence because I was the First Lady and I knew I had to stand by Pastor Lucas and the ministry no matter what. And yes, there were times when I lost myself in the process. But it was well worth the sacrifice.

"I finally told Pastor Lucas how I felt and he apologized for his insensitivity. I was finally able to put it behind me. I realized I just couldn't fulfill the sexual part of our marriage because of all the pain. I also realized that it was unfair of me to expect Pastor Lucas to remain celibate. He and I finally came to an agreement about his indiscretions. He had to be discreet and never flaunt his liaisons in my face. Being a part of the ministry and raising my children has been fulfilling enough for me. Now I have the grandchildren too and I feel my life is complete." Sharon's face had gone from disbelief, to sympathy, to understanding. *Good,* thought Viola. *Now we can get off me and my marriage and on to the more important issue of your marriage to my son.*

"Don't ruin your marriage, Sharon. Go to God. He didn't put you two together to be torn apart by one mistake. Go to counseling. Do whatever you have to do to keep your marriage together. Talk to each other. You must stick by your husband's side no matter what. I have never lied to you, Sharon; I tell you these things because I think you need to hear them… Pastor Lucas isn't here now, but when he gets home I'll tell him all that you've told me. There is no need for you to have to tell him something like this. I know it would be uncomfortable for you."

Sharon was in a quandary. She loved Richard Jr., she felt certain that he loved her, and she wanted her marriage to work. She knew that Viola and Richard Jr. shared a close relationship and that he admired her greatly. She couldn't believe that he spoke of her with his mother on a regular basis and the thought made her feel special.

The most unbelievable thing that Viola had shared with her was her knowledge of Pastor Lucas' indiscretions. Who knew she had a problem with painful sex? Sharon couldn't imagine being unable to enjoy love-

S.E.C.R.E.T.S. VOLUME II by: *Pastor Shirley*

making. How empty Viola's life must be. However, Pastor Lucas could be a little more discreet. Everyone knew of his indiscretions and his attraction to Latin women.

Sharon tried to envision herself telling Pastor Lucas about Richard Jr. having sex with another man and the thought made her just a tad nervous. She had a good relationship with Pastor Lucas, but he could be overbearing and had a tendency to be condescending in his interactions with women. With everything else she was going through, she had no desire to add Pastor Lucas' archaic mindset concerning women to the list, so she decided to let Viola relay the information to him, especially since she'd offered to do it.

Sharon told Viola that she would accept her offer to tell Pastor Lucas about the things they'd discussed. Feeling that the visit had come to an end, she gathered her purse, stood, and hugged her mother-in-law. She thanked her for listening and kissed her on the cheek. Feeling much better, Sharon left.

From her living room window, Viola watched her back out of the driveway. She grinned from ear to ear and shook her head in satisfaction. She had lied through her teeth but she had done and said whatever was necessary to keep Sharon from leaving Richard Jr. It was true that he really loved Sharon. It was also true that he was bisexual and not gay.

Viola had known about Richard Jr. since he was 13 years old when she'd caught him and a boy who lived down the street, fondling and kissing one another. She had sent the boy home and had a long talk with Richard Jr. She told him she loved him and that he could *not* openly pursue this lifestyle. He was the one who would one day succeed his father and he couldn't do that if people knew he was having sex with men. Richard Jr. had been terrified that Viola would share his sexual preference with his father. Viola reassured him she would never share anything negative about him to anyone and that she would always protect him.

Over the years, Viola had "rescued" Richard Jr. from several similar situations. Each time she had scolded him about the need to be discreet and reminded him that he was to be the future leader of the ministry. He had to keep that in mind and always work toward that end. Any time rumors about him surfaced, Viola quickly and efficiently obliterated them. She never told Pastor Lucas because she knew that he would disown Richard Jr. and she simply couldn't allow that to happen. The ministry was *everything* to her. *Nothing* else was as important. Even as she told Sharon that she would relay the information to Pastor Lucas, she had absolutely no intention of letting one single word of their conversation escape her lips.

Viola had carefully worked behind the scenes to guarantee that Richard Jr. would inherit the leadership of the ministry after Pastor Lucas' demise. Though she had no influence over Pastor Lucas, she had a large amount of influence over her son. She had deliberately cultivated her relationship with him to ensure that he always felt that he needed her and owed her because she had protected his awful secret…and had done so repeatedly.

All that stuff about painful sex and Pastor Lucas treating her like a queen was something she concocted on the fly. She really liked Sharon and she couldn't bear the thought of her looking at her with pity in her eyes. So she had come up with an explanation. A good explanation even if she had to say so herself. Viola grinned toothily. She knew that her plan was finally coming together.

Viola called Richard Jr. on his cell phone. She told him everything that had transpired and everything she'd told Sharon. She admonished him for not having called her beforehand and she then advised him on his next course of action. After hanging up the phone, she went into the family room to watch her favorite cooking show, "Down Home with the Neelys." She loved the meals they cooked and the fact that Pat understood that it took nothing away from his manhood to let the world know that he adored his wife. *Oh, what I would do to have a man think of me in that way,* Viola mused. She burrowed into the cushions and clicked the television on. After all, there was nothing else she or Richard Jr. could do now except wait.

****

S.E.C.R.E.T.S. VOLUME II by: *Pastor Shirley*

Three weeks after Sharon caught Richard Jr. engaged in gay sex, Pastor Lucas had a massive heart attack and was hospitalized. Two days later he died, and Richard Jr. succeeded his father as leader of the ministry. In the midst of all the family turmoil, Sharon was caught up in assisting Viola with the many details of the enormous funeral. Pastor Lucas was well known and people would be attending from far and wide. To Richard Jr.'s utter relief, Sharon momentarily forgot about his repenting in front of the church and their attending counseling. He, of course, did not remind her.

The day of the funeral, Richard Jr.'s jaw was fully healed and no longer required bandaging. He was able to render a lively, upbeat eulogy.

Holding a tray with two steaming cups of Sharon's favorite Colombian coffee heavily laced with cream and sugar, Viola called Sharon into Pastor Lucas' office at the church. They had been extremely busy and she figured they could both use a breather. She put a cup of the fragrant brew in front of Pastor Lucas' chair and one in front of the visitor's chair on the other side of the desk. Viola took a seat in Pastor Lucas' large chair and motioned Sharon into the chair opposite the desk. His chair gave Viola a great sense of power and it radiated from her in waves. Sharon noticed something different about Viola though she couldn't quite put her finger on what it was. She seemed somehow more confident, which was ridiculous because she knew confidence was the one thing Viola did not possess.

Viola smiled and began. "Sharon, I just wanted to thank you for all your help. Without you I don't know how I would've been able to organize this huge affair." She nonchalantly picked up her cup and took a leisurely sip of her coffee.

"But that's not why I called you in here. I wanted to talk to you. What I'm about to say may shock you, but I'm telling you these things because you need to hear them." Sharon had no idea what Viola was about to say, but with an opening like that, she steeled herself for the worst.

"Pastor Lucas' dream was always that Richard Jr. take over the ministry if anything ever happened to him. Richard Jr. is ready and he has taken control. He will be a much better leader than Pastor Lucas and that's really saying something. Under his leadership, the ministry will reach heights you can't even dream of. You are now the First Lady of this church and this ministry. Richard Jr. needs you by his side and the ministry needs you. He cannot be effective and focus on the ministry if you're not here to lend your sound advice and he only sees his kids on the weekends." It was Sharon's turn to adopt an air of nonchalance.

Viola continued. "You must smile even when you're crying on the inside. You must hold your head high even when you want to run and hide. If Richard Jr. is having a hard time making it up a hill, you must get behind him and push. I've had to do all these things and more during my time as the First Lady. I even turned a blind eye when Pastor Lucas fathered several children by other women in the church."

Viola noticed Sharon's nonchalance quickly change to shock. "Yes, Sharon, Pastor Lucas has always been honest with me about his other life and his other kids. He has several other children and two of them even grew up in the church right along with our own children. There were many Sundays I looked out over the congregation and I hated the mothers and their bastard children." The amount of venom in Viola's voice shocked Sharon. She'd never seen her show any type of strong emotion in the past.

"But I realized that I could not allow my personal feelings to get in the way of the growth of the ministry. I could not allow a scandal of that magnitude to destroy all the work we had done over the years. No one would have understood my agreement with Pastor Lucas and I certainly didn't want everyone knowing the intimate details of our marriage. I did what I had to do, and suffered in silence, because I was the First Lady. I stood by him because it was my duty to stand in the gap for my husband. There are many other instances I could share with you, but they don't matter anymore." Both Sharon and Viola took sips of their coffee. Sharon set her mug on the desk and leaned back in her chair.

"Sharon, I have come to realize that very few things are as they appear. I have interacted and networked with hundreds of First Ladies over the

S.E.C.R.E.T.S. VOLUME II by: *Pastor Shirley*

years and most of them will fall into one of three categories.

1. They have been THERE.
2. They will go THERE.
3. Or they are already THERE.

"Where is 'THERE' you're probably thinking? 'THERE' is the secret life all First Ladies will lead at one time or another. 'THERE' is the horrible existence where the First Lady is smiling on the outside and crying on the inside. 'THERE' is what every First Lady does to protect her home, her ministry, and her lifestyle. 'THERE' involves areas like adultery, mental abuse, physical abuse, drug use, incest, and a whole host of other unpleasant issues. Many First Ladies are dealing with multiple situations.

"You must remember that no matter how First Ladies look, act, or dress, they are all dealing with secrets. Some are more dreadful and bizarre than you can imagine. Sometimes it hurts and it's not easy being THERE. But you can be thankful you've only had one area to deal with and you've only had to deal with it one time. Richard Jr. loves you and his family so much. He would never dream of disrespecting you, so at least you don't have to worry about that. Yes, he made a mistake, albeit a big mistake. But he realizes he made a mistake and he won't do it again.

"Now, you must look at the big picture. Being the First Lady of the ministry will afford you many luxuries and perks. Luxuries you can't even imagine. The first perk being that you will no longer have to work a job outside the home. I know you find being a lawyer fulfilling, but you won't have time to be a lawyer AND be an effective First Lady of this thriving ministry. Richard Jr. was going to tell you that after the funeral, but I just had to tell you now. I didn't take advantage of many of those luxuries, but you must do so and enjoy it. You will have assistants, household servants, drive the best cars, and eat at the best restaurants. You will take regular vacations to exotic locations and wear only designer clothes. Your children will attend the most prestigious private schools and associate with other children of rich and famous people. You will receive a large amount of respect just because of your position as the First Lady. Use it wisely and don't abuse it. You cannot turn your back on God. You cannot turn your back on the ministry. And you cannot turn your back on Richard Jr. You will reap many benefits for all of your hard work, dedication, and devotion."

Viola's voice had now taken on a hard edge, the likes of which Sharon had never heard her use before. "Sometimes, Sharon, you just have to suck it up. Sometimes, you just have to look the other way. No matter what he does, no matter what you see, it is your responsibility to keep it all together and to protect your husband and the ministry at all costs. Nagging and complaining have no place in the life of a First Lady. My husband worked too hard in this ministry to let it fail now. I never found it necessary, but if it pleases you to do so then take a lover on the side. Just be discreet. Do whatever you have to do in order to maintain the public image of a loving family." Sharon could no longer maintain her façade of nonchalance. She stared at Viola in open-mouthed shock. Viola noticed Sharon's reaction and inwardly smiled. *Surely,* Viola thought, *you are not a prude, Sharon. We are two grown women, for heaven's sake!*

Outwardly, Viola continued in a much louder voice. "YOU MUST STEP UP TO THE PLATE! You must always appear in public with your head held high, proud, and tall. After all, YOU ARE NOW THE FIRST LADY!"

Viola paused and wiped her brow with her ever-present linen hankie. "Sharon, you must never forget there is always some other woman waiting in the wings to take your place. There is always some other woman who will be willing to overlook any number of indiscretions and do whatever is necessary in order to reap the rewards and respect of being the First Lady of the ministry, especially a large, thriving ministry like this one will become under Richard Jr.'s leadership. Pastor Lucas arranged that upon his death, an extremely large sum of money would go to the ministry to assist Richard Jr. and put him on the rise. You are Richard Jr.'s wife and you have the intelligence and practicality needed to assist him in leading the ministry to new and exciting heights. Yes, you may have to perform a few unpleasant tasks along the way, but oh the rewards you will reap will be more than worth it. If you cannot get over this incident on your own, think of your children. Would you deprive them of a lavish lifestyle and the chance to rub elbows with other wealthy children?" Before Sharon could answer, Viola answered her rhetorical question. "No, you wouldn't deprive your children of this great opportunity. Never forget that, nor take your eyes off the prize."

Sitting quietly in her chair opposite Viola, Sharon was in major shock. Viola was essentially dangling a carrot in front of her face. Keep her mouth shut, support Richard Jr. no matter what he did, and she would reap untold financial benefits and fame as a result, not to mention the power! She knew that her husband was an excellent steward and the ministry would indeed thrive as a result. But, could she do that? Could she just forget that she had seen her beloved husband having sex with another man in her bed, just to reap financial gain? She would still demand a battery of blood tests and counseling. If she was going to try to forget this wicked mess, the least he could do was cooperate on those points.

And what about her children? Did she want to deprive them of such a lavish lifestyle? No, she didn't and she wouldn't. And what about her job? All the "ands" and "buts" swirled in and out of Sharon's mind.

Viola watched Sharon intently. She could plainly see her examining and discarding different scenarios as her brain evaluated the pros and cons of all she'd just heard. Nevertheless, Viola wasn't worried. She had made a calculated bet on a winning candidate. Sharon really did love her son and her children, *and* she was extremely materialistic. She worked hard as an attorney to afford the designer clothes and other items she deemed important. Sharon loved being an attorney, but it was stressful and regularly required long hours. So Viola had done what any intelligent person would do; she had dangled in front of Sharon's face all the things she knew were important to her. She had essentially told Sharon that she could live way more lavishly without having to work 80 hours a week to pay for it, as long as she remained with Richard Jr. and supported him in the ministry. She knew that Sharon would not be able to walk away from the lifestyle she'd just described. She also knew that she had to feel as if she had come to the decision on her own.

Having gone through myriad scenarios in her mind, Sharon appeared to come to a decision. She looked Viola in the eye. "I understand everything you've said to me, Viola. I will follow your sound advice and I will do whatever I have to do in order to serve and protect the ministry." She smiled brightly and Viola returned the smile in kind. "However," Sharon continued bringing an abrupt end to Viola's 'cheesefest.' "There are four things I must have in order to put Richard Jr.'s gay episode behind me and they are non-negotiable."

Viola felt a prick of irritation and the first stirrings of anger. She had just offered this simple woman the world on a platinum platter; a world that she'd certainly never had, and she had the audacity to present her with non-negotiable demands? Viola carefully schooled her features into blankness, something that came easily to her after two decades of practice. "What are the four things you want, Sharon?" She asked in a calm voice.

"What you are asking me to do is going to be extremely difficult," Sharon began, effectively setting the stage for her requests. Viola's features remained expressionless. *So,* thought Viola, *she is going to use Richard Jr.'s dumb actions to her advantage. Smart move and smart woman.*

Sharon continued, "I came home from work and caught the man I love in *my* bed having sex with another man. That memory constantly haunts my days and my nights. I can't seem to stop thinking about it. It's like a horrible movie that won't stop playing over and over in my head. In order for me to get over this, I'm going to need some professional help. Richard Jr. and I must go to counseling."

Viola said nothing. She picked up her coffee and took a small sip, never shifting her gaze away from Sharon's face. When Viola didn't respond, Sharon detailed her other demands. "I want Richard Jr. and I to have full physicals complete with blood tests for all sexually transmitted diseases, especially AIDS. There is no way I can continue my marriage on any level until I am certain we are both healthy and disease free.

"Regarding my job, I'm not going to resign. I love what I do, Viola. I worked too hard and paid too much for my education to just walk away.

S.E.C.R.E.T.S. VOLUME II by: *Pastor Shirley*

However, the ministry will be my priority, so I will entertain reducing my work schedule to accommodate its demands; but I'm not going to quit. If in the future, I realize there is no way I can do both, we can revisit the issue.

"And lastly, I cannot continue to sleep in the house where I caught Richard Jr. in bed with another man. I can't put the incident behind me if I have to repeatedly confront the 'scene of the crime.' I can barely stand to enter that house let alone continue to live my life there. I'm going to need a huge new house, completely furnished, of course."

Viola mentally reviewed Sharon's requests. She had underestimated the little minx. Though she would never admit it, she was truly impressed. She briefly wondered if Sharon would prove to be a formidable opponent in the future. Viola quickly dismissed the absurd notion with a mental wave of her hand. No matter what, she could handle Sharon.

Sharon's first two demands were reasonable and she would certainly tell Richard Jr. to comply. But her refusal to leave her job angered Viola more than she cared to admit. *How dare she tell me that SHE will revisit the issue in the future if SHE realizes she can't do both! Who does SHE think she is? It's not about her. It's about the best interests of the ministry!* Sharon needed to be taken down a peg or two. Unfortunately, she couldn't afford to do that at this time. Right now, she needed Sharon to take her place beside Richard Jr.—at least for a year or two until she was ready to implement her master plan. Viola decided to ignore Sharon's ridiculous notion of continuing to work outside the home. She would see soon enough how difficult that was going to be.

Sharon's last demand presented a small problem. Viola could tell that Sharon fully expected the ministry to pay for the new house and its furnishings. Knowing Sharon, all would be extravagant and expensive. Viola seethed at the thought. Because of Pastor Lucas' history of mismanaging finances, she was certain there was little if any money in the church coffers. However, due to Richard Jr.'s talent of making money grow quickly and efficiently from the most unlikely sources that would not be the case for long. Viola would simply have to pay for the house out of the money she would receive on Pastor Lucas' life insurance policies.

Unbeknownst to her husband, she had maintained two separate life insurance policies on him for over twenty years. The payment of one policy alone totaled over five million dollars. Viola knew that she could meet the greediest of Sharon's stipulations. She would ensure that Richard Jr. understood that the money she spent on their new house was a loan and required repayment after he straightened out the ministry's finances. Though annoyed, Viola was also silently amused that Sharon honestly thought that what she was demanding was some form of punishment for Richard Jr.'s bad behavior. In all actuality, it was a small price to pay for keeping Sharon's silence and ensuring her total cooperation regarding her First Lady duties. That cooperation was the first step that would enable Viola to implement the plan she had been crafting for over a decade. The benefits of this "investment" far outweighed Sharon's petty desires.

Viola slowly rose and walked to the front of the desk. "Everything you've asked for is reasonable and doable. You can start looking for a new house next week. I'll talk to Richard Jr. about it. But not to worry, you will have your new, fully furnished house." She hugged Sharon warmly.

Sharon said, "Again, I understand everything you've said. I won't get sidetracked and I won't allow a woman, or anyone else for that matter, to take my place or provide fodder for the church gossips." Sharon stepped back from Viola and looked her directly in the eye. "I will do everything you have advised."

Sharon hugged Viola again and went back to the banquet hall to supervise the meal. As she left, Viola sat back in her husband's chair and smiled to herself. Yes, she had known that she would outlive Pastor Lucas. In fact, she had counted on it. He was 15 years her senior and he'd spent his entire life in and out of bed with a variety of women. She felt certain he would've caught something with all that bed hopping. But, wouldn't you know it wasn't his bed hopping that finally brought him down but his faulty heart?

This came as no surprise to her either considering his affinity for junk food and lack of exercise. He was so busy virtually ignoring Viola that he failed to notice how well she took care of her physical body. Her body was her temple and she treated it with kindness and reverence. She adhered to a strict vegetarian diet and she refused to put anything artificial in her body. She never called attention to her preferred eating plan by making separate meals for herself. She cooked regular meals, put a little of everything on her plate, but she only ate those items that nurtured her body. Pastor Lucas never noticed she wasn't partaking of the fattening, artery-clogging favorites he loved and ate with gusto.

Viola also maintained a six-day a week alternating walking, weight training and Pilates exercise regimen. As a result, she had the body of a 25-year old. The walking resulted in a firm tone, the Pilates gave her extreme flexibility, fluidity, and balance, and the weight training carved her lean, flexible limbs into pure muscle.

She wished Pastor Lucas would have paid more attention to her and that he had treated her with love. She would never forgive him for not treating her with love and respect and for subjecting her to public humiliation due to his many and continuous liaisons. She would never forget how he constantly told her that she was ugly and once even required her to affix a picture of a naked and fully exposed harlot out of a smut magazine to the wall above her head while he had sex with her. He then made her turn her face so it would not interrupt his line of vision. Viola hated him for all the cruelty she'd endured at his hands and she began plotting her revenge and her comeback years ago when she first caught Richard Jr. with the boy down the street. Patience was a virtue and she had it in spades. After all, she had nurtured it for years for just such a time as this.

She had meticulously cultivated her relationship with Richard Jr. She constantly praised him and made sure he knew she loved and supported him. She made sure he knew she accepted him regardless of his attraction to men. She made sure he knew that he could tell her anything and tell Pastor Lucas nothing. She wanted Richard Jr. to be emotionally and irrevocably tied to her and through years of painstaking planning, she had succeeded.

Over the years, Viola had found a measure of fulfillment in being a mother. But she had found the most fulfillment in being the First Lady of the ministry. Ugly or not, she was afforded a large deal of respect because she was the First Lady. It was to that end that she had patiently worked. She had waited years to implement part two of her plan. It was now time to do just that.

Viola knew that people looked at her and wondered what Pastor Lucas had ever seen in her. She knew that they laughed at her behind her back. They called her ugly, stupid, and dumb. But she was none of those things, she thought with a smug smile. She would soon make those same ignorant people eat crow. She was VIOLA LUCAS! It was her turn! And they would all regret their cruel, insensitive words. They would envy her and want to be her.

She rose to leave the office. She looked around one last time. One regime had ended. THANK GOD! A new regime was about to begin with her at the helm. She looked forward to it.

She walked out and closed the door softly behind her. As she walked to the banquet hall, her mind was busy making plans for her future. And oh what an exciting future it would be… at least for her. Woe unto anyone who even *thought* to step in the way of her new empire!

To find out what happened to Viola Lucas, Richard Lucas Jr., and Sharon Lucas, be sure to read S.E.C.R.E.T.S. of the First Ladies, Trilogy. Available soon in a bookstore near you.

Chapter 13

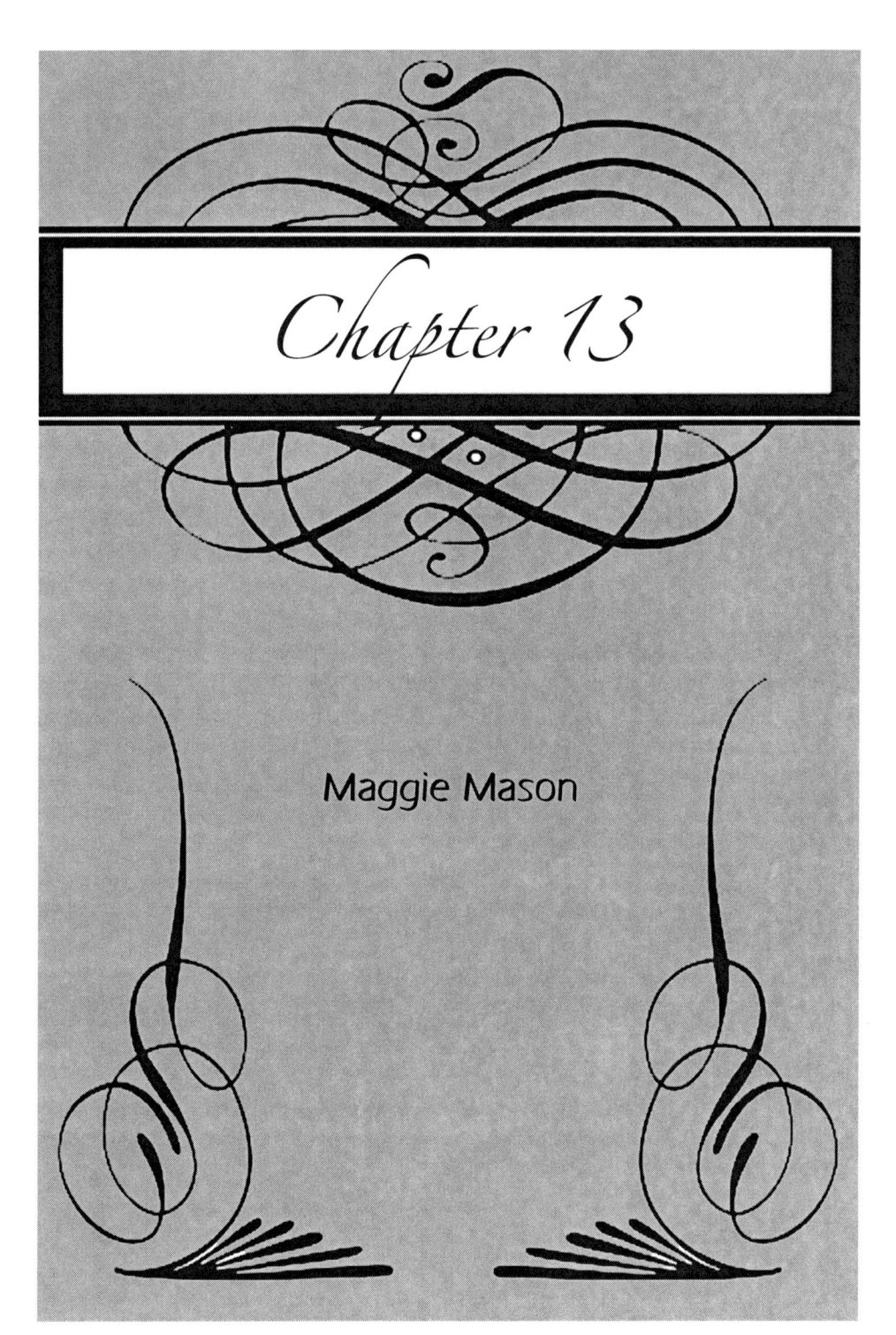

Maggie Mason

S.E.C.R.E.T.S. VOLUME II by: *Pastor Shirley*

Maggie Mason
628 Sherwood Pass

Maggie Mason

Maggie…
Your mind is ablaze
With hazy thoughts
Reaching desperately
For the peace you've always sought

A new woman, a new home
new clothes, new love
Yet all you have is old and worn
And you are sadly alone

Concocting a disease
To explain your appearance
To try and cover up
The other woman's interference

You'd be tempted to laugh
If there weren't so much pain
Hopes, dreams, ambition…
completely gone down the drain…

S.E.C.R.E.T.S. VOLUME II by: *Pastor Shirley*

First Lady Maggie Mason is approximately 5'7" tall, slender in form, wears her hair shoulder length, and is considered a conservative dresser. She has been married to Pastor Robert Mason for 10 years and together they have pastored a small ministry for the last five. Though she is acknowledged as quiet and reserved, she loves the church members and they adore her.

Pastor Robert Mason is approximately 5'9" tall and somewhat overweight. He is outgoing, has a penchant for playing practical jokes, and can be extremely manipulative if he thinks the situation warrants it. Robert is a man who only devotes time to those things that he deems important. Unfortunately, his style of dress didn't make the cut. He couldn't care less what he wears as long as the items are clean.

Because the ministry is small, Maggie wears many hats and fills in whenever there is a need. And there is *always* a need. Maggie is the soloist, the choir leader, the Wednesday night youth teacher, the Sunday school teacher, the hospitality leader, and the usher. She wears so many hats that it sometimes slips her mind that she is also the First Lady.

The Masons had a stormy marriage from the beginning, which resulted in both of them backsliding as well as a seven-year separation. During this separation, Maggie met another man, Noah, and fell in love. Noah was the exact opposite of Robert. He was kind, loving, and supportive. Noah treated her as if she were the most important person in the universe. And to him, she was. He proudly introduced her to his family and friends. He refused to listen to his family regarding her marital status, stating firmly that it was between him and Maggie and no one else. She had finally made the decision to divorce Robert so that she could marry Noah and live her life happily with him, a life that she eagerly looked forward to. When she told Noah of her decision, he screamed loudly, picked her up, and swung her around the room. Two days later, after a routine visit to her doctor, Maggie was ecstatic to learn that she was pregnant with Noah's child.

Maggie called Noah at work and told him that they were going out to dinner that night. She asked him to meet her at Vincenzo's, an upscale Italian restaurant. Noah said, "Sure, are we celebrating something?" Maggie smiled and answered, "We certainly are!" And then hung up the phone to keep from answering further questions and spoiling her surprise.

When Noah arrived, Maggie was waiting for him. She was dressed in a sexy, low-cut black dress, tall black high heels, and her hair was piled on top of her head in a sexy upsweep. This style of dress was totally out of character for Maggie, who normally favored more conservative fashion. Noah took one look at Maggie and said, "WOW! You look amazing! I can hardly wait to find out what we're celebrating so we can go home and really celebrate." He threw her a come-hither look and waggled his eyebrows suggestively as he finished his sentence.

Maggie made him wait until dessert before she told him the news because she knew that once she did, they were leaving regardless of how much they'd eaten. However, she hadn't anticipated Noah's response. When she told him they were going to have a baby, he went completely silent. He didn't say a single word as he stared mutely at her. When he failed to respond, Maggie misinterpreted his response as negative and burst into tears. Maggie's outburst jolted Noah back to reality. He jumped from his seat, ran around to her side of the table, and engulfed her in a loving embrace.

Having heard Maggie burst into tears, the entire restaurant now blatantly observed as Noah held her and hastily explained. He told her he was beyond happy about the baby. He'd always wanted a baby with her but was afraid she didn't want one with him because of her marital situation. He was so stunned when she'd told him that she was giving him something he'd wanted so badly, it had rendered him completely speechless. But it was a speechlessness born of pure happiness.

When Maggie realized that he was happy about the baby, she stopped crying and hugged him. Noah picked her up and began screaming that they were going to be parents. The entire restaurant erupted into applause for the happy couple that was so obviously in love. The manager even sent over a beautiful, complimentary chocolate cake. Noah told him to box the cake to go because they were leaving to go celebrate.

S.E.C.R.E.T.S. VOLUME II by: _Pastor Shirley_

That evening, as they lay in bed after a particularly tender bout of love-making, Maggie thought she could never be happier than she was at that moment.

Two months later, Noah was killed in a freak accident at work. All the dreams she'd had of spending her life with this wonderful man were now over. Her baby conceived in love would never know how wonderful his/her father was, or see his beautiful smile or experience his love and support. Maggie was absolutely distraught.

Maggie had not seen Robert in years, but a few months after Noah died, she ran into him at the grocery store. He paled as his eyes swept over her very pregnant belly. He was furious that she'd had the audacity to take up with another man and become pregnant when they were still married. He conveniently forgot all the sexual interludes in which he'd been involved and that he had also fathered several children by different women during their separation.

Seeing her made Robert realize how much he'd missed her. He knew he hadn't treated Maggie as well as he should have. He told her that he wanted her back and that he was determined to do a better job as a husband. He told himself the fact that she was pregnant with another man's baby was of no consequence. If they reunited, he would raise the child as his own, even giving the child his name. He thought he was being particularly generous considering Maggie's obvious betrayal.

After Noah's death, Maggie realized that she needed God in her life and began attending church again. She repented and was reconciled to God. Maggie went to church regularly and Robert soon realized that if he was going to see her, he would have to attend church too. He also realized that in order to be a part of Maggie's life again, he would have to do more than just go to church; he would have to get saved. This he pondered. Did he want to get saved again? Yes, he decided that he did. He had to admit that his life had been much better with God in it. With his mind made up, the next time Robert attended church, he repented and was reconciled to God. Soon thereafter, much to his delight, he and Maggie moved back in together.

Maggie was in the advanced stages of pregnancy and more than anything she needed rest. She was tired and looked haggard because she was not sleeping at night. Robert kept her up every night drilling her like a common criminal. He even went so far as to move the dining room table, put a chair under the light fixture, and demand that she sit in the chair to answer his questions. Maggie looked at him like he was demented and she refused. Robert became obsessed and continued to question her. He wanted her to confess to everything she'd done while they'd been separated. He wanted to know dates and times. He wanted to know everyone she had kissed, gone out to dinner with, had sex with, or even smiled at. He wanted to know every aspect of her life with Noah and, most importantly, about their sexual relationship. He wanted Maggie to compare his lovemaking to Noah's and then tell him he was better in bed than Noah had been. He wanted to know how many times a week they had made love, how long it had taken for her to reach a climax, if they had engaged in oral sex, and even the positions that they had enjoyed.

After weeks of incessant questioning, Maggie had had enough. She could not go on with the small amount of sleep she was getting. That night, when Robert came in from work, Maggie said, "Robert, I'm glad you're home. Come sit in the living room. I want to talk to you." Robert shrugged and indicated the kitchen. Noticing his gesture, Maggie smiled and said, "Dinner's done. We can eat when we finish talking. I felt like cooking today so I made fried chicken, mashed potatoes and gravy, biscuits, and cabbage, and for dessert I baked a peach cobbler."

Robert's stomach grumbled. Maggie was a wonderful cook and he was looking forward to dinner. They both sat down and Maggie took a deep breath. "Robert, I'm in the last stages of my pregnancy and I just cannot continue to exist on one or two hours of sleep a night. These marathon-questioning sessions have got to end. They aren't doing either of us any good. Anything we did while we were separated and unsaved is under the blood. God has forgiven us and we said we forgave each other when we got back together. There is no purpose in rehashing past events, yours or mine. Since nothing good can come of all the questions…" Maggie paused before continuing, "I will not answer any more questions about

S.E.C.R.E.T.S. VOLUME II by: *Pastor Shirley*

anything that happened in the past."

Maggie saw a flicker of irritation quickly flit across Robert's face. She knew that he was not happy about her telling him what she was and was not going to do; but when it came to this matter, she had to put her foot down or she would go insane. She kept talking, albeit at a faster pace. "I've never asked you about what you did while we were separated and I know you were living with other women and you even had several children. You said you have forgiven me and I know I have forgiven you. In order for our marriage to work, we have to leave our past behind and move forward. When we got back together, you said you wanted to raise this baby as yours. Have you changed your mind?"

Robert was angry that Maggie had dared to bring up his other children and was attempting to dictate to him. It was as if she thought she was on the same level as he, which clearly she was not. But if he pushed her about her proper role as the wife now, she might leave him again and he certainly didn't want that. He felt that it was best to boost her confidence and deal with the task of molding her later. Robert was silent for a few moments longer, knowing that it was making Maggie uncomfortable. "No," he began slowly as if composing his thoughts as he spoke. "I haven't changed my mind. Because the baby is a part of you, it will be my baby too. I'm excited about that. I agree with you. We have to leave the past behind and move on. I'm sorry about all the questions." Lying through his teeth, he continued, "It won't happen again."

Maggie heaved a huge sigh of relief and smiled. She got up from her chair, hugged Robert, and kissed him on the cheek. She went into the kitchen to fix their plates. She had high hopes for their future. Sadly, her optimistic hopes were premature.

Robert had ceased his questions but he began keeping her up at night in other ways. Every time Maggie began to doze off, Robert roughly elbowed her in the side to wake her up. Maggie's side soon became badly bruised from all the poking. It was as if he was deliberately trying to keep her from getting a good night's sleep.

104

A few weeks later, Maggie gave birth to a healthy baby boy. True to his word, Robert was the doting dad and gave the baby, Troy, his last name. Maggie wanted to name him after his father, but knew the gesture would totally disrupt her marriage, so she kept the thought to herself. All appeared to be going well. Robert began pastoring a small church and he and Maggie became absorbed in the ministry and raising their son.

When Troy was just a baby, Maggie noticed a change in Robert. He became increasingly silent and withdrawn and he began doing things to deliberately frighten and subdue her. He bought two large dogs, a Rottweiler and a pit bull. He named them Joy and Pain and trained them to pounce at his command and to only take orders from him.

Robert trained the Rottie, Joy, to guard the front door and she wouldn't move unless he commanded her to do so. Thus, when he wasn't around, Maggie was a prisoner in her own house. Joy did not react if Maggie simply walked past the door, but if she tried to go out the door, Joy began growling and baring her teeth as if she were going to rip Maggie's throat out. Surprisingly, Joy loved Troy and allowed the baby to climb all over her and to pull her ears and docked tail. Much to Maggie's relief, Joy never moved, growled, or made any hostile gestures toward the baby. Robert's obsession with controlling her continued to escalate. One night, Robert and his killer pit bull, Pain, followed Maggie and her sister, Erin, to a visiting church. When the church service was over, Maggie and Erin were driving home with both of their children sleeping in the back seat. It was very foggy and difficult to see so travel was slow and tedious. Out of nowhere, a car flew by them so fast that it almost ran them off the road.

"Maggie, that car that almost ran us off the road looked just like Robert's car. And it looked like he had someone else in the car with him," Erin

S.E.C.R.E.T.S. VOLUME II by: *Pastor Shirley*

said with disgust.

Maggie peeled her eyes away from the foggy landscape and chanced a momentary glance at her sister before answering nervously, "Erin, I know you and Robert sometimes butt heads, but you can't possibly think he'd run us off the road. Besides, it's so foggy out here you couldn't have gotten a good look at the car. Trust me, Robert is at home. That couldn't have been him."

Erin was adamant. "This has nothing to do with me and Robert not getting along. I'm telling you I got a good look at that car and it was Robert and someone else. Just to prove it to you" Erin said, suddenly making a quick left onto an even darker road, "I'm taking a shortcut and we're going to beat Robert home."

Maggie leaned forward in her seat. She clutched the dashboard as she peered out the window desperately trying to see in front of them. She prayed that Erin knew where she was going and that she wouldn't run them into a ditch. There was nothing more for her to say because Erin would not be satisfied until she either proved her point or was shown that she was wrong.

Erin took a few quick turns and arrived at Maggie's house just as Robert was pulling into the driveway. Next to him sat, Pain, his killer pit bull that Erin had mistaken for another person.

"Well, well, well!" Exclaimed Erin. "I told you that was Robert and he had someone in the car with him. How was I to know he had that stupid dog with him?"

Maggie was absolutely horrified! She jumped out of the car and yelled, "What is wrong with you? You almost ran us off the road back there. Why would you feel the need to spy on me? And why in the world is that dog sitting up front next to you?"

Robert slowly got out of the car followed by Pain, who sat immediately next to him awaiting further instruction. Robert glanced at Erin sitting in her car observing the conversation between him and Maggie. He turned toward the house and said to Maggie over his shoulder, "I'm not discussing this in front of an audience." Robert motioned to Pain and they both entered the house.

Maggie turned sheepishly to Erin, too embarrassed for words. As she retrieved Troy from the back seat, she tried to cover up Robert's rudeness. She smiled and said, "Erin, everything's ok. You go on home and I'll call you tomorrow and fill you in on the details."

However, Erin was unconvinced. "Ok, I'm going, but if you need me any time of the day or night, you just call me. Christian and I will be over in a snap," she said snapping her fingers for emphasis. "I'll be praying for you and I love you." Maggie waved to Erin as she drove off.

Maggie entered the house and found Robert and Pain reclining on the couch in front of the television. "Robert, I told you I didn't want that dog on the furniture." Robert didn't even acknowledge her presence; he began playing with Pain.

As Maggie turned to leave, Robert jumped to his feet, anger transforming his features, and yelled, "Don't ever think you can talk to me like that, especially in front of your nosy sister. She's just looking for something to gossip about to the rest of the family. As far as the questions you asked me outside, I went for a drive. I never saw you. Where were you?"

Maggie looked at him not believing anything he'd said. "How could you not know it was us? You know Erin's car. Why were you following me? You didn't believe me when I told you we were going to church with Erin?"

"I told you," Robert said slowly and evenly, "that I was just out for a drive and I never saw you and Erin. And no, I was not following you. For what?" Maggie knew that he was lying but decided to let the incident pass before it blew up into something much worse.

Over the next few weeks, Robert began acting even more strangely and his every action was shrouded in jealousy. He questioned everything Maggie said and everywhere she went. The bouts of nightly marathon

S.E.C.R.E.T.S. VOLUME II by: Pastor Shirley

questioning resumed, and went on night after night after night. Maggie was worn down both mentally and emotionally and she felt as if she could not breathe. Robert was so preoccupied with Maggie and her schedule that she was unprepared when she discovered that he was having an affair.

Money became scarce in the Mason household, and Maggie was unable to pay the household bills. In past years, they'd had no problem meeting their financial obligations as Robert had been an employee at his company for over 10 years and made a good salary. She just couldn't understand where the money was going. She had since given birth to their daughter, Elizabeth, and no longer worked outside the home. Maggie asked Robert why money was so tight all of a sudden. Robert told her that the reason they were running short on money was because he hadn't submitted the paperwork for all the overtime he'd been working. Over the years, whenever his overtime paperwork fell behind, Maggie went to his office and completed the paperwork for him knowing that he wouldn't be paid for his overtime hours until it had been submitted. As Maggie sat looking at a stack of unpaid bills, she knew that they couldn't continue this way. She decided to go down to Robert's office to help him to get his paperwork in order. She had been a regular fixture at Robert's office in the past and no one would think it strange if she showed up now.

She went to Robert's office to fill out the necessary forms and realized that his overtime was drastically less than she had originally thought. Obviously, there was some mistake. She made a mental note to ask Robert about it and filled out the forms for the few hours she was able to confirm. As she finished, Robert walked into the office to see Maggie behind his desk and several of his time cards spread out in front of her. He was furious. "What are you doing here? I don't need you spying on me. I can't do my job with you looking over my shoulder and rifling through my things. Besides, there is confidential company information on my desk and I could be fired if someone saw you going through my paperwork. If you want to be a bookkeeper so bad, then go get a job somewhere else. I don't need you trying to be one here!"

Maggie looked at her husband disbelievingly. "I didn't come down here to spy on you. Why would I want to do that? I came down here to fill out your overtime paperwork like I've always done whenever you got behind. There is no money in the checking account. How am I supposed to buy food or pay bills?"

"I told you I was behind on my overtime paperwork and I meant that. I will get the paperwork submitted by the end of the week."

"And what am I supposed to do in the meantime? How are we supposed to buy food and pay utilities?

"I told you I would get the paperwork turned in by the end of the week and I will. I don't need you here standing over my shoulder. As far as the money to buy food, I don't have any to give you. And, if you are so gung ho to do my work, go get a job somewhere else. Or better yet, just go home."

Maggie was hurt and stunned by his reaction to her desire to help him. She gathered her car keys and her purse and quietly left Robert's office. While driving home, she prayed for God to intervene on her behalf. She asked God to unite them together in love and to bind every hindering spirit that might come to destroy their marriage. Though Robert's behavior at home changed drastically, it did not change one bit at church as he continued to preach, pray, and teach.

One Sunday, Maggie's two sisters, their husbands, and their children came to her house for dinner, after which time they were all going to visit Robert's church for the evening service. Everyone had eaten and the children were downstairs. Maggie went to the top of the stairs to check on the children when she heard her two oldest nieces, Rhonda and Deana, talking about Robert. She stopped, observed, and listened.

Rhonda was painting her fingernails when she said, "I hate going to Uncle Robert's church and I hate his preaching. Can you get more boring than him? As soon as he gets up to preach, everyone takes out a pillow. Girl, I put a search-a-word puzzle book in my purse just so I can stay awake. You know how Mom and Dad have a fit if I fall asleep." Rhonda stopped

S.E.C.R.E.T.S. VOLUME II by: *Pastor Shirley*

polishing her nails and began to blow on the hand she'd painted.

Deana rolled her eyes to the ceiling. "I don't know anyone who enjoys going to his church. That must be why he has so few members. They get sick of going to church to be put to sleep. Girl, give me a couple of pages out of your puzzle book. At least I'll have something to do too." Both girls laughed.

Maggie stood at the top of the steps contemplating her nieces' words. The girls were right. Robert was a boring preacher, though she had never admitted it to anyone, not even herself. Maggie yelled down to the girls and asked about kids. "They're fine, Aunt Maggie!" They yelled back in unison.

Maggie went back to the room where the adults were laughing and talking. Her mind was far away from the conversation at hand, as Maggie was mentally taking a long, hard look at their ministry. They had been working for over five years and what did they have to show for it? Not much. Their membership never seemed to grow. And why was their ministry not growing? There was no way they should still be at square one after five years of hard work. And what about her marriage? She couldn't quite put her finger on it, but she knew there was something seriously wrong as there were too many unanswered questions, too little money, and a definite change in their relationship.

Several days later, Maggie was at home. She had not heard from Robert all day, which was odd. At about 5:30 pm, she called his office to find out how much longer he was going to be.

"Hello," Robert answered curtly.

"Hi Honey. It's so late and since I hadn't heard from you all day and you still weren't home, I got worried. I have a good dinner waiting. How much longer are you going to be?"

"I have been really busy all day and I didn't have a chance to call you. I won't be home until late tonight because I have to catch up on my overtime paperwork and the district manager will be here in two days to do an inspection. You know what that means, more overtime for me and the guys as we get this facility ready."

"Ok, I'll put a plate in the microwave for you. I love you."

"Thanks. You too, bye." Robert hung up before she could speak further.

At 10:00 pm, Robert still hadn't come home. At this point, Maggie was very worried because he had never been that late before. She called his office and got no answer. She figured he must be on his way home and she went back to sleep. When she awoke at about 2:30 am, Robert was still not home. She was beyond scared now. She got up, got dressed, put her two sleepy children into the car, and drove down to her husband's office. It was completely dark and Robert's car was nowhere in sight. Maggie drove back home, put the children back to bed, and sat at her kitchen table. She made a pot of coffee, paced the floor, and prayed that nothing had happened to her husband. She called the office every 30 minutes but the phone just rang and rang.

At 7:30 the next morning, Robert finally answered the phone. Relief flooded through her as she said, "Robert, I have been calling for hours. Where have you been? Are you alright?"

"I had a lot of work to do to get ready for the inspection. I worked through the night."

"Robert, I was so worried when you hadn't come home I put the kids in the car and drove down there. The building was completely dark and your car was nowhere in sight."

"That was probably when I stepped out to get a bite to eat."

"What restaurant is open at 2:30 in the morning?"

"Denny's is open 24 hours."

"Well, why didn't you answer the telephone? I have been worried sick about you!"

S.E.C.R.E.T.S. VOLUME II by: *Pastor Shirley*

"I turned the ringer off. I didn't want to be disturbed. I needed to stay focused to get all this work done. I didn't know I would be working all night and it never occurred to me that you would be calling. I thought you would be asleep. I'm sorry I worried you."

Maggie contemplated Robert's explanation and it seemed reasonable, but something in her gut told her that there was more to the story. She ignored her gut feeling. "I was just so worried about you. Do you want me to bring you lunch?"

"No, no don't bother. I'll grab a sandwich."

"What time will you be home tonight?"

"The usual time. Oh I've got to go; my boss is calling." The line went dead without even the courtesy of a goodbye.

But Robert didn't come home that night either; using the same excuse he'd used the previous night. The next morning, Maggie called her husband and said, "Robert you're working so hard. Me and the kids would be happy to come down there and keep you company. We really miss you."

Robert blew up and began screaming, "First of all, I'm not alone, I'm surrounded by employees and I brought Joy and Pain down here. They love to run around this big warehouse at night and the boss likes that they guard the premises. Second, I don't need you down here spying on me and checking up to make sure I'm working. I am a grown man and I don't need another mother!" He slammed the phone down and left Maggie's ears ringing.

Maggie's jaws dropped to the floor. Where was all this anger coming from? She'd only wanted to help; to keep him company so he wouldn't be alone. This will blow over. It certainly can't get any worse. I'll just leave him alone and keep praying. But Maggie had no idea that it would be a week before she saw Robert again.

On Sunday morning when Maggie woke up, Robert still hadn't come home. She got up and got the children ready for church. When she arrived, Maggie was relieved to see Robert was already there. She hadn't seen him all week and her emotions ranged between being happy that nothing had happened to him and angry that he hadn't come home. As they approached, Robert was engaged in a conversation with Deacon Ward. The children ran to greet their father. "Daddy, Daddy, we missed you. Where have you been? Are you coming home tonight? You missed my baseball game," Troy told his father. The children fired questions at Robert, not giving him a chance to answer. He bent and hugged them both.

Deacon Ward noticed the kids' enthusiastic greeting. "I didn't know you were out of town, Pastor."

Robert smiled and responded, "No. . uh . .I. . um . . haven't been out of town . . I've just been working long hours." The lie then rolled easily off Robert's lips, "I'm up before the kids get up in the morning and get home after they have gone to bed. I'm thankful for the overtime hours but this schedule is killing me."

Maggie hurried up the sidewalk to have a few brief moments to speak with Robert. When he saw her approaching, he hurriedly walked inside the church without so much as a 'hello'. During the entire service, he never even looked in her direction. After he preached and prayed for the members in the prayer line, he made an announcement that shocked both Maggie and church members. "Before we dismiss church today, I need to inform you of some upcoming events. There will be no church tonight or for the next four weeks due to some badly needed renovations at the church. We don't want anyone getting hurt while the work is going on. However, you are free to visit other churches during that time. If you need anything, contact Deacon Ward, who will be in touch with me daily."

Maggie and the church members were stunned. Maggie's mind raced. Renovations? What renovations? Where was the money coming from to finance these renovations? Certainly not from their household. They could barely pay their bills as it was.

S.E.C.R.E.T.S. VOLUME II by: *Pastor Shirley*

Robert dismissed the service and before Maggie could get to him to discuss his whereabouts for the last week as well as his bombshell announcement, he jumped into his car and drove off. Maggie gathered the kids and went home.

After that, things deteriorated, as Robert still had not come back home. Maggie kept calling his job to attempt to talk things out, but to no avail. Robert said they had nothing to talk about. Maggie was desolate. She paced the floor night and day worrying about the welfare of her husband and her marriage. She was not eating and barely drinking, existing only on coffee and Pepsi. Since she was slender to begin with, she now looked drawn and even more haggard.

By now, Robert had been gone for two months and had refused to come home. Maggie decided to go to his job and confront him about his non-existence in their home. When she arrived at his job, he was in his office talking to Glen, one of his employees. Robert took in her gaunt appearance and carelessly flicked his eyes over her shrunken frame. He finished his conversation with Glen and asked him to close the door as he left.

As soon as the door closed, Maggie launched into the speech she'd rehearsed on the way over. "Robert, we have to talk. We can't go on like this. You've been gone for two months and you haven't left any money for food or bills; bills we need to pay because the creditors are calling every day and I have no idea what to tell them."

"Maggie, I don't need you coming down here nagging me and embarrassing me in front of my workers. Can't you see I'm trying to work? As far as money is concerned, I don't have any to give you and I don't know what to tell you except GET A JOB!" He walked around his desk and stood directly in front of her. "I've been thinking over the last two months. I needed that time to get my head together and decide if I still wanted to be married." Maggie gasped. His words had a devastating effect on her and it showed on her face. He was glad and felt powerful; his words had hit their mark. "But I'll tell you what. I will agree to come back home if you stop spying on me and get a job. I want you to pay half of the household bills and I will come and go as I please." Robert's voice dripped with animosity.

Maggie was shocked into silence. She could not believe all he'd just said. This wasn't a request. It was the foolish ramblings of a cruel and petty man. Had he conveniently forgotten that he'd been gone for two months? "Robert, you seem to forget that you told me repeatedly that you didn't want me to work. You wanted me to quit my good job as a teacher and stay home with the kids and take care of the house, which I have done well. I don't mind getting a job and helping out because our marriage is important to me. Which brings me to the I-will-come-and-go-as-I-please thing. How can we possibly have a good marriage with that kind of arrangement? No. That, I won't agree to."

Robert was furious that Maggie had the nerve to turn down his generous offer. He glared at her. "Maggie, my terms are not up for discussion. Take it or leave it." He paused and looked at Maggie. "Well, what's it going to be?"

Maggie did not answer Robert's question. She jumped to her feet abruptly and turned to leave her husband's office.

"I guess your answer is no," Robert said to Maggie's retreating back. He shrugged and picked up the labor report on his desk.

Maggie didn't know what to do now. As she drove home, she broke down and cried. She needed someone to talk to and she was so glad that Erin had finally returned. She had gotten a new job as a district manager, which required her to do one month of training, spending one week at each of the company's four divisions. During Erin's month out of town, she had spoken to her often; however, she absolutely refused to ruin this exciting new time for her sister by telling her how awful Robert was treating her and the kids. She was ever so happy now that Erin was back. She called her and Erin said that she would come right over.

Fifteen minutes later, Erin parked in front of Maggie's house. She got out of her car and began walking up to the front door. Maggie must have heard her arrive because she opened the front door as she stepped up on

S.E.C.R.E.T.S. VOLUME II by: *Pastor Shirley*

the porch. Upon seeing Maggie's emaciated state, Erin stopped dead in her tracks in stupefied shock. Maggie was barely recognizable as the person she had been one month ago. She appeared to have aged at least 10 years and had lost at least 20 pounds. Since Maggie was naturally thin, a 20-pound weight loss left her looking sickly and skeletal. She had dark circles under her beautiful eyes, her clothes were hanging off of her like clothes hang off a clothes rack, and her eyes were puffy and red.

Though Maggie looked terrible, Erin dared not tell her so. She took the last steps to the front door and grabbed her sister in a loving hug. Maggie burst into tears and Erin cried with her. They sank to the floor, holding each other and crying. Erin then began to pray and Maggie soon joined in with her. After a powerful, impromptu prayer session, they got up off the floor, shut the front door, and went to Maggie's kitchen table.

"Erin, I am so happy you're back in town. I really missed you. Mother always said we were so close we should have been twins".

Over hot tea, Maggie told her sister everything that had been going on, leaving out nothing. Erin listened in silent anger. *How could Robert treat my sister so horribly?* Thought Erin. *He should be thankful Maggie is even interested in his fat self!*

Erin sipped her tea and forced herself to listen to Maggie, as opposed to telling Robert off in her head. When Maggie told Erin that she had no idea how she was going to pay bills or buy food, Erin told her not to worry about it. She and the other members of the family would help her.

"I can't accept help from the family," Maggie wailed. "It's just too embarrassing."

"Maggie," Erin said calmly, "There is absolutely nothing to be embarrassed about. We are family and we help one another out of love because that's what we do. No one will think any less of you because of this awful situation. You never complained or hesitated to lend your financial support when Cara needed it. Or Jacey, or Samantha, or Evan and his wife or—"

"Alright," Maggie said sheepishly, with the faintest of smiles gracing her mouth, "I get your point."

"Your family loves you and we will get through this. This too shall pass," Erin said with finality.

When she finally left a few hours later, Maggie had eaten, showered, and was talking like her old self. Erin gave Maggie more than enough money to buy groceries and promised to come over the next day to get a handle on her financial situation. As Maggie waved goodbye to Erin from her front porch, she felt better than she had in weeks.

As promised, the next day Erin arrived with her checkbook, her favorite pen, a calculator, and some breakfast in hand. After they ate, Maggie cleared the table and brought out her mountain of bills. Erin deftly divided them into three piles: Pay now, pay later, and hell-will-freeze-over-before-we-pay-it. She even had little index cards with the headings printed on them.

She explained that the family was more than happy to assist Maggie and the kids, but that they were not paying Robert's bills too. All of his bills were placed on the "hell-will-freeze-over-before-we-pay-it" pile.

Two hours, numerous checks, and several cups of tea later, they had a handle on Maggie's finances. Erin then told Maggie that the private school that her children attended was looking to hire a first-grade teacher. Because it was a private school, it paid its teachers better than the public

S.E.C.R.E.T.S. VOLUME II by: *Pastor Shirley*

school system, it came with excellent benefits, and if she was hired, both of her children could attend at a 75% discount.

Maggie was ecstatic. Not only could she support herself and her children, but they could attend a prestigious private school as well, and at a significant discount! God was so good. In one of her darkest hours, He'd opened up a door to light her way and give her hope. No, she didn't have the job yet; however, she did have faith in God, which meant that as long as she was persistent and did her part, she would find a job because good teachers were always in demand. She hugged her sister and thanked her profusely.

Erin laughed and said, "Maggie, I haven't done anything. All I did was tell you about a job opportunity. You still have to apply and actually get the job."

Maggie was so overcome with emotion that she couldn't speak for a moment. One large, fat tear seeped out of her eye and rolled lazily down her left cheek. Wiping it away with the back of her hand, Maggie said, "You are the best big sister anyone could have, Erin. Here I am grown with my own kids, and you're still looking out for me. I know I have to apply for the job but you made me remember that I am educated and I have skills that people are willing to pay me for. You made me remember that I have a lot to offer and I don't have to sit around here waiting for Robert and being treated like less than a human being."

"AMEN!" Erin said as she jumped from her chair acting as if she was in church. They both erupted into a fit of laughter as they relived memorable church services from their childhood. Sometime later, Erin began gathering her items to leave. She grabbed the stack of envelopes containing Maggie's bills along with her purse, keys, pen, calculator, and index cards. Seeing that Erin had picked up the bills, Maggie said, "I can buy the stamps and mail those, Erin. They are my bills and you guys have done enough already."

"It's not a problem. One of the places I need to go to today is the post office so I might as well take these with me." Maggie gave her sister a fierce hug, hoping that it conveyed all the love and emotion she felt.

The following day, after dropping the kids off at school, Maggie drove to the school that Erin's two children attended. She had dressed carefully and prayed in the car on the way over, asking God to give her favor and grant her the job. As she walked into the school with her revised résumé in hand, she appeared to be much more confident than she actually felt.

A few days later, a member of the church, Sister Mathis, called Maggie to check on her. "Hello, Sister Mason. How have you been?"

"I've been just fine, Sister Mathis. Thank you for asking," Maggie said as warmly as she could, desperately trying to sound like her normal self.

"I wanted to call and check on you. I was at the grocery store yesterday and I ran into the pastor. I asked him how much longer the church is going to be closed. I asked him about you and he told me you had been very ill and had lost a lot of weight. He alluded to the fact that you might have an incurable disease. Are you all right, Sister Mason? Are you ill?"

Maggie thought she had heard everything. An incurable disease?! How could Robert spread such a vicious rumor about her? Well, she would put a stop to this madness right now. "No, Sister Mathis, I do not have an incurable disease and I have not been ill. I don't know what possessed him to say such a thing. I have lost a lot of weight because he and I have been having marital problems and I haven't had an appetite. But I do appreciate your concern. I haven't talked to Pastor Mason about the church, though; what did he say?"

"Oh, he said that the renovations weren't done yet. I told him that I drove by there and I hadn't seen anyone working. He said the repairs are being done inside the church and the workers are entering and leaving from the back entrance. I'm so glad you're not ill. I'll be praying for you that things work out for you and the pastor."

After Maggie hung up the phone, she called Robert at his office. He answered anxiously on the first ring as if he was expecting someone's call. When he heard Maggie's voice, his tone changed to one of great

S.E.C.R.E.T.S. VOLUME II by: *Pastor Shirley*

disappointment. Maggie ignored the instant change. "Robert, why did you tell Sister Mathis that I had an incurable disease?" She asked without preamble.

"Maggie," he said as if talking to a small child, "you do look like you're dying since you've lost all that weight."

"Robert how could tell people such an awful lie?"

"Like I said, you look sick, but more importantly, why are all these bill collectors calling my job?"

Maggie ignored the question about the bill collectors and asked some questions of her own.

"How am I supposed to pay bills at the house and buy food? You haven't left any money for the house in months. And what about the church? What are you going to do about the members? Sister Mays came by the house yesterday asking about the church and she said she couldn't reach you and Deacon Ward wasn't able to tell them anything."

"I'm not sure what I'm going to do about the church yet. I haven't decided. More importantly, it's none of your business because I'm the pastor. As far as money in the household is concerned, you need to get a job and support you and the kids. My money now has to support me. I'll pay you what I can to help out with Elizabeth, because she's mine. Troy never was and he's your responsibility… I've been thinking of starting a new church with new members and a new wife. You are supposed to be a helpmeet, not a burden and, Maggie, you are one great big burden around my neck."

"What do you mean a new wife? Robert, what are—" Before she could finish her sentence, he slammed the phone down.

The next day, as Maggie dropped the kids off at school, her mind was miles away thinking about her last conversation with Robert about a new wife. As she passed Walmart, she thought she spotted Robert's white Cadillac in the parking lot in the far south corner. She quickly made an illegal U-turn in the middle of the street almost hitting one car and causing another to come to an abrupt stop. The occupants of both began screaming obscenities at her while vigorously giving her the finger. Maggie ignored the screeching tires and angry shouts as she turned into Walmart.

As she drove closer, she realized that it *was* Robert's car and… he was with a woman. She drove around slowly looking for a spot from which she could observe them unobtrusively. Finding one, she promptly parked. Maggie watched in horror as they hugged, kissed, and laughed. They were so engrossed in their teenaged make-out session that neither noticed Maggie walk up to the passenger side of the car and violently snatch the door open.

"ROBERT, WHAT IS GOING ON AND WHO IS THIS WOMAN?" Maggie screamed.

Robert was so shocked that his mind refused to provide him with a suitable lie. So he told the truth. "This is Debra. Debra Perry. I'm in love with her and I want to be with her. I'm tired of sneaking around and I want the world to know I love her."

Maggie completely lost all conscious thought, so astounded was she by his earth-shattering statement. All these months,

- Robert had no money for their household, and Debra was the reason.
- Robert had made her feel as if she was inadequate, and Debra was the reason.
- Robert had been absent from their home, and Debra was the reason.
- Robert had lied to her and disrespected her, and Debra was the reason.
- Robert had been lying to the church members, and Debra was the reason.

Before Maggie could speak, Debra jumped out of the car with a smirk on her face. She said, "So this is your little wifey pooh. I see why you left home and came running to me. Look at her, she looks awful." Debra

S.E.C.R.E.T.S. VOLUME II by: *Pastor Shirley*

laughed menacingly. "Honey, only dogs want bones. You see all this lusciousness?" She asked, gesturing to herself from head to toe. "Look at what he's got now. Look at these firm breasts and these long, thick chocolate legs. And every night your husband's face is buried between them enjoying the sweet nectar inside. That's right, baby! The darker the berry, the sweeter the juice, and the nectar in this flower is syrupy sweet and he's addicted to it. He just can't seem to get enough of it." She finished her speech by placing her hands on her hips and glancing at Robert for confirmation. Robert sat mutely looking from one to the other, his mouth agape.

Rage welled up in Maggie and erupted viciously. Her eyes blazed and she screamed, *"OH NO YOU DIDN'T, YOU GUTTER SLUT!"* Maggie forgot that she was saved and picked up a piece of rusted pipe lying on the ground by Robert's car. She then began swinging it wildly at Debra with all her might. She hit Debra several times with the pipe, causing her to release a series of blood-curdling screams. Debra's screams finally pierced Robert's mind-numbing shock and jarred him into action. He jumped from the car, ran around to the passenger side, snatched the pipe from Maggie's hand, and threw it into nearby bushes. He grabbed Maggie in a bear hug, trapping her arms at her sides, and began screaming at her. While she struggled to free herself, Debra ran forward and viciously slapped the taste out of Maggie's mouth, sending her head flying back with the sheer force of the slap.

Robert immediately released Maggie and turned to enfold Debra in his arms. He ushered her to the passenger side of the car to sit so he could see the extent of her wounds. There was blood and he didn't know where it was coming from. He was absolutely scandalized by Maggie's violent, out-of-character behavior. He was scared to death as he pulled a handkerchief from his pocket and applied pressure to the most vicious looking wound on Debra's arm to staunch the flow of blood. It seemed to work. Thank God it wasn't serious. Robert spun around and directed his anger toward Maggie, whose eye had begun to swell and color from the brutal slap she'd received. He cursed her out and told her that if she ever touched Debra again he would beat her down with his own hands.

Reality set in as Maggie stood to the side watching Robert tend to Debra's wounds and whisper tender words of solace and love to her. Maggie's heart broke further. In all their years of marriage, Robert had never spoken to her like that. Only Noah had spoken to her that way. The rage that had earlier consumed Maggie dissipated like air seeping from a balloon. She immediately apologized to Debra and Robert and ran back to her car with tears blurring her vision. She got into her car and sped out of the parking lot. *Oh God, I could have killed that woman,* she thought. Maggie now knew the meaning of temporary insanity.

Realizing what she had done, upon entering her home, Maggie fell prostrate on the floor of her living room and repented to God. She prayed for strength and guidance. She prayed according to Philippians 4:7, that the peace of God which passeth all understanding would keep her mind and her heart. Maggie knew that no matter what happened in her life, nothing was worth losing God for, and nothing was worth her going to jail for either. Maggie prayed for Debra's shoulder and that she would not go to the police to press charges against her for assault.

After praying, Maggie went into the bathroom.

As she washed her hands, she looked into the mirror over the sink. She was astonished by her appearance; her right eye was black and blue, swollen half shut, and had a small cut underneath it. She was instantly alarmed. How was she going to explain these wounds to Erin and the rest of her family? What was she going to tell her children? Time stood still as she scrutinized her battered appearance in the bathroom mirror.

When she again became aware of her surroundings, she was a complete bundle of nerves. Every sound, real or imagined, sent her running to the living room window, terrified it was the police. Since her children were visiting their Aunt Erin, she was alone.

Clutching her living room drapes in a white-knuckled grip, she began to quote Psalms 118:17 repeatedly: *"I shall not die but live to declare the salvation of the Lord. I shall not die but live to declare the salvation of the Lord. I shall not die but live to declare the salvation of the Lord."*

S.E.C.R.E.T.S. VOLUME II by: *Pastor Shirley*

He will not get the best of me! He will not destroy me! Greater is He that is in me than he that is in the world! I am a woman of God and I know He has not brought me this far to leave me!

Oh my God! Are those police sirens I hear in the distance? Are they coming to arrest me?

To find out what happened to Maggie and Robert Mason, be sure to read S.E.C.R.E.T.S. of the First Ladies, Trilogy. Available soon in a bookstore near you.

Chapter 14

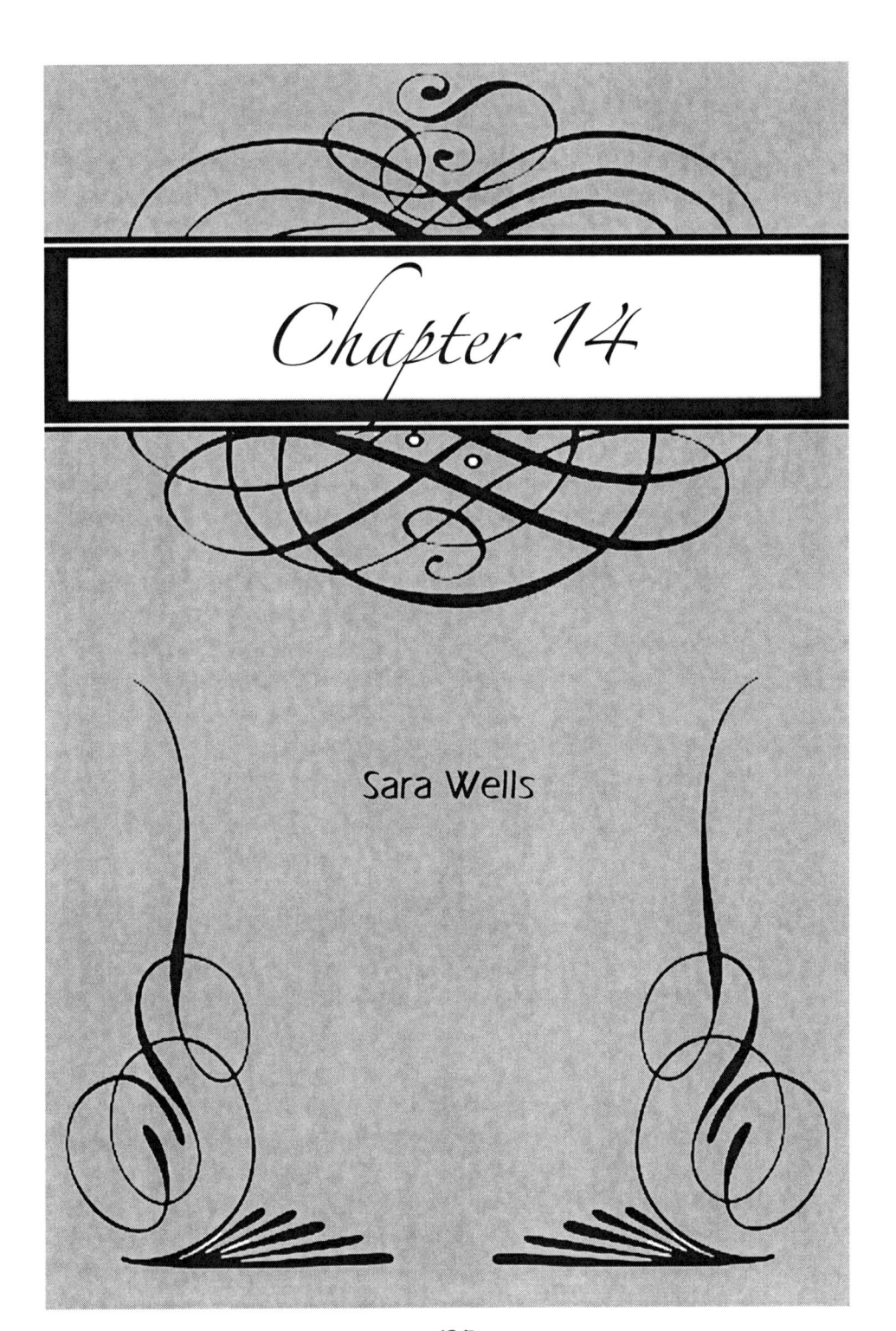

Sara Wells

S.E.C.R.E.T.S. VOLUME II by: *Pastor Shirley*

Sara Wells
67921 Star Point Road

Sara Wells

Sara…

As a child you try to sleep
While your stomach is cramping
Not understanding why the hunger pains
And dizzy spells are happening

We all have things
We are ashamed to reveal
Afraid of letting others know
And pretending our past isn't real

To finally escape the pain
of hunger's constant rule
To experience happiness
And not be treated so cruel

But slowly things occur
Making you feel uneasy
the origins of those thoughts
only make you fell queasy

To have a child/woman
Aspire to upstage you
To stare at you with cunning eyes
As you decide what to do

S.E.C.R.E.T.S. VOLUME II by: _Pastor Shirley_

Sara Wells is a short, dumpy woman with long flowing hair. However, no one would ever know how long her hair is because she wears it in only one style—pulled back severely from her face and twisted into a bun at the nape of her neck. The long silvery strands of gray give her hair a shimmery, dramatic effect.

Sara couldn't care less about her appearance and usually just wears whatever her hand touches when she reaches into her closet. Matching colors and patterns and figure flattering styles are concepts she doesn't fathom. She neither cares nor understands women's preoccupation with the latest style trends. However, Sara's unorthodox attitude regarding fashion is a direct result of her upbringing in poverty.

Sara was raised in an extremely large family of 18 children. Surplus was something none of the siblings even realized existed until they grew up and left home. Sara was no exception.

Each meal was a virtual battlefield of pushing, yelling, and shoving just to get a piece of bread. Sara's mother, Connie, prepared the family meals, put the food on the table, called the kids to the table, and quickly got out of the way of the stampede of screaming kids. She left the room, allowing the kids to eat by themselves. Unfortunately, the older kids took advantage of the situation by pushing the younger ones out of the way until they'd eaten their fill. The younger ones spent the entire time running around the table looking for an opening in which they could snatch something to eat before everything was eaten. When they were finally allowed access to the table, they would be lucky to find a few scraps of bread. If they were successful, they then had to dodge the slaps and hits of their older siblings who tried—and most often succeeded—to take what they'd managed to snatch. The younger kids, who were simply no match for their older, taller, stronger siblings, went hungry many a night while the older kids went to sleep with full bellies.

After meals, Sara, who was child number 15, spent most of the time in a corner crying, hungry, and angry. There was just no way she would ever be able to eat a meal in peace when she had to battle an army just to get a scrap of bread. Sometimes her older brother, Danny, would have pity on her and the other three little ones and make the older siblings share a meal with them. But this only happened maybe once a week. The younger kids were so hungry by then that they inhaled the food, fearful that Danny might change his mind, while the older kids looked at them with outright malice in their eyes. The older children felt that the younger kids were eating food that rightfully belonged to them.

Most nights before falling asleep, Sara fantasized about food. She visualized herself living in a pretty house and having enough food for seconds and thirds; and, if she really wanted it, having enough food for fourths! She turned on her side, clutched her pillow to her chest, and amid the sounds of her grumbling stomach, fell asleep dreaming of food. Her dreams did not include nice cars, pretty clothes, or makeup. Her dreams were filled with her eating anything she wanted nonstop for days at a time.

Sara's clothes consisted of whatever was passed down to her from her older sisters. In a house with that many kids, colors didn't matter, matching didn't matter, and size and fit were never a consideration. If an older sibling outgrew a pair of shoes or article of clothing, it was passed down to the next child in line until it finally wore out. Clothing was only discarded if it could not be sewed, glued, patched, or repaired. Personal likes and dislikes were not requested or considered.

One day while in school, Sara's teacher, Mrs. Pratt, called on her to come to the chalkboard to work out a math problem. Sara was excited because she loved math and she was the only one in the classroom who knew the answer. She was dressed in a tattered threadbare dress and a pair of extremely worn shoes that were two sizes too big. Not giving her clothes a thought, Sara rose from her desk and began walking to the front of the classroom. Each time she took a step, her overly large shoes slipped off her feet and made a "flip flop" sound that brought peals of laughter from her classmates. As she passed Lily and Dawn, two girls from affluent families, she heard them snickering. Then she heard Lily, the leader, say, "Look at that ugly dress she's wearing! Can you believe she had the nerve to leave her house looking like that? And look at those ugly shoes. They have holes in them and they're so big they keep flopping off her feet. Please shoot me if you ever see me looking that bad in public," she

S.E.C.R.E.T.S. VOLUME II by: *Pastor Shirley*

finished dramatically.

Sara flinched at the cruel comment. She tried to walk more quietly, but didn't have much success. She completed the problem and went back to her seat as quickly as possible. For the rest of the day, Sara didn't hear anything that Mrs. Pratt said. It was that day that she really took a good look at her family and realized just how poor they were. It was that day that Sara died inside and withdrew into a protective shell where no one could hurt her. It was that day that she swore to herself that she would one day have nice clothes and enough food to eat.

It was also that day that Sara stopped participating in class. When Mrs. Pratt called on her, she dropped her head and mumbled "I don't know the answer," even if she did. Sara swore to herself that she would never, ever put herself on public display in front of her class where her classmates would laugh at her again. Oh how she wished she could make herself invisible!

That day had a profound effect on Sara's life forever. By far, it was the most humiliating day of her life and one that she would never forget. Even after she became a grown woman, reflecting on that day still caused pain and humiliation to wash over her body as if the entire horrid incident had just occurred. For this reason, Sara went through her life in a protective shell until she met and married Deacon Xavier Wells.

Deacon Wells noticed Sara long before she noticed him. At the time, she wore her long, beautiful hair parted at the side and hanging loosely to her waist. She was a beautiful woman, but she was totally unaware of her physical beauty and extremely shy and withdrawn. It was apparent that Sara had constructed a protective wall around herself and had not allowed anyone to penetrate it. But Deacon Wells loved a challenge and set out to tear that wall down and get to know this beautiful, mysterious woman.

Deacon Wells was a dapper dresser and after looking at Sara's shapeless wardrobe of dull, faded colors, he mentally redressed her in stylish, properly fitting clothing in bold, jewel-toned colors. He added some curls to her long, silky tresses, and perhaps a little rouge to her cheeks just to add a hint of color to her pale complexion. He also decided that she needed to add about 15–20 pounds to her frame, as she was extremely thin. But first things first…

Deacon Wells proceeded slowly so that he would not frighten Sara away. He escorted her to church events and dinners, as well as on long walks, to the movies, and on afternoon rides. It took him 1½ years to tear down the protective wall that Sara had painstakingly built around herself. Shortly thereafter, Deacon Wells proposed marriage and Sara accepted.

So embarrassed was she by her childhood poverty that she never fully explained the details of her unhappy childhood to her husband. Though she told him enough for him to extrapolate that there was never enough food to eat, she considered her childhood another place and another time. To think about it or revisit her past in any way was to inflict cruel and unusual punishment on herself, which she had absolutely no desire to do.

After they were married, Deacon Wells derived great pleasure from giving Sara gifts. It was the way that her eyes widened and the huge smile that spread across her face when he presented his latest offering to her. It was the almost childlike glee that she exhibited when ripping off the wrapping paper. And it was the profound appreciation that she expressed to him no matter what he gave her. When she first entered the house they were to share, she lay on the floor, ran her hands along the nap of the carpet, and exclaimed how soft it was. She wore her new clothes with pride and even learned how to style her hair attractively.

But it was the food that most interested Sara. She went from cabinet to cabinet looking at all the food. She opened the refrigerator and was surprised to learn that it, too, was filled with food. Food that was all hers. Food she didn't have to share. Food she could eat whenever she wanted. Food she could eat without having to engage in a fight. One day, Sara ate so much that she was sick and vomiting for days. Realizing what she'd done and why, Xavier said, "Sara, the food belongs to you. It's not going anywhere. No one is going to take it away from you and you don't have to share it unless you want to. There is too much food for you to ever eat in one day, so there's no reason for you to eat until you make yourself sick. We will always have enough food. When we get low, I'll buy more. We won't ever run out. So, take it easy." Sara nodded her head in acknowledgement. But she just couldn't get over the fact that all of that food in the overflowing cabinets was hers.

Over the years, Sara became addicted to food. Clearly, it was her "drug" of choice. When she wasn't at work at the furniture store or at church, she spent all of her free time researching food, trying new recipes, and experimenting with herbs, spices, and new techniques. She became an amazing cook and enjoyed cooking fabulous meals and desserts for Xavier every day. Food dominated her very existence and, as a result, Sara gained a great deal of weight.

Xavier worked for the town doctor, Dr. Brinkman for over 15 years in whatever capacity the good doctor deemed necessary. He picked up and delivered medicine, observed treatment procedures, scheduled patients, and cleaned the office. After years of observation and discussing medical procedures with Dr. Brinkman, he now also diagnosed minor ailments and assisted the doctor in making home visits to ailing patients. When Sara had not become pregnant in the two years they had been married, it was to Dr. Brinkman she went to get answers.

After many tests, he informed her that she would be unable to have children. Sara was crushed and immediately overtaken by a deep bout of depression because she knew that Xavier desperately wanted a large family. Though she'd never voiced her opinion to him, she had only planned to have one or two children. Her unhappy childhood was filled with memories of poverty, tattered clothing, and constant hunger. They were just too vivid for her to overcome and she would never put any kids of hers through that type of unhappiness.

Xavier was privy to all patient information passing through the office so Sara didn't have to inform him of her inability to have children. Sara was crushed beyond words and she sobbed uncontrollably as Xavier embraced her. He told her that he loved her deeply and that her inability to have children didn't change his love for her.

Sara loved her husband and whenever he was around children, the pain in his eyes was evident to her. Xavier simply adored kids. It was his love for children that prompted Sara's agreement when her nephew, Darren, begged them to adopt his daughter. Ashley was six weeks old and neither Darren nor Iris, his girlfriend, were of a mind to parent a child. Darren explained to Sara that Iris had dropped the baby off on his doorstep in a basket with a note that read, "I been playin' the mommy. Now it's your turn to play the daddy." He further explained that he didn't know the first thing about taking care of an infant. He begged them to take Ashley and raise her as their own, saying that he and Iris would sign papers relinquishing all claims and parental rights.

Darren was clearly relieved and ecstatic when Sara and Xavier agreed to adopt Ashley. Though he didn't want the responsibility, he wanted Ashley to have the best home possible and the only people he knew who could provide that were his aunt and uncle. He knew that they desperately wanted children, but had been unable to have them.

Since neither of them knew the legalities involved with adoption, Xavier spoke to Dr. Brinkman and requested his advice. Dr. Brinkman referred him to his personal lawyer and told him to mention his name when he went to see him. The lawyer was extremely helpful and prepared the necessary documents at a significant discount. Xavier and Sara met with Darren and Iris for them to sign the papers. They had already taken possession of Ashley one week prior. Darren and Iris couldn't sign the papers fast enough.

From the beginning, Xavier doted on Ashley and took complete responsibility for her care. He happily bathed her, combed her hair, fed her, changed her diapers, and even got up at night for her midnight feedings.

S.E.C.R.E.T.S. VOLUME II by: *Pastor Shirley*

Nothing was too great or too small for him to do for his daughter. Sara bragged to her sisters, brothers, and friends about how great a father Xavier was, how involved he was in Ashley's care, and how blessed she was that she didn't have to lift a finger to take care of Ashley when he was home. She often joked that she could be a mom with none of the pain of childbirth and none of the work involved with a small child.

The result of Xavier's constant focus was that Ashley lived for his attention and approval. When Ashley was being potty trained, she would walk right past Sara and go straight to Xavier with a diaper clenched in her chubby hand. When she wanted a bottle, she cried if Sara tried to give it to her and ate nothing until Xavier could feed her.

As soon as Ashley could walk and talk, she began misbehaving and talking back to Sara. When Sara mentioned Ashley's antics to Xavier, Ashley would begin wailing at the top of her lungs and call Sara a liar to her face. The first time Ashley called her a liar, Sara almost passed out. Both she and Xavier were raised to believe that children did not use that term, especially to adults. After regaining her composure, she was preparing to reprimand Ashley when she ran to Xavier and flung herself into his waiting embrace. Xavier scooped her up, kissed her, and rocked her until she quieted down. Sara stood there with an incredulous look on her face. How could he cuddle her when she had misbehaved and disrespected Sara in the process? Sara faced her husband and said, "Xavier, this is not the way to handle Ashley. She's been acting bad, talking back all day, and now she has the nerve to call me a liar. A LIAR! You know she shouldn't be using that word. We cannot allow her to get away with this type of behavior."

Xavier stopped rocking Ashley and said, "Look Sara, I don't condone Ashley acting bad or disrespecting you and I will deal with that. But spanking her for saying the word 'lie' is a little over the top. I don't think we've ever told her that she shouldn't be using that word so how can we spank her for it now? We can't and you know it."

Sara glanced at Ashley in her father's arms. Her head was on Xavier's shoulder. Sara looked again. Was there triumph in her daughter's eyes?

Surely she hadn't seen that?

From that point on, Sara began to notice a considerable change in Xavier. He got extremely angry whenever she tried to discipline Ashley. He would tell Sara not to touch her and to leave the disciplining to him.

****

At church, Ashley sat with Sara and the rest of the congregation and Xavier sat in the deacon's pews located at the front of the church to the right of the pulpit. When Ashley was four years old, they were in church during testimony service. Sara noticed that Ashley was moving to the end of the pew and thought that she was moving closer to her friend, Hannah. When the next song began and Sara stood up to sing and clap her hands, Ashley chose that moment to dart right past her. She boldly walked right into the pulpit, straight to the pews where the deacons were, and sat down next to Xavier.

Sara was absolutely horrified. Ashley had darted past her so quickly that she hadn't had a chance to catch her. Children were not permitted in the pulpit unless the pastor summoned them. Ashley's brazen entry into the pulpit, especially in front of the whole church, was just unacceptable.

To Sara's further amazement, Xavier didn't seem the least bit disturbed by Ashley's little foray into the pulpit. In fact, he seemed proud. He happily scooted over to make room for her. Looking at her daughter, Sara had to admit that she did look like a little angel. She was dressed in a frilly yellow dress, yellow socks, black patent leather shoes, and had beautiful yellow ribbons on her long ponytails. Xavier leaned over and rearranged her dress to cover her little knees showing her how to sit properly. Unlike when Ashley sat with her, she never moved during the entire service. She was the perfect little lady.

****

When Ashley was eight years old, she was at the kitchen table supposedly doing her homework. Sara was running later than usual because she had worked an extra hour at the furniture store. She now rushed about

S.E.C.R.E.T.S. VOLUME II by: *Pastor Shirley*

preparing dinner, completely absorbed in her task. It took her a couple of minutes to notice that Ashley was no longer working on her homework, but staring at her and following her every move instead. When she looked into Ashley's eyes, what she saw frightened her to her very core. The eyes staring back at her were not the eyes of a child but the knowing eyes of a woman. *No,* Sara mentally corrected her first assessment. *Not the eyes of just any woman, but the eyes of the 'other' woman. As if she is sizing me up.* The hairs on the back of her neck stood on end. She shook herself. *Surely I'm losing my mind. How can an 8-year-old girl be the 'other' woman? And more importantly, Ashley isn't old enough to compare herself to me on an equal level!* Sara thought. *Silly me!*

Sara's assessment of Ashley was correct, though she didn't know it at the time. However, the conversation that she was about to have with Ashley would definitely confirm her suspicions. She was about to find out that even at eight years old, Ashley didn't consider herself Sara's equal, but rather her *superior.*

To mask her earlier fear and to lighten the mood in the kitchen, Sara turned to Ashley, smiled, and said in as calm and confident a voice as she could muster, "Ashley, honey, what are you staring at? What is going through your little head right now?" She then wiped her hands on her apron and took a seat at the table to Ashley's right.

Ashley stared at Sara for a long moment, her eyes cool. Ashley didn't turn away. She didn't blink. She didn't smile. And, she didn't answer Sara's question. Instead, she got up from her chair next to Sara, moved to the chair opposite her, sat down, and leaned back casually, all the while maintaining her piercing stare. Sara was feeling extremely uncomfortable with the long silence and Ashley's direct, all-too-knowing gaze. She could feel fear rising again and this time it was lodging in her throat. *This is silly,* Sara thought as she continued to stare at her silent daughter. *Why would I have reason to fear my child?* Sara jettisoned the thought from her mind and forced a smile onto her face.

Sara's fear and discomfort were almost palpable and did not escape Ashley's shrewd scrutiny. The edge of Ashley's lips rose slightly, barely discernible. It disappeared so suddenly that Sara wasn't even sure she'd seen it. She suddenly jumped to her feet almost knocking over the chair she'd previously occupied. She grabbed the back of the chair to steady it before it crashed loudly to the floor. Embarrassed that she'd shown her nervousness to Ashley, she spoke again in an elevated voice. "I said, what are you staring at?!"

A smirk came across Ashley's little face before she answered in a quiet, confident voice. "You. I'm staring at you."

"I can see that," Sara snapped. "*Why* are you staring at me?"

As Ashley turned to look out the bay window overlooking the backyard, she smiled slyly. A beautiful purple and gold butterfly chose that moment to flit aimlessly across the window. Ashley watched its flight intently, remaining silent as she did so. She knew that Sara was on pins and needles awaiting her response. But she would not be rushed. She watched the butterfly until it flew out of view. She then turned back to her mother and leaned forward, resting her little forearms on the table. In the same confident tone she replied, "I know why the butterfly smiles, do you?" Ashley gave her mother a dazzling smile. "Well, do you?"

"Ashley, butterflies don't smile, but even if they did, that has nothing to do with what I just asked you." Planting both of her hands firmly on the back of the chair, Sara leaned over the chair and asked, "Now, why are you staring at me?"

"I'm staring at you because I won't be like you when I'm Daddy's wife."

Sara flinched and angled her head. "What…did…you…just…say?" Sara spat the words out through clenched teeth.

Ashley leaned back again pushing her homework aside. She picked her doll up and began carefully arranging its pretty pink dress. When she was satisfied that the doll was properly attired, she looked Sara directly in the eye and said, "You heard me."

"What do you mean?" Sara yelled, abandoning all attempts at main-

S.E.C.R.E.T.S. VOLUME II by: *Pastor Shirley*

taining her composure. "What do you mean when you become Daddy's wife?" Sara leaned over the chair and pierced Ashley with a hard, knowing stare.

Ashley wasn't intimidated in the least. "I mean I will not be fat like you. I will be trim and good looking for Daddy. I will have lots of babies for him. And when you die, I will sleep with him in your bed every night. Daddy won't have to come to my room at night anymore because I'll always be with him. And we can take baths together whenever we want, and hold hands whenever we want, and have fun whenever we want."

The color drained from Sara's face and her knees buckled as she blindly slumped into the nearest chair. She was too stunned to speak and breathing had become extremely difficult. She wrapped her arms around her waist and simply stared at her daughter, who sat watching her every move intently. Finally, she demanded, "What are you saying, Ashley?" Her voice barely above a whisper and dripping with sorrow.

Ashley smiled broadly, absently fiddled with her ponytail and said, "You are the wife, and you should know what I'm saying." With those words, she got up from the table and walked out of the kitchen without so much as a backward glance.

Sara laid her head on the table, her face toward the bay window. She looked off into space as if in a trance. Her head suddenly felt as if someone had stuck a knife through her temple causing a sharp, piercing pain. Had her daughter just told her that she and her husband were engaging in sexual acts? That her husband went to her daughter's room at night on a regular basis? She felt as if she were about to vomit as she recalled the sickening words that her 8-year-old daughter had just shared with her. Sara began taking deep breaths in an attempt to calm her nerves and settle her queasy stomach, but it didn't work. There was no way that she could make it to the bathroom, so she grabbed the kitchen trash can just in time to catch the contents spewing like a geyser from her stomach.

This was the way that Xavier found Sara when he came home from work. Concern riddled his face as he approached her heaving body. "Are you ok, Sara? What's wrong?" Before she could answer, Ashley burst into the kitchen and flung herself into Xavier's arms. "Daddy, Daddy, I missed you. Will you come into my room and play with me? Please, please, please Daddy come now, come right now." She wrapped her arms around his neck and kissed him repeatedly on the cheek.

"Ok, ok, ok Ashley," Xavier said laughing and kissing Ashley. "Just for a little while." He bounced off to Ashley's room carrying her in his arms, completely forgetting that he'd just found his wife throwing up in a trash can when he'd arrived home from work. When the dry heaves finally abated, Sara turned just in time to see Xavier's retreating back and looked right into Ashley's waiting eyes. This time Sara didn't have to question the look in Ashley's eyes; she knew beyond a shadow of a doubt that they were filled with triumph.

About an hour later, Xavier came out of Ashley's room and asked Sara about dinner. For the first time in Sara's life, she couldn't have cared less about eating or food. She'd simply turned off the pots and pans and sat at the kitchen table staring out the window with a far-off look in her eyes. Never taking her eyes from the window, she said, "Before dinner, you need to know what Ashley said to me today." As Sara repeated what Ashley had told her, she turned from the window and carefully watched Xavier's facial expression. It never changed in the least. When she finished her story, she had clearly worked herself into a tizzy.

Xavier studied Sara closely for a moment. Calmly, almost too calmly, he said, "All little girls love their fathers and fantasize about them. Dr. Brinkman has repeatedly told me about incidents similar to this with his patients. There is nothing unusual or malicious about Ashley's story and she didn't tell it to you to upset you. If you're upset in any way, then you're telling me that you think there's more to Ashley's story. That you think there is something else to our relationship than that of a father and daughter. And I know you aren't suggesting such a horrible thing. I'm a deacon in the church and I take my relationship with God and my position in the church seriously. Such a thing would never even occur to me."

Xavier was looking at Sara with a hard stare. He was daring her to dispute what he'd just told her. Xavier knew that Sara would not question him further as long as he took a hard stance and dismissed the subject. "Enough said about this. Let's eat." Sara sat in her chair staring at Xavier. Had he just dismissed her and all she'd said with a few sentences? That was it? But Sara had never stood up to Xavier in her life and she wasn't about to start now. Though she was not satisfied with his explanation, what could she do? With unshed tears shimmering in her eyes, she stood up and walked to the stove to complete dinner.

Unbeknownst to Sara and Xavier, Ashley was outside the kitchen listening to the entire conversation. She didn't understand why her father had just lied to her mother. Her father told her every day that he loved her and wanted to be with her all the time. Why hadn't he admitted it to her mother? Then she figured that maybe she wasn't old enough yet to take care of her father. She would just have to grow up and then her father would tell her mother the truth. She went back to her bedroom until dinner was ready.

The topic was never discussed again. But Sara began to watch Xavier and Ashley like a hawk.

****

When Ashley was 11 years old, Sara told Xavier that she was too old for him to continue bathing her and selecting her underwear. Xavier was obviously upset and said, "Stop trying to make a mountain out of a mole hill. All fathers take care of their daughters like this." Sara didn't know any fathers who treated their daughters the way Xavier treated Ashley. Her father certainly hadn't treated her or her sisters like that.

The following Saturday, Xavier was sorting laundry in the washroom. When Sara walked by, she thought she noticed blood on a pair of Ashley's panties. "Oh my God!" Sara exclaimed. "When did Ashley start her period?" When she reached for the panties, Xavier quickly grabbed them and said, "No, Ashley hasn't started her period yet. I cut my finger the other day and ran into the washroom to get something to wrap around it. I reached into the hamper and pulled out the first thing my hand touched, which happened to be a pair of Ashley's panties. When I noticed I had grabbed them, I was embarrassed and threw them back in the hamper and pulled out a towel instead." Though Xavier's excuse sounded extremely weak, Sara didn't comment further.

Sara decided that perhaps it was time to talk to Ashley about the birds and the bees. She found Ashley in her bedroom lying across the foot of her bed watching television. Though Ashley was aware that Sara had entered her room, she didn't acknowledge her entrance in any way. It took Sara a full three minutes to realize that Ashley wasn't going to voluntarily acknowledge her, so she noisily cleared her throat and asked Ashley to turn the TV off so that they could talk. Instead of obeying, Ashley simply used her remote to lower the volume. She then turned to face her mother. When Sara tried to broach the subject of sex and the various processes that the body underwent, Ashley's eyes widened, and she fell back across the bed hooting with laughter. Since she was already uncomfortable speaking to Ashley about this, Sara was horrified by her daughter's response. Finally regaining her composure, Ashley sat back up and with supreme amusement in her eyes said, "You are soooooo late. Daddy already talked to me about this a long time ago." Before Sara could respond, Ashley turned the volume up on her television and turned back over onto her stomach to continue watching her favorite program. Sara was so embarrassed that she quickly left Ashley's room, not even realizing that her 11-year-old daughter had just dismissed her.

****

Xavier had long since stopped having sex with Sara or giving her money with which to run the household. Also, if she needed personal items, such as stockings, Sara had to beg Ashley to ask Xavier for the money because he never refused his daughter anything.

By the time Ashley was 12 years old, her buttocks had rounded and filled out, her stomach was flat, and her breasts were large and full. She had a trim, shapely body that any grown woman would envy. When Ashley was 15 years old, she began vomiting in the morning and missed some days

S.E.C.R.E.T.S. VOLUME II by: *Pastor Shirley*

from school as a result. Sara told Xavier that there was something wrong with Ashley and that she was going to take her to see Dr. Brinkman. Xavier told her that he had noticed the changes in Ashley, had made an appointment for her to see the doctor that afternoon at 1:00 pm, and that he would take his daughter there. When they returned home that afternoon, Ashley went straight to her room, climbed into bed, and stayed there for a week. Xavier told Sara that Ashley had the flu and would be home for a few days recovering. Dr. Brinkman had prescribed some antibiotics for her and after a few days' rest, she would be just fine. Xavier further told her not to bother or upset Ashley in any way and that he would take care of her. He took breakfast to her every morning, came home and prepared her lunch, and brought her dinner each evening, staying longer and longer in her bedroom each time.

When Ashley was 16 years old, she got the flu three times that year and each time, stayed home for one week in recovery. That same year, Sara quit her job at the furniture store when she became deathly ill with uterine cancer. Xavier immediately moved her from their bedroom to the guest room saying it would be easier for her to get to the kitchen and bathroom. She didn't understand his rationale because their bedroom had a bathroom and the kitchen was only a few doors down the hall.

Sara's health deteriorated rapidly. She was soon largely confined to her small twin bed in the guest room and needed assistance with meals and going to the bathroom. Sometimes, Sara lay in her bed for hours begging for food, water, and help to the bathroom. It was during these times that her childhood came back to haunt her with full force. Having enough food to eat and liquids to satisfy her thirst completely consumed her thoughts. Xavier and Ashley seemed to forget that she was in the house and often did not bring her food until 5:00 or 6:00 pm. She was wasting away. Literally. She was always hungry and thirsty, which left her uncomfortable and in pain most of the time.

Though the pain of hunger was agonizing, it was nothing compared to the excruciating emotional pain that Sara experienced every night. She could hear Xavier and Ashley laughing and splashing in the bathtub and then retiring to what used to be her bedroom, which they now both shared.

While she lay in bed, she could clearly hear Xavier and Ashley having sex. They were loud, vocal, and vulgar, not caring that Sara was in the next room. She lay in her bed sobbing through her grief and pain. Xavier and Ashley didn't notice, or they seemed not to care.

One day, Sister Janice, one of the ladies from the church, came by the house unannounced to visit Sara.

Sis. Wells
It's me
Sis. Janice

Sara, who had always been plump, now lay in the bed with her skin tightly drawn over her bones. Sister Janice was simply shocked at her skeletal appearance. She had brought Sara some homemade chicken soup and quickly put some into a bowl and fed it to her. Sara ate heartily. While she fed Sara, Sister Janice began to pray for her. She was surprised at the dirty condition of her gown and sheets. She helped Sara into the tub to bathe and changed her bed linen. While she helped Sara bathe, she told Sara that she had been asking Deacon Wells for months if she could come over to visit and he always told her that it was better for her to rest and not exert herself by receiving visitors. "Today, I decided to take a chance when I knew he would be at work, and I'm so glad I did."

"She called Dr. Brinkman to come to the house to look at Sara and told Sara and Dr. Brinkman that she would gladly pay the bill. Since they lived in a small town, Dr. Brinkman was not above making house calls and told Sister Janice that he wouldn't think of charging Sara for his visit. Because Xavier was picking up supplies for the office, he was unaware that Sister Janice had called or visited Sara.

S.E.C.R.E.T.S. VOLUME II by: *Pastor Shirley*

When Dr. Brinkman arrived, he, too, was shocked at Sara's haggard appearance. He asked Sister Janice to wait in the living room while he examined Sara. "Why haven't you been to see me?" Dr. Brinkman asked with genuine concern in his voice.

Averting her eyes, Sara said, "I really didn't have the strength to go into town."

"Then why didn't you have Xavier tell me to come to you? You shouldn't have waited so long without seeing me."

After thoroughly examining Sara, Dr. Brinkman said, "I'm going to give you some pills for the pain. Take them every day. And you need to eat more, Sara. You are much too thin." He gave the pills to Sara and took a seat in the overstuffed chair next to the bed.

"I want to talk to you about something else. I have been talking to Xavier for some time about the need for Ashley to take better care of her young body. Xavier brought Ashley in the other day for a checkup. Some quack had done six abortions on her and the last one just about killed her. I keep telling Xavier that this is wreaking havoc on Ashley's body and because she's had so many abortions at such a young age, it may have damaged her ability to have children in the future. Due to the large amount of scar tissue from the multiple abortions, if she is fortunate enough to have children, and that is a big if, at the very least, she will have a very difficult time carrying a child to term."

Dr. Brinkman shook his head and then continued. "He told me you were aware of Ashley's abortions so I wanted to encourage you to talk to Ashley about abstaining from sex for a while and allowing her body to heal. Or if she insists on having sex on a regular basis, try to get her to use some form of birth control so she doesn't keep getting pregnant."

Sara nodded in horrified shock. *Abortions?! What abortions?* She thought. *Xavier said Ashley had had the flu! He never said anything about her being pregnant!*

Dr. Brinkman made Sara promise to see him on a regular basis. He then gathered his black leather medical bag, and left. Sister Janice came back into the room with orange juice and more soup. Sara ate the soup gratefully, thanked Sister Janice, and collapsed back on the pillows, totally exhausted. Sister Janice promised to visit again the next day to help Sara with her meals so that she could regain her strength. She then prayed with Sara and left. As she walked down the street toward her house, she knew that she was going to visit Sara every day because it was obvious to her that she was getting absolutely no help from Deacon Wells or Ashley. The woman was practically starving to death. Well, she had no intention of letting that happen. She would gladly take care of her.

After Dr. Brinkman and Sister Janice left, Sara lay zombie-like in her bed. Random thoughts zoomed in and out of her head nonstop as she thought of all the things she had overlooked. The signs had been there, but she had either ignored them or hadn't taken them seriously. Maybe she should call the police and have Xavier arrested. But who would believe her? Ashley would certainly never testify against her father, nor would she ever do anything that would put Xavier in jeopardy.

Sara lay in her bed reliving what Dr. Brinkman had told her. Everything suddenly made sense to her. Ashley's unnatural attachment to Xavier even as a child. All the times Ashley had the "flu." Ashley telling her she was going to be Xavier's next wife. A 2-year-old Ashley telling her that Daddy had a tail between his legs. Sara had laughed and brushed it off as childish gibberish. Now she knew that wasn't the case. Ashley had seen Xavier's hanging penis and had called it a tail. This 'Christian' man of hers was a child molester! Xavier had been molesting Ashley since she was a baby. She remembered all the times he had set her on his lap and held her close. He was probably deriving some sort of sexual pleasure from her squirming in his lap. The realization made Sara ill. How could she have missed what he was doing to their child? Xavier had raised Ashley up in sex and perversion and God help her, Ashley loved it! Ashley had never had any boyfriends; she hadn't even been on any dates. Yet she'd had six abortions! Xavier had never told her about that because he was the father of all those aborted babies.

S.E.C.R.E.T.S. VOLUME II by: _Pastor Shirley_

Later that evening, Xavier marched into her bedroom and said, "I need to talk to you." He paused for a minute noticing her changed sheets and clean nightgown, though he didn't care enough to comment on them. "Anyway, Ashley is pregnant and the father of her child is Brother Levi. When she was babysitting for him last month, he forced himself on her and now she is pregnant."

Sara sat up in the bed and said, "WHAT? How could Ashley be pregnant? She's never even had a boyfriend!" She said firing the questions at Xavier in quick succession.

Irritated at being questioned by her, Xavier replied, "Will you at least try to follow along, Sara? Ashley is pregnant. I didn't want her around him because I noticed how he was lookin' at the young girls at church. I'm going to the pastor and tell him about this. I don't want him ruining anyone else's life with his disgusting perversions. I might even go to the police. I haven't decided yet. Ashley is a kid and what he did is statutory rape in this state." Not giving her a chance to ask questions or respond to his announcement, he turned on his heels and stalked out of the room.

Sara just lay there limp and shaken. She was afraid, but the emotion was not for Xavier or Ashley, but for the plot of lies they had concocted to frame Brother Levi. It had not escaped Sara's attention that Brother Levi was, in fact, sexually interested in young girls. Everyone in the church was aware of his misplaced interest in teenage girls. But Sara knew one thing for certain; if Ashley had in fact slept with Brother Levi, he'd been smoothly set up. Xavier had orchestrated the entire thing to blame the baby on him and throw the suspicion off his own heinous actions. She thought how terrible Xavier was to have instructed his daughter to have sex with a grown man. Then she thought how terrible Xavier was to be having sex with a young girl, his own daughter. Her mind racing, Sara finally fell into a fitful sleep with the sounds of Xavier and Ashley's love-making ringing loudly in her ears.

The next morning, Ashley graced Sara with her presence, which was a rare occurrence. She sat in the chair opposite the bed and said, "I'm pregnant and Brother Levi is the father of my baby."

Sara stared at Ashley for a moment and turned her face to the wall. The sight of Ashley made her sick.

Ashley jumped from her chair and shrieked, "Why are you turning your face away? You don't believe me? I just told you that your teenaged daughter is pregnant by a grown man and your only response is to turn your face to the wall?"

Sara turned back to her daughter, who was now standing by her bed. "No, Ashley, I don't believe one word you've said. I also know that if you had sex with Brother Levi, your daddy told you to do it."

Ashley's eyes widened in shock. She quickly regained her confident composure and looked deep into Sara's eyes. *She knew! She knew the truth!* Ashley thought. The realization startled her for a moment, but it was quickly replaced by happiness and calm. She was glad that Sara knew. It was time she died and allowed her to be the wife she could certainly never be. Ashley shrugged nonchalantly and walked to the mirror over the dresser. She took a brush out of her pocket and began to brush her hair in slow deliberate strokes. Though she appeared to be totally engrossed in the task, Sara knew that Ashley was watching her closely through the mirror.

"Do you like my hair? I just had it cut into a new style. Daddy picked it out. He said it complemented my eyes," she said while arranging the silky strands. Sara didn't respond. She just continued to watch Ashley in the mirror. Ashley wanted to annoy Sara because her calm and silence were getting on her last nerve. She took out a tube of bright red lipstick and applied it generously to her pouting lips. Ashley knew that Sara didn't like her to wear red lipstick saying it made her look too old—which is exactly why she wore it every chance she got.

She turned from the mirror and faced her mother, leaning her hip lazily against the dresser. She locked eyes with Sara. "About Brother Levi, yeah you're right. Daddy did tell me to do it with Brother Levi so people won't talk about us. But I really don't care what they say because when you finally die, I will be Daddy's wife and then we can have lots of ba-

S.E.C.R.E.T.S. VOLUME II by: *Pastor Shirley*

bies." With those cruel words, Ashley agilely pushed from the dresser and regally walked out of the room with her head held high.

Sara felt the hot sting of tears on her face as they rolled unchecked down her cheeks. She picked up the telephone and dialed. She heard the soothing, raspy voice of Pastor Richards as he said, "Hello and praise the Lord."

"Pastor Richards, this is Sara Wells."

"Sista Wells, how you doin'? We been prayin' for you that the Lord would grant you a full recovery. Deacon Wells said you are coming along just fine and he asked the church not to visit you because even the smallest things tend to tire you out. He thanked the congregation for lettin you get your proper rest."

Thank you, Pastor, for all your prayers. Please keep praying for me." Sara paused for a brief moment as she worked up her nerve for the next statement. "Pastor, I really need to talk to you as soon as possible. There are some things I must tell you. This is a matter of life and death."

Pastor Richards was a little taken aback by the urgency in Sara's voice. "Well certainly, Sista Wells. Is 10:00 this morning ok with you?"

"Yes, Pastor, 10:00 is fine. Also, please don't tell Deacon Wells about my appointment with you. He might forbid it saying I need my rest. But, I have been resting for months and having a conversation with you won't tire me out at all. What I have to talk to you about is urgent."

Again, the pastor was a little shocked. But since her explanation seemed plausible, he agreed to her request.

To find out what happened to Sara Wells, Deacon Xavier Wells, and Ashley Wells, be sure to read *S.E.C.R.E.T.S. of the First Ladies, Trilogy.* Available soon in a bookstore near you.

Chapter 15

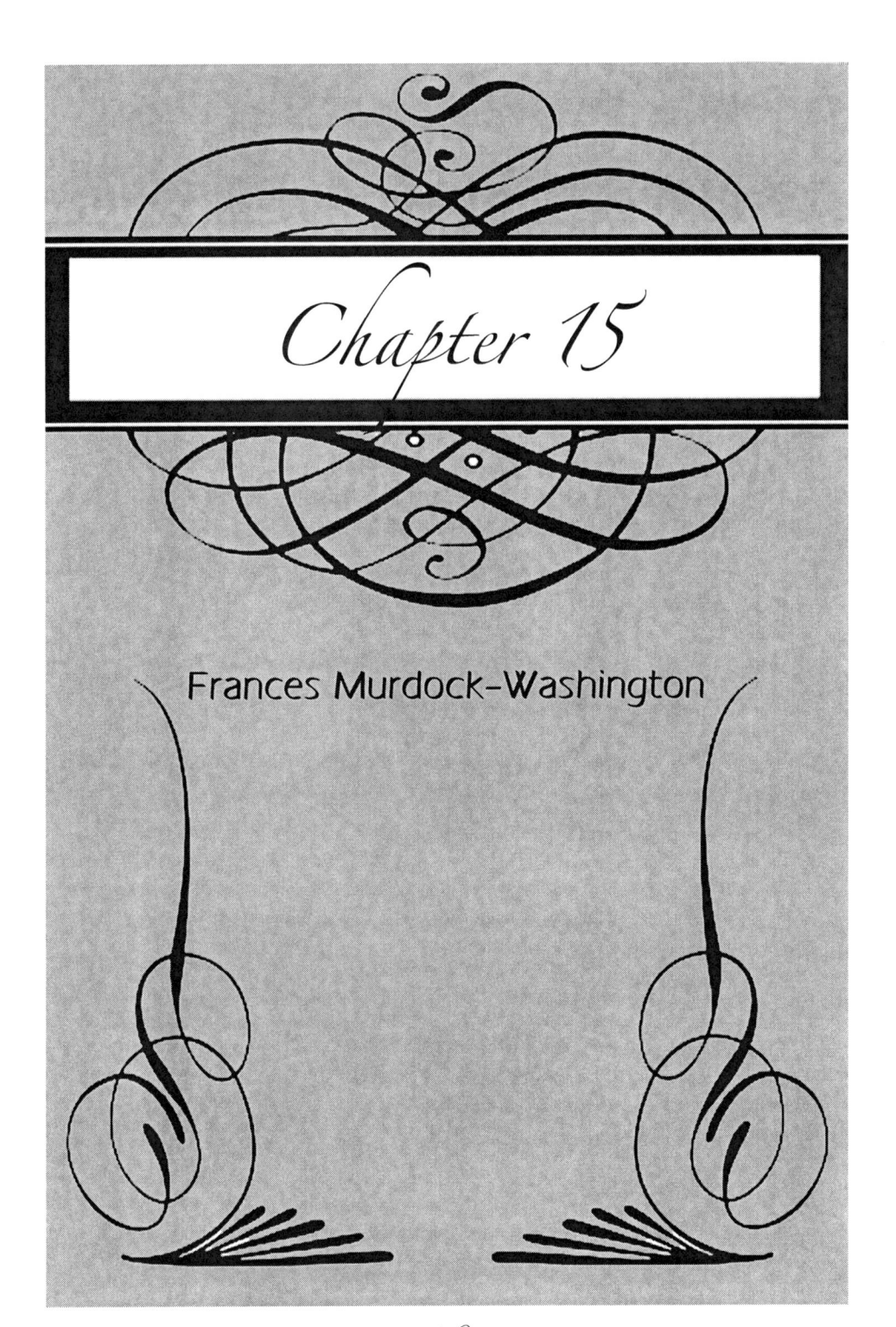

Frances Murdock-Washington

S.E.C.R.E.T.S. VOLUME II by: *Pastor Shirley*

Frances Murdock-Washington
169725 Silvius Parkway

Frances Murdck—Washington

Frances Murdock-Washington

Frances
Have you ever heard
Of a functioning alcoholic?
It's not just a term,
It's also symbolic

Who is truly
Falling and stumbling?
Who is really
Staggering and tumbling?

How does it feel
To live in such shame?
To use your career and activities
To mask hidden pain?

S.E.C.R.E.T.S. VOLUME II by: _Pastor Shirley_

Frances is the Vice President of Sales and Marketing for a major national drug company. She is saved, sanctified, Holy Ghost filled and married to Bishop Mitchell Washington. Talk about having it all! Frances lives in a fabulous home, has a vacation home, a housekeeper, a cook, a personal trainer, a pool boy, a gardener, a personal assistant, a large bank account, and she drives a snow-white Mercedes CL65 AMG ,a silver Porsche GT2 RS, and a 1969 BMW classic convertible. She had the car restored to its original glory and it is her favorite. Her houses and automobiles are all paid for thanks to her knack for investing and her careful management of her salary and household funds.

Frances has the illusion of beauty and for a woman standing at 5'10½ " is considered tall. She is proud of her height and wears three-inch heels every day, bringing her height to over six feet. She is naturally slender and has never had a weight problem in her life. She practices Pilates 30 minutes twice a week and eats healthily because it makes her feel good and ensures her energy level remains high.

At her job, Frances is one of only two women who have achieved such a high position. She is highly respected and is considered a whiz when it comes to devising motivational tools to inspire her team. In addition to all her personal and professional achievements, she is married to an incredibly handsome man. The love they share is evident to all whom they meet. They agreed early in their marriage that neither of them wanted children. Because Frances has money, drives beautiful cars, lives in a beautiful house, and is married to a gorgeous man, she is the envy of all the women in her church as well as the other First Ladies in the circuit of churches in which they interact.

Bishop Mitchell Washington is an extremely handsome man and a dynamic preacher. He is 5'8", wears a meticulously groomed beard and mustache, and takes equal care of his physical health. Mitch is secure in his manhood and couldn't care less that his wife is over two inches taller than he is. The fact that he is shorter than Frances has never been an issue for either of them. His love for his wife and devotion to the ministry are paramount to him.

Mitch's childhood memories are painful because he grew up in a home in which his father constantly cheated on his mother. As a child, he and his siblings often witnessed violent fights and bellowing arguments between their parents. He witnessed his mother's heartache and her resulting low self-esteem. He vowed that he would never do that to his wife when he got married. And he never has—no matter how attractive the female might be. He always says that remaining faithful is a choice. A conscious choice. One he has to make sometimes on a daily basis; sometimes on an hourly and even minute-by-minute basis. But he chooses his wife and his marriage every single time. It hasn't always been easy, but he remains faithful to his wife whom he loves dearly.

****

Early one Saturday morning, Frances sat in her home office staring at the computer screen. She was supposed to be reading and returning office email; however, she had been looking at the same message for the last hour. She was looking at the screen but her eyes were not focused on it. She was reviewing the messy situation that her life had become. So many people envied her for her loving marriage and the prosperity that she and Mitch enjoyed. Boy, if they only knew! The old saying was true. You simply cannot judge a book by its cover!

Frances loved Mitch and knew that he loved her. She also knew that he was dedicated to the ministry. Regardless of these things, she was living a lie. Her happy life was just a facade. She was at her wits' end and didn't know how much longer she could go on pretending. She knew that Mitch couldn't continue to hide behind the scripture of being slain in the spirit every time he fell or passed out in the pulpit.

Reflecting on her marriage, Frances knew exactly when the problems began. She remembered when they were first married and how happy they were. They were both from the "old school" of Bible teaching. They believed that drinking and smoking were wrong and against the teachings of the Bible and that anyone who did these things was not saved. Therefore, neither she nor Mitch touched alcohol, drugs, or tobacco products.

S.E.C.R.E.T.S. VOLUME II by: *Pastor Shirley*

It was several years later that Mitch was introduced to Prophet Ray. He called himself a true prophet of God. He and Mitch became fast and close friends. However, Prophet Ray did not believe that drinking alcohol was wrong. He quoted and stood on the scripture found in I Timothy 5:23, *"Drink no longer water, but use a little wine for the stomach's sake and thine other infirmities."* Prophet Ray always drank cocktails before dinner, wine with dinner, and port after dinner. Shortly thereafter, Mitch started drinking wine with dinner only, quoting the same scripture in I Timothy to Frances. Frances looked at Mitch with total incredulity. They had often discussed how people could find a scripture in the Bible to corroborate wrongdoing if it was taken out of context and now he was actually doing the same thing. Frances was horrified when Mitch began teaching the members that it was ok to drink wine with dinner. Some of their members also from the "old school" way of thinking felt that this practice was a sin and consequently left the church.

Shortly thereafter, Mitch purchased a liquor cabinet and filled it with various top-shelf liquors. He began casually sipping wine all day. He carried an expensive flask from Tiffany's to ensure he always had his wine on hand. Then, he began drinking cocktails before dinner. Soon, Mitch was drunk all day, every day.

Frances begged him to quit drinking and to go to Alcoholics Anonymous or rehab. But he refused, insisting that he didn't have a drinking problem and that he only drank in moderation.

Reflecting on the past had given Frances a terrible headache. She shut her computer down and spent the rest of the day in bed mentally preparing herself for the stress-filled day to come.

The next day, Sunday, began just like every other Sunday had for the past three years. She got up two hours earlier than necessary in order to get

Mitch out of bed, showered, and dressed in time for church. Since her cook and housekeeper had Sundays off, she went to the kitchen, made a pot of strong coffee, and ate a light breakfast of toast, fruit, and orange juice. She then spent the next hour trying to get Mitch out of bed. After much prodding, he finally opened his eyes. Frances then went back downstairs to get him a cup of strong black coffee.

Gripping the edge of the mattress, Mitch swung his legs over the side of the bed and tried to acclimate himself to an upright position. He waited a moment for his alcohol-saturated brain to float in the general direction of functioning consciousness. It took a while to get there. With much effort, Mitch forced his heavy eyelids open. It took several blinks to bring the spinning room into focus. His head felt as if someone had taken a sledgehammer to it. He closed his eyes again and reached for the bottle of vodka that he kept hidden in his nightstand drawer. He opened it and took a long, chest-burning swig. He no longer drank wine. He drank straight vodka all day because it was not detectable on the breath. At least he hoped that was the case since he drank it even while he was at church. He had long ago traded in his first flask for a much larger one, which he now kept filled with vodka.

Mitch had no idea how he was going to make it through the day and no idea how he was going to address the church. He was getting worse. He was blacking out and unable to account for large chunks of time. It seemed as if he could no longer function in any capacity unless he had a healthy dose of vodka. He knew he had to do something before everything fell completely apart.

Mitch heard Frances coming up the stairs and quickly put the bottle back in the drawer. He smiled as she entered their bedroom. She handed him a cup of strong black coffee, which he gratefully accepted and immediately began to sip. He then stumbled into the bathroom and directly into the shower. After his shower, he felt a little better. Upon entering his bedroom, he saw that Frances had already selected what he was to wear and had laid everything out neatly on the bed for him.

He was grateful, as he could not have performed even this simple task in

S.E.C.R.E.T.S. VOLUME II by: *Pastor Shirley*

his current state. He was barely able to dress himself and lay back across the bed to wait for Frances. As he lay there, he remembered when he used to make breakfast and make love to Frances on Sunday mornings before church. Now he couldn't even pick out his clothes or drive her to church. Moreover, he couldn't remember the last time he'd made love to her.

They arrived at church and Frances went into the sanctuary while Mitch tried his best to walk normally to his office. He purposefully missed Sunday school on a regular basis in an effort to get himself together before he had to take the pulpit. He drank more vodka to calm his nerves, and then again switched to strong black coffee. His members assumed he spent the time during Sunday school in prayer and consecration. Obviously, the assumption was incorrect; however, he certainly didn't set the record straight.

Much too soon, Mitch heard the first chord of the organ signaling the end of Sunday school and the beginning of morning service. He left his office and went to the pulpit. He sat with his fingers steepled in front of him and his head down. It was a practiced pose that he'd adopted to discourage members from approaching him. They assumed he was praying. This façade worked because no one approached him while he "communed with the Lord."

When it was time for him to preach, Mitch stumbled in the direction of the podium. He realized that he was acting strangely and thus raised his hands to the heavens as if he was under the anointing of the Spirit of the Lord. However, before he made it, he tripped over his own feet and smashed his temple on the side of the podium. Blood was gushing from his head and seeping into the carpet. Frances jumped up and ran to the pulpit. She applied pressure to the wound in an effort to stop the bleeding. Someone called 911 and an ambulance arrived rather quickly. Frances accompanied the ambulance to the hospital.

The church was abuzz about how this could've happened if Bishop Washington was slain in the spirit and under the anointing of God. The assistant pastor, Minister Kenyon, just dismissed the service and told the church to pray for the pastor because he was under attack.

Mitch was a wonderful husband and pastor until he started drinking. His drinking had now become life threatening, as evidenced by the amount of blood he'd lost and his unconscious state. Whenever he got up, his steps were clumsy and his speech slurred. She knew that he wasn't fully in control, but she didn't know how bad it was until today.

Frances stood by Mitch's bedside in the hospital. He was in a coma, hooked to several machines, and his head was heavily wrapped in bandages. As she stood looking down at her husband, she felt the weight of the heavy burden she'd been carrying. Frances began to sway under the weight of it and grabbed the rail of Mitch's bed to steady herself.

- And then… she wept.
- She wept for this great man of God who'd been deceived by the devil.
- She wept for her husband and her marriage.
- She wept for her lover and her friend.
- She wept for the ministry.
- She wept for the members who'd been deceived and led astray through false teachings.
- She wept because getting him help would expose his problem and destroy his standing in both the church and community.
- She wept for all the secrets and lies she'd been forced to keep.
- She wept because she didn't see a way out of her secret existence.
- She wept for the code of silence by which she'd been forced to live.

Looking through eyes blurred with tears, a chest tight with strain and fear, and a heart heavy with shattered hope and binding silence… Frances wept.

S.E.C.R.E.T.S. VOLUME II by: *Pastor Shirley*

To find out what happened to Frances Murdock-Washington and Bishop Mitchell Washington, be sure to read S.E.C.R.E.T.S. of the First Ladies, Trilogy. Available soon in a bookstore near you.

Chapter 16

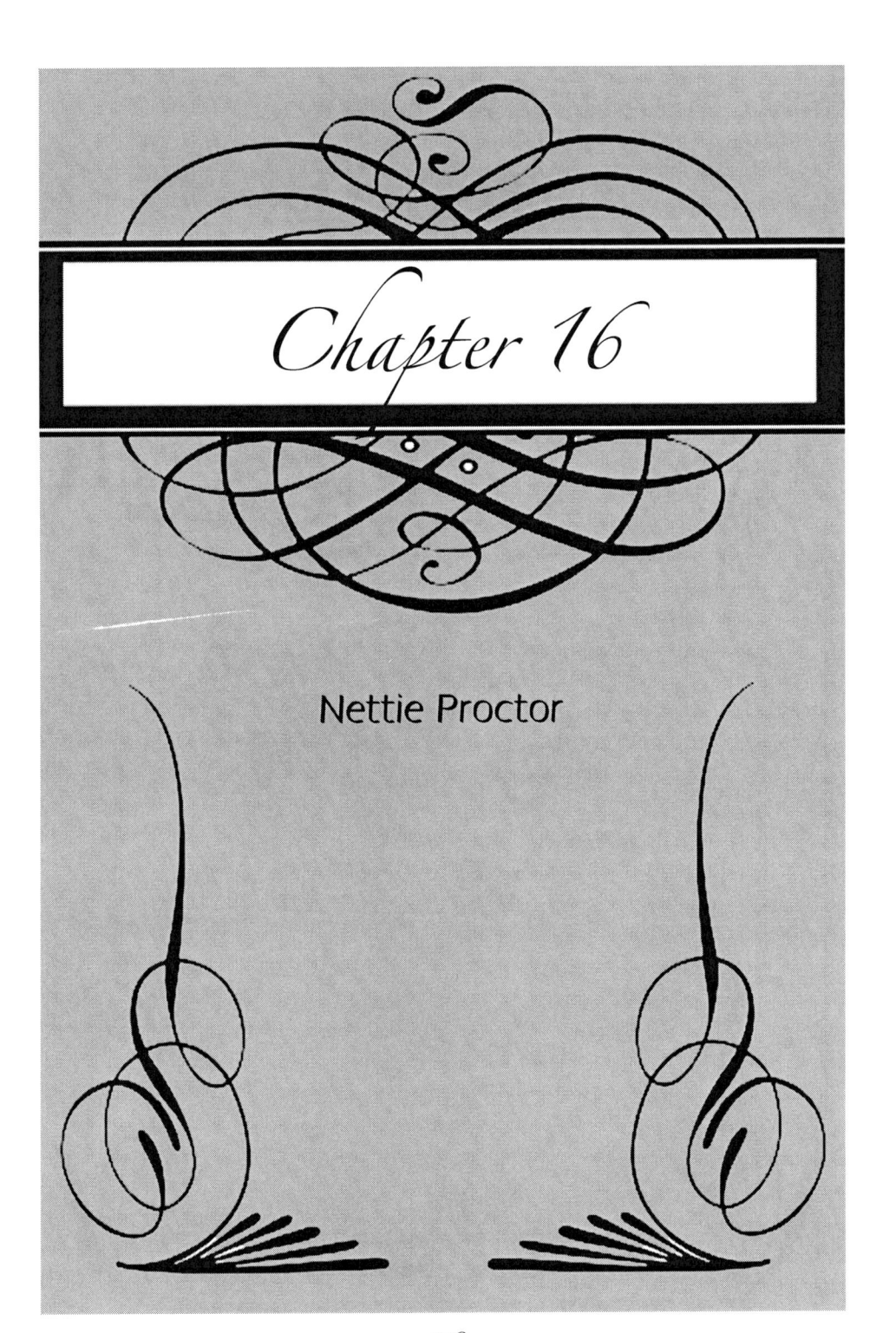

Nettie Proctor

S.E.C.R.E.T.S. VOLUME II by: *Pastor Shirley*

Nettie Proctor
410 Sedgewick Street

Nettie Proctor

Nettie...

Tick tock... tick tock
Look... look at the clock
The minutes are passing
With the speed of light
But you only feel the blanket
Of your overwhelming fright.

Tick tock... tick tock
The time is narrowing on the clock
Your mind is racing,
Your feet are pacing
Knowing this day is worth erasing
The hands on the clock
Are bearing down
Your once bright smile
Is now a dark frown

Tick tock... tick tock
There's no more time
On the clock
Was it really worth the gamble?
Time's now up!
And your life is in shambles...

S.E.C.R.E.T.S. VOLUME II by: *Pastor Shirley*

*N*ettie Proctor is married to Pastor James Proctor. Nettie is a tall, attractive woman with a slender build and a kind smile. Nettie's mother had fostered a strong sense of self-worth in her only daughter, telling her that she had the power to do whatever she wanted to do with the help of God. Nettie's shoulder-length black hair always looks healthy and stylish due to her regular visits to the neighborhood salon.

Nettie works for a national retail giant as a customer service manager. Although her job requires irregular hours, she doesn't mind because she enjoys it. She likes being able to help her customers. Though some customers try her patience, she's found that they are the exception, not the rule.

Pastor James Proctor is a tall, attractive man. He takes great care of his appearance, and as a result, looks at least 10 years younger than his actual age. He exercises regularly, eats in a relatively healthy manner, and always dresses impeccably. His church members love him because he is what they refer to as "real." He is a down-to-earth man who loves God and is doing God's work, as opposed to being a judgmental, self-righteous leader.

In addition to overseeing the church, Pastor Proctor also works at the correctional facility at the edge of town. The inmates like and respect him because he treats them like men as opposed to animals and he doesn't take advantage of them like so many of the other officers have done. Pastor Proctor likes and values his job because it is the first "real job" he's ever had. Prior to this opportunity, he made money sporadically, traveling as an evangelist, preaching wherever he could. He also receives funds from the church treasuries.

Nettie has worked diligently in the church for years. She is always the first to volunteer her time, service, and finances. She always makes certain that God's work and His house come first. It is because of her dedication to the ministry that she was appointed financial secretary years ago. Nettie is detail oriented and her financial records are always in perfect order. She accounts for every dime of church income, and never wants anyone to accuse her or her husband of mismanagement of church funds. Because of her money management and record keeping skills, she's been able to make several large investments for the church, which are now paying off big time! Nettie is ecstatic about this.

****

However, there is a noticeable change in Nettie lately. She is apprehensive about praising God and letting her gift flow in the Spirit the way she used to do. Pastor Proctor repeatedly tells her that "it don't take all that." He tells her not "to be holding up" his Sunday service by speaking in tongues because he has to be up delivering his message by a certain time in order to be out by the time he'd set.

Nettie has such an anointing when she sings that people are blessed all over the church. However, she rarely sings these days because Pastor Proctor told her to let the younger members of the church sing.

One Sunday, a visitor sent a message to the organ player requesting that Nettie sing a solo. Nettie, shocked by the request, remained in her seat. However, she couldn't deny the request per Pastor Proctor's edict because the congregation began clapping and calling her name. As she walked to the microphone at the front of the church, she nervously chanced a quick look at Pastor Proctor. He was definitely not happy and pointedly looked at his watch indicating that he wanted her to finish up as quickly as possible so that he could remain on schedule. As Nettie reached the microphone, she heard the spirit of the Lord say to her "It is better to obey God rather than man." That's all she needed to hear. She decided to go for broke and let God have his way. She was going to give it her all as befitting a servant of God. As Nettie began to sing, the Spirit of the Lord came down upon the congregation. The members began to praise God. Some members were rejoicing, others were speaking in tongues, and still others were slain in the spirit. When Nettie finally took her seat, it took the praise and worship leader an additional 20 minutes to calm the church down and regain control of the service, and people were saved and delivered.

After church, members were rushing up to Nettie telling her how anointed

S.E.C.R.E.T.S. VOLUME II by: *Pastor Shirley*

she was in the gift of song and that the Lord had greatly blessed them. They told her that she should sing more often as it was such a blessing to everyone. Nettie accepted their compliments with grace, never taking credit for anything the Lord had done.

As she walked to the car, she felt honored to have been the vessel that God had used to bestow a blessing upon the church. She felt proud that God had chosen her. She felt good. When she got into the car, Pastor Proctor was uncharacteristically quiet. He didn't say one word on the entire drive home. His obvious anger put a damper on what she felt had been a success. Once in their home, he let Nettie have it with both barrels. As they walked to their bedroom, Pastor Proctor said over his shoulder, "Didn't I tell you not to sing on Sundays and to let the younger members in the church sing? You deliberately disobeyed a direct order from your husband and your pastor. Don't you ever do that again! I don't appreciate your delaying my service!"

Nettie knew that Pastor Proctor was angry as evidenced by his silence in the car. However, she didn't appreciate his placing the blame on her shoulders. "I was asked to sing. The church started clapping and calling my name. What was I supposed to do? Make up a lie about why I couldn't sing? Or better yet, tell them that you FORBADE me to sing anymore? How could I refuse under the circumstances? Besides, the church was blessed and the Lord had his way."

Pastor Proctor stopped walking abruptly and whirled around so quickly that Nettie almost bumped into him. His face was twisted in anger. "God didn't have his way! YOU had your way! THAT WAS ALL YOUR DOING, NOT GOD'S! If ever you're called upon again, DO NOT GET UP! How hard is that?" He changed directions and stormed out of the house instead. Nettie sat in the middle of her bedroom floor in total bewilderment. She loved her husband and she loved God. Why was he so jealous of something that really had nothing to do with her? She was merely a vessel for the Lord's use. She pondered these things in her heart as she lay down to rest before the evening service.

When Nettie got up some time later to go to service, she couldn't locate her car keys. Thinking she must have misplaced them, she went to find her purse where she always kept a spare set. Those were gone as well. Then it dawned on her that her husband had taken them so she'd have to stay home. But why did he want her to stay home? This was too much for Nettie to comprehend. She decided to wait up for Pastor Proctor and ask him about her keys. He was gone until well past midnight. When he came in, he was not dressed in the suit that he'd been wearing earlier that day.

"That's not the suit you had on earlier today. Why did you change?"

"Woman, I don't need to ask your permission to change my clothes. For your information, after our argument, I went down to the church and locked myself in my office. I was praying for the church and consecrating myself. The suit I had on doesn't fit as comfortably as I would like so I changed into my spare suit, which you know I keep in the office. It is because of your constant nagging and harping that I stayed at the church."

Nettie flinched at his accusing her of nagging. She was a very easygoing person and nagging was not her way. "When I got ready to go to evening service, I looked all over the house and couldn't find my car keys. Then I decided to use the spare set I always keep in my purse. They were missing too. You wouldn't happen to know anything about that would you?"

"I accidentally took both our keys when I left after our little spat this afternoon. I didn't notice it until church was over and I went back to my office. I wondered why you hadn't come to the evening service. I thought you were just pouting and stayed home to piss me off so I'd have to deal with the members' questions about your absence. Now, I am not going to be grilled by you or answer any more questions. Will you ever let me get some peace?! Is it too much to ask for a man to get some peace in his own house?"

Nettie was angry. She had never engaged in such trivial, immature games the entire time they'd been married. He'd obviously said the last part to make her mad. He knew she did not approve of using the term "piss me off." She felt such language was not befitting a pastor and man of God.

S.E.C.R.E.T.S. VOLUME II by: *Pastor Shirley*

He usually only used it when he was trying to pick a fight with her. However, she wasn't going to rise to the bait. Someone had to keep a cool head. "The spare set of keys I keep in my purse was missing too. Why did you take those? And if you were so concerned about my absence at evening service, why didn't you call?"

"I have more on my mind than you and your little grandstanding efforts. I have a church to run and a ministry to oversee. Like I said, I thought you were staying home on purpose. To piss me off. As far as your spare set of keys, you keep so much junk in your purse; I'm surprised you can find anything." Pastor Proctor turned his back to her and began pulling his shirttails free of his pants.

"I thoroughly searched my purse earlier. The keys were not in there."

"Look again."

Nettie got out of her bed and went to get her purse, which she always kept on the hall table by the front door. She knew this was a wasted effort because she had dumped everything out of her purse when she'd been looking for her keys earlier; but the keys were in the main compartment on top of everything else. She knew beyond a shadow of a doubt that she had not left them there and that he'd taken them. She always kept her spare set of keys safely out of sight in the zippered pocket on the side. Why did he not want her to leave the house? What was really going on here?

Walking back into her bedroom, Nettie said, "The spare set of keys are in my purse now, but they weren't there earlier."

"What are you trying to say? Are you trying to say I stole your keys? Why would I do that? You have said some dumb things in the past, but this takes the cake, Nettie."

Struggling to maintain her composure, Nettie replied, "I'm saying the keys weren't there earlier. Why are you so late getting home? It's almost one in the morning and church was over hours ago."

"I am not a child and I will not be raised by my wife. I come and go as I please and you have nothing to say about that. Because it amuses me to do so, I will tell you where I was after church. I went back to my office and continued my praying and consecrating. Now I'm tired and I'm going to bed."

Nettie didn't believe him for one minute. Pastor Proctor had never been a great prayer warrior. That was not his spiritual strength. It was hers. So why now all of a sudden was he locking himself in his office for hours praying? Yeah right, as if she really believed that! Nevertheless, why was he lying to her? Why had he taken her keys? What had he been doing all this time both before and after church? All of these questions played and replayed in her mind, like an audio on repeat.

Nettie knew where he'd been and with whom he had been with. *HER*. *HER* was the woman Nettie had heard rumors about off and on for years. *HER* was the woman Pastor Proctor had a baby with, though he'd never once mentioned *HER* or the baby to Nettie. Whenever she asked him about *HER*, his reply was always the same, "Woman, you must be crazy. I'm not involved with anyone. You must be losing your mind. You are always accusing me of something."

Nettie knew she was not wrong and the drastic changes in Pastor Proctor's behavior proved it. All of the signs were there:

1. He was no longer interested in sex with her.
2. He was spending more and more time away from home.
3. Looking younger was his major focus. He dyed his hair, mustache, and beard every two weeks and inspected them daily for any missed gray strands.
4. He went on a diet and lost weight.
5. He purchased trendy new clothes on a regular basis.
6. He couldn't account for large chunks of time.
7. He couldn't account for large amounts of household funds.
8. He was overly critical of Nettie and her appearance.
9. He lied constantly about everything.
10. He went into another room or left the house completely to talk on his cell phone.

11. He used the computer secretly and alone.

12. He was very concerned about Nettie's schedule and whereabouts.

13. The final straw was that his Viagra usage had significantly increased.

Nettie had no idea about the last one until two weeks ago. While visiting her doctor for a routine checkup, he teased her about her husband's increased sexual appetite. He said Pastor Proctor was refilling his Viagra prescription every two weeks! This was news to Nettie because he certainly wasn't sleeping with her! She couldn't mention this to Pastor Proctor because he was quite vindictive and would probably bring the doctor up on charges for violating the Health Insurance Portability and Accountability Act (HIPAA), which prohibited doctors from sharing patient information unless given express permission.

Nettie knew, beyond any doubt, that the signs were there that her husband was cheating. She no longer recognized Pastor Proctor. Who was this stranger who shared her bed? She was caught between a rock and a hard place. She wanted to leave him but she loved him dearly. Every time she tried to discuss the matter with him, he made her feel as if she were losing her mind. She just didn't know what to think anymore.

****

Approximately six months had passed when Pastor Proctor decided that some changes needed to occur. Instead of the trustees handling the finances as they'd done previously, Pastor Proctor took control of all church finances. He told Nettie that the Lord was leading him in a new direction because he could not trust people. He also said that he had to take all the finances in hand so that he could make sure everything was where it should be. Nettie told him that she didn't think the trustees were going to go along with his decision.

Nettie was right. The trustees didn't go along with Pastor Proctor's announcement at all. In fact, they were angry and insulted. They repeatedly stated that they were not going to put money into a church where they had no say as to where the money was going. Pastor Proctor would hear no one on this matter. He was adamant about taking over all treasuries in the church. For this reason, many people left the church and never returned. Pastor Proctor told Nettie that he really didn't care about the members who'd left. He said the trick was in keeping more coming in the front door than were going out the back door. He was correct in that respect. However, once the new members saw that there were no trustees and no member involvement in the church finances, they, too, soon left.

Nettie felt so helpless. She'd worked by Pastor Proctor's side for many years helping to build their small church into a thriving ministry. And now with one decision, a decision with which she adamantly disagreed, the ministry was going up in flames. Pastor Proctor never consulted her about anything anymore. She tried to talk to him about it but he nastily told her that God had called him to pastor the ministry, not her. Though his flippant reply shocked her, she was determined to discuss the matter with him. She waited until he came in for the evening and she broached the subject again.

"James, I want to talk to you abou—"

"If you want to talk about the church finances," he said, cutting her off in mid-sentence, "my decision has not changed and it's no longer up for discussion."

"James, I am not a child that you can decide which topics are and are not up for discussion. The church finances are exactly what I want to—"

"I am SICK AND TIRED of you asking questions about the money coming into the church!" He shouted. "The church I pastor, not you. If you don't like the way I'm running this church, you can leave too. After all, there are plenty of women waiting in the wings hoping you'll mess up so they can step into your shoes." With those words, he marched into his office, slamming the door loudly as he went. Nettie went into her living room, lay on the floor, and began to pray. She felt hopeless and she prayed, "Please, God give me strength and guidance."

****

S.E.C.R.E.T.S. VOLUME II by: *Pastor Shirley*

Several days later, Nettie was headed home from work when she realized that she'd left her events calendar in her office at the church. She was actively planning the upcoming pastors and wives conference and needed the addresses of several churches she wanted to invite. She decided to stop by the church to retrieve the calendar.

When she arrived, she noticed her husband's grey Navigator in the church parking lot along with a big, red, shiny truck she'd never seen before. Nettie parked her car and walked to the back entrance of the church. She unlocked the door and headed in the direction of her office. She looked up the hall and noticed that Pastor Proctor's office door was open. Angry voices filtered out into the hallway. Nettie froze in her tracks. She heard a man whose voice she didn't recognize say; "You've got to be out of the house in two weeks. We have waited long enough and we aren't waiting any longer. There will be no more extensions. If you wanted unlimited extensions, you should've borrowed the money from a bank, not from us. Either you pay back the loan or the house will belong to us."

Nettie was in shock. Her church calendar forgotten, she backed silently down the hall and out the door. She ran to her car and got inside. She sat there staring into space. After about five minutes, which seemed like hours to Nettie, Pastor Proctor came out of the administrative offices followed by his visitor, who promptly got into his big red truck and sped off. *Oh my God!* Thought Nettie.

Nettie was reeling from this news. She was so engrossed in her thoughts that she hadn't noticed Pastor Proctor banging on her car window.

"What's wrong with you? Are you deaf? I've been calling your name for what seems like hours!" Nettie rolled her window down. Pastor Proctor then asked, "Why are you here?"

"Oh, I left something at the church and I came by to get it." Nettie said, not meeting her husband's probing eyes.

"Well? Are you going into the church or not?" He demanded indignantly.

"No, no," Nettie stammered.

Nettie Proctor

"Well, I'll see you at home then." Pastor Proctor got into his Navigator and drove off. Nettie's head was spinning. She could not believe he hadn't mentioned one word about his visitor. Not a single word. Well two could play the silent game. She wouldn't say a word about it either.

When the first week went by and Pastor Proctor said nothing about the man or their house, Nettie began to think that perhaps she had misunderstood the conversation she'd overheard. Perhaps they were talking about someone else's house. In all honesty, she had no idea what other properties her husband owned. She reasoned that if they were about to lose their house, surely he would've said something to her by now. Therefore, she began to relax.

Tuesday of the second week, Nettie noticed Pastor Proctor's Navigator in the driveway as she arrived home from work. *Strange,* she thought. *He doesn't usually get home until after 8 pm.* She drove her car into the garage and entered the house via the kitchen. As she walked to the entry hall to put her purse and keys on the small table, she noticed Pastor Proctor sitting in the family room. She walked in and said, "Hey" as she lightly brushed his cheek with a kiss. When he didn't answer, Nettie assumed it was because he was engrossed in the sports program he was watching. *Nothing unusual about that,* she thought. She turned in the direction of their bedroom when Pastor Proctor said, "Wait a minute, Nettie. Before you go, I need to talk to you." Nettie turned back around and took a seat on the sofa. She didn't like the feel of this. What was he getting ready to tell her?

Pastor Proctor rose from his chair and walked to the window. With his back to her he said, "This won't take long. Something's happened that I'm not proud of… But everyone makes mistakes and I've made a big one. In six days' time, we won't have a place to stay anymore. We have to be out of the house by then."

Nettie jumped off the couch, "What are you talking about? How can that be?! What do you mean in six days' time we have to be out of the house? What did you do?" Nettie was yelling at the top of her lungs.

S.E.C.R.E.T.S. VOLUME II by: *Pastor Shirley*

"Do…not…raise…your…voice…at…me…woman." Each word was punctuated with a stab of his finger. "I am trying to tell you something. Are you going to listen? Or keep running off at the mouth?" He yelled the last two questions.

Nettie sat back down on the couch shaking her head in disbelief. She was trying to take it all in…if that was possible.

Pastor Proctor continued. "Now, as I was saying before you threw your hissy fit…In six days' time, we won't have a house to live in. The people I owe money to won't give me any more extensions."

Pastor Proctor was quiet for a moment and it was apparent that his mind was a million miles away. He began again, his voice soft with memory, "At first I was winning. Then I got confident and I started playing more often. Then I started losing so I stopped playing in regular games and started playing in high stakes games trying to win back my losses."

Cutting into Pastor Proctor's explanation, Nettie shrieked, "Are you talking about gambling? Since when did you become such a big time gambler and how did you find out where games like this are even held?"

Pastor Proctor thought for a moment. He was clearly contemplating exactly how much to tell her. "I started playing poker at work to pass the time. In the beginning, we didn't play for money. Eventually, we added monetary bets to spice up the game. I beat everyone at work. Then I learned there was an inmate, Romero, who played poker real good. I started letting him out of his cell to play with us. He began teaching me everything he knew about the game of poker and he was brilliant. After a while, Romero told me he thought I was ready to play in the big league. When I asked him what the big league was, he told me where to go to play high stakes cash games with real poker players. I was exhilarated! I began to play and I began to win!

172

"Then I started losing. Each time I lost, I told myself that all I had to do was play one more game and I could win back everything I'd lost. But, that never happened. I just kept on losing. I got desperate and began selling our assets to enter other games. After I'd sold everything, it occurred to me that I could use the house as collateral and get a loan from the bank. I went to the bank, but without your physical presence to sign the note, they wouldn't authorize enough to pay the entrance fee let alone actually play in the biggest game of the century. I was so desperate, I even contemplated getting someone to act as you and sign the note. But since everyone in that bank knows you personally, that plan was a no-go."

Pastor Proctor paused for a minute to rub his temples. "I mentioned this to Romero and he told me of some 'businessmen' he knew who would loan me the money. I went to them, and they gave me the money I needed." Again, the faraway look entered his eyes. "I played brilliantly that night. I really did. The game got down to just me and Glass. I had a pair of sevens in my hand and the first three community cards were a nine, an eight, and a seven. I was ecstatic! I had trips!" Seeing Nettie's confused expression, he explained. "I had three of a kind. Three sevens. It's a very good hand. My luck was finally going to turn around. I could feel it."

Pastor Proctor's voice took on an excited edge. "I made a modest bet while keeping my face void of emotion, not wanting to alert Glass that I had a good hand. However, Glass was a difficult player. I had never played with him before that night and I wasn't able to read him. He didn't display any of the subconscious gestures other players did to give them away when they had a good hand. Glass called my bet and raised it slightly."

"I was feeling on top of the world. He obviously felt he had a good hand, but surely he didn't have as good a hand as I did. The dealer turned over the fourth community card, also known as the turn card. It was a five. This card didn't help me but at least I still had three of a kind. If I bet again, it might indicate to Glass that I was pretty confident about my hand, so I checked. Glass looked at me a long moment. Then he did the same and checked too. I thought this meant that he wasn't as confident as

S.E.C.R.E.T.S. VOLUME II by: *Pastor Shirley*

he wanted me to believe because he hadn't increased his bet. The dealer turned over the last community card. It was a three. Again, it didn't improve my hand and I was pretty certain that Glass didn't have as good a hand as he'd like me to believe. It was time for me to place my final bet and I put all my chips in. I was confident I was going to win and I tried to keep the smile off my face. The pot had over $350,000 dollars in it, more than enough to recoup all my losses. It was Glass's turn to bet. I expected him to fold. He didn't. He pushed in all his chips too."

Pastor Proctor broke out in a sweat, reliving the big game all over again in his mind. "For the first time since the game began, I felt the first stirring of alarm. Glass would have never put in all his chips unless he had a very good hand. I could feel sweat trickling down my back under my shirt. I struggled to remain calm. It was time for me to reveal my hand. 'Three of kind!' I said triumphantly flipping over my pair of sevens. Every eye in the place turned to Glass. He stared at my sevens for a long moment. The time seemed to stretch on forever and my nerves with it. Then he raised his eyes and said one word—'straight'—while turning over a jack and a ten."

Having never played poker, Nettie had no idea what 'three of a kind' or a 'straight' meant, and her puzzlement was clearly evident on her face. Pastor Proctor interpreted her confusion and plowed on with the rest of his story.

"HE HAD A STRAIGHT! FIVE CARDS IN SUCCESSION!" He said throwing his hands into the air. "He had the jack and the ten and there was a nine, eight, and a seven on the table. What are the odds he would have that? He had beaten me and he was busy scooping the large pile of chips in his direction. As he did so, I saw my life intermingled with those chips. I stood to leave so the guys wouldn't see me break down. When I got outside in the car I...I...cried. I cried for all the things I'd lost because Glass got lucky. I prayed to God to help me get through this. Then I remembered that I had taken a loan against the house." He bowed his head in defeat much like he did on the night of the game.

After a pregnant pause, he continued. "The people I thought were just 'businessmen' were loan sharks and they didn't take kindly to the fact that I couldn't pay back my loan. They started pressuring me. They started calling me at work and then they started coming to my job. I even saw them in the congregation a few Sundays at church."

He paused, then blurted out, "I'm sorry, Nettie. We're flat broke."

Nettie sat in confusion, her mind furiously working to make sense of all Pastor Proctor had told her. "What?" Nettie said. "Back it up…Back…it…up." Surely she hadn't heard what she thought she'd just heard. "Did you just say you mortgaged my home, our home?"

Pastor Proctor ignored Nettie's question and plowed on. "Look. Before you go and get all upset, I found us a nice two-bedroom apartment we can move into tomorrow." Seeing Nettie's look of pure fury, he said, "Or we can rent a hotel room for a while. Before you start hurling insults at me or blaming me for this mess we're in, we needed to move anyway. The house was going to need a lot of work…a new roof…new windows and siding, and the plumbing needed to be updated. It will be a little tight for us financially for a while, but we can save our money and buy a new place in a better neighborhood closer to the church." Pastor Proctor stopped his jabbering and looked at Nettie trying to gauge her reaction.

Nettie just stared at Pastor Proctor as if he were a stranger. She said nothing for a full two minutes. She just looked at him. Hard.

He finally asked, "Don't you have anything to say?"

Nettie eventually found her voice. "I cannot believe you've been so irresponsible that we have lost our beautiful home. If you expect me to leave my five-bedroom, three and a half bathroom house and move into a two-bedroom apartment you have lost your mind. And since we're sharing, what did you spend all the money on?"

"What?!" He asked incredulously.

"You heard me. WHAT DID YOU DO WITH ALL THE MONEY YOU GOT FROM THE LOAN SHARKS?" Nettie yelled. "I never saw a penny of it. You never paid a house payment. You never paid a light bill. In fact, you never paid any of the household bills."

"I put it into the church," he replied in a pious tone.

Nettie jumped up off the couch and began walking toward the master bedroom taking Pastor Proctor completely by surprise. "Where are you going?"

"If you can't be honest with me and tell me everything, I'm leaving. I have weathered many storms with you over the years. I worked by your side to support our home and the ministry. Then you have the nerve, the audacity to lose our home in a poker game of all things?! You have wasted money many times over the years, but this takes the cake! I'm sick of it!" She turned toward the bedroom.

"Ok," Pastor Proctor said in a voice barely above a whisper. He hung his head in defeat, but Nettie didn't see it because she was halfway up the stairs.

Nettie stopped. But she didn't turn around. "OK...What?"

He knew that he needed Nettie to get through this mess. It was she who made the lion's share of the household income and also provided them with medical benefits having been employed at her job for over 15 years. His salary certainly wouldn't allow them to live in the style to which he'd become accustomed. He also needed her to remain visible at the church. He wouldn't be able to keep this humiliating incident a secret unless she was by his side.

The events of the last month had taken their toll on him. He was physically and mentally worn out. He didn't know how much more he could stand. The numerous secrets he'd been carrying around with him had become too much of a burden. He decided to unload all of them now. He knew that Nettie loved him and would support him if she felt that he was telling her the truth. He just hoped that she could deal with the truth.

"OK, I will tell you the truth." He paused a moment to gain his courage.

He wearily sat down on the last step and put his head in his hands. He couldn't bear to look at her as he told her this part. "About the time I got… She came to me and—"

"She who?" Nettie asked tonelessly.

"Sister Terry Hayes came to me… I know you are aware that she and I have a baby together. I never wanted to hurt you, Nettie. I got caught up in a bad situation. I stopped seeing her before the baby was born. Anyway, she came to me and told me that she was getting evicted from her apartment and her car had broke down."

He paused again, knowing that Nettie was going to have a fit over this next bit of information. "I wanted to ensure my baby had a place to stay. I bought her a small two-bedroom house in her same neighborhood. She is only responsible for the taxes, utilities, and insurance. Sister Hayes can handle that on her small salary and I don't have to worry about my baby being put out on the street. It isn't the baby's fault that she was conceived. It was my carelessness. I didn't want her to be penalized for my mistake." He paused again. "I also bought her a small car. Nothing fancy. I got her a used Honda. I paid for the car in cash and paid the insurance for a year. Now she can get back and forth to work and take the baby to daycare. I didn't do any of those things for Sister Hayes. I did them for the baby." This part wasn't true, but Nettie didn't need to know that. "With the rest of the money, I entered the big poker game I just told you about. That's the whole truth. I swear it!"

Nettie whirled around in utter disbelief. Pastor Proctor had never before admitted his affair with *HER* and now *HER* not only had a name, but *HER* had a baby as well. His baby. Nettie was so mad that she could barely see straight. She stomped back down the stairs, folded her hands behind her back, and began to pace in a tight, agitated circle. "WE HAVE LOST OUR HOME BECAUSE YOU WERE OUT BUYING HOUSES AND CARS FOR YOUR WHORE?" Nettie yelled. "How could you do that to me? Your wife! The woman who has worked by your side for years. You put HER, THAT WOMAN, BEFORE ME, YOUR WIFE!" Nettie had never been prone to physical violence in the past, but, oh how she

S.E.C.R.E.T.S. VOLUME II by: _Pastor Shirley_

wanted to punch him in the face for the first time in her life. She was yelling. She was pacing. She was throwing things at him. "Let me tell you something, I am not moving into a two-bedroom apartment, and I am not sticking around while you throw our life away to support your mistress and kid. Yes, I know about HER. I have always known… Of course you should support your kid. That's your responsibility. But you should've paid child support to do that like every other man who has a baby on the side, NOT gamble away my life and house to do it! You expect me to stick around after this?" Nettie ran out of things to throw. "After all this?" Nettie began pacing again.

Abruptly, Nettie ran from the room going into the garage. She grabbed a hammer and three cans of black spray paint. Pastor Proctor heard the door to the garage open and assumed Nettie was so upset that she was leaving the house—but he was wrong.

Nettie came back into the house and stood in the kitchen. She looked at the walls she had lovingly painted just the perfect shade of robin's egg blue and the coordinating curtains she had painstakingly selected. The totality of her loss washed over her like a hard spring rain drenching every crevice of her body and replacing the love she had previously held for her home with hatred. She ripped the curtains from the windows and flung them to the floor. Grabbing a bucket from under the kitchen sink, she quickly filled it with items she would need to ravage her home. She threw several screwdrivers, two knives, a hammer, a mallet, and paint into the bucket, and then she put on her leather work-gloves. She vigorously shook a can of spray paint and began painting the windows and the walls. She used her hammer to gouge large holes into the walls. If she wasn't going to be able to enjoy the soothing environment she had lovingly created, no one else would either. She intended to utterly destroy every room of the house she had once loved.

Pastor Proctor heard the commotion in the kitchen and went to investigate, passing Nettie as he entered. He was astounded to see the results of her anger. The walls and windows sported large gaping holes and were covered in graffiti-like black spray paint. The curtains were missing from the windows, the floor was now missing several tiles, which she had obvi-

Nettie Proctor

ously chiseled out with a hammer and screwdriver, and the light fixture was ripped out of the ceiling and dangling from its socket. Pastor Proctor stood in shock, not believing his eyes. He would never have thought that Nettie would do this to the house he knew she loved. He was jarred back to reality by the sound of pounding in the dining room. He ran to the room to ask Nettie exactly what she was doing. He had to scream in order to be heard over the banging of her hammer.

Nettie stopped punching holes in the wall and threw the man she had married a scathing look. She didn't speak for a long moment and then replied in a low menacing voice, "You have the nerve to stand in my presence and ask me what I'm doing? You have gambled away our home, my home, and bought your whore a new house and a new car. I AM GOING TO BE PUT OUT IN THE STREET, BUT YOUR WHORE HAS A NEW HOUSE AND A NEW CAR?!! How dare you feel you can ask anything of me? I helped pick out this house; I selected all the wall colors, window coverings, themes, and furniture. I did those things, not you. My income paid the house payment for over ten years and now you have the nerve to tell me that I no longer have a place to live and that I have to be out of my beloved home in six days? YOU ARE SELFISH! YOU ARE INSENSITIVE! YOU ARE IRRESPONSIBLE AND IMMATURE! AND I AM SICK AND TIRED OF YOU AND YOUR MESS!!!!!! Thanks to your irresponsibleness, I have to leave my home, but I will not allow someone else to enjoy the beauty I have so lovingly built and you would do well not to speak to me." She then flung the mallet in her hand with all her might, catching Pastor Proctor over his right ear.

Blood squirted in all directions. But none of this fazed Nettie. Without further comment, she turned from Pastor Proctor and started shredding the carpet with a butcher knife being careful not to scratch or damage any

S.E.C.R.E.T.S. VOLUME II by: *Pastor Shirley*

of the furniture, which she planned to take with her.

Pastor Proctor clamped his hands to his ear and screamed "Look what you have done to me, Woman! I'm bleeding like a hog! What's wrong with you? Are you trying to kill me?!" He then ran to the mirror to assess the damage that Nettie had wrought to his ear. Bright red blood stained the front of his shirt. The right side of his face was throbbing mercilessly and blood continued to gush from the wound over his right ear. Eyes frantically searching the room, he grabbed the long scarf from his coat that was lying over a chair. He tied it tightly around his head to staunch the bleeding. While recovering from his shock at seeing Nettie vigorously determined to annihilate their home, he became very angry. How dare she throw a mallet at him? She could've killed him! She had a lot of nerve yelling and threatening him, too. So what if he had made a mistake? She made mistakes too, and at least he had apologized. *He* was the man of this house. And why was she taking her anger out on the house? He couldn't turn this house over to loan sharks in a vandalized condition. They would interpret receiving a destroyed house as a direct insult, and rightly so. They would have to retaliate in order to maintain their reputation, thus, guaranteeing his demise.

The next order of business was to immediately get control of the crazed lunatic he'd married before she completely destroyed their house. She had finished shredding the carpet in the first area and had now moved to another. The only way he could think of was to jolt her back to reality.

"Nettie," said Pastor Proctor. She never looked in his direction or acknowledged his presence. She just continued her carpet shredding. He thundered her name again. "NETTIE!" She paused momentarily but then vigorously returned to shredding in a new, untouched area.

Pastor Proctor crossed the distance between them, snatched the knife from her hand, and roughly hauled her to her feet. He marched her into the family room and none too gently dumped her on the couch. "Take your hands off me NOW!" Nettie spat.

Pastor Proctor's face was thunderous. "Listen to me, Nettie. I know I made a mistake but I can't undo it now and I can't turn over this house to loan sharks with holes in the walls and the carpet cut to shreds. These are not bankers I'm dealing with; they are thugs and they would take my turning over the house all jacked up as an insult. An insult they would not allow to go unaddressed. I'm sure they would choose to address such a large insult with the payment of my life. Do you really want me to die over a house, Nettie? I know I've made a mistake—" Nettie flung her husband a vicious look filled with hatred. Holding up his palm to stop her from voicing that hatred, he said, "Okay, okay, I've made a huge mistake. But I have apologized and I'm sorry. We have to figure out a way to get out of this mess and save face in front of the congregation."

"Is that all you can think about right now? You have destroyed all I have worked for and hold dear and you are thinking of 'saving face'? NEWSFLASH, Playboy! I will NOT help you find a way to get out of the mess YOU got yourself into just so you can 'SAVE FACE'," Nettie screamed.

Then something strange happened. The glazed look in her eyes receded and she looked at him with a mixture of shock and curiosity. "What's... wrong with your face? Why are you bleeding? Who hurt you?" She asked in a voice barely above a whisper.

"Don't worry about me. I'm fine and everything will be fine. Just don't go running off at the mouth and blowing everything out of proportion."

By now, Pastor Proctor was quite concerned at Nettie's erratic behavior. He studied her for a moment. He *never* expected this. He had no idea how he was going to fix this. He knew she would be angry. But this? He knew in that moment that she was coming unraveled. He also knew he had to get to the emergency room. Blood had soaked through the scarf and was apparently flowing again. He explained to Nettie that he had to go to the hospital and would be back as soon as he could. He knew he was in trouble when she looked at him blankly and asked why he needed to go to the emergency room.

After Pastor Proctor left, Nettie sat on the couch plotting her revenge.

S.E.C.R.E.T.S. VOLUME II by: *Pastor Shirley*

When Pastor Proctor returned, she would apologize and promise to help him straighten out this mess. She would even offer to repair the damage she had done. However, she had no intention of doing either. In four days' time, Pastor Proctor was scheduled to attend a weekend conference two hours away. He was due to leave on Friday and return on Sunday afternoon. During that time, she was going to have a moving company back a large truck up to the front of her house and pack every stick of furniture inside. After they took her furniture and loaded it into the storage facility she will have rented by then, she was going to totally demolish the house room by room.

Nettie couldn't control her menacing thoughts and the need to punish her husband. It was as if someone or something else had taken control of her mind and body. She smiled as she envisioned using fire in a metal trashcan to create smoke damage and turning on the sprinklers inside the house to create water damage. He better hope he returned to the house during daylight hours because she had every intention of having all the utilities turned off, turning off his cell phone, and canceling all his credit cards. After all, these things were in her name because she was the one who had paid for everything, not him.

Let him deal with the thugs who loaned him the money. He was stupid for getting involved with people like that in the first place. If they took their payment out of his hide, so be it. He deserved whatever he got.

If he could buy houses and cars for *HER*, he could certainly take care of himself. He could even move in with *HER*. After all, he was the one who'd paid for *HER* house and car while he carelessly gambled away their marital home and future.

Again, Nettie felt as if she was on the outside of her body watching a total stranger. She knew she was at the point of no return. She knew she had reached her limit and was no longer thinking rationally or logically. But, at that moment, she didn't want to be rational or logical and she quickly pushed any attempt at rational thought from her mind. She was a woman scorned and she was headed to a place where sanity and rationale were not welcome! She knew it… and she reveled in it.

Nettie Proctor

To find out what happened to Nettie Proctor and Pastor James Proctor, be sure to read S.E.C.R.E.T.S. of the First Ladies, Trilogy. Available soon in a bookstore near you.

Chapter 17

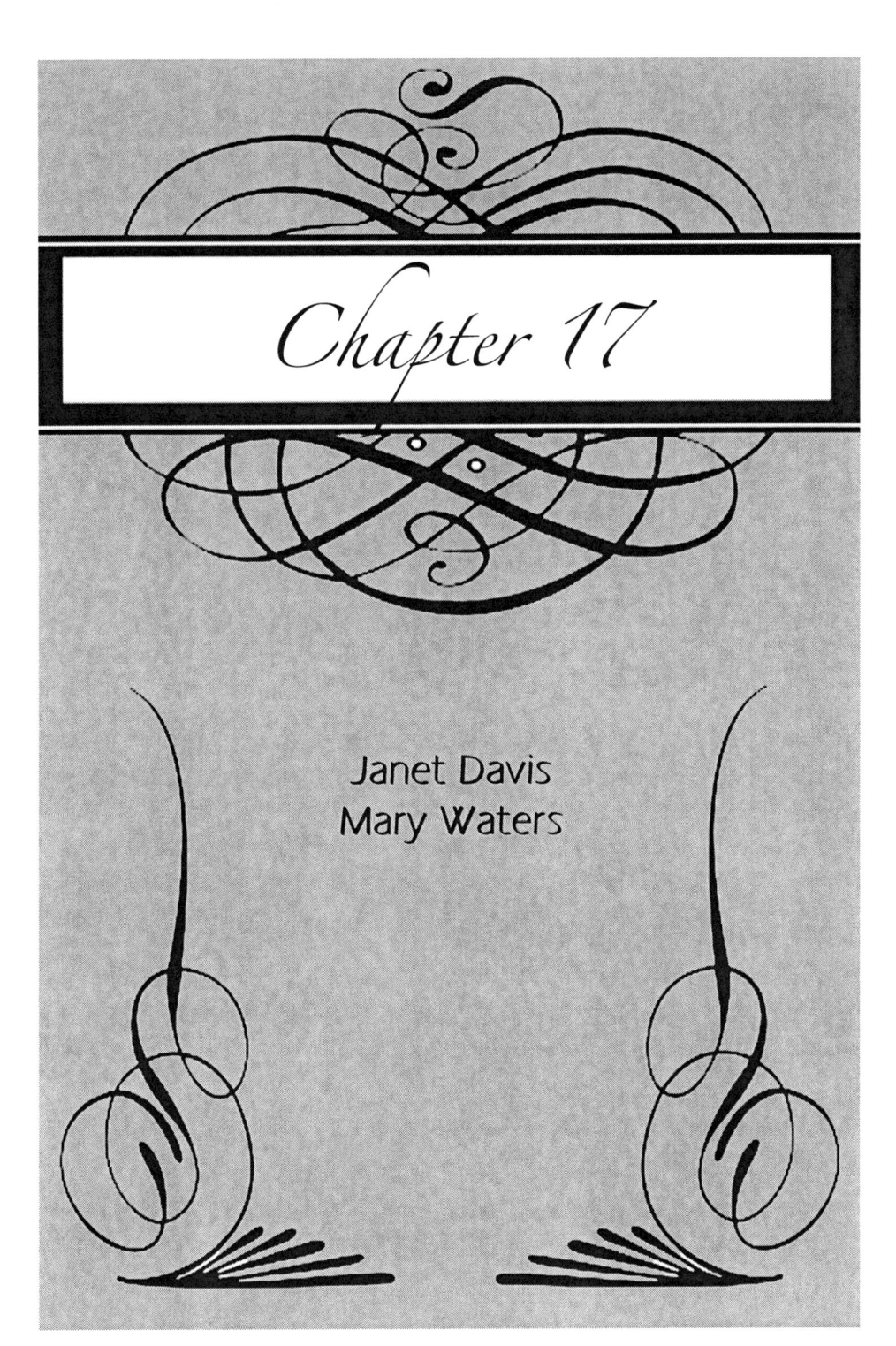

Janet Davis
Mary Waters

S.E.C.R.E.T.S. VOLUME II by: *Pastor Shirley*

Janet Davis
153 Susquehanna Road

Janet Davis and Mary Waters

Mary Waters
1007 Starwood Lane

Mary Waters

S.E.C.R.E.T.S. VOLUME II by: *Pastor Shirley*

Janet and Mary...

What do you do
in the face of such pain?
Leave or stay?
Nothing to gain.

Two lives,
seemingly far apart
Two bodies
harboring a broken heart

Who's to say
which way to go?
Turn left or right
on this empty road.

The phone hums
and then connects
What to expect?
will silence unfold?
Or maybe the unholy shriek
of a tortured soul...

First Lady Janet Davis is married to Apostle Eddie Davis. Janet is approximately 5'3" tall and grossly overweight with short braids and a sweet smile. Janet has been on every diet imaginable, only to gain more weight each time. She finally just gave up trying to diet and began to fool herself into believing that she was content with her immensely large size. She is often heard saying, "I've just got more meat in the pot." Janet has learned to take such disingenuous compliments like, "You have such a pretty face" in stride; though she feels the slap of the backhanded compliment.

Janet is very jovial and fun loving. She has a great sense of humor and always has a quick reply. She is the type of person whom everyone wants to be around because she is considered the life of the party. When Janet first met Apostle Davis, she was at a church Sunday school picnic. Apostle Davis was 19 years old and she was 17 and soon to graduate from high school. Apostle Davis was very intelligent and excelled in all things academic. He'd graduated from high school at the age of 15 and was now graduating from college. Of all the young men at the picnic, Janet noticed Eddie because of his mature attitude and the confident way in which he carried himself. Janet just knew he was someone special. He was already a young minister and was promised a church as soon as he graduated from college.

Many of the young girls at the picnic were aware that he was in college and that he had already been promised a church. They had dreams of being an apostle's wife and the First Lady of a thriving church. Thus, they went out of their way to get Eddie's attention. He was not the least bit interested in any woman who aggressively pursued him. However, he made it a point to be polite to the girls and then to promptly ignore them.

Janet was different. She acted as if he didn't exist. She was regaling a group of teenagers with a humorous rendition of a sermon given last Sunday at her church. The members of the group, which now also included a few adults, were laughing so hard that they were practically in tears.

Eddie noticed Janet. He noticed her spunk and sense of humor. He noticed her pretty face and her slender body. He noticed her charisma, her

S.E.C.R.E.T.S. VOLUME II by: *Pastor Shirley*

zest for life, and her easy command of the group around her. But the most important thing he noticed about Janet was that she *hadn't* noticed him—or at least she gave no indication that she had. Eddie was intrigued.

They began a whirlwind courtship and married right after Janet graduated from high school. They were so much in love and had high hopes for the future. Eddie got the church appointment and Janet set out to make a happy home.

Janet got pregnant on their wedding night. She really had a hard time with the first baby and was inactive for most of her pregnancy. She was so disgusted with herself because she had gained 80 pounds during the nine months. However, all the pain, suffering, and weight gain was well worth it when 7lb. 15 oz. Steven was born. He was such a sweet baby and so cuddly. Janet just loved his baby smell and she doted on him constantly. Janet had weighed only 135 pounds when she got married. After Steven was born, her weight had ballooned to 215 pounds. She went on a diet and lost only 18 pounds. She was so discouraged by the paltry weight loss after weeks of deprivation and starvation that she just gave up the notion of trying to diet.

Steven was six months old when Janet discovered she was pregnant again. To her dismay, she was carrying triplets! Due to the multiple births, she was again forced to remain in bed for the entire pregnancy. Janet had an extremely hard time during both the pregnancy and the birth of the triplets. She was blessed in that she had the support of her family, which proved to be invaluable. Due to the additional weight and pregnancy complications, her family had to be with her on a constant basis. By this time, Janet was over 100 pounds heavier than she was with her first pregnancy. She desperately hoped that after the triplets were born she would be able to lose the additional weight.

Her beautiful babies were born right on schedule. She had two handsome sons, Kai and Kaden, and one beautiful daughter, Kendall. When Janet left the hospital, she topped the scale at 302 pounds. However, she was so wrapped up in her babies that she put weight loss on the back burner. She told herself that she would lose the weight later.

As time passed, Janet became even more disgusted with her failure to lose weight. Because of her 5'3" frame, she appeared to be much larger than she actually was. She had endured not only looks of disgust on the faces of others, but that same look of disgust on the face of her husband as well. He never missed an opportunity to ridicule her about her weight and make her feel unattractive. He called her "baby elephant," "Henrietta the hippo," and "Orca the whale." He also referred to her clothes as "circus tents" and said anything else that he could think of to describe her weight in a negative manner. He told her that no one else would possibly be interested in her and that she was lucky that he was still with her. Apostle Davis had long ceased to make love to her, telling her that he just couldn't stand looking at her bloated body. He instructed Janet not to undress in front of him saying that the sight of her was nauseating and repulsive. Janet hadn't known the meaning of the word repulsive, though she knew it was nothing positive. When she looked it up the next day and discovered that it meant extremely disgusting, she burst into tears. To think the man whom she had married thought the body that had borne his four children was *extremely* disgusting, eradicated any self-esteem she had left. His cruel and uncaring comments hurt her badly and affected her deeply. However, her husband never seemed to notice and kept right on preaching.

Janet cried herself to sleep many nights. Had it not been for her children and her love of the Lord, Janet would have had a nervous breakdown. She prayed daily that the Holy Spirit would keep her and comfort her. Her favorite scripture, Philippians 4:7, *"And the peace of God, which passeth all understanding, shall keep your hearts and minds through Christ Jesus,"* got her through so many lonely days and nights. She also prayed for her physical health. She'd had a cold for three weeks and it wasn't getting any better. Her energy level was extremely low and she had a persistent, moist cough. She had to get better because there was no one else to take care of her children.

Janet began to notice that Apostle Davis was spending more and more time at the church during the day. Thinking that he was swamped with the organization of the many outreach ministries and associated administrative tasks, Janet asked if she could help him at the office. Apostle Davis cruelly told her that a woman's place was in the home. Janet winced at his harsh reply, but shook her head in defeat.

Approximately six weeks later, unannounced and unexpected, Janet dropped by the administrative offices at the church. Sister Ellen, the church secretary, was not at her desk so Janet went directly to her husband's office. She opened the door and, to her utter shock, found the secretary straddling her husband's lap, her skirt hiked up around her waist, and her blouse unbuttoned. Janet was so shocked that she just stood there in disbelief. When Apostle Davis looked up and saw Janet standing in his office, he abruptly jumped up causing his secretary to fall unceremoniously to the floor in an untidy heap.

As Sister Ellen began to right her clothing, Apostle Davis said nothing. His mind was working furiously to come up with a plausible explanation. Then he questioned in a cold voice, "What are you doing here, Janet?"

"I...um...came—"

"You came to my office unannounced. Why did you do that?"

Janet was temporarily stunned into silence. Was he actually acting as if *he* was angry with *her?* As if *she* had done something wrong?

"What is going on here?" She blurted out before she lost her nerve.

By now, Sister Ellen, again fully dressed, had quietly retreated to her desk. Apostle Davis turned his back to his wife. She heard the unmistakable whir of his zipper as he refastened his pants. When he turned back around to face his wife, she saw, to her dismay, that he had not only regained his composure, but his anger as well.

"You want to know what is going on here?" He asked her sharply. "I'll tell you what's going on here." He sneered. "I am doing the Lord's work, which you so rudely interrupted. I was laying hands on the sick."

Janet could not believe her ears! He actually had the nerve to tell her that he had been laying hands on the sick?! She saw exactly what type of hands he had been laying and exactly where he'd been laying them.

Janet turned on her heels and quickly left the office with tears streaming down her face. As she passed Sister Ellen's desk, Janet tucked her head down further, not wanting the secretary to witness her total humiliation. She went home and immediately began to eat to pass the time. However, she was hurting so badly that she didn't even taste the food. She felt as if someone had ripped her heart out. She had never before felt such pain, not even when she'd delivered her precious babies.

She conducted her motherly duties as if in a trance. Her mind was totally on Apostle Davis and what she had witnessed. She expected him to come home that evening after having repented to God and then to ask for her forgiveness. She had decided that she still loved him and would forgive him when he asked her to do so. She would suggest that they attend therapy as a condition of her forgiveness. She knew they needed help with their marriage and perhaps therapy was the answer.

She was totally unprepared for the scene that unfolded before her eyes when Apostle Davis finally came home. He walked into the house, three hours late, in a fit of anger. When the children ran to greet him, as they normally did, he yelled at them and sent them to their rooms. Their little faces were crushed. Janet was heartbroken for her precious babies. But Apostle Davis didn't notice his children's disappointment or Janet's resulting anguish.

After the children had run out of the room as fast as their little legs could carry them, he whirled around to face Janet. He approached her menac-

S.E.C.R.E.T.S. VOLUME II by: Pastor Shirley

ingly and pointed his finger in her face.

"How dare you spy on me! I have taken care of this family and done the Lord's work for years. I have put up with your disgusting weight issues since the beginning of our marriage. Who else will have you? Who else can afford to buy food to feed you? What do you possibly have to offer another man except an overweight, disgusting body and a bunch of kids? You have no skills. You've never worked. You can't even keep house. It's never clean, my dinner is rarely prepared well, and I am always running out of clean shirts. You're so dumb that I can't even discuss church issues or current events with you. That's one of the things I like about Sister Ellen. I can talk to her about the church as well as politics, art, literature, or whatever else I'm interested in. She didn't feel well today so I was praying for her." This whole laying-hands-on-the-sick story sounded ridiculous even to his ears. But he had begun with it and he was sticking with it. He knew Janet wouldn't dare question him as long as he put his foot down and made her feel bad about her weight.

"I will not put up with your spying and your troublemaking. You are to NEVER, EVER again come to my office unannounced! Do I make myself PERFECTLY CLEAR, SHAMU?!" Janet nodded mutely understanding his reference to Shamu the whale. "Now get my dinner and clean up this kitchen."

Janet could not believe her ears. He was blaming his infidelity on *her!* He had not taken responsibility for any of his actions. Janet was feeling so many emotions; she didn't know how to go about dealing with any of them. Her mind began playing tricks on her. Had she really seen her husband in the middle of a sexual interlude? Could he possibly have been praying for Sister Ellen?

The following Sunday, Apostle Davis preached as if it was his last chance. Sister Ellen kept jumping up and yelling, "Hallelujah! Preach the word!" As she stole glances at Janet with every outburst. Janet just sat there hiding behind the mask that she wore so well. The mask, a practiced look of love and support, was plastered on her face. On the outside, she nodded her head and murmured "Amen" at the appropriate times. On the inside, she was screaming and crying with the weight and pain of her situation. She thought *How can he stand at the pulpit and preach as if he has done nothing wrong? And someone please tell me why Sister Ellen keeps jumping up. I can barely look at her without wanting to slap her teeth down her throat.*

Janet's sense of right and wrong was in contradiction with what she had been taught as a small girl. All her life, she had been taught that wives supported their husbands no matter what they did. She had been taught that to suffer for Christ was to reign with Him and, yes, this included marriage problems. She had been taught that a saved wife obeyed her husband and stood by him even if that meant denying her own feelings and wellbeing. She was also taught that good, saved wives kept silent, fasted, and prayed for their husbands.

By observation, Janet had learned from her mother that a dutiful and supportive wife turned a blind eye even to her husband's infidelity. Because of this ingrained belief, Janet had turned a blind eye to Eddie's cruelty and infidelity. Who could she possibly tell? Who would believe her? Infidelity was not discussed and certainly no one ever admitted to experiencing it. All the First Ladies she knew never said anything negative about their husbands. Like her, they were all smiles and big hats.

As Janet sat in church listening to her husband preach, she tuned him out completely and reflected on her marriage. She was honest with herself during her assessment and she didn't like what she saw. Unfortunately, she had to admit that she had let her physical appearance go. She remembered when she wore a size 6-8 dress, kept her hair cut in a short, attractive style, and wore makeup daily. Now she wore a size 5X (and some of them were snug), she kept her hair braided because it was easy (not because it was attractive), and she wore no makeup at all. She realized that these changes had not resulted in an improved look for her. She wondered if she had been a better wife, a better lover, and had not gained so much weight, if Apostle Davis would still have strayed repeatedly over the years. What if, what if, what if?!

Janet was so completely absorbed in her thoughts that she didn't realize

S.E.C.R.E.T.S. VOLUME II by: *Pastor Shirley*

that her husband had completed his sermon and that she was being called to the front to acknowledge the visitors. As the First Lady, this was a job she usually enjoyed. Today, however, she performed her duties by rote, without her usual energy and humor. She spoke the words that were expected of her, finished her task, and took her seat.

Apostle Davis stood again to dismiss the service. Before doing so, he acknowledged Sister Crawford and how nicely she was dressed. Janet's heart burst into a million little pieces. She would have given all the money in the world to have her husband utter those words to her. Janet couldn't remember the last time Apostle Davis had given her a compliment for any reason. Because he told her almost daily that she was nothing and would never amount to anything without him, she now believed this to be true. Janet remembered the many occasions that her husband told her that she should be down on her hands and knees thanking God that he was her husband and that he was still with her. He repeatedly told her that no one else would ever want her because she was fat and ugly. Because of these hurtful words, Janet cried out to God many nights, praying for the strength just to make it through another day.

All of these things Janet hid from the church congregation, her family, her friends, and sometimes even herself. She always smiled and acted brave, but she was at the end of her rope. She now asked God to lead her, guide her, and give her the strength to do what she had to do. Whatever that was.

On a cold, rainy day in November, Janet woke up feeling badly as if she had the flu. Her head felt like someone had squeezed it in a vise, her body ached all over, she had a high fever, and she was vomiting. She was so weak that she could barely get out of bed. When Apostle Davis came into the bedroom to get dressed for the day, Janet told him how bad she felt and asked him to stay home to care for the children. In the middle of her explanation, Janet dashed past Apostle Davis and into the bathroom as another violent bout of vomiting came crashing down on her. After emptying all the contents of her stomach, Janet walked slowly and unsteadily back into the room, feeling both weak and dizzy. As she entered, she saw Apostle Davis now fully dressed and reaching for his car keys. "Eddie, I really need you to stay home and help me with the children today. I'm so weak, I can barely stand up," Janet said while wiping her brow and slowly getting into bed.

Apostle Davis turned around with a look of repugnance on his face. He stood for a moment looking at Janet and said nothing. He then casually leaned against the bedroom door and said, "It's not the flu that's causing you to have trouble standing, it's all that extra weight. You're as big as a house. How do you think you're supposed to feel?" Apostle Davis straightened and walked to the bed where Janet was laying.

"I don't have time to babysit you and the kids. Get your fat elephant butt up and out of bed and take care of the kids and this house. It's a mess." Apostle Davis leaned forward and sneered, "When I get home today, I don't want to hear you were too sick to fix my dinner. I don't need you bothering me with menial domestic tasks. I need to keep my mind clear to study God's word for my sermon on Sunday."

Apostle Davis stood up and walked to the mirror. He critically examined his hair. Not liking what he saw, he put his car keys on the dresser, picked up the brush, and brushed his hair for the umpteenth time since entering the bedroom. He continued spewing his callous, hateful words as he brushed. "Besides, I can't stay home today because I promised Sister Ellen that I would take her out to lunch. She's been doing such a good job and I want to show her that I appreciate all of her hard work and dedication." Apostle Davis gave his hair one final pat, picked his car keys up, and walked out of the bedroom without so much as a backward glance. Janet soon heard his car start and pull out of the driveway.

Janet lay in the bed in a shocked and shaken state. Then she began to cry. What began as a simple crying jag became a huge, body-racking sobbing fit. She knew that this was not helping her feel better. In fact, she knew that it would make her feel weaker. But try as she might, she just couldn't stop crying. What was she going to do? How was she possibly going to make it through the day? How was she going to care for the kids, clean the house, and cook dinner when she could barely stand up on her own? As Janet pondered these thoughts, the phone rang. She picked up the

S.E.C.R.E.T.S. VOLUME II by: *Pastor Shirley*

phone to hear Sister Waters' loving, motherly voice on the other end. "Sis Janet, it's me, Sis Waters from the church. How you doin', baby?" Not giving Janet a chance to answer, she went on. "The Lord been layin' you on my heart real heavy like. I jus' had to call and check on you. Are you all right? Is there anything I can do for you?"

Janet tried her best. She tried to hold back the tears. But she was unsuccessful. She began to sob on the phone making it difficult, if not impossible, for Sis Waters to understand what she was trying to say. Eventually through Janet's tear-filled response, Sister Waters was able to gather that Janet was very sick with a fever, chills, and vomiting and that she had no one to take care of her or help her with the kids. Sister Waters then said, "Say no more, honey. I'll be right over and I'll be happy to take care of you and them babies."

Sister Waters was one of the sweetest ladies at the church. She was a widow and all of her seven children were grown. She had 22 grandchildren and doted on all of them. She was very wise in her dealings with the younger ladies in the church and she often joked with them saying that she had attended the "school of hard knocks" and had learned her lessons well. She had been married for 39 years before her husband died and they had pastored a church together for 20 of those years. Sister Waters remembered the hard times that she had endured with her husband in the early years of building the ministry. During that time, she had longed for someone to talk to and confide in about her problems; someone who would have prayed with her and kept her situation private. She hadn't had a person like that so she had shouldered the heavy burden alone.

Sister Waters had been watching her First Lady for quite some time. She had been praying that God would give her the strength to endure. Sister Janet had not confided in her concerning her personal life; however, she really didn't have to. Sister Waters was older and well seasoned, and she, too, had been a First Lady. This is why she could read all of the telltale signs in Sister Janet's eyes. No matter how expensive the suit, how large the hat, or how wide the smile, there is a haunting look of pain in the eyes of every First Lady that can only be read and recognized by another First Lady.

As Sister Waters drove over to care for her First Lady, she knew that Sister Janet was in a great deal of emotional pain. This brought back memories of her marriage and her husband. She hadn't thought about them in a long while. Rev. John Waters was a big, brown-skinned bear of a man standing approximately 6'5" in height and weighing approximately 285 pounds. He was reasonably good looking and was always described as a dapper dresser. He had an infectious laugh that immediately lit up a room. He was jokingly referred to as a "gentle giant" by Sister Waters and the "Jolly Green Giant" by others. Sister Waters was barely 5 feet tall, chubby, had a quiet confidence about her and a sweet disposition and attitude. The old saying that opposites attract was certainly true in this instance as Rev. Waters was big, tall, and boisterous, while Sister Waters was short, round, and quiet. They were so happy together that people often said it was as if God himself had put them together. Many other married couples often envied the Waters' openly loving relationship, saying that they lived in a fairytale world where making each other happy was their main concern—which it was. They freely gave of themselves to the ministry and to their children. After God, their marriage was most important to both of them and it showed.

Rev. Waters doted on Sister Waters and his children. He never wanted her to work outside the home, saying that God told him to take care of his family and that was exactly what he was going to do. His large family lived comfortably due to Sister Waters' money and household management skills. With Sister Waters' help, he was able to manage his time to include his children's many activities, church duties, work, and his marriage. In the area of family, he was an excellent example to the younger men not only at his church but in his neighborhood as well.

Sister Waters loved caring for the children, managing the house, and surprising her husband with special meals. They loved each other in and out of the bed and, as a result, they shared an enjoyable and fulfilling sex life. When it came to making love, they based their sexual relationship on the Bible passage stating that "marriage is honorable and the bed is undefiled." They had no hang-ups or inhibitions when they made love. They always said that they were made to love each other. Sister Waters

S.E.C.R.E.T.S. VOLUME II by: *Pastor Shirley*

especially loved the time they shared laying in each other's arms after they'd made love. Rev. Waters always made her feel so beautiful telling her that God had created her just for him and that he loved every inch of her body. Rev. Waters always made her feel desirable and sexy never once mentioning her weight because it wasn't an issue for him.

They had been pastoring for approximately 10 years when a new family joined the church. Sister Reeves was a single mother with two small sons. She was a good worker in the church and regularly visited the pastor and his wife. Sister Reeves was considered plain looking. She was the type of person who could easily blend into a crowd, as there was nothing about her that stood out or grabbed your attention.

One Sunday, Sister Reeves stood up and made a special announcement. She said that the Lord had laid Rev. and Sister Waters on her heart and that she wanted to lead the Pastor's Aid Committee. However, she wanted to change the name to the Pastor's and Wife's Aid Committee because they were one and shared in the leadership of the church. She went on to say that the Lord had given her a burden for her pastor and his wife.

When she sat down, Rev. Waters stood and said that Sister Reeves should be commended for her devotion to her pastor and wife. Sister Waters was also flattered. She was used to the members carrying on over the pastor, but no one had ever given such attention to her.

Initially, Sister Reeves worked quite hard in her new position. She organized special programs in honor of the pastor and his wife and she never missed an opportunity to remind the congregation how special their leaders were and that they were blessed to have them.

However, after 11 months, things began to change. Sister Reeves again stood up in the church to make an announcement. She said that she was being led by the Lord to start focusing the committee's efforts on the pastor alone because he was the one who carried the burden of leadership for the church, not his wife. Also, she was changing the committee's name back to the Pastor's Aid Committee.

Sister Reeves took it upon herself to place water on the podium during the pastor's sermon as opposed to leaving it on the small table by his chair, stating that the pastor shouldn't have to reach very far if he wanted a drink. Whenever the pastor preached, she insisted that he go directly to his office to change his clothes where she always had another set of clothes waiting for him.

Later, in addition to having access to his regular clothes, Sister Reeves asked Sister Waters for undergarments for the pastor as well. She explained this unusual request by stating that if the pastor changed his outer clothes and left on his wet undergarments after he ministered, he could still catch a cold. Sister Waters loved her husband and she certainly didn't want him to get sick. Knowing how her husband perspired heavily while ministering, Sister Waters provided the undergarments and articles of clothing to be placed in her husband's office. Shortly thereafter, Sister Reeves began insisting that she take the pastor's clothes, including his undergarments, home to personally launder them. She even had a new lock put on the pastor's office door. She gave one key to the pastor and she kept the other one for herself.

Sister Waters realized that the situation had clearly gotten out of hand when she went to enter her husband's office and her key no longer worked. When she learned that Sister Reeves had a key and she didn't, it became quite obvious to her that Sister Reeve's pastor's aid "ministry" had an ulterior motive. She had always shared a relationship with Rev. Waters in which good communication was encouraged and valued. She felt certain that Rev. Waters would straighten everything out once this situation was brought to his attention.

That evening when Rev. Waters came home, she told him that she wanted to talk to him after dinner, which is when they usually spent time talking to one another. Once in their bedroom, Sister Waters told him exactly how she felt, warned him to be careful and not to fall into the devil's trap. However, she was blindsided by her husband's explosive response. Never in all the years she had been married to Rev. Waters had she seen him this angry. He jumped up out of his chair and began gesturing wildly with his hands, yelling at the top of his lungs, and pacing back and forth.

S.E.C.R.E.T.S. VOLUME II by: *Pastor Shirley*

If his actions weren't enough to upset her, his words certainly were. He was a big man and his out-of-character actions were frightening her. She had never had this type of intense anger directed at her.

He stopped pacing and said, "You're just trying to run around and start trouble in the church. Sister Reeves is trying to do the Lord's work and take care of her pastor. I wish I had more members who were as concerned about their leader as she is. She has proven to be a willing worker, a woman who is led by the Lord and who flows in the spirit. You'd best keep your lies and your accusations off this spirit-filled woman of God. Stop running around trying to stir up trouble. My God, woman, you're supposed to be helping me build up the ministry, not tear it down from the inside." He then yanked the bedroom door open and walked out of the room and out of the house.

Sister Waters was at a loss for words. She felt as if someone had knocked the wind out of her. How had this situation gotten so out of control? She had never seen him this angry and unwilling to discuss a problem head on. He had never refused her input in the past nor had he ever accused her of trying to tear the ministry down. The comment about the ministry hurt badly. If there was one thing Rev. Waters knew it was that she loved the Lord, was a praying woman, and that she was totally dedicated to the ministry.

When Tuesday night came, Sister Waters purposefully arrived at the church early in order to speak with Sister Reeves. She found her in the lobby on her way to the pastor's office. "Hello Sister Reeves," she said in a cheery voice that she didn't feel. "Do you mind stepping into my office for a moment? I need to talk to you."

Sister Reeves stopped, rolled her eyes, sighed loudly, and said, "Make it quick. There are things in the pastor's office that need my immediate attention."

Sister Waters noticed the sighing and eye rolling but chose to ignore it for the moment. She was determined to take the high road when she handled her business. Sister Reeves followed Sister Waters to her office and noisily plopped down into the chair facing the desk. With difficulty, Sister Waters ignored Sister Reeves' overall air of disrespect. She began in a kind voice.

"Thank you so very much for your dedication to my family—"

Sister Reeves abruptly cut her off. "As I've already said, the Lord is leading me in a new direction. I am being led to focus my care just on the man of God. After all, he is the one with the burden of the people and the church, not you. The pastor needs someone by his side every moment and every step of the way. And since we're talking, I have noticed that you have become real slack in caring for and ministering to the man of God. It is because of your lackadaisical attitude toward your husband that he is not as happy as he used to be. I couldn't stand by and do nothing. I had to step in to make sure that everything was taken care of so he can focus on the church and the ministry."

Though Sister Waters was in absolute shock, with much effort, her face remained blank. She'd felt her anger rising from the very beginning of Sister Reeves' little speech. *Was this woman crazy?* She thought.

She took a few deep breaths and a sip of water to get her anger and her voice under control. She did not want Sister Reeves to know that she had the ability to upset her to such a degree. If she thought it before, she now had confirmation that this woman was definitely after her husband. She deliberately took great care in the wording of her response so that the devil wouldn't get the victory.

"Sister Reeves, again, I thank you for your devotion to our family in the past, but you are completely out of line here. I am Pastor Waters' wife, not you. I don't need you, or anyone else for that matter, to tell me how to care for my husband. I am perfectly capable of taking care of him as I have always done for many years. What you need to do is focus on your life and your sons and leave the care of Pastor Waters to me. I don't want you tending to him in the church or washing his clothes anymore, and I want the key to his office."

S.E.C.R.E.T.S. VOLUME II by: *Pastor Shirley*

The look of total shock was evident on Sister Reeves' face as she digested this unexpected information from Sister Waters. The look then turned from shock to triumph. "That's not what Rev. Waters told me today when he took me to lunch. He said you would pull something like this." Sister Reeves jumped to her feet and stormed out of the office, slamming the door with such force that Sister Waters' beloved picture of the last supper went crashing to the floor.

You could have knocked Sister Waters over with a feather. On top of that, she now had a splitting headache. After surveying the broken photo and the other pictures that now hung crookedly on the wall, she slumped down in her chair and put her head in her hands.

LUNCH?! Did that wretched woman just say my husband has been taking her out to lunch? Thought Sister Waters. Why had Rev. Waters taken Sister Reeves to lunch, and more importantly, why hadn't he mentioned it to her? What reason could he possibly have for spending personal time with Sister Reeves? Why was he fueling the situation by spending unchaperoned time with her? What did Sister Reeves mean by "that's not what Rev. Waters told me" and "He said you would pull something like this"? Pull something like what? What had he told her? Come to think of it, why was her husband discussing his personal business with Sister Reeves? Why were they discussing his home life? What was really going on here?

She knew that the only person who could answer her many questions was Rev. Waters, but since Tuesday night prayer meeting was about to begin, she wouldn't get them answered until it was over. She threw the broken picture into the garbage can and straightened the other crooked pictures on her wall. Sister Waters checked her appearance in the mirror, opened the door, and walked out with her head held high.

She could hardly wait for the prayer meeting to end that night so that she could go home and confront Rev. Waters. They had driven separate cars because Sister Waters had wanted to arrive earlier than usual in order to talk to Sister Reeves. When the service was dismissed, she took only a few moments to speak to some of the members as she hastily walked to her car and drove off. She was sitting in a chair in the living room, her back ramrod straight, when Rev. Waters got home about 30 minutes later. He walked in, took note of her stiff posture, realized that she was upset, and immediately became irritated.

"What are you so huffed up about?" He asked with annoyance dripping from his voice as he walked past her to their bedroom.

"Huffed up?" She retorted as she jumped up from the chair and followed him into the bedroom. "You bet I'm 'huffed up' as you call it. Why did you take Sister Reeves to lunch today?" Not giving him a chance to answer, she continued, "And why were you discussing our personal life with her?" Rev. Waters had begun to take his church clothes off and his movements were stiff and jerky. Clearly, he was angry, which only irritated Sister Waters further.

"There you go again, stirring up a bunch of mess," he said disgustedly as he threw his shirt and jacket onto a chair. "Since when do I have to report to you when I talk to a church member? And for your information, I was not discussing our personal life with Sister Reeves. She just asked me about my children and grandchildren."

"Sister Reeves said that you were not as happy as you used to be." She stood facing him with her hands on her hips. "Well?! Did you say that?"

Rev. Waters hesitated, clearly uncomfortable with the direction that the conversation had taken. "I told her that there was a time when I was happier and that was all I said about that subject. As always, you are blowing everything out of proportion." He had now sat down on the side of the bed and was removing his socks and shoes.

Sister Waters couldn't believe what she was hearing. He *had* been discussing their personal life with Sister Reeves. "What do you mean there was a time when you were happier?"

Needing time to get his thoughts together, Rev. Waters went into the bathroom and turned on the shower. Walking back into the bedroom he said, "She just said that I looked unhappy and she asked me if I was happy, that's all." He said in an absent tone, attempting to dismiss the weak answer he'd just uttered in a blanket of nonchalance.

Sister Waters was clearly angry as she asked, "What has happened over the years to cause you to be so unhappy all of a sudden? You were fine before Sister Reeves got here. Now you're soooo unhappy? What has changed?"

"It's you!" Rev. Waters shot back as he removed his watch and put it on top of his wallet on his dresser. "You've changed."

"What do you mean I've changed?" Sister Waters replied. "Changed how? Maybe YOU are the one who's changed! Did that ever occur to you? No, it didn't because you're too busy taking Sister Reeves out to lunch. Just so you know, I told Sister Reeves that she would not be attending to you anymore and that I wanted the key to your office. If anything needs doing, I'll do it."

"WHAT?" He shouted, walking toward Sister Waters and stopping directly in front of her. "Who do you think you are? Since when do you give MY members orders? You have overstepped your bounds and you have put your mouth on a woman of God."

Sister Waters hopped onto a chair, as she often did, to get closer to Rev. Waters' massive height. Facing him with hands on hips, she replied, "Are you blind? Open your eyes! This woman is not sent from God, but from the pits of hell. She's come to steal your testimony, kill our marriage, and destroy the ministry! Can't you see that?!"

"No! I can't see that! What I see is a jealous woman hell-bent on stirring up trouble and running good members away from the church. You should be ashamed of yourself for even saying these things. You don't tell my members what to do. I DO! Tomorrow, I'm going to tell Sister Reeves that she is only to take directives from me and no one else. I am the leader of this church and this ministry. Not you! You need to remember that!" He then snatched his clothes from the chair, hastily redressed, and stalked out of the house. Sister Waters slowly stepped down from the chair and went into the bathroom to turn the shower off. She undressed, changed into her nightclothes, and went to bed.

Rev. Waters did not return home the next day until dinner time. He went into the bedroom, took a shower, changed his clothes, and left without a word.

Sister Waters was extremely hurt by Rev. Waters' behavior. As she cleaned up the kitchen and put the food away, she thought about her marriage. She could not believe that this was happening to her. It was as though her world was crashing down around her ears. Why hadn't she or Rev. Waters seen what *that* woman was up to before now? The Bible said to watch as well as pray. She had forgotten to watch, and so had her husband.

Sister Waters realized that she had not been eating very much at all because she simply had no appetite. Though she still cooked dinner every day for her youngest son, she rarely ate. As a result, she lost about 30 pounds. She looked good, even if she had to say so herself.

In a very short period, Rev. Waters had changed completely. He became very concerned with his physical appearance. He went on a diet and lost weight. Sister Waters had to admit that he looked amazing. She had never seen him so trim and fit looking. Rev. Waters began dyeing his hair. He inspected his hair and mustache regularly to make sure there were no telltale gray strands to give away his advancing years. He changed his style of dress, buying a host of new clothes. He exchanged his normal style of clothes for sportier, more youthful ones. He began wearing a gold chain around his neck and he got new glasses saying that they made him look and feel younger.

Since the wonderful sex life they'd previously enjoyed had been regulated to once in a blue moon, Sister Waters decided to surprise her husband with new lingerie on her now slimmer figure. When Rev. Waters came in that evening, he barely looked at her, giving her the answer he normally did—"I'm too tired to make love. I've had a really long day." Sister Waters was crushed. He didn't even notice that she had lost weight, nor did he notice her beautiful new lingerie, in blue, his favorite color. There was

S.E.C.R.E.T.S. VOLUME II by: *Pastor Shirley*

a time when he'd notice if she fixed her hair in a different style. Now he wasn't noticing major changes, and, he had never repeatedly turned down sex. Something was definitely wrong. If he was not getting it at home, she knew that he was getting it someplace else.

At church, Rev. Waters became livelier and more animated, as if he was always on fire for the Lord. But at home, he was always tired, rude, and cruel. Rev. Waters spent less and less time at home and he had almost no time for his children and grandchildren.

A few months later, Sister Waters noticed that Sister Reeves was gaining weight. Sister Reeves, a woman of average weight, had begun wearing loose dresses and large sweaters. Then Sister Waters noticed that Sister Reeves' stomach was getting larger. Her worst fear was realized when a couple of weeks later, Sister Reeves stood before the church and made an announcement. She clutched a handkerchief in one hand and said tearfully, "I stand before you today to ask for your forgiveness. I have sinned in the eyes of the Lord and the church. Instead of allowing the Lord to lead me, I started leading myself. I am pregnant by a man I was dating. He has since left town and I am now alone with my two sons and a baby on the way. I didn't mean to make the church look bad in any way. Again, I ask for your forgiveness. I have repented to God and He has forgiven me. Please pray my strength in the Lord."

Sister Reeves sat down to a stunned church. The pastor had been singing this woman's praises for so long that the members didn't think Sister Reeves was capable of doing such a thing. Rev. Waters stood up and began telling the church not to judge Sister Reeves too harshly. He also reminded them that according to the Bible, he who is without sin should cast the first stone. He continued by applauding her sense of courage because she had stood before the church to ask for forgiveness. Also, since she had repented to God and to the church, the congregation should forgive her and not judge her.

Sister Waters instinctively knew that Sister Reeves' announcement was a lie. She looked at her husband at the pulpit. He had succeeded in keeping his face void of any emotion whatsoever. This in and of itself was out of character for him. His face was usually quite expressive. It was obvious to her that they had hatched up this lie together in order to throw the suspicion off him. She knew that they had to say something and that they hadn't had much time because everyone would have known she was pregnant very soon judging by the size of her belly. By getting Sister Reeves to make the 'I-have-sinned-please-forgive-me speech', he could continue his affair with her and still have Sister Waters at home to take care of his home. In effect, he had found a way to have his cake and eat it too!

But Sister Waters had had enough! When they got home from church that day, she told him that she knew that he was the father of Sister Reeves' baby. At first, Rev. Waters got upset and repeatedly denied ever having an affair with, let alone impregnating, Sister Reeves. After much bickering, he finally admitted that it *was* his child and that he was in love with Sister Reeves. He then dropped a bombshell by saying that he was leaving the ministry and leaving her for Sister Reeves.

Sister Waters was completely blindsided by this revelation. She had expected him to ask for her forgiveness and to beg her to allow him to stay so that they could work things out. She tried to reason with him. She told him that she had forgiven him and that God would do the same if he just repented. They could get past this mess together if he would only give their relationship a chance and allow her to be what Sister Reeves had become to him. She begged him to think of the children if he couldn't think of her. The entire time that Sister Waters was begging him to stay, Rev. Waters wasn't even giving his wife the courtesy of speaking to her face to face. He stood stiffly with his back to her.

Rev. Waters wanted to laugh out loud. He couldn't believe his ears. There was no comparison between Sister Reeves and his wife. His wife could never be to him what Sister Reeves had become. Sister Reeves was beautiful, exciting, sexually aggressive and, best of all, made him feel young. He couldn't get enough of how he felt when he was with her. That feeling was like a drug and he was definitely addicted to it. Nothing else mattered to him now. He turned to his wife and said in a brutal voice that was much harsher than he'd intended, "First of all, you can't do what Sister Reeves does for me. She is so easy to talk to and I can tell her anything. She

S.E.C.R.E.T.S. VOLUME II by: *Pastor Shirley*

doesn't judge me like you do. She doesn't nag me night and day. I don't care about this house or the ministry or anything else. I care about Sister Reeves. As far as the kids and grandkids are concerned, I love them and I will still be a part of their lives." Not caring about how his sharp words had lacerated her heart, he packed his suitcase and left the house.

The pain that Sister Waters endured felt almost too heavy to bear. Everything she thought she knew about her life and her world was no longer relevant. Though she cried out to God night and day, she told no one else what had happened and she carried on as if nothing had changed. The church assumed that Rev. Waters was traveling on the evangelist field, and since no one asked her directly, Sister Waters allowed them to keep on believing it. Two months had passed before Sister Waters called the bishop to inform him that Rev. Waters had left and that, as a result, the church would need new leadership. The bishop even tried talking to Rev. Waters, but to no avail. The word finally got out that Rev. Waters had left Sister Waters and the church for a woman and that they were now living together.

A few months later, Sister Waters was in the bathroom stall at church when two 13-year-old girls came in. She recognized the animated voices of Cheryl and Joann, two girls who were always gossiping and in grown folk's business. Not checking to see if the door to the bathroom stall was closed, which would have indicated that they were not alone, they continued their conversation.

Adjusting her skirt, Cheryl said, "Girl, I heard my momma tell Sister Betty Jean that Sister Reeves had twin boys on Friday. Rev. Waters is just beside himself. Since he already have a son with his name, Momma said he gon' name one boy after his father and the other after Sister Reeves' father. Momma said they seem to be happy together and that the pastor looks younger than he ever did when he was pastoring and that he didn't even ask her about Sister Waters."

Joann squealed and said, "I wonder if my momma know about this. Girl, I can't wait to get home to tell her."

The girls left the bathroom after primping in the mirror and adjusting their hair. Sister Waters finished in the bathroom and instead of returning to the service, she left through the side door and went home because she just couldn't bear to face anyone. Every time she heard about Rev. Waters and Sister Reeves, it was as if someone had thrust a knife into her heart all over again. *Of course Rev. Waters looks younger now! He dyes his hair every other day and wears the same style of clothes his sons wear!* She thought. It hurt her that the girl had said that Rev. Waters hadn't asked about her. She hadn't seen him since he'd left, although he had continued to pay the household bills. She thanked God every day for that. Regardless of his horrible behavior, Sister Waters refused to divorce him. Instead, she opted to keep praying for him, saying that God hadn't told her to divorce him and that she was waiting on the Lord to lead her and guide her in this matter. She said that he was still her husband in the sight of the Lord and that she would be patient and wait for God's word on the matter.

The children were also negatively affected by Rev. Waters' actions, as he had been very involved in their lives and had been such an example to them in the past. Unbeknownst to Sister Waters, her two eldest sons, John Jr. and Cameron, got together and decided to have a meeting with their father. They tried to reason with him and begged him not to leave their mother and the church, saying that a mid-life crisis wasn't reason enough to lose his entire life.

They were surprised at the person Rev. Waters had become. They didn't even recognize the man they had called Dad all these years. He became so angry that his eyes turned red, his nostrils began to flare, and his lips were quivering. He told his sons, "I have already been raised by my parents and I will not be raised by my kids. Whatever I do is my business and no one else's. I will NOT discuss my personal life with my kids, and no one in my family, including my kids, can tell me what to do. You two have a lot of nerve even calling this little meeting and thinking you could question me about anything I *may* have done. This ridiculous conversation is over." He pierced each of his sons with a scathing look and stormed out of the door.

S.E.C.R.E.T.S. VOLUME II by: *Pastor Shirley*

The boys went directly to Sister Waters' house. She was in the kitchen visiting with Terry and Alex, her oldest and youngest daughters. John Jr. and Cameron rushed into the kitchen and, without speaking to their sisters, launched into the details of their secret meeting with their father. They told Sister Waters that they didn't even know their father anymore. He was rude, uncaring, and had completely lost his mind. They begged her to divorce him and move on with her life. They said that they would never speak to their father again and that as far as they were concerned, he was dead.

Sister Waters angrily whirled around and faced her sons. "Both of you sit down and listen to me! No matter what your father has done, he is still your father. He has always been a good father and provider. Instead of hating him, I want you to pray for him because he is very confused right now. Don't judge him too harshly. You just have to love him in spite of what he's done." Her four children gaped at her. She could clearly read the question in their expressions. "And yes, I meant what I said when I told you to pray for your father."

Sister Waters took a seat at the table across from her sons. She took a sip of her coffee and continued in a much softer voice. "Remember when your father played in the yard with you two for hours? How about when he played ball with you and the fact that he never missed any of your games? Remember the time he hitchhiked for miles after he had a flat tire just to see John Jr. pitch his first game? What about how jealous the other kids in the neighborhood were because of your relationship with your father? It was your father that taught you both how to drive and, against my wishes, insisted you each have a car."

After a pause, during which Sister Waters pointedly stared at both of her sons, she said, "What about you, Cam? Remember how happy you were when you won the state championship competition in swimming? It was your father that coached you night and day until you learned the skill and gained the speed necessary to win. We all used to laugh at him because his skin was so wrinkled after all those hours in the pool. He is, and always will be, your father. He has been a good father to his kids. God does not want us to hate him but to love him. He has just gotten off on the wrong track."

Her sons agreed, though grudgingly, to pray for their father. Their two sisters, who until now had been silent, spoke up. Terry, the oldest daughter, spoke for both of them.

"Mom," Terry began with a hard edge to her voice, "I have listened to everything you told Cameron and John Jr.; however, that doesn't take away the fact that we are appalled by Dad's actions and his response when the boys asked him about it. I saw him the other day and I barely recognized him. He looked ridiculous. He is spending too much time trying to look and act young." Terry's voice had now significantly increased in volume. "This whole situation has the church in an uproar. Dad has caused a scandal!" Terry was now loudly going on about how the entire neighborhood was privy to their problems. Seeing movement in her peripheral vision, she glanced at John Jr., who was rolling his eyes heavenward and pantomiming the action of a fisherman reeling in a fish. This was an old family sign that they often used in church; it meant to 'reel it in,' or more to the point, finish up and sit yourself down. Terry realized that she was getting worked up and needed to end her speech before John Jr. interrupted her.

Terry paused for a brief second. When she began again, her voice had softened considerably. "Mom, I know it's been hard on you. The kids had a meeting and we agree that you have our full support. What we really want to know is what you are going to do about this situation. You can't just sit around and do nothing. More importantly, what can we do to help you, Mom?"

Before Sister Waters could answer, Alex, her outspoken baby daughter, sighed loudly, jumped to her feet and said, "All this love and support stuff is great, and Mom, you KNOW I got your back, but I can't guarantee that I won't jump on the heifer if I see her on the street. I just want to open up a can of whup— I mean a can of beatdown on her and run her out of town. At the very least, I want to tell her off. Then Dad will come back home and everything will go back to normal. It may not be Christian-like but since I ain't claiming to be saved, it's all good. Forget about them tired old Rolaids. A good beatdown will set anyone straight. Now, that's how

S.E.C.R.E.T.S. VOLUME II by: _Pastor Shirley_

I spell relief!" Alex finished in a singsong voice and sat back in her chair.

Terry dropped her head to hide her smile. Leave it to Alex to say exactly what was on her mind. Most times, she did so *before* she had given the situation adequate thought. But in this case, she agreed in theory with Alex's little speech, though she couldn't tell her sister that. The reality is that someone would end up seriously hurt, in jail, or both. Alex had a promising future and sometimes Terry, as the big sister, had to protect Alex from herself. So she didn't comment on it.

Knowing her children well, especially her youngest child's proclivity for announcing a plan and following through if she did not object, Sister Waters reiterated everything she had told her sons earlier but added that they most certainly were *not* resorting to physical violence! She said the last statement while looking directly at Alex. Seeing her mother's look, Alex dropped her eyes, but Sister Waters still saw frustration in their depths. The foursome agreed not to resort to violence and that they would pray for their father. Sister Waters breathed a sigh of relief as they all took their leave.

After three years without Rev. Waters, Sister Waters had finally adjusted to living alone. She had continued to lose weight and now she looked and felt much better. The funny thing is that she hadn't been trying to lose weight. It just seemed to come off on its own. Boy, if she could bottle whatever it was that had taken away her appetite, she could sell it and become a millionaire overnight. Lost in her thoughts, she was brought back to reality when she heard a knock on the door. When she opened the door, to her surprise, Rev. Waters stood on the other side. A look of shock briefly flitted across his face before he asked to come in and talk to her. As Sister Waters led the way to the family room, Rev. Waters noticed how nice the house looked. Sister Waters had obviously done a little re-decorating. He also noticed how nice *she* looked. Had she lost this much weight before he left? Had he been that wrapped up in Sister Reeves that he hadn't noticed? As he sat down on the new sofa in the family room, he realized that there were many things that he hadn't noticed three years ago.

He began by saying that he was very sorry for the way in which he had treated her and the children and he asked her to forgive him. He begged her to take him back, stating that he had left Sister Reeves. He said that he would continue to take care of his sons and be a part of their lives, but that his relationship with Sister Reeves was definitely over.

Sister Waters felt like his confession was an answer to her prayers. She allowed him to come back home and he began attending church again. By this time, Rev. Cook had been appointed to pastor the thriving church that Rev. Waters had so callously left behind. Rev. Waters had a hard time fitting into the church as a lay member and he constantly found fault with the way in which Rev. Cook pastored. He often said that he could do a much better job. After a few months, Rev. Waters told Sister Waters that the Lord wanted him to pastor again.

Rev. Waters found a small building and started pastoring. She and the children followed him to his new church to help with the ministry. Soon thereafter, Sister Waters noticed that there was a difference in Rev. Waters' preaching. Something was definitely missing. He just couldn't seem to flow in the Spirit as he once had. She just kept on praying for him and asking God to completely restore and deliver him.

It was approximately one year later when the front door of the church opened, and Sister Reeves walked in followed by her four sons. She walked all the way to the front of the church and took a seat in the front row of pews. One look at Rev. Waters and it was plain to see that her unexpected appearance had clearly shaken him. He could hardly preach his sermon.

After church was over, Sister Reeves waited around to talk to Rev. Waters alone.

S.E.C.R.E.T.S. VOLUME II by: _Pastor Shirley_

Shortly thereafter, Sister Waters began to see changes in Rev. Waters. Again. In fact, he was acting exactly like he did the first time he was having an affair with Sister Reeves. He soon left the church and Sister Waters to attempt to make a life with Sister Reeves for the second time.

Again, Sister Waters was devastated! She went about the dismal business of putting her life back together. She vowed that no matter what happened in her life, she would never let go of God.

Three years later, Rev. Waters once more appeared on her doorstep. Once more, he begged Sister Waters to take him back, stating that he had left Sister Reeves for good. He said that he had grown a lot emotionally and that he was ready to do the right thing by his wife. Hoping that Rev. Waters had indeed come to his senses, Sister Waters allowed him to come back home. Unfortunately, soon after his return, he began acting strangely and saying that he had to work longer hours. A few months later, he left for the third time to move back in with Sister Reeves.

Over a number of years, Rev. Waters was in and out of Sister Waters' life five more times. Each time he cried and promised that his relationship with Sister Reeves was over. Each time he left her and went back to Sister Reeves. However, the sixth time Rev. Waters came to her house begging her to take him back, Sister Waters had finally had enough. She listened to Rev. Waters cry and beg her to allow him to come back home. She listened dispassionately as he went through his familiar spiel. She said nothing for a moment. She then told him that she would not allow him to hurt her, humiliate her, or send her and the kids on another emotional roller coaster ride. Sister Waters walked him to the door, looked him squarely in the eyes and said, "I don't know why it has taken me years to say this to you, but I thank God I finally have the courage to do so. Hit the road, John, and don'cha come back no more!"

Though the conversation with Rev. Waters had caused her some pain, she was proud of herself for finally standing her ground. Rev. Waters left and went back to Sister Reeves for the final time. Sister Waters heard that he was preaching here and there; however, his ministry was never the same. Sadly, when he died a few years later, he was still not free of Sister

Reeves.

****

When Sister Waters turned onto Sister Davis' street, she was still reflecting on her past and as she thought of Janet, she had a definite feeling of déjà vu. As she arrived at her First Lady's house approximately 20 minutes later, she began to pray for Janet. She walked to the front door and found it open. She walked in calling Sister Janet's name and found her in the bathroom vomiting violently. She helped her get back into bed and put cold compresses on her face and forehead. Almost instantly, Janet fell into a deep, fitful sleep. She tossed and turned constantly.

As she sat by Janet's bedside, Sister Waters knew what she had to do. She had to pray for her, gain her trust, and figure out a way to get her First Lady to confide in her. She couldn't bear the thought of Janet going through this situation alone. She was deep in thought when she heard the children playing in the living room. She took another look at Janet and went to check on the kids.

Later that evening, as Sister Waters sat by her bedside, Janet finally opened her eyes.

"How do you feel?" Sister Waters asked Janet.

"Oh I feel so much better than I did this morning. Thank you so much for coming over and helping me today. Where are the children? It's so quiet in here," she said as she began to cough uncontrollably.

"Oh, those sweet babies are jus' fine. Don't you worry none about them. While you was restin', we played some games in the house for a while. Then they had some lunch, took a nap, watched a little TV, and ate dinner. I gave them baths, read them a bedtime story, and put them all down for the night."

"Oh my goodness!" Janet shrieked while attempting to throw the covers back. "What time is it? I'm so sorry that you've been here all day! I didn't mean to—"

S.E.C.R.E.T.S. VOLUME II by: *Pastor Shirley*

"Hush chile!" Sister Waters said in her soothing motherly voice while pulling the covers back up over Janet. "I was glad to do it. I could see you was really sick and exhausted and you needed the rest. Your body was jus' plain run down and that was its way of gettin' you to settle down and rest."

"But I didn't mean for you to spend your whole day here with me and the kids. I never even heard the kids or the phone ringing or anything?"

"The phone didn't ring none today. No one called." Sister Waters could plainly see the pain and hurt in Janet's face as she realized that Apostle Davis had not called all day.

"What time is it now?" Janet asked, her voice barely above a whisper.

"9:13 pm. Now that you awake," Sister Waters said in a bright voice, "I want to help get you cleaned up. I made some good ole-fashion chicken soup. I want you to try and eat some. Now let's get you up, showered, fed, and lookin' pretty before Apostle Davis get home."

Janet burst into tears. Sister Waters moved to the head of the bed and hugged her. She said, "There, there baby. It can't be that bad. You jus' lay back and rest. I'll stay with you an' the kids until Apostle Davis get home."

Janet was comforted by Sister Waters' soothing words and motherly embrace. She lay back against the pillows and closed her eyes. Her thoughts were on Apostle Davis. *Where is he? How could he do this? What could he possibly be doing at this time of night and with whom? He knew I was sick this morning when he left. Why didn't he call to check on me today? What if something had happened to me or the kids? Thank God Sister Waters came over today. I don't know what I would have done!* She realized that she needed someone to talk to. She was so tired of carrying this heavy burden alone and acting as if everything was ok. She so wanted to remove the mask she had worn for so many years. Sis Waters was once a First Lady; perhaps she could talk to her. She needed a friend in whom she could confide.

As these thoughts went through her mind, Janet felt the hot tears well up in her eyes and seep through her closed eyelids. After a while, she opened her eyes. She could hear Sister Waters in another part of the house. She wearily pulled the covers back and went into the bathroom to shower. The cool water soothed her feverish skin. Janet stood there for what seemed like hours lost in thought. And pain.

Janet was jolted back to reality by the loud knocking on the bathroom door. A concerned Sister Waters asked her if she was alright. Janet told her that she was fine and would be out shortly. She then turned the water off, dried her body, and brushed her teeth and hair. When she came out of the bathroom dressed in a clean nightgown, Sister Waters was changing the sheets on her bed.

"There you are. Don't you look pretty? Thought you would rest much better with some nice dry sheets on the bed seein' as how you had sweated and them other ones was pretty damp." Sister Waters had now finished remaking the bed. Janet saw a tray on the nightstand with a bowl of soup and a glass of orange juice.

Janet was overwhelmed by Sister Waters' kind words and unselfish actions. She crossed the space separating them, hugged her, and thanked her profusely for her help. "Oh, I've got to go and see about the children," Janet said as she turned toward the bedroom door.

Sister Waters wanted to ease her anxiety. "Now, Sis Janet, you jus' get back in that bed and rest. I already done took care of everything for you. Remember that the children have already been fed and put down for the night. Now it's your turn to eat. You ain't ate nothin' all day. You can't get better if you don't eat."

Sister Waters gently placed the tray on Janet's lap. Janet continued to protest, stating repeatedly how sorry she was that Sis Waters had been there for the entire day and much of the night.

"Now you jus' hush up that nonsense, baby. I am here because I want to be. You are my friend and my First Lady. Besides, I don't have no husband or babies at home. So don't you worry none about me. I am jus' fine. You jus' try to eat some of that soup, drink your juice, and rest."

"Did my husband call since I woke up?" Janet asked with a hopeful look on her face.

Sister Waters' heart grieved for Janet and the pain she was obviously feeling. "No, honey. He still ain't called."

Janet's heart sank at Sister Waters' words. She lay back on the pillows and closed her eyes. When she heard Sister Waters leave the room, she opened her eyes again and looked down at the bowl of soup. She wasn't hungry, but she knew that she would recover much more quickly if she ate. She forced herself to eat a few spoonsful of soup. It was very good, as she knew it would be. After she drank all of her juice and set the tray back on the bedside table, she closed her eyes again. It seemed she had only lain there a few minutes before the blessed numbness of sleep engulfed her.

Janet was awakened the next morning by the sounds of her children's happy voices as they played in the backyard. She rolled over and looked at the clock on her bedside table. It read 10:35 am. Seeing the time, Janet was jolted into action. *Oh my goodness!* She thought. *I have never slept this late! Sister Waters must think I am the laziest thing on earth. I have got to get out of bed and take care of the children and the house!*

As she struggled to stand up, she realized that she felt worse today than she did yesterday. She felt dizzy and weak and her head was pounding. She looked down at her nightgown. It was damp with perspiration. She sat back down on the side of the bed.

She looked up as Sister Waters knocked on the door. "Good morning, Sis Janet. How you feel today?"

"Not good at all." Janet lay back down on the bed. "My head is spinning and I feel worse today. It's day outside again and my kids—"

"Sis Janet don't you worry 'bout a thing. I stayed the night and I already took care of the kids today. I'll be here for as long as you need me."

"Where is my husband?"

"I don't know, baby. He never came home."

Janet began to sob uncontrollably. "He…never…came…home?" She forced out between sobs. She began to cough and gag. Sister Waters walked to the bed and tried to console her. When she embraced her, she realized that Sister Janet's clothes were wet and her body temperature was entirely too high. She knew that this was not good. She helped Janet to change into suitable clothes and called Apostle Davis' office; someone had to tell him that his wife was very sick and needed to be taken to the hospital. When she got no answer at the church, she left a detailed message for Apostle Davis, informing him that he needed to come to the hospital. She then called a neighbor to watch the kids and drove Janet straight to the emergency room. The physician on duty took one look at Janet and began an immediate series of tests. Two hours later, she was admitted to the hospital after being diagnosed with a very high temperature of 104.3 and an extremely severe case of walking pneumonia.

Davis, Janet
B206

Apostle Davis never responded to Sister Waters' message. On the sixth day of her ten-day stay in the hospital, he finally came to visit her. He only stayed for 20 minutes, telling her that he had too much work to do for the Lord and that he certainly couldn't waste time sitting around in a hospital.

S.E.C.R.E.T.S. VOLUME II by: *Pastor Shirley*

Janet was dismayed at his behavior and lack of concern. She could have died for all he cared. She knew that she had to have a strong talk with her husband. She just couldn't go on like this. She was at her breaking point.

Janet's recovery was slow. Four weeks after she had been hospitalized, she still felt the effects of her illness. Though her energy had increased somewhat, it was nowhere near back to normal. The smallest of tasks completely exhausted her and she still had a nasty sounding cough. Janet just prayed for the day that she would feel normal again and be free of her aggravating cough.

Janet called Apostle Davis at his office. She asked him to come home immediately after the office closed because they needed to talk. Apostle Davis told her that he would be home quite late because he had a couple of meetings, after which he would be visiting home-bound members. He ended his response by saying that he would see her whenever he saw her. For the first time in their marriage, Janet stood her ground. She told him that if he didn't come home, she would come to his office but that either way, they were going to talk that day. He reluctantly agreed to meet her at the house that evening.

Apostle Davis breezed into the house two hours later than usual. He was dressed as if he had spent the day casually strolling and looking at antiques—an activity that he enjoyed—instead of working at the office. He did not greet Janet and he ignored his children. He quickly walked into the bedroom, automatically assuming that Janet was following him. Janet made popcorn and put in a movie to keep the kids occupied while she talked to Apostle Davis.

Apostle Davis went straight to the mirror and began combing his hair. When he heard Janet enter, he turned to her and without preamble bluntly said, "What the hell is your problem? You're always looking for something to complain about. What is so important that I had to stop doing the Lord's work in order to come straight home and babysit you and your fragile feelings? In the future, do NOT threaten me again." Seeing Janet's confused look, he expounded on his statement. "Do not try to manipulate me into doing what you want me to do by saying you will come to my office. You are not to come to my office unless I invite you. I don't need you there interrupting the progress of the ministry."

Janet was shocked; not by his condescending attitude or even his warped moral code—after all, she had been dealing with those almost from the beginning of their marriage. Rather, she was shocked that he had cursed at her. He had never done that before. Ignoring that bit of information for the moment, Janet held fast to her resolve and plowed on. "Eddie, I am fed up with your cruel attitude, demeaning treatment of me, and your numerous affairs. I—"

Abruptly cutting her off, Apostle Davis immediately jumped to the defensive and said, "Affairs? What affairs? You can't prove anything. You have never caught me in the act of adultery. You are going crazy, that's what your problem is."

Since she was getting nowhere fast on the current path, Janet decided to try another angle. "Eddie, I am neither stupid or crazy. I have always known what you were doing, though I didn't always have the guts to admit the truth. Why would you give up your wife, children, home, and ministry just to keep having affairs? You are a powerful man of God. You are anointed to do the Lord's work. But He is not going to bless you in your mess. You have to do your part. All you have to do is repent to the Lord and me and turn from the situation. We should also go to counseling so that we can work out our marriage problems."

"Repent to you?" Apostle Davis asked as he burst into laughter. "*You* should be repenting to *me*! You have turned me off sexually since the kids were born. You're fat and ugly and no one else could possibly want you. You should be grateful to me that I have stuck around all these years!" As Apostle Davis spoke, it was as if a hazy cover had been lifted from her mind and her eyes. She finally saw him clearly for the first time in her life.

Apostle Davis continued. "You bet your bottom dollar I am a man of God. I am also a man and a man has needs that must be fulfilled. The Lord understands that you are in no way capable of taking care of my needs. He does not hold it against me if I have to get those needs filled elsewhere. I have nothing to repent to God about and it's comical that you think I possibly have anything to repent to you for. If you were a real woman, I wouldn't be forced to get my needs filled elsewhere. If you didn't look like a massive bloated pig in the nude, perhaps I could find a way to rise to the occasion."

"As far as counseling is concerned, I don't need to pay $200 dollars an hour to have someone tell me what I already know. All our problems are your fault and they could easily be solved if you would stop eating like a pig, get some exercise, and lose some weight. You are my wife in name only and that's as far as it goes."

Janet thought she had prepared herself for anything that may have come out of his mouth. But, she was wrong. Though her eyes filled with tears, she was determined not to give him the satisfaction of seeing her cry. She blinked several times to clear her eyes.

Switching conversational gears again, she said, "If you do not feel comfortable going to counseling, perhaps we should speak to the bishop about our problems. I'm sure he could—"

Before Janet could finish her sentence, Apostle Davis grabbed her and put her in a headlock. He squeezed her neck so tightly that she could barely breathe. "If you ever say a word to anyone about our personal problems, I will personally make you wish you hadn't. You will obey me in this matter and keep your mouth shut! There is no reason to bother anyone else because of something you can fix. Lose some weight and everything will be ok."

With those heartless words echoing in her ears, Apostle Davis shoved her away from him roughly. Janet screamed as she hit her head on one of the children's toys as she fell to the floor. She touched her head and her hand came back with a smattering of blood. Apostle Davis never looked in her direction, acting as if he hadn't heard her scream. He straightened his slacks and smoothed his hair down. He walked out of the room, through the living room past his children and out the door. He ignored his kids as they yelled, "Bye, Daddy!" Janet then heard his car backing out of the driveway.

Janet lay on the floor and finally allowed herself to sob. She just could not go on this way any longer. Her physical safety, as well as her sanity, were now in jeopardy. She now knew that Apostle Davis was crazy and that he certainly didn't care about her or the children.

As Janet struggled into a sitting position, pain shot through her head, and her wrist felt extremely tender as well. She hadn't noticed her wrist before now. She realized that she must have hurt it when she'd tried to break her fall. When she tried to move her wrist, the pain was excruciating, but since she didn't see any visible bones, she hoped that she hadn't broken any.

Janet scooted in the reverse direction so that the bed supported her back. She began to cry as she contemplated her marriage. She had to do something. If not for herself, she had to save her children. They were blameless in this, yet they were also paying a very high price.

What am I going to do? Who can I talk to? Where do I go for help? Am I the only First Lady to ever experience something like this? The First Ladies I know are always happy and smiling. Some wear big hats and are immaculately dressed. Some sit on the front pew and some share the pulpit with their husbands. Some are public speakers, missionaries, evangelists, and even preachers. But, they always seem happy in the church and in their marriages! Janet concluded that they could never have experienced the horrors that she was going through. She reasoned that she must have done something wrong and that this was her punishment and burden to bear. But Oh, God! It is just so heavy. . .

Janet painfully pondered her thoughts. Then it felt like the Lord touched her heart, soul, and mind and breathed life back into her. After years of mental, emotional, and now physical abuse, Janet knew that this was the last day she would ever wear the mask of silence. She realized that it was not the will of God for her to endure this type of suffering. No woman should. She mentally removed her mask and flung it with all her might across the room, watching with a new resolve as it shattered into a

S.E.C.R.E.T.S. VOLUME II by: _Pastor Shirley_

million tiny pieces.

She rose to her feet and began to recite the 23rd Psalms,

"The Lord is my Shepherd,
I shall not want.
I shall not want for peace,
I shall not want for happiness,
I shall not want for love,
I shall not want for safety.
I shall not want."

And then she picked up the telephone. From this day forward, her grueling, painful existence was not going to continue. After flinging off her mask of silence for the first time in her married life, she realized that she did have something to say about it. She would no longer remain silent, she thought, as she dialed the numbers that would change her life forever.

To find out what happened to Janet Davis and Apostle Eddie Davis, be sure to read S.E.C.R.E.T.S. of the First Ladies, Trilogy.
Available soon in a bookstore near you.

Chapter 18

Leta Byron
Mei Li Byron

S.E.C.R.E.T.S. VOLUME II by: *Pastor Shirley*

Leta Byron
5598 Serenity Way

Leta Byron

Leta Byron and Mei Li Byron

Mei Li Byron
5598 Serenity Way

Mei Li Byron

S.E.C.R.E.T.S. VOLUME II by: _Pastor Shirley_

Leta...

Now I know what you're thinking
"What in the world was he drinking?"
How could he risk all?
My, my, my, how the mighty do fall...

And yet you wonder...
where was her voice?
Why did she stay?
She did have a choice!
But confusion pushes
and pulls her psyche
Perhaps she didn't know
what to believe.

The truth is too terrible
to easily comprehend
So it's easier for some
to allow "the blend."

You try to believe all is well
or soon will be
You shut your eyes tightly
to the painful reality.

230

Leta Byron and Mei Li Byron

*L*eta Byron is a big-hearted woman who loves God. She has caramel-colored skin and a freshly scrubbed, all-American, girl-next-door kind of look. Upon seeing her for the first time, most people would describe her as cute. Leta is of average height and average weight and works long hours on her feet as a hairstylist. Leta excels in providing her long list of clients with precision cuts and undetectable hair weaves.

Leta is married to Pastor Nick Byron. He is about six feet tall with a small belly bulge. Thin for most of his life, it frustrates him that his weight is now something that he has to monitor and work to maintain. He is reasonably good looking and maintains a sporty wardrobe in order to relate to the large number of young adults and teenagers who make up his church. According to Pastor Nick, "A church with no children, teenagers, and young adults, is a church on the road to certain death." Pastor Nick is the leader of a thriving flock and his members often boast that they have a leader who actually lives what he preaches. Pastor Nick loves his wife and is proud of her accomplishments in her chosen field.

Leta loves children and has always wanted to have lots of her own. Unfortunately, that was not to be the case. When she was five months pregnant, a drunk driver ran a red light at an intersection and plowed into Leta's car. Leta lost the baby and hovered on the brink of death for several weeks as the doctors worked frantically to save her life, which they were only able to do with extensive surgery. As a result, Leta would never be able to have children. Due to the severity of the pain in her back, Leta's doctor prescribes Vicodin, a derivative of opium and highly addictive. Initially, the Vicodin completely relieved her pain. But as time went on, it took more and more of the pills to give her the same pain relief.

Leta's recovery was slow and painful. For weeks she was in a state of depression as she tried to deal with the notion of being unable to bear a child of her own. She was so lost during this time that she didn't even notice the number of pills she was mindlessly taking, and she avoided children at all costs. The very sight of their happy little chubby faces caused her personal pain to resurface with a vengeance.

S.E.C.R.E.T.S. VOLUME II by: *Pastor Shirley*

Whenever Leta saw a pregnant woman, she experienced a deep hurt beyond words, which caused emptiness and a void that nothing seemed to fill. The nameless pregnant women reminded her that she would never experience the joy and wonder of motherhood for herself. Often, no matter how hard she tried, tears welled up in her eyes and spilled over onto her cheeks. At night, thoughts of her unborn child flooded her mind and caused her to cry herself to sleep.

Nick was so worried about Leta that he suggested she teach a children's Sunday school class. At first, she adamantly refused. But Nick was patient and persistent and he finally got her to agree to teach a class of four year olds. His plan worked. It didn't take long for Leta to completely shed her shell of depression and begin to enjoy her life again. She openly doted on her class and went out of her way to plan activities that would allow the children to have fun and learn about God. She always brought them snacks to ensure that they were not hungry during the morning service. Her class adored her in return.

Nick never dwelled on Leta's inability to have children. In fact, he often told her that she was more important to him than 10 children. This comment always made her laugh because she just couldn't imagine her home filled with 10 children running around, although she would welcome such a gargantuan responsibility with open arms.

It was Leta's loneliness and love of children that persuaded her to agree to adopt two frightened little girls of mixed Asian and African-American heritage. Their African-American father, James, and his wife Jennifer, were both in the military and assigned to the base in Taipei, Taiwan. Shortly after arriving, James embarked on a torrid affair with their 19-year-old housekeeper, Ling Su. Upon learning of her husband's betrayal, Jennifer was extremely hurt and angry at the blatant disregard for their wedding vows. She told James in no uncertain terms that she would not be disrespected nor would she sit idly by while he had an affair. Jennifer, immediately moved out, filed for divorce and requested to be transferred to a military base in Germany. Jennifer never looked back and James never heard from her again.

Leta Byron and Mei Li Byron

Ling Su continued as James' housekeeper and eventually bore him two daughters. James was so enamored of Ling Su that he married her even after confirming that she had been seeing other military men behind his back.

Their marriage was rocky from the start with a great deal of yelling and fighting. Ling Su spent most of her time partying and drinking and James spent most of his trying to keep up with his wild wife. Things got progressively worse after they were sent to a military base in the United States. After four years, Ling Su had tired of being a wife and a mother. She left her husband and two daughters and went back to Taiwan.

Faced with the responsibility of raising the two girls alone, James broke under the pressure and turned to drugs and alcohol to cope with his issues to the exclusion of everything else. This resulted in his being dishonorably discharged. Because the girls had no other known family, they were put into the foster system.

It was these frightened little girls who now stood huddled together in Leta's living room staring at her with eyes full of wariness. They were 7 and 8 years old, extremely thin, and although their clothes appeared to be clean, they were threadbare. The older girl, Mei Li, (pronounced may-lee) had beautiful eyes that were an unusual shade of brown, though they were sunken in and alert with wisdom she shouldn't have had at only 8 years old. Her younger sister, Jun Ping, (pronounced june-ping) was a classic study in contrasts. Though she talked freely and acted as if she was unafraid, she clutched her sister's oversized, worn shirt in a death grip, as if she feared being separated from her.

The girls looked like little castaways and Leta's heart melted. She couldn't have been happier if she had been given her weight in gold. "Yes," Leta thought, "I will love them and raise them as my own daughters."

Over the next few years, Leta and Pastor Byron loved the girls and taught them how to act like little ladies. By the time they were 12 and 13, they were totally unrecognizable as the two frightened, malnourished girls who had initially entered their home. They were doing well in school,

S.E.C.R.E.T.S. VOLUME II by: *Pastor Shirley*

had many friends, and had generally adjusted into fine adolescents.

It was about this time that Leta noticed a change in Mei Li. She wanted to spend all her time around Pastor Byron. Wherever he went, she wanted to go. Leta mentioned this to Pastor Byron. He explained that the girls didn't remember much about their biological father, so they were naturally drawn to him because he loved them and spent time with them.

Though Pastor Byron's explanation seemed logical, Leta continued to notice negative changes in Mei Li. It was as if Mei Li resented Leta's very presence. She became extremely mouthy and rebellious to everyone except Pastor Byron, her grades took a serious nosedive, and she began to get into trouble at school. When Leta again voiced her concern to Pastor Byron, he said that he would talk to Mei Li about it. The situation did improve, but only for a short period. Leta hoped that perhaps Mei Li was just going through a phase.

When Mei Li was 16 years old, Leta overheard her talking to Matthew Zane, a 17-year-old boy, in the back of the church. Leta was a couple of pews away speaking to Sister Elsie about the upcoming bake sale and overheard Mei Li say, "There's no way I'm going to a movie with you, Z. I don't date boys. I only date men." Mei Li then swung her waist-length, jet-black hair to the other side and eyed Matthew flirtatiously.

Leta excused herself from her conversation with Sister Elsie and quickly guided Mei Li to the office in the back of the church. Once inside, she jumped all over Mei Li for making such a brazen comment to Matthew. Later, as they dressed for bed, Leta told Pastor Byron what she'd overheard. He shrugged the situation off and told her that she was overreacting. Leta didn't agree, but she hoped that Pastor Byron knew what he was talking about.

Unfortunately, Mei Li got bolder by the day. After a particularly loud argument between Pastor Byron and Leta about his being unable to account for income equal to one month of household expenses, Mei Li sat listening on the floor in the next room while working on her laptop.

Leta Byron and Mei Li Byron

After a while, she had had enough of Leta jumping in Pastor Byron's case. She got up, went into the next room and said,

"You don't need to be talkin' to Pastor Byron like that. He don't need you upsettin' him about all this small stuff. You need to be more caring where he's concerned."

Leta had had enough of Mei Li's mouthing off. Whirling around to face Mei Li with her eyes ablaze with fury she yelled, "You have completely overstepped your bounds, young lady! You are a child in this household, not an adult. Your behavior of late has been unacceptable and I, for one, will NOT accept any more of your disrespect or your acting like you think you're grown. What goes on between me and Pastor Byron is none of your business and you'd best remember that because if you EVER stick your nose into our business again, not only will I smack you into next week, but I will put a whuppin' on you that I'm sure your behind can't stand. Do we understand each other, missy?!" Both Mei Li and Pastor Byron were shocked not only by what Leta said, but the volume and venom with which she said it. Pastor Byron was quiet but he thought his wife was overreacting and being a little hard on Mei Li. She was just a misguided kid after all.

Mei Li thought Leta was crazy for threatening to put her hands on her. She also had to admit that she had never seen Leta this angry. Since Pastor Byron hadn't said anything in her defense, she thought she'd better cool it for a while. She rolled her eyes at both of them and strode angrily from the room. Mei Li never let a slight go unaddressed and she certainly had no intention of starting now.

S.E.C.R.E.T.S. VOLUME II by: *Pastor Shirley*

The next day, Leta's back was killing her. She had stints of dizziness, frequent bouts of blurred vision, and she was nauseated a lot lately. She didn't know what was wrong with her and her pain medication just wasn't working as well as it used to. She increased the number of pills she was taking, thinking that more pain medication would result in more pain relief. It did; however, Leta had no idea that her pain medication was also having an adverse effect on other parts of her body. She had no idea that the Vicodin had fundamentally changed the way in which her brain worked and had begun to take over its normal pleasure and motivational systems. She also had no idea that the stress of dealing with Mei Li had increased the adverse effects on her body.

Leta had never been so happy as she was the day that Mei Li turned 18, went away to college, and moved out of her house. However, her happiness was short-lived. Mei Li got pregnant immediately and was back home three months later. Her attitude was even worse than it had been before she left. She was mean to her sister, refused to help in the house, and was disrespectful to everyone—except Pastor Byron.

Leta was at her wits' end. She had had her fill of Mei Li's disrespectful attitude. Mei Li argued with her about everything and even the smallest of issues were blown into a test of wills. When Leta suggested that Mei Li go to their family doctor, Dr. Sutton, for her prenatal care, Mei Li flew into a rage. "I don't need you to tell me what doctor to see. I am perfectly capable of choosing a doctor. Go to Dr. Sutton? I don't think so! For what? So he can tell you everything going on with me and my business? I want a doctor we don't know so my baby's daddy can go with me to my checkups."

Leta was truly confused. She was just trying to ensure that the girl had a good doctor to take care of her and her baby. What was the deal with all this other nonsense? "What does your choice of doctor have to do with who your baby's daddy is or if he goes with you to your checkups? What's the difference?" Asked Leta.

"WHAT'S THE DIFFERENCE?" Mei Li shouted. "I'll tell you what the difference is and why it should make a difference to you. My baby's daddy is your husband!"

Leta thought perhaps her mind and her hearing were playing tricks on her. She regained her composure and said "What did you say?"

"YOU HEARD ME! I SAID Pastor Byron is the father o' my baby," Mei Li shot back venomously. "Are you deaf as well as stupid? Pastor Byron has been messin' with me since I was 13 years old. He taught me all about sex and all the things he likes. If I didn't do it right, he made me keep doin' it until I got it right. Now I know what he likes and how to touch him with my hands and my mouth."

Mei Li noticed Leta's stricken face and for the first time in her life, felt a pang of compassion. When she began speaking again, her voice had lost its hard edge. "We really didn't want to hurt you. We knew what we were doing was wrong. We tried to stop, but we just couldn't. We love each other."

Mei Li was about to leave Leta standing in shock when she remembered something else. "Oh, by the way, when you leave every year for a week to go to the First Ladies' retreat, I sleep in your bed with Pastor Byron. I wait until Jun Ping falls asleep then tip toe down the hall and get into your bed. Me and Pastor Byron have a great time then I get back into my bed before Jun Ping wakes up the next morning."

Leta's head was reeling at Mei Li's revelation. She thought of the time she'd found one of Mei Li's bracelets in her bed. Pastor Byron happened to be in the room when she discovered it and seeing the baffled look on her face said, "Mei Li has been looking for that bracelet. She asked me if I'd seen it and I told her I hadn't but I would help her look for it. It must have fallen off her arm when me and the girls were in here watching a movie." Holding out his hand he continued, "I'll give it back to her and tell her you found it." Leta handed the bracelet to her husband and climbed into bed. It was a couple hours later when it occurred to her that the bracelet had been under the sheets, not on top of the comforter.

Mei Li's voice shifted Leta's focus back to her. Mei Li said, "Haven't you noticed I've never had a boyfriend? Pastor Byron wouldn't let me.

237

S.E.C.R.E.T.S. VOLUME II by: *Pastor Shirley*

He wanted me all to himself. When I went away to college, there wasn't a week that went by that Pastor Byron didn't come and spend at least one night with me." Seeing the shock register on Leta's face again, Mei Li went on to explain.

"Where did you think he was?" Mei Li held her hand up in order to end further comment from Leta and said, "Don't answer that. I know where you THOUGHT he was. He told you that one night a week he was going to be shut in at the church fasting and praying and you were not to call or come by because you would be taking him away from his time with the Lord. Well, he wasn't spending time with the Lord. He was in my dorm room riding me or I was riding him.

He was so jealous and protective of me. It was like he was totally obsessed with me. He didn't want me to meet someone my own age at college and leave him. He wanted me to get pregnant right away so I could come back home. So I stopped taking my birth control pills." Mei Li abruptly stopped talking and turned to look at Leta. Seeing the disbelief on Leta's face, she continued.

"Oh I know you don't believe me. Pastor Byron said you would never believe any of this because you were just too deep; always goin' thru the church and the house prayin' and speakin' in tongues. Pastor Byron always laughed about that. He said you were so heavenly minded that you were no earthly good. Every time you went off in them exotic tongues, me and Pastor Byron would look at each other and laugh. Even if we were at church, we would catch each other's eye and nod. It was our secret. One time we was laughin' about you speakin' in tongues at church and we almost got busted by Mother Fenton. She kept lookin' at me and then at Pastor Byron. She knew something was up." Mei Li smiled to herself at the memory.

Leta's head was spinning. She knew in her heart that Mei Li spoke the truth. It all made sense now— Mei Li's hostile attitude toward her, Pastor Byron's lack of interest in sex, and his unaccounted for chunks of time and money. Leta had to grab the back of her dining room chair to keep from falling. She certainly didn't want to faint in front of Mei Li. She felt hot, nauseated, and lightheaded.

Leta sat down in the chair. How could this atrocity have taken place in her house, right under her nose and she not be aware of it? The worst part of it was that this mess had been going on for years. YEARS! She wanted to run. She wanted to cry. She wanted to scream. She wanted to kill someone. Anyone. No, not anyone—Pastor Byron! How could he have disrespected her in this vile manner? She had been a good wife to him; perhaps too good. The more she processed these thoughts, the angrier she became and the closer she felt to going over the edge.

As tears streamed down her face, Leta turned to Mei Li and said in a calm voice, "I don't make it a habit of explaining myself to children because they are not on my level and I won't start now." Leta saw Mei Li bristle at being called a kid. "I want you out of my house. I don't care where you go or what you do, but you are no longer welcome in my home. If you don't go now I will kill you… You better go, slut!" Leta's message was all the more chilling because it had been delivered in a calm voice and not the dramatic screaming that Mei Li had expected. She lifted her head and walked past Leta and out the front door as if she were the Queen of Sheba. She walked out as if being thrown out was of no concern to her.

Mei Li got into her sporty little car, which Pastor Byron had bought for her when she went away to college, and drove off. Leta called Pastor Byron but it went straight to voicemail. She left a message asking him to come home immediately because they needed to talk.

Her back hurt more and more often lately, making her feel as if she was never pain free. She was now taking two weeks' worth of Vicodin in five days. Her doctor was threatening to stop her prescriptions altogether, saying that she was showing all the signs of prescription drug addiction. She vehemently denied his allegation, saying that she needed the Vicodin for bona fide back pain only. He agreed to refill her prescription once more, but after that he would no longer write them for her. She had no idea what she was going to do then or how she was going to make it through the day without her pills. Her doctor had asked her if she was experiencing blurred vision, lightheadedness, dizziness, constipation, nausea, vomit-

S.E.C.R.E.T.S. VOLUME II by: *Pastor Shirley*

ing, or severe confusion. Though she denied having any of them, she was actually experiencing *all* of them and the thought alarmed her. After this mess with Mei Li was over, she would give her health some serious attention. However, for now she shoved several pills into her mouth and washed them down with a swig from her ever-present bottle of Diet Pepsi.

She paced the floor of her dining room for what seemed like hours. She rehearsed over and over in her mind what she was going to say to Pastor Byron. When he finally arrived, he lit into Leta, not giving her a chance to say a word. He accused her of being petty and overreacting. He then said, "How could you put Mei Li out?! I cannot believe you did that! Mei Li was just a child when she came to us. How could—"

After a few moments, Leta had recovered from her initial shock at Pastor Byron's verbal attack. He actually had the nerve to be angry with her? Cutting him off mid-sentence, Leta angrily shouted, "Are you the father of Mei Li's baby?"

Pastor Byron looked at her as if she had lost her mind. "What! Listen to yourself. I am a man of God, a preacher of the gospel. Do you really think I could do something like that? Do you really think I could stoop so low as to have sexual relations with a kid? My own daughter? Woman, you are crazy!" Pastor Byron walked past Leta and took a seat at the dining room table.

Leta turned so that she was facing him. "I am not crazy and she's not your daughter. She's a girl who came to live with us at a young age. There's no blood between you. However, that shouldn't have mattered. In the eyes of the court and the church, you are her father. Besides, why would Mei Li say such things if they weren't true?"

Pastor Byron's eyes blazed with barely suppressed fury. "Woman, I don't know what goes on in the mind of young people these days."

"Mei Li said the baby is yours. She said she is pregnant with YOUR child!"

"Now I know you've lost your mind if you believe that mess. You should see a shrink because something is wrong with you if you're even repeating this ridiculous story. Mei Li called me when she left here and told me that you'd put her out of the house with no money and no place to go. So, before I came home, I had to go take care of *our* pregnant daughter that *you* so carelessly threw out into the street. I got her something to eat and a hotel room for the night. I told her to wait until tomorrow when you'd had a chance to cool off and then she could come back home."

"WHY IN WORLD WOULD YOU TELL HER THAT?!" Leta screamed, looking completely horrified at the very thought. "Mei Li can *never* come back here." Leta's voice increased in volume. "This is my house too. Mei Li is grown and she is not welcome here anymore. Whether what she said was the truth or a lie, she cannot live under the roof I help to provide. Where I come from, children do not act like this and disrespect their parents and elders."

Pastor Byron stood up and pierced Leta with a penetrating stare. Narrowing his eyes he said, "Look around you, Leta. Open your eyes. You're not in Mississippi anymore, are you? You are in good ole Sea Crest and the rules are very different here. You do not rule this house, I DO! You do not decide what will and will not go on here, I DO! The only rule that is the same is that you do not tell me, the husband and head of this house, what to do. I tell you and I'm telling you I will bring Mei Li home tomorrow because it's obvious to me she has a problem and needs our help. We certainly can't turn our backs on her now. She needs us now more than ever. Mei Li and Jun Ping are our daughters. How could you throw your own daughter out in the street?"

Leta stood, anger clearly evident on her face. "You would bring her back here after everything she said to me? After the blatant disrespectful manner in which she talked to me? After she said she is carrying your child and that you've been HAVING SEX WITH HER SINCE SHE WAS THIRTEEN YEARS OLD?!"

Pastor Byron's facial expression never changed. It was as if he hadn't even heard the accusation of his having sex with a minor child, which of course she knew he had heard because she'd screamed it at him. His

S.E.C.R.E.T.S. VOLUME II by: *Pastor Shirley*

voice was hard when he said, "I don't know who you think you're talking to but you need to take all that volume out your voice." He paused. The anger radiating off him was palpable. "And stop making everything about you. This isn't about you!" he spat pointing at her. "It's about Mei Li and the fact that she needs us right now. I already told you she obviously has some kind of problem if she's spouting tales like this. This house is in MY name and I WILL bring her back tomorrow. What would people say if they knew the pastor and his wife put their pregnant daughter out in the street?" Pastor Byron turned his back on her and walked into the kitchen, a clear sign that he had ended the conversation and she had been dismissed. Leta could not believe this was the same man she had married. What happened to the kind, loving man who had promised to take care of her and love her always?

Leta was so upset that she ran out of the room sobbing. Reaching for her bottle of Vicodin, she shoved several pills into her mouth and swallowed them without the aid of liquid. After a while, she fell asleep. When she woke up, the clock on her bedside table read 10:34 pm. Leta got up to get a glass of water and noticed that Pastor Byron wasn't home. He finally arrived around midnight saying he'd been out visiting the sick and shut in.

When Leta got home from work the next day, Mei Li was sitting in the family room in Leta's favorite chair, casually thumbing through a magazine. She looked up as Leta entered the room. Mei Li smiled triumphantly at Leta, daring her to say something about her being back in the house or being in her favorite chair. She'd purposely chosen to sit in that chair to drive home her point: *Pastor Byron cares about me and he doesn't care what you think or say.* Leta stared at Mei Li for a long moment. Finally, she turned around and went to her room.

Mei Li's behavior was totally out of control. Her attitude was nasty and she was so disrespectful to Leta that even her sister, Jun Ping, commented on it. She adamantly refused to help in the house in any way. When Leta got home from work each day, the kitchen was a mess and the sink was always filled with the dirty dishes that Mei Li had used. When Leta asked Mei Li to clean up after herself and to load the dishwasher, Mei Li told her, "I'm pregnant. I can't be on my feet loadin' no dishwasher. It's your job to keep this house clean, not mine. Besides, Pastor Byron said I ain't no maid and to leave the cleaning to you."

Did this vile girl just have the nerve to tell me my husband told her not to clean up after herself? Leta thought. She would be talking to Pastor Byron about that when he got home. In the meantime, she didn't want Mei Li to know that her comment had angered her. With a great deal of effort, she kept her face expressionless. "You are pregnant, not an invalid," Leta said evenly. "You are perfectly capable of loading your dirty dishes into the dishwasher and cleaning up after yourself."

"And how would you know about that?" Mei Li sneered. "How would you know what pregnant women go through? Have you ever been pregnant? Oh, I forgot. You were only pregnant for a few months. But, you can't get pregnant anymore, CAN YOU?"

Mei Li's comment hurt Leta to her very soul. Tears sprang to her eyes and rolled down her cheeks. Before she thought about her actions, Leta backhanded Mei Li with all her might. Mei Li now lay sprawled on the floor, clutching her burning cheek in complete shock. Sobbing, she ran out the front door, got into her car, and drove off.

She could no longer have children and now this girl with her distended pregnant belly had painfully reminded her of everything she had always wanted but would never have. She wasn't a whole woman. Is that why Pastor Byron wasn't as responsive lately? Was he really the father of Mei Li's baby? She didn't know. She didn't know anything anymore. She went to her room and sobbed her distress at the top of her lungs. The sound coming from her bedroom was so distressing and filled with pain that it tore at Jun Ping's heart. She became afraid for her mother. She called Pastor Byron and told him what had happened between Leta and Mei Li and suggested that he might want to come home and check on her. Pastor Byron told her that Mei Li had already called him and told him what had happened and that Leta shouldn't have jumped on Mei Li.

Holding the phone in her hand, Jun Ping pulled it away from her ear and looked at it in total disbelief. She put it back to her ear and said, "Obvi-

S.E.C.R.E.T.S. VOLUME II by: *Pastor Shirley*

ously Dad, Mei Li didn't tell you everything. Mom didn't jump on her or mistreat her like I'm sure she told you." June Ping then recounted the events exactly as they had occurred, and ended by explaining that Leta had slapped Mei Li out of utter frustration. "She only hit her one time, and frankly, I wondered how come it took her so long to do that because Mei Li has been saying awful, disrespectful things to her for months when you're not around. It wasn't the beatdown Mei Li deserved and I hardly think that qualifies as 'Mom jumping on Mei Li'. Now Mom is a wreck and I really think you should come home and check on her."

Pastor Byron was shocked. Mei Li's story was nothing close to what Jun Ping had just told him, but he knew that Jun Ping was telling him the truth. Leta was sensitive about not being able to get pregnant anymore, and rightly so. He hated having told Mei Li about Leta's medical history. He would have to deal with Mei Li regarding that, but first he needed to see about Leta. Though he'd done some things of which he definitely wasn't proud, he really did love Leta. It was never his intention to hurt her. It was like he was on a roller coaster ride and couldn't get off. The ride was exciting and thrilling and made him feel younger than he'd felt in years.

He left his office at the church and went home. He found Leta exactly as Jun Ping had described. He reassured her that her inability to have a baby had nothing to do with his feelings for her. He loved her and had always loved her. He told her that he did not blame her for the baby that they lost and that he was definitely *not* the father of Mei Li's baby.

Four weeks later, Mei Li announced that she had found an apartment and was moving out. Leta was extremely relieved, though she tried not to let it show. Even though they'd been at odds, Leta loved her and was worried about her. She was concerned about how Mei Li was going to support herself since she had no job. When she asked Mei Li this, her answer was, "That's none of your business. But if you must know, I don't have to work. My man is taking care of me."

"Who is this man and where is this new place of yours?"

Mei Li smiled and said, "That's my business and it's for me to know." She then turned and walked out the door, never looking back. She didn't say goodbye to anyone; not even her sister.

****

Once Mei Li moved out, Pastor Byron never arrived home before 11:00 pm. He said that it was full-time work taking care of the people in the ministry and visiting the sick. However, Leta was not buying this excuse anymore. She questioned everything he said and was suspicious of everything he did. She just couldn't trust him anymore, especially when he told her that he didn't know where Mei Li's new apartment was located.

Leta's behavior became increasingly irrational, even to her. She couldn't help herself and felt totally out of control. At the slightest infraction—whether real or imagined—she yelled at Jun Ping, whom she loved dearly and who had never given her a minute's trouble, as well as at Pastor Byron, who, on the other hand, was giving her more than enough provocation. Pastor Byron chalked up Leta's illogical behavior to her stress over the situation with Mei Li so he didn't give it much thought. It never occurred to him that there might be another cause.

One day, Leta decided to play detective, so she rescheduled all her appointments for the rest of the day and took off early from work. She drove to the church and parked so that she could see Pastor Byron's car but he couldn't see hers. About 45 minutes after her arrival, Pastor Byron came out of his office and got into his car. Unbeknownst to him, Leta followed him. He stopped at a floral design shop, went in, and came out carrying an enormous bouquet of red and yellow roses in a beautiful crystal vase. He then drove to a luxurious apartment complex on the other side of town. He got out carrying the roses and let himself into the apartment with a key. He was in the apartment for about 30 minutes when Leta called him on his cell phone. He answered and said, "Oh Leta. I was going to call you because I have to visit some people at the hospital so I won't be home until late. In fact, that's where I am now."

"Really? Well, you did manage to get one thing right; someone *is* going

S.E.C.R.E.T.S. VOLUME II by: _Pastor Shirley_

to need a doctor. I'm looking at your car and I'm coming to the door now. Open up because I want to talk to both of you. Now!" Leta got out of her car and knocked on the door. No one answered. She then banged it loudly and still no one answered. So she called Pastor Byron on his cell phone again. When it went straight to voicemail she hung up. She then yelled at the top of her lungs, "I'm not going anywhere. If you don't come out, I will call the police and all the church leaders, and I will make a big scene. You decide how you want to handle this."

After about 20 minutes, the door opened and Pastor Byron came out, clearly angry. Before he could say anything, Leta shouted, "Is that your baby? Are you the father?" Pastor Byron rushed right past her without saying a word. He just got into his car and drove off.

Two months later, Mei Li gave birth to not one, not two, but three baby boys. She was so proud that she told anyone who would listen that she was the mother of three beautiful baby boys and that Pastor Byron was the father. Needless to say, the news spread throughout the church like an out-of-control forest fire, and soon everyone knew that Pastor Byron had been sleeping with Mei Li since she was a child and that they were now the parents of triplets.

This took its toll on Leta. She lost so much weight that her clothes, which used to fit her snugly, now hung off her body. The members of the church wondered why she stayed with Pastor Byron. They said that she was a fool to stay with someone who treated her like dirt and blatantly disrespected her.

The church emptied like a deflated balloon. When the church doors opened the Sunday following the birth of the triplets, the only people present were Pastor Byron and Leta. The church members left and never came back. Instead of closing the church doors, they kept right on having church, hoping that the members would return. But they never did. However, this did not seem to bother Pastor Byron in the least. After all, he had three sons now.

Leta's doctor had refilled her prescription for Vicodin several more times only because she'd doggedly begged him, even resorting to violent crying jags. However, after several months, he finally refused to write any additional prescriptions and Leta was feeling the effects of withdrawal, though she had no idea her numerous symptoms were all related to her addiction to Vicodin. She was restless, had trouble sleeping, and was suffering from cold flashes and diarrhea. She felt awful and her behavior was becoming more and more irrational. She thought that it was all attributed to the stress that she was enduring due to Mei Li and Pastor Byron's sordid affair.

Pastor Byron was so caught up in playing the daddy role that he lost sight of everything else, including God. He doted on the triplets and aggressively ensured that neither they nor their mother wanted for anything. In a final thoughtless deed, Pastor Byron asked Leta to be involved with his sons as well.

"What do you mean 'be involved' with your sons? Do you mean play mommy to them? Feed them? Change their diapers? Are you crazy? How could you even ask me to do something like that?" Leta was now screaming her frustration and hurt at her husband. "These boys are the result of your sexual relationship with your so-called daughter. And now you have the nerve to ask me to 'be involved' with them?" Leta threw Pastor Byron a scathing look. "You have finally lost what little bit of your mind you had left," she said disgustedly.

Pastor Byron looked at his wife. He was so caught up in the joy of being a father that he had forgotten how difficult it had been for Leta. He desperately wanted to bring the boys to the house and do "daddy things" like film home movies and take pictures of them in their carriers with stuffed animals sitting beside them. They were just so beautiful and he adored them. But, in order to do those things, he had to get Leta's buy-in and it appeared it was not going to be forthcoming. He couldn't blame her though. After Leta's accident, he had long ago given up hope of becoming a father. And now he had three beautiful baby boys. *His* baby boys. He knew that what he'd done was wrong and that it had been humiliating for Leta, but he just couldn't help himself. Pastor Byron sighed. He just had

S.E.C.R.E.T.S. VOLUME II by: *Pastor Shirley*

to get Leta to allow Mei Li and the boys to visit. He would just have to find a way to convince her and he wouldn't give up until he did.

Leta got into her car and drove aimlessly around her neighborhood with unseeing eyes. Leta's thoughts returned to the last conversation she'd had with her husband. She just couldn't believe that Pastor Byron had asked her to play mother to his sons. Those boys were not of her body and the fact that he had committed incest and statutory rape to conceive them seemed to have escaped his memory. How could she possibly forget? Since the birth of the triplets, Leta awoke each morning with the most unbearable pain in her heart. It seemed that the entire neighborhood knew of Pastor Byron's betrayal and Leta was so ashamed and humiliated that it was difficult for her to hold her head up in public.

As Leta drove, she contemplated her future. Should she go or should she stay? Should she stay and fight for her marriage? Did she even have a marriage? Should she stay and pray? So many questions and no answers. Leta thought of her beloved family so many miles away. She missed them and needed their love and support so much right now.

Leta felt as if she had traveled to hell and back. She fasted. She prayed. Then she fasted and prayed some more. *Oh Lord, give me an answer. Please. How much am I supposed to take and still remain in your will? How much am I supposed to suffer? How much more of this must I allow?* She knew that the Bible said the Lord would not put more on you than you could bear, but just how much was she supposed to bear before she got the green light from God to walk away from this mess and save herself? But to leave her marriage was against everything she had been taught. More than anything else, she wanted to be saved and to please God. But, she was so confused. Oh God, it hurt so bad! Leta felt as if her heart had been completely ripped out of her chest and torn to shreds. She knew that there was no pain on earth greater than the pain of infidelity. The hurt was more intense because Leta knew that she had been a good and faithful wife.

Leta stopped at a red light at a major intersection. Suddenly, her legs began moving involuntarily and she was terrified. How could she drive her car if she couldn't control her legs? The light turned green but Leta was so engrossed in trying to control her legs that she didn't notice. The cars behind her began angrily blowing their horns. Leta broke out into a cold sweat. She was desperately trying to get her legs to obey her, but they just weren't listening. The light turned red again and the people in the cars behind her began shouting obscenities and giving her the finger. She clutched the steering wheel in a white-knuckled grip as she struggled to keep her right foot on the brake pedal. She lost that battle as her foot slid right and slammed onto the gas pedal. Leta's car bolted into oncoming traffic as if it had been shot from a cannon. She was terrified and so focused on her legs that she didn't see the large yellow Hummer barreling toward her.

To find out what happened to Leta, Mei Li and Pastor Byron, be sure to read S.E.C.R.E.T.S. of the First Ladies, Trilogy. Available soon in a bookstore near you.

Chapter 19

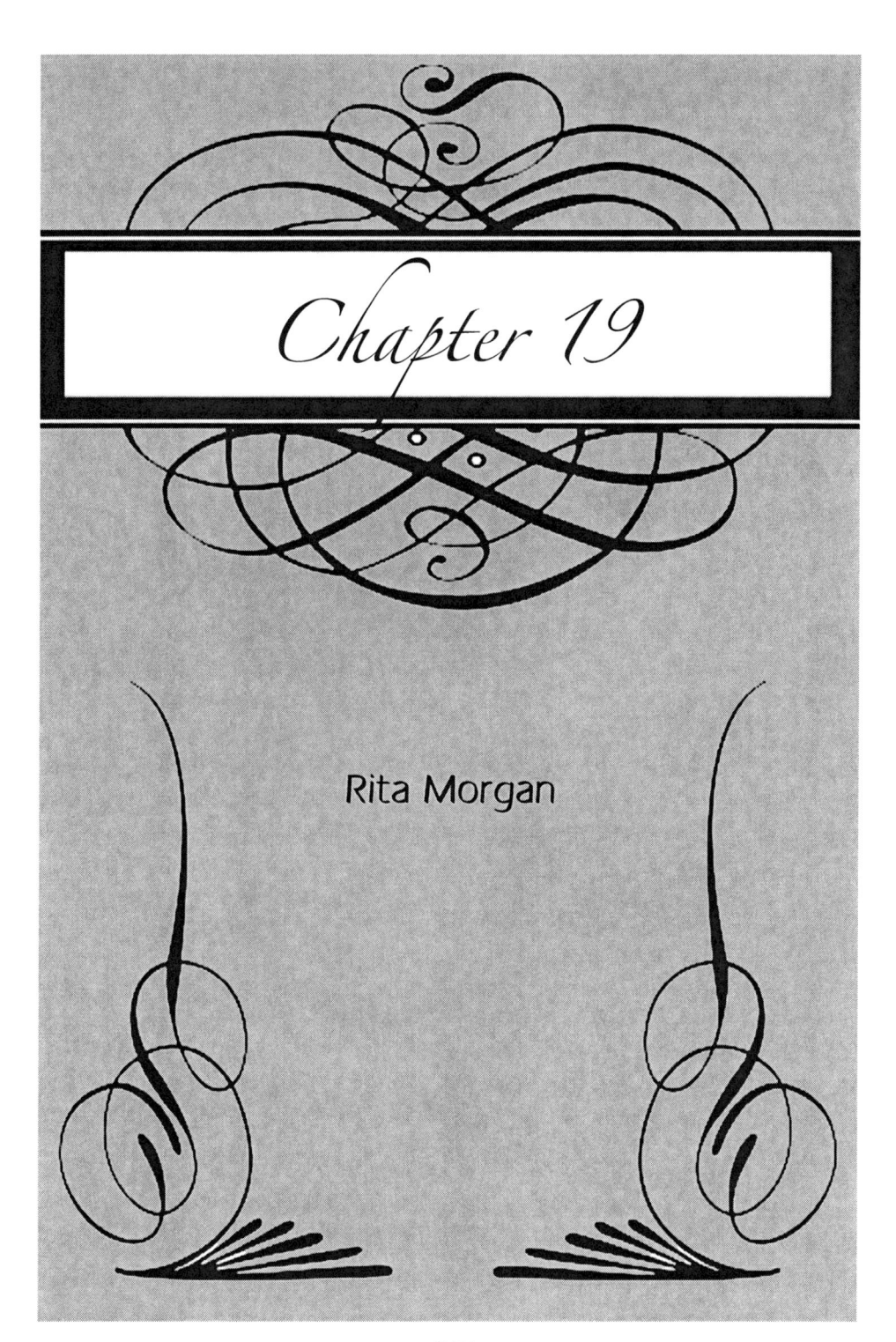

Rita Morgan

S.E.C.R.E.T.S. VOLUME II by: *Pastor Shirley*

Rita Morgan
3609 Spiralwood Street, #C153

Rita Morgan

RITA…

How do you get rid of Satan?
That's the question
We're all debating

When he lives in the very same home
Strutting around
Caring not that his cover is blown.

He chooses and speaks
on the most disgusting of topics
His eyes dare you
to interrupt or object
His mouth is always fixed in a vicious sneer
Feeling a rush each time
he sees your fear

His mind Is as cunning as a snake
You wonder how much more
can you possibly take

How do you rid yourself of Satan?
That's the question
we're all debating…

S.E.C.R.E.T.S. VOLUME II by: *Pastor Shirley*

*F*irst Lady Rita Morgan, also known as Evangelist Morgan, is married to Elder Simon Morgan. Rita is a stunningly beautiful woman. She has long flowing black hair, a gorgeous figure, dancer's legs, and a million dollar smile. She had only been saved a year when she met Simon. She was a dynamic soloist, an all around worker in the church, and she was on fire for the Lord.

Elder Simon Morgan is a reasonably handsome, dark-skinned man of above average height and trim build. He is known for his lively "fire and brimstone" sermons. He was single and visiting one of the churches in the district when he saw Rita and couldn't take his eyes off her. She was gorgeous. He openly stared at her during the service and smiled when he caught her eye. Rita smiled back and quickly looked away. Though she was trying to keep her mind pure and on the Lord, she was also wondering who he was.

Rita and Simon lived approximately two hours apart and only saw each other sporadically at district church functions. Rita knew that Simon was smitten with her and the feeling was quite mutual. However, that was the extent of their relationship. One year later, after church, Simon walked right up to Rita and asked her out to dinner. Rita happily accepted and waited in anticipation until the time came for Simon to pick her up. They had a wonderful dinner and getting to know one another was easier than either of them would've thought.

Rita told him the story of the death of her first husband and son. After high school, Rita had gone away to college to fulfill her academic dreams. In her second year, she met and fell in love with Drew. Rita had gotten pregnant immediately and they planned to get married when the baby was born. Shortly after the birth of her beautiful son, Drew Jr., they got married and were extremely happy. They decided to continue their academic pursuits and threw themselves into their classes with a vengeance. They lived on campus in the married student apartments and Drew got a part-time job to help supplement the income they received from their school grants.

Rita Morgan

When Drew Jr. was six months old, Drew Sr. decided to take him to visit his parents to give Rita some quiet time to study for final exams. Unfortunately, her husband and son never made it to his parents' home. A drunk driver ran a red light and hit Drew's car knocking it into the path of oncoming traffic. Her husband and son were killed instantly.

For an entire year, Rita walked around in a nightmarish fog. It was as if she was operating under a cloud from which she could not escape. She was so distraught that she did not want to live. Her best friend, Chloe, was worried about Rita's state of mind. Chloe was saved and prayed for her friend constantly. She checked on her daily and forced her to eat as she was dropping weight at an alarming rate. Chloe decided that Rita had to get out of the house and badgered her until she agreed to accompany her to a tent revival at her church one night.

REVIVAL TENT MEETING

Church was the absolute last place Rita wanted to go. She had been walking around in a zombie-like state for so long; she didn't know what to do to rejoin the world around her. She wasn't living; she was merely existing. What would she possibly do at church? She called Chloe and attempted to get out of going to church, but her friend wouldn't take no for an answer. Feeling she had no other choice, Rita finally agreed to go. Rita sat through the entire service numb from head to toe. She told herself that she would never attend another church in her life. Rita was so engulfed in her thoughts that she didn't realize that someone was calling her name. Chloe was tapping her on the shoulder pointing to the speaker for the evening. Startled, Rita looked up, amazed to see that the woman was standing di-

S.E.C.R.E.T.S. VOLUME II by: Pastor Shirley

rectly in front of her. When did she leave the pulpit and walk over here? Rita thought. The speaker, Evangelist Allen, asked Rita to stand. Rita complied. She took Rita's hands in hers and looked directly into her eyes. When she had Rita's full attention, she began to speak. "You are not here by accident. God told me you were coming and I have been waiting all day to meet you. God brought you here to save your life, deliver you, and set you free because He has great work for you to do. He loves you so. He was so concerned about you that He sent you a word through me.

"I know you have suffered a great loss. Since then you haven't known what to do or even which way to turn. God knows best and you have to remember that the Bible says all things work together for the good to them that love God and are called according to His purpose.

"God wants to save you and give you the gift of the Holy Spirit. He wants to welcome you into his family. You will no longer be lost and not know which way to turn. Wait on the Lord. He will be your comforter and your guide. Counterfeits not sent from God will come, but wait on the Lord!"

"Needless to say, the Lord saved me," Rita said, at the end of her story. "He filled me with the Holy Spirit. He has been my friend and comforter ever since. That's why I am so excited about Him and why I will never leave Him. He must be a part of my life. He did for me what no one else could do. I don't know if I would even be alive had the Lord not seen fit to save my life." Rita said the last sentence so low that Simon had to strain to hear the words.

For a moment, Simon felt awkward. Was he the one the Lord had warned Rita about? Was he the counterfeit? In deep thought, he exhaled loudly. Of course he wasn't. He was a man of God. How could he be a counterfeit if he was a man of God?

Simon felt relaxed as he conversed with Rita. He'd never felt this comfortable with anyone in his life. He decided to share his past with her. He just hoped it wouldn't taint her opinion of him. He shoved his hand through his hair and began. "Well, here goes. I grew up in a really bad and really poor neighborhood. I was in and out of detention homes beginning in the fifth grade so I was considered a 'bad boy.' Throughout my childhood, I had only been exposed to illegal, easy ways of making money. It never occurred to me and no one ever told me there were legal ways to make a living that didn't involve going to college because no one in my neighborhood ever went to college.

"Anyway, I began selling drugs. Eventually, I tried them. I found out that using drugs eased the pain I had been carrying around for a long time. Soon, I was hooked and I couldn't make it through the day without drugs. I was walking aimlessly around the streets one day and wandered into a church. The Lord saved me and filled me with the Holy Spirit. He saved me from my drug addiction immediately." He finished his story and looked at Rita hesitantly. When she said nothing, he said, "I really hope my past hasn't frightened you off because I am really interested in pursuing a relationship with you." His voice dripped with sincerity. "Hopefully you are not as interested in my past as my future. And since God holds my future in His hands, I know I have a bright future. I don't share my past with too many people because they would judge me for what I have overcome with God's help and what he's already forgiven me for. Rita, you are so easy to talk to. It's so difficult to find someone who isn't judgmental."

Rita looked directly into his eyes, reached across the table, and took his hand in hers. "No, your past hasn't scared me off. It's not your past that matters most to me."

Simon and Rita dated regularly for the next 10 months and got married one year after their first official date. Rita moved to Simon's hometown and joined his church. Simon excitedly prepared to become an ordained elder. They got a tiny apartment and Rita was able to get a job as a bank teller. Simon also got a job but lost it three months later. He found another job and proceeded to lose it, too, after only four months. In the midst of his unsuccessful job search, he went before the bishop and the board of elders and received his license to become an elder. Though he was happy about this, he was depressed over his employment situation.

Eight months into their marriage, Rita began to notice a tremendous change in Simon. He became very demanding, treating her like nothing more than a servant whose job it was to cater to his every need. She overlooked it, thinking he was probably under a great deal of pressure because he couldn't find a job.

Rita got pregnant ten months after they were married. She kept working but it was extremely difficult because she was so ill and had to stand on her feet all day. She dared not quit because Simon still hadn't found a job and if she were honest with herself, he didn't seem too interested in finding one. One day after coming in from work feeling sick and totally exhausted, she finally worked up the nerve to ask Simon about his seemingly non-existent job search. He became furious and barked, "I am an ordained man of God doing God's work. It is a full-time job preaching the gospel. I cannot be weighed down with things that don't concern the word. Besides, you're working and you can continue to work. In the Bible days, women worked while they were pregnant and you are certainly no different. Having a baby is a woman's burden sent from God and you'll just have to bear it. God didn't give that burden to the man."

After finishing his warped speech, he sat down in front of the television and ordered her to fix him something to eat; as if he'd been the one working all day with an aching back and swollen ankles.

Rita looked around the apartment. It was an absolute mess with newspapers and his clothes strewn all over, and the sink was overflowing with dirty dishes. In an attempt to stay ahead of the housework, for which she was solely responsible, she had cleaned the entire apartment last night before going to bed. She had hoped that Simon would see how clean the apartment was and would assist her in keeping it tidy. No such luck. *Well,*

there's no way I'm cleaning it tonight, Rita thought. She just felt too bad. As she went into the kitchen to make something for dinner, she wondered what had happened to the kind and thoughtful man she'd married.

Because all of their meat was frozen and she felt terrible, Rita chose a meal that was filling, but more importantly, quick to prepare. She made grilled ham and cheese sandwiches, tomato soup, and a tossed salad. However, Simon didn't appreciate her efficiency. He said the dinner was not fit for an esteemed man of God. He disgustedly threw his food on the floor and demanded that she cook him some "real" food. "Make me some fried chicken, mashed potatoes, gravy, and cornbread. And none of those nasty instant mashed potatoes either. I want the real stuff." As an afterthought, he threw over his shoulder, "And wash all them dirty dishes and clean up that mess you made on the floor." Taking note of the disbelieving look on Rita's face he said, "Yes, the mess YOU made. If you'd made me some real dinner, I wouldn't have thrown that mess you called dinner on the floor. So it's all your fault. You made me do it so you can clean it up."

Rita was too sick and too tired to argue with Simon. She got up and put some chicken legs in the kitchen sink to thaw. She peeled potatoes and opened a box of Jiffy cornbread mix, quickly hiding the box in the trash. She didn't want him complaining about boxed cornbread too. She'd take help wherever she could get it. One hour later, she called Simon to the dinner table. He ate with gusto and got up from the table to return to the couch and the television. He'd left his plate on the table for her to remove. Rita was really sick now but she dared not go to bed without cleaning up the kitchen. After she had finished, she fell exhaustedly into the bed.

A few weeks later while preparing dinner, Rita was contemplating the birth of her baby and thinking of the baby she had lost. Her due date was drawing near and she was becoming increasingly concerned. There was no extra money for a bed, or diapers, or clothes for the baby. And Simon didn't seem to care one way or the other. What were they going to do? It took every dime of her meager paycheck just to pay the rent and keep the utilities on. She took a few deep breaths to fortify her courage before she voiced her concerns to Simon. He never took his eyes from the television as he replied, "God will provide" in a distracted voice.

S.E.C.R.E.T.S. VOLUME II by: *Pastor Shirley*

Rita was scared and angry. Something had to change. "Simon, YOU are the husband and you should be the one to provide. According to the Bible, you are supposed to take the lead in the household, not me. I shouldn't hav—"

But before Rita could continue her sentence, she found herself in excruciating pain lying flat on her back on the floor. Her mouth was bleeding and her back felt as if it was broken, which she prayed was not the case. She was dizzy and was having a hard time focusing her vision.

"Why did you hit me?" She asked, momentarily forgetting that she was dealing with a violent man.

Simon stood over her screaming every obscenity known to man at the top of his lungs. Rita had never heard Simon use such foul language and it terrified her. Paralyzed with terror, she lay on the floor staring up at him. She had neither the will nor the strength to do anything except lay there and stare up at the crazy stranger in front of her. This was not the man she'd married.

With clenched fists, he ranted, "I don't need you to tell me what to do. Only God can do that. ONLY God can judge me. You are not important enough to address me about my responsibilities. If you know what's good for you, you won't do stupid things to provoke me to hit you, because it will be your fault if I have to straighten you out and help you remember your place. You'd best remember that!"

Rita was terrified. Simon's eyes were rolling to the back of his head and his nostrils were flaring. "Now get your lazy @!%#-- up and fix dinner. I have to preach at church tonight and I don't want to be late." He went back into the living room to wait for her to prepare dinner. She was in so much pain and so large with child that even the simplest tasks required extra time. She was afraid that she would not be able to finish in time for church.

She dragged her complaining body up and went into the bathroom to wash her face and survey the damage. Her lip was split and swollen and there was a slight bump on the side of her head. Thank God it's not too bad, she thought. At least she wouldn't have to cover any bruises with makeup. As she quickly washed her face, she prayed that she would be able to complete dinner, be ready in time for church, and not further infuriate Simon in the process. She felt that God had smiled on her because it was only by an act of God that she'd made it. Although barely.

That night at church, before he got up to preach, he said, "I would like for my beautiful wife to come and render a solo." Rita could not believe her ears. You just cursed me out and busted my lip and now you want me to come up and sing a solo? She thought scornfully. Though singing was undeniably the last thing she felt like doing, she dared not refuse. After she returned to her seat, Simon preached, danced, and spoke in tongues all over the pulpit. As Rita watched him from her seat in the pew, she desperately hoped that her disgust at his hypocrisy didn't show on her face.

As was the practice, the senior pastor raised an offering for Simon. The offering totaled $22.50 because the members just didn't attend service during the week like they did on Sundays. All the way home, Simon complained about the measly offering he had received. His complaints went in one ear and quickly out the other because Rita had other things on her mind. She was extremely scared that she was going to lose her job. She could barely stand and perform her job but she begged her boss to let her continue to work because she desperately needed the money. Reluctantly, he agreed. She thanked God for favor.

The next morning, Rita was getting ready for work and put her hair up in a ponytail. Her hair was long and thick, and the ponytail gave her a small measure of comfort, especially in the summer time. It felt good to get her hair out of her face and off her neck when she drove to work because their car was on its last leg and had no air conditioning. As she awkwardly bent to kiss Simon on the cheek, he took one look at her hair and slapped her across the face. Rita jerked backward, her hand flying to her stinging cheek. Simon stood up and hit her again, sending her sprawling to the floor. He screamed, "Didn't I tell you never to wear your hair up?" As he bent over her viciously yanking the rubber band out of her hair, taking large tufts of hair with it. "You will always wear your hair down. I like women with long flowing hair. That's one of the reasons I married you.

S.E.C.R.E.T.S. VOLUME II by: *Pastor Shirley*

If you weren't so stupid, you would have figured that out by now. Now don't make me hit you again. NOW GIT! And you better not be late for work." Rita was barely able to get up off the floor by herself. She went into the bathroom to look at her face and to quickly apply makeup if it was needed. It was needed; Simon's handprint was clear on the right side of her face. She was going to be late now and she just hoped her boss would understand.

Considering the physical abuse she had endured the last two days, it was no surprise when Rita woke up at 2:00 am the next morning, her body riddled with excruciating pain.

Oh no! She thought. I can't be in labor now. It's not time yet. What could've happened to cause the baby to come four weeks early? Then it hit her like a ton of bricks. Yesterday, when Simon hit her and knocked her on the floor, it must've caused such a jolt that the baby was coming early.

Rita woke Simon and told him that the baby was coming. On the way to the hospital, she prayed and prayed. Lord, don't let me lose my baby. Please, don't let me lose my baby. Then she began to cry. She thought about the death of her first baby and first husband. She simply could not bear to lose another baby.

When they arrived at the hospital, Rita was immediately taken into the emergency room. But before they could get her upstairs to the delivery room, the pain became extremely intense and she had the urge to push. Doctors and nurses were screaming and running in every direction. When the baby was born, the doctor looked at the nurse. She took the baby and ran from the room. Rita was beginning to get frightened. No one said anything to her about the welfare of her baby.

"What's wrong with my baby?" She screamed. The doctor looked at Rita and down at the birth canal and his eyes almost popped out of his head. "Oh my goodness! There's another baby coming! You're having twins!"

"No I'm not!"

"Well, tell that to the baby coming out now. Didn't you know you were having twins?" The doctor asked.

"NO!" She shrieked as she strained to push the second baby out. The nurse took the second baby and once again ran from the room.

"Doctor," said Rita, "What is going on with my babies?" The doctor looked at Rita and said, "Because your twin sons were approximately four weeks early, we need to get them into the neonatal unit immediately. As it is, it will be touch and go for the next 48 hours. I don't know who you rely on when you need strength, but I advise you to call on him now." Rita began to cry convulsively.

The doctor had already informed Simon of the twins' fragile health. As the doctor walked away, Simon walked to Rita's bedside. He looked down at her with none of the usual love and emotion that would normally be shown to a wife who had given birth for the first time. He leaned close to her so that only she could hear his next words. "What did you do to make the babies come four weeks early?" He hissed. "You had better pray that they do not die because if they do, I WILL HOLD YOU PERSONALLY RESPONSIBLE FOR KILLING MY BOYS!" He pinched her viciously on her arm for emphasis. Rita screamed out in pain. But before the nurse could come over to see why she'd yelled, Simon stormed out of the emergency room and didn't return until late the next day.

The next morning, Rita was moved to a semi-private room. She picked up the phone to make a call and was told by the hospital operator that there was a charge to turn the phone on. "Didn't my husband pay the charge?" She asked the operator. "No, he didn't."

"Well, how much does it cost?" Rita asked.

"$20.00," the operator answered.

"Thank you," Rita said and hung up the phone. She began to cry in earnest and Stella Gavin, the lady on the other side of the room, could not help but overhear her emotional sobs.

S.E.C.R.E.T.S. VOLUME II by: *Pastor Shirley*

Stella and her new baby girl, Ashley, were being released. She was dressed and ready to go. She walked to Rita's bedside and said, "I'm not trying to interfere, but you can use my phone." Rita tried to stop the flow of tears long enough to respond to her generous offer. Before she could answer, Stella's husband, Dennis, strode proudly into the room. Seeing the love for his wife in his eyes, Rita started crying all over again. How she longed for Simon to look at her like that.

Dennis asked Stella what was wrong. She told him that Rita's husband hadn't paid the $20.00 charge and that she couldn't use the telephone. She told him that she'd offered to let Rita use her phone, but now she noticed that Rita still had an IV and couldn't get out of bed. She told Dennis that Rita had given birth to twin sons yesterday and that the babies were not well enough to go home or to receive visitors. She also told him that she felt really bad for Rita because her husband hadn't visited her or the babies. In fact, no one had visited her since she'd arrived.

After listening to his wife, Dennis looked at Rita crying in her bed and hooked to a gazillion tubes. The sight touched his heart and he knew that he had to help her in some way. He patted her hand. "Don't worry about the phone, Rita," he said looking at the name card over the bed. "I will happily pay the charge for your phone to be turned on. When I sign the discharge paperwork for Stella and Ashley, I'll pay it then. You just need to wait about 20 minutes and then you can make your call." Rita cried harder and mumbled a 'thank you' through her tears. "Stella and I will pray for you and the health of your beautiful babies." Rita looked up then. "Yes, I saw them when I went to visit Ashley. They're beautiful. Remember we're praying for you and may God bless you."

The nurse came to push Stella to the entrance of the hospital in a wheelchair. They both waved at Rita as they left. Rita waved back. Her crying had subsided. True to Dennis' word, the phone was on 20 minutes later. She picked it up and dialed her mother, Alexandra Green. When she heard her mother's voice on the other end, she just could not hold back the tears. All her mother could hear on the phone was sobbing. She knew it was Rita and that she needed her. She patiently waited for her daughter to gather some control so she could find out what was going on. Finally,

Rita was able to say, "Mom, please come now. I'm in the hospital, Cedar Valley on Syracuse Road, and I need you." Alexandra said, "I'm on my way, baby. I'll be there real soon."

As Alexandra drove to the hospital to see her daughter, her mind was racing. What's wrong with Rita? Since Rita wasn't due to have the baby for another month, she hoped that her ignorant husband hadn't done something to her. Rita didn't visit her family often because none of them cared for Simon or the way he treated Rita. She hadn't wanted Rita to marry him because neither she nor Rita had known enough about him or his past. What was the rush to get married? If she wasn't pregnant, why the unseemly haste? Get to know the man first. Then decide if he is suitable marriage material. Alexandra had relayed all these things to Rita, but she hadn't listened. She was in love. And now she was in the hospital crying. Where was Simon? Did he even have a job yet? Probably not. Alexandra put all these thoughts to the back of her mind as she pulled her cream Lexus SUV into the visitor's section of the hospital parking lot. Regardless of how she felt about Simon, she was determined to be cheerful and pleasant when she saw her daughter.

When Alexandra walked into Rita's room and saw her daughter hooked up to numerous hospital machines, and that her eyes were red and puffy from crying, her motherly heart was touched as only a mother's can be when seeing her child in distress. Since Rita hadn't seen her, she quickly retreated. She walked down the hall to the waiting area and called her husband on her cell phone. He hadn't accompanied her on this trip because he'd been at work. But she knew if there was a need, he would be there at a moment's notice.

"Hello," Jake answered anxiously.

"Hi honey, it's me" Alexandra said. "I'm here at the hospital and Rita looks awful. She is hooked up to all these machines, she looks as if she hasn't slept in months, and her eyes are all puffy and red. I'm concerned about her. She looks really bad although I would never tell her that."

Jake did not profess Christianity and immediately went into a cursing fit

S.E.C.R.E.T.S. VOLUME II by: *Pastor Shirley*

blaming Simon for his daughter's current state. Remembering that Alexandra was still on the phone, he pulled himself together and said, "Have you talked to her yet? What's going on with her?" He asked with genuine concern in his voice.

"No. I haven't talked to her yet. I took one look at her and came to call you. She hasn't seen me so she doesn't know I'm here yet. But I'm really concerned," Alexandra said fearfully.

Jake and Alexandra had been married for many years and he knew her well. Her call to him was to fortify her courage. She needed to be strong when she faced Rita. He began to do just that, saying that whatever was going on, he was certain she could handle it. He ended the call by telling her that he loved her dearly and to call him again when she knew what was going on. At Alexandra's request, he grudgingly promised not to resort to physical violence should Rita's situation prove to be as bad as they both suspected.

After hanging up with Jake, Alexandra said a prayer before she walked into her daughter's room. She felt stronger and she now felt ready to deal with whatever Rita had to say. She went straight to her bed and enveloped her in a warm, loving embrace.

"Mom", Rita cried. "I just had twins. Two beautiful twin boys and I didn't even know I was carrying two babies. They were not due for another month and now my beautiful babies are struggling in the neonatal intensive care unit. I am so scared, Mom. I just cannot stand to lose another child. I should have gone to the doctor more, but since we can't afford health insurance, I went to the county clinic whenever I could spare the fee. Obviously, it wasn't often enough if I didn't even know I was carrying twins!" Rita wailed. *Oh, God,* Rita thought, *please, don't let my babies die.*

Alexandra said nothing, sensing that her daughter needed her love and, for now, her silence. She knew, as a mother knows, that something wasn't right in her daughter's marriage. In fact, she knew that something was very wrong. But she was determined not to bring the subject up unless

Rita initiated it first. Until now, though it killed her to do so, she had maintained her silence and let Rita live her own life.

Alexandra looked at her daughter and saw the fatigue, exhaustion, and helplessness in her child's face. She didn't yet know what was going on, but she was certain of one thing—there was more to this situation than met the eye. Something had happened to Rita since she married Simon. She no longer had the glow in her eyes and the excitement in her voice that she'd had all her life.

Rita eventually quieted and slipped into a fitful sleep. Alexandra eased her down on the pillow and decided to go see her new grandbaby. After dressing carefully in sterile hospital scrubs, she was led into the neonatal unit. She was delighted to learn that Rita had had twins! They were the most beautiful babies she had ever seen. She knew that she was biased; however, that didn't stop her from sharing her thoughts with everyone present.

Before Alexandra went back downstairs to Rita's room, she called her husband knowing he would be worried about Rita until he heard from her again. She told him everything and he listened raptly. Upon entering her daughter's hospital room, she walked to the window and looked out focusing on nothing in particular. She was praying for her daughter and her grandsons' welfare. She asked God to protect them as only He could.

Alexandra thought about how happy Rita had been as a child. Rita was her fourth child and she was born happy. She was the best baby she'd ever had. In fact, she was the best baby any mother could ask for. Even though she was the youngest, she was the peacemaker among her siblings. She was always trying to help people and animals. She was forever bringing home stray animals in need of care. She said that they were God's creation too, even though they had temporarily lost their way.

Alexandra heard Rita softly calling for her. She turned from the window to see that Simon had entered the room. He was standing next to Rita's bed. He said an uninspired "Hello" to Alexandra and then spoke to Rita. "When are they going to let you out of this place? You can lay in bed at

S.E.C.R.E.T.S. VOLUME II by: *Pastor Shirley*

home. We don't have that kind of money! I'm tired of trying to cook for myself. You need to get out of this place so you can take care of me and the apartment. It's a wreck."

Rita glanced nervously at her mother. She'd dared not tell her what had been going on in her home. She knew that her mother didn't really like Simon so she tried to cover up Simon's telling remarks. "Oh, Simon, you are such a kidder," she said with a weak smile. Alexandra looked at Simon. He wasn't kidding. He was dead serious. Rita's attempt at covering up Simon's insensitivity and meanness didn't fool Alexandra at all. As Alexandra's grandmother, Sallie, was fond of saying, "she was too old a cat to get slapped by a kitten," which meant she saw Simon for what he was and neither Rita nor Simon could fool her with their cover-up attempts.

Alexandra could see fear all over Rita's face. This man calling himself a preacher was cruel and mean to her daughter. Alexandra decided to change the subject to something more pleasant in order to ease the tension in the room.

"I am so delighted you had twins. My grandsons are so adorable. You will have two babies in the crib, not one. How exciting. I guess I had better run out and get another outfit for you to take the second baby home in. I know you have one of everything, now you'll need two."

Rita looked more nervous. She said, "Mom, will you please get two outfits. I never got a chance to shop."

Alexandra shrugged and said, "Sure. I'll be happy to. But don't you have some things at home? You know, some basic things like blankets, T-shirts, bottles, a crib, etc.?" Before Rita could answer, Simon jumped in, "We wanted to wait to see what the sex of the baby was before we bought anything. As far as a crib is concerned, we can use two dresser drawers to make beds for the boys. And as far as bottles, we don't need them. God gave Rita everything she needs. She has two breasts and two boys. She can do her duty as a woman."

Rita tried to laugh it off by saying, "Simon stop kidding. You're embarrassing me." But Alexandra knew he meant everything he'd said. Nothing for the babies? Nothing at all?! Alexandra knew that Rita was working, but what about Simon? She spoke to Rita. "Taking care of one baby is extremely difficult. Two is even more so. I can stay a couple of weeks to help you while Simon is at work. That way you can get some rest. Those midnight feedings can really take it out of you," she said laughing.

Simon cut her a sharp look. "I am doing God's work, not man's work. Rita will be going back to work in a few weeks and I will just have to sacrifice and keep the boys until she gets home."

"But you said Rita was going to breast feed. How is she going to do that if she goes back to work immediately?"

"Rita will just have to pump the milk at night and I will just have to take time from my day and take care of the boys."

"What exactly is Rita supposed to be pumping this milk into? You didn't buy any bottles," Alexandra said pointedly. She saw anger in Simon's stony expression and cold fear in her daughter's eyes. Deciding that she had to ease Rita's obvious fear, she apologized. "Look Simon, I'm not trying to be sarcastic or to anger you in any way. I am just merely trying to help you think this through so that everyone is taken care of. Have you ever taken care of an infant? Not one but TWO at the same time?"

"Everything I need to know, God will teach me," Simon spat out.

Alexandra curbed her tongue to keep from giving Simon a good tongue-lashing for laziness, meanness, and insensitivity. After all, this was Rita's husband and she was just the mother-in-law. Simon left saying that he had some studying to do.

Alexandra tried but she just couldn't keep her vow of silence. She had to discuss Simon's ignorance. "Rita, I can see there is something very wrong in your marriage. I have tried to stay out of it, but I just can't bear to see you being mistreated by your husband." As if having an epiphany, Alexandra's face lit up and she said, "Look, Rita. Why don't you and the twins come home with me for a couple of weeks? Your father and I

S.E.C.R.E.T.S. VOLUME II by: _Pastor Shirley_

would love the company and you know how your Daddy loves babies and kissing their little cheeks. He has never had a problem changing diapers or warming bottles or even the late-night feedings. Come home and let us take care of you and the twins."

"Mom, though your offer is much appreciated and highly tempting, I can't. What would Simon do without us? Besides I think it might be better if I start out caring for the twins. That way when you leave, I'll be used to the work involved." Rita's answer made absolutely no sense to Alexandra and she could plainly see that Rita was afraid of her husband; but she let the matter rest.

"Well, if you change your mind, the offer is always open. Whether it's today, tomorrow, or next year, your father and I are here for you. Now, I am going on a baby shopping trip the likes of which this town has probably never seen. I will have everything you need for those babies delivered to your home. After all, what are grandparents to do except spoil their grandchildren?" She said with forced cheerfulness.

Rita began to cry again. "Thank you so much, Mom. I do not mean to be a burden to you and Dad. We had planned to shop for the babies, but time just got away from us. Then they came a month early…"

"Don't worry about a thing, Rita. You are never a burden to your father and me. We love you unconditionally." Alexandra kissed Rita's cheek, gathered her purse and keys, and left the hospital room. After exiting the elevator, she pulled out her cell phone and called Jake to update him on this unbelievable situation.

Four days later, Rita was released from the hospital; however, her babies were not strong enough to be released until 2½ months later.

After two weeks, Simon forced Rita back to her job saying that they needed the money. She was so exhausted that she didn't think she was going to be able to make it through the long day. When the boys finally came home, Simon did not assist her with the midnight feedings, saying that "taking care of squealing brats" was her job. The fact that they were also his "squealing brats" didn't seem to matter to him.

After getting up every two hours to feed and change the boys, Rita could barely stand. She often slept during her lunch hour because it was the only time she could sleep uninterrupted.

One day, she didn't wake up until it was time to go home. When she realized the time, she was terrified that she was going to lose her job so she went to see her boss to explain. He reassured her saying that she'd looked so exhausted that he knew she needed the rest. So he'd told everyone to let her sleep. Though he wanted no one else to know, she was even going to be paid as well. Rita just cried and thanked him profusely. The extended rest was wonderful and she felt better than she had in weeks. She stopped right then and there to thank God for the favor He had given her with her boss.

In addition to being forced back to work after only two weeks, Simon also forced himself on Rita sexually. Though her doctor explained to both of them that they needed to wait six weeks, he didn't care. Rita begged him saying that her body had gone through a great ordeal and needed to heal. He would hear none of it. Simon told her that she was his wife and that she was there for his pleasure. As such, she had no say in the matter. Rita suffered through his rough lovemaking sessions in silence. Her body was still extremely tender and it hurt terribly. Many times when he finished, she was crying and bleeding.

It came as no surprise to Rita that six months after the twins were born, she was pregnant again. How was she possibly going to support another baby? As it was, ends were not meeting at all! Simon's behavior fluctuated often, which kept Rita off balance. It was difficult for her to predict his mood from day to day, which caused her to be stressed all the time. When he was belligerent, she was cowed into submission. When he apologized and tried to be loving, her heart soared thinking that perhaps he meant his apology and the physical abuse would end. But, it never did.

Simon picked up a little money here and there when he preached at visiting churches. However, he never used the money to help in the household. He always found something else that he needed to spend the money on, like a new suit or pair of shoes for himself. He never paid a bill, bought food, or even diapers for the boys.

One Sunday evening, Simon was asked to preach at a neighborhood church. The offering was much higher than usual and Rita calculated in her mind that the money could buy a two-week supply of much-needed Pampers for the boys, pay the phone bill, and buy a week's worth of groceries with enough left over to fill the car with gas! Rita was ecstatic at the prospect.

That night after she had put the boys to bed, Rita said, "Simon, I'm really glad you received a good offering at church tonight. I could really use some help with the household responsibilities." She then recounted all the things that they could do with the money before continuing, "That would be such a big help, and I need some help supporting this family, Simon. I just can't do it all by myself anymore. It was hard enough when we didn't have the boys. Now it is virtually impossible."

Suddenly Simon was in front of her. He grabbed her long hair with one hand and began punching her in the face with the other. Rita was caught completely off guard. She tried to defend herself, but the force of the punches rendered her helpless. While he rained punches on her head and face, he screamed every foul name he could think of at her. He told her it was her responsibility to support this family and that the money he received for doing God's work was his to use to keep him looking good at the pulpit.

Rita slumped against the wall and slid to a sitting position. Simon kicked her viciously on the side of the head. The force of the blow sent her careening into the coffee table. Rita was dazed and had trouble focusing her vision. Through her haze, she saw Simon rushing toward her again. She scrambled to get out of his way, but wasn't able to do so in time. With all his might, Simon kicked her brutally, squarely in her pregnant stomach. Pain exploded throughout her entire body and she couldn't move her hands and legs. Thankfully, blackness rose up to meet her as she fainted.

Rita had no idea how long she lay unconscious. When she regained consciousness, she just lay there staring up at the ceiling. The helplessness and hopelessness of her situation were like a 1,000 lb. weight. Full of anger and fear, which she was unable to vent, she considered her life. What could she do with two small babies and another one on the way? She began to cry and rub her stomach. Please, please God do not let my unborn baby die. It's not his fault his father is crazy.

It was a long time before Rita could drag her body, which was screaming in pain, into a sitting position. The pain continued to wash over her in nauseating waves. By the time she accomplished this, her head was bathed in perspiration and she felt like she was going to vomit. After getting her bearings, she was able to stand. She stumbled in the direction of the bathroom, each step causing her debilitating pain. But before she could make it there, she heard a knock at the door. She turned and gingerly made her way to the front door. As she walked, she suddenly noticed how quiet it was in the apartment. Where were her baby boys?

She opened the door and was surprised to see her upstairs neighbor, Eve. She had the twins in their stroller and she looked uncomfortable and embarrassed. Eve took one look at Rita's face and her expression first registered surprise then shock. She stammered apprehensively, "Rita, I'm so sorry to bother you. I didn't mean to disturb your rest. I know you must be tired."

Rita just stood there trying to concentrate on what she was saying and wondering why she was apologizing to her. And most of all, why did Eve have her babies? Eve could see that Rita had been beaten. Judging by her bruised and swollen face, neck, and arms, the beating had been severe. There was blood splattered all over the front of her dress and bruise marks in the shape of hands on her neck. Had her husband choked her? Then Eve found her voice, "Rev. Morgan came over four hours ago and brought the twins. He asked me if I minded keeping them for a few hours while you slept because he had a very important appointment he couldn't miss. He said you were ill and exhausted with the twins, being pregnant, and working. He also said that he had tried to wake you up, but you were just out of it. I told him no problem and that I'd be glad to help out. I wouldn't have bothered you but my daughter's school just called. Cheyenne has a fever and is throwing up. I have to go pick her up. By the way, I just fed

S.E.C.R.E.T.S. VOLUME II by: *Pastor Shirley*

the twins lunch and changed them so they should be full and about ready for their afternoon nap." Eve paused, her eyes pools of concern. Her next phrase was uttered in a hushed and nervous tone; "Rita… um… are you alright? Do you need me to call your family or someone?"

Rita said "Oh no, I'm fine," then thanked her profusely and apologized for having bothered her. She was thankful that the boys had been fed and she immediately put them to bed for their nap. Rita was in so much pain that she could barely walk. She sat gingerly on the bed and tried to figure out what she was going to do. She was at her wits' end.

She picked up the phone, called her sister, Meagan, and told her what had happened. True to her extroverted nature, Meagan was livid. She told Rita to call the police and their parents. Rita knew that she couldn't tell her father what had happened. Again, Jake wasn't saved and did not live by the 'turn the other cheek' principle. Oh no; her father lived by the 'I'm going to do unto you MUCH WORSE than you did unto me and, if I can help it, BEFORE you do it unto me' rule. He carried a pistol at all times and had no qualms about using it.

She was sure… make that, somewhat sure, that her father wouldn't kill Simon; but she had no doubt that Simon would, at the very least, find himself seriously injured. Her father's favorite place to shoot a person was in the kneecap saying nothing brought a man down and broke his spirit like a shattered kneecap.

Meagan told Rita to throw some things into a bag for her and the twins and that she would be there to pick her up in 30 minutes. Rita was scared to death as she tried to quickly pack a bag. She was in so much pain, she could only hobble about to pack, which made her take more precious minutes than she felt she had. She prayed that Simon wouldn't come home before Meagan arrived. Thank God, he didn't.

Meagan took Rita and the twins to her house. While she helped Rita to take a shower, her husband, Nicolas, took care of the twins and their own two daughters, Lori and Reese. Meagan was appalled at the myriad bruises crisscrossing Rita's pregnant body. Some were new, most were older. She was horrified. She said that Simon should be put under the jail for what he had done to Rita. She helped Rita to wash her long, flowing hair and to lotion her body. She tucked her into bed and brought her some dinner. After Rita finished eating, she fell into a deep, fitful sleep.

When Meagan went downstairs, the twins had eaten dinner and Nicolas was giving them a bath. She looked lovingly at her husband. He was truly a rare breed; a good man. He looked up as Meagan entered the bathroom and smiled back. She helped him to finish their baths and put them to bed.

The next morning, she went into Rita's room. "Good morning, baby sis. Are you feeling better today?" When Rita nodded in the affirmative, Meagan continued. "Simon called four or five times yesterday demanding to speak to you. I told him he will call my house with respect or not call at all and I told him NO he couldn't talk to you, due to the fact that you were badly beaten, totally exhausted, and you needed your rest. I asked him did he have any idea how you got in that condition? You know he lied and said he had no idea. I said someone had to take care of you and make sure you got some much-needed rest. I was just the one to do that and if for any reason I couldn't handle it on my own, Nicolas would be more than happy to jump in.

He threatened to come and get the boys even if you didn't want to come home. I told him I was NOT afraid of a coward like him, and that if I see him within 200 feet of my house I am calling the police and telling them that a man masquerading as a preacher had badly beaten a pregnant woman. I told him I had taken pictures of your injuries and if he didn't want to go to jail for assault and battery he'd better leave us all alone. I then told him he should be ashamed of himself for calling himself a preacher and behaving like a hood on the street. He hung up on me but, trust me, I'm not offended," she said laughing.

Rita began to cry and Meagan rushed over to console her. She told her that everything would be OK. Rita finally quieted just as Nicolas poked his head in the door bearing a tray filled with breakfast for both Meagan and Rita. There were thick slices of maple-cured bacon, fluffy scram-

S.E.C.R.E.T.S. VOLUME II by: *Pastor Shirley*

bled eggs, crispy hash browned potatoes, his famous homemade biscuits dripping with butter, two small individual pots of homemade strawberry jam, freshly brewed gourmet coffee, and freshly squeezed orange juice. Meagan thanked her husband with a deep kiss, which he returned. Rita looked at Meagan and said, "Meagan, you are so blessed. You can see the love Nicolas has for you in his eyes. I would give a million dollars to have Simon look at me like that. He has a good job and he doesn't mind helping you with the kids and the house. But more than anything, he is crazy about you."

Meagan set her coffee cup down and studied her sister for a moment before responding. "Yes, I'm blessed. But if you remember, I waited on God to send me a husband. I was really, really tired of being single, but I was determined to marry the man God had for me. People used to laugh at me behind my back saying I would be an old maid before I ever got married. But I stood on the Word of God. Because I waited, and believe me it wasn't easy waiting, I am now very happy. I have a good man. A kind man. A man who is supportive of me and who loves his kids. But most of all, he loves God. By the way, he told me to tell you that you are welcome to stay with us as long as you want.

"You know, Rita, when I was in college living in the dorm, we had to go to numerous meetings when we first arrived. Most of the meetings were about self-defense, campus safety, and other stuff like that. But I found one meeting really interesting and I have never forgotten what I learned. It was called how to identify a loser; in other words, how to identify a no good man.

First they abuse you. Beating a pregnant woman is definitely abuse.

Second, they use you. Simon is the man of your household. He should be supporting you, not the other way around. I don't know how you have been working this long being as large with child as you are. He is lazy and doesn't want to work. The Bible says a man that doesn't work and support his family is worse than an infidel. You've never said it but I know you do all the cooking and cleaning too. He is using you Rita.

Last, they accuse you. You can't tell me that Simon doesn't somehow make it your fault that HE beats you. Cowardly men do that. It's always someone else's fault when they beat women. Those same cowardly men do not beat on other men. Oh no, they only choose targets they consider weaker than they are."

Rita hung her head in shame. Meagan scrutinized her sister shrewdly and realized that Rita had the exact same look that she did as a child when she was trying to avoid something unpleasant. Because this particular topic of conversation made Rita uncomfortable, Meagan decided to change the subject. Again, Meagan stated, "You can stay with us as long as you want. Nicolas adores the twins, and Lori and Reese love the boys as well. We can help you get on your feet, though we wouldn't even think of that until after my new niece or nephew deems to honor us with his or her arrival and you've had a chance to completely recover. Nicolas makes a lot of money. Believe me, your staying here won't affect our household finances at all. I don't want you thinking you would be a burden or anything like that." Meagan hugged Rita and, sticking her tongue out, continued, "I know how you get." Rita laughed at her sister's silliness and realized that this was the first time that she had laughed in months.

"Thank you," she replied. Before she could answer further, Nicolas came back into the room pushing the boys in the stroller, followed closely by Lori and Reese. The boys had been fed, dressed, and were smiling happily. He said that he was taking the kids to the park and then to a movie, so Meagan and Rita could spend some quiet time together. Rita looked nervous. "Nicolas, the twins can be a handful. Are you sure you can handle four kids?" Nicolas smiled and said, "I was very involved with the girls as babies. I did everything. I can more than take care of the twins. Besides, I am an expert diaper changer. Although I have to admit," he said laughing, "I have to change the twins' Pampers much quicker than I did the girls or else I find myself dodging a stream of urine. What is it about a rush of air that makes them want to go right then?" They all laughed.

 Nicolas took the kids as promised and Meagan and Rita spent the day shopping. Meagan paid for everything with her credit cards. She bought Rita eight new maternity outfits. Rita was overjoyed. She'd never had

S.E.C.R.E.T.S. VOLUME II by: *Pastor Shirley*

maternity outfits before and marveled at how much more comfortable they were. She even wore one out of the store. Meagan then bought lots of new clothes for the twins as well as a month's supply of Pampers and baby food. Rita had never seen so much baby food and Pampers in her life. She cried as Meagan continued to shop. They finally went back home, happy and exhausted.

Rita and the twins had been at Meagan's house for two weeks. Two beautiful weeks filled with love, safety, food she didn't have to cook, and church. Rita was rested and the twins were happy. She called her job, told her boss what had happened to her, and requested a little time off. Her boss suggested that she take some vacation time so that she would be paid. Surprised and pleased at his suggestion, Rita thanked him profusely and again thanked God for favor.

After repeated phone calls, Rita finally consented to speak to Simon. He kept calling and begging her to go out to dinner with him until he wore her down. After another week, she agreed but refused to allow him to pick her up. She said she would drive herself so that she could leave whenever she wanted. She arrived at the restaurant and Simon was waiting anxiously for her. He noticed how good she looked. She was wearing a maternity dress, makeup, and her hair was up. She looked fantastic and he told her so.

After a good meal and easy conversation, Simon knew that he had to address his violent behavior. "Rita, I'm so glad you agreed to have dinner with me tonight. I have missed you and the boys so much. I am so sorry for what I did to you. It will never happen again, I swear." Tears were steadily sliding down his face. "I don't know what came over me. But I do know it will never happen again. I have repented to God and He has forgiven me for my terrible behavior and treatment of you."

"I want my family back. I want my wife and boys back. I miss you all so much." Simon noticed that Rita was hesitant. He didn't want to push his luck so he said, "OK, ok, you don't have to make up your mind or answer now. Take your time. I'm willing to be patient. But I do have something to ask of you. I have to preach at a visiting church on Sunday night. I would like you to be by my side and sing before I come forth. Would you at least do that? Please."

Reluctantly, Rita agreed. Simon really preached at the service and they had a high time in the Lord. Rita was glad she went. The service provided even more spiritual food for her soul. That night after the service, Simon did something he'd never done in the past. He counted the money he'd received in front of her. Then he gave Rita $75.00 of the $112.00 offering saying that it was for her and the boys. He said that they were a team and that he was now prepared to do his part financially with the upkeep of the house and caring for their children.

Rita was shocked. Maybe Simon had changed. Maybe he really did love her and the boys. Maybe he was ready to be the man with whom she had fallen in love. Rita loved Simon and wanted her marriage to work. So she decided to give Simon another chance. Her marriage vows were important to her. She had pledged before God and her family to marry Simon for better or worse. She had seen enough of the worse to last her the rest of her life. Surely, the better had to be just around the corner. Besides, she couldn't live with herself if she didn't give her marriage a second chance.

Over the next few weeks, Simon treated Rita extremely well. He was attentive and kind. He helped with the boys and two or three times a week he had dinner prepared when Rita came home from work. He was even looking for a job on a regular basis. Of the money he received for preaching, 75% of it went into the household. Rita thought that all of his income should have gone into the household as hers did. But she didn't want to cause friction between them since they had been getting along so well. Besides, she told herself, he was making an effort, which was more than he'd done in the past, and she appreciated it. Rita was as close to happy as she could get in her marriage.

Two months had passed since Rita's return home when she began noticing a change in Simon's behavior. It was difficult for her to decipher, but she instinctively knew that things were about to change for the worse. She was right. He was quiet and grouchy. Nothing she did pleased him.

S.E.C.R.E.T.S. VOLUME II by: _Pastor Shirley_

Rita again lived in fear of saying or doing the wrong thing. She didn't know how to deal with him and the smallest comment or gesture sent him into a fit of rage. She decided that the safest way to deal with him was to limit her communication to answering his questions. All other conversation might lead to an explosive outburst.

That night around 1:00 am, Rita awoke and immediately knew that something was amiss. She didn't know what it was, but she could feel it in her spirit. The Lord spoke to Rita and said, "Look at the window." She turned her head to stare at the window. Seeing nothing but darkness, she turned to go back to sleep before it was time for her to get up for work. The Lord spoke again, this time in a thunderous voice, "LOOK AT THE WINDOW!" Shaken out of her sleep-induced stupor, Rita looked at the window again. It got very bright and then got dark again. Knowing something was terribly wrong, she jumped out of bed and saw that her bedroom was engulfed in swirling layers of thick, black smoke. Oh my God, the apartment building is on fire! She looked out of the window and was able to see that over half of it was ablaze. If God hadn't woke her up and told her to look at the window, they would've died. PRAISE BE TO GOD! Rita continued to praise God inwardly as she woke Simon and the kids and rushed out of the apartment. Because of God's warning, Rita and her family were able to make it outside just before the entire building was consumed and collapsed right on top of their apartment.

As they stood watching their home burn, Simon seethed with fury. His mind was racing with irrational questions. Why would God wake Rita and not him? He was the man of God. He was the head of his household.

Rita Morgan

Not Rita. She was just a housekeeper, a cook, and a breeder.

The fireman walked up to Simon and said, "You got your family out of that apartment just in the nick of time. One more minute and you wouldn't have been able to make it to safety."

Simon replied through gritted teeth, "I am a preacher and God should've told me to wake up and look at the window, not my wife."

Rita stood there in disbelief. She couldn't believe that Simon was sharing his immature view with the fireman. The fireman looked at Simon as if he needed to be in a straitjacket. He spoke up and said, "Hey man, if I were you, I wouldn't care who warned me just as long as they did. I would just be glad for the warning and that me and my family got to safety in time. You should be proud of your wife. Maybe she has an inside track to God. I've seen so many families perish in fires like this. Just be thankful you're all alive." He laughed, but Simon saw no humor in the situation at all.

After the fire, Rita saw a huge change in Simon. They moved in with Elder and Sister Burton, friends from the church, until they could find another place in which to live. Simon again refused to get a job, saying that God would provide. Rita envied Elder and Sister Burton's relationship. They had the kind of loving, supportive relationship of which she'd always dreamed.

One night as they were lying in bed, Simon wanted to make love. Rita was apprehensive because the twins were still awake and they all slept in the same room. She was very large with child as her due date was rapidly approaching. Plus Simon had been really rough with her lately when making love and sometimes the pain was unbearable. She did not want him to hurt her. Being in the Burton household bolstered Rita's courage as she felt that he wouldn't hit her while they were staying there. Feeling safe from physical violence, for the first time in their marriage, Rita refused saying that she didn't feel well with her due date so close.

Simon went ballistic. Because they were in the Burtons' house, and he didn't want them to know about his abusive behavior, he knew that he had to do the next best thing—mentally intimidate his wife and ruthlessly ter-

S.E.C.R.E.T.S. VOLUME II by: *Pastor Shirley*

rorize her. He wanted to crush her head with his bare hands and knew that he had to get inside her mind to make her feel his frustration and anger. He leaned in and began to talk in a slithering hiss, and his eyes sparkled in malicious triumph as he saw Rita cower and her flesh actually rise with goose bumps. Rita then saw parts of Simon's personality that she never knew existed.

Feeling power and exhilaration coursing through his veins, Simon began revealing things about his past. "Before I married you, I was homeless. The pastor let me sleep at the church and the members never knew I was living there." Rita was shocked. She hadn't known this either. "After church was over, I would go into the sanctuary and sleep on the benches. There were many nights I wondered what it would be like to have sex in the sanctuary, on the altar. Right in front of God." Rita's mind was reeling. She knew he was crazy now. She felt like she was suffocating. Her large belly made every movement awkward so struggling into a sitting position took her a few minutes.

Simon eyed her as he continued. "I finally did it. I convinced one of the sisters at the church to have sex with me on the altar. It was so… amazing. I felt like I owned the world. I felt like I was God!" As he told her this demonic story, he became aroused and began masturbating while he looked at the expression on Rita's face. "So you see, Rita, there are many women who will happily submit to sex with me. Anywhere I want them to. They don't come up with dumb excuses about being sick just to get out of it." Rita moved to get out of the bed, not wanting to view this repulsive display, and was thankful that the twins were too young to know what he was doing. But Simon moved faster and clamped his hand on her arm, "You stay right here until I'm finished. If you aren't willing to have sex, you can at least provide an audience for me. I wonder how it would have felt to have YOU in every position imaginable on that alter…" Rita was scared to move. She was forced to watch and after a few minutes of intense masturbation, he finished with a disgusting groan and cleaned himself thoroughly with the edge of her nightgown. His eyes gleamed with sinister satisfaction as he blew her a kiss.

Feeling sick to her stomach, Rita scrambled from the bed and went into the bathroom. She threw off her nightgown and sat on the toilet staring into space for what seemed like hours. What had she gotten herself into by marrying this deranged man? This had to be a nightmare and she desperately wanted someone to wake her. NOW! She didn't want to be in this dream any longer. She thought for the umpteenth time, I should have listened to my mother. I shouldn't have married Simon without getting to know who he really was or at least asking someone about him. As Rita sat on the toilet, she contemplated her life and her marriage. She'd had such high hopes when she'd married Simon. They all seemed like a joke now. She didn't know what her next move should be, but she was sure of one thing—something was wrong with Simon; he was in need of psychiatric treatment. Unfortunately, she couldn't even suggest this to him without him using the suggestion as an excuse to physically abuse her. She prayed that God would give her an answer.

Rita and Simon stayed with the Burtons for two more weeks before they found another apartment. Rita's co-worker told her of an apartment in her development that would be vacant in two weeks. When Rita met with the landlord, she knew that God had given her favor with him. Even though Rita didn't have the money for the security deposit, he still rented the apartment to her. Somehow the landlord knew that he had to help her, but he didn't understand why.

Rita and her family moved into the new apartment. She went about getting everything set up with renewed energy, excited for a new start. She was determined to help Simon to find his way back to the Lord by remaining by his side. She knew it was a long shot, but it was all she had so she took the gamble.

Two months after moving into the new apartment, Rita gave birth to a bouncing baby girl she named Kendall. Rita was disgusted with herself. After three babies, she was now 50 pounds overweight. She desperately wanted to lose the weight because Simon had taken to calling her names. Just this morning he'd said, "You are as big as a house. You aren't sexy anymore. How do you expect me to make love to a pig? If you don't lose the weight soon, and get your figure back, I will be forced to look for sex

S.E.C.R.E.T.S. VOLUME II by: *Pastor Shirley*

elsewhere. It's your responsibility to always look good for your man." Rita left for work with tears streaming down her face.

Rita began to worry about Simon's aggressive attitude toward sex. Even with his ultimatums and hurtful name-calling, when she came in from a long day after work, he expected her to immediately fall into bed and have sex with him. Rita tried to explain that she was tired and that the children were up and running around. She begged him to be more understanding and considerate of her. She tried to explain that if he just allowed her to take a few minutes to rest after she got home from work, she would be very grateful and much more sexually responsive. But Simon refused to understand and told her that she was being selfish.

Rita was worried about the bills because her meager salary wasn't enough to pay them and Simon was again showing absolutely no interest in finding a job. The new apartment was higher in rent than the previous one, their car barely made it to and from work, and they never had enough food or Pampers. She lived in fear that the electricity was going to be turned off when she arrived home. So far it hadn't been, but the gas had been turned off for three weeks, causing her to have to heat water on the stove for bathing and washing the dishes. Thank God she had an electric stove.

Rita came in from work one day and noticed a card sitting on the kitchen table. It had been sent by her mother and addressed to her, but it had been opened. A cheerful card inside said, "Rita, we are sending you a check for $300.00. I hope it will help you in some way. We love you. Mom and Dad."

Rita read the card again. She was so happy. She could pay the phone and electric bills, and she could buy the twins two much-needed pairs of shoes. She looked for the check, but it was not to be found. She looked on the floor thinking that perhaps it had fallen from the envelope by accident. At that moment, Simon walked into the room. He said, "Oh, by the way, your mother sent us some money. We sure did need it. I cashed the check today and bought me a pair of shoes and a new shirt and tie. I really needed those things so I can look my best when I preach. I'll use the rest of the money to buy me a pair of pants and another shirt."

Rita was so angry, upset, and disappointed that she again forgot that she was dealing with a very violent man. She exploded, "You did what?! My mother sent that check to me, not you. You had no right to open a letter addressed to me or to cash a check addressed to me. The gas is turned off, the electricity and phone are about to be turned off, I have no gas to get to work, and the twins need shoes and Pampers, and all you can think about is yourself! I am sick and tired of totally supporting this family and doing all the housework. Simon, I can do bad all by myself!"

In a sudden burst of motion, Simon flew across the room and slapped Rita savagely across the face. "WHO DO YOU THINK YOU'RE TALKING TO?!" He grabbed her hair and began punching her in the face, head, and throat. The last punch took her breath away and she thought her throat canal might be crushed. She couldn't seem to get enough air into her lungs and she feared she might suffocate. Through her pain, Rita saw the twins huddled in the corner terrified. Simon was screaming obscenities and had begun to kick her as well. He told her over and over that he was going to kill her and she really thought she was going to die.

She looked across to the counter and saw the scissors she had used the day before when she'd been sewing patches onto the boys' pants. By this time, Simon had picked her up and thrown her across the room. She landed on her neck and pain exploded through her body. She struggled to her feet and grabbed the scissors. Rita looked at Simon approaching her ominously and was truly afraid that he was going to kill her. He reached for her again and Rita began stabbing him with the scissors. Her only thought was to get him off of her before he killed her. She stabbed him several times in the shoulder and arm. Blood gushed everywhere. When Simon realized he'd been stabbed, he ran out of the house screaming like a woman.

One of the neighbors called the police and before Rita knew it, her apartment was filled with police officers and paramedics. One of the police officers asked her what happened, and she explained everything, telling him that she thought that Simon was going to kill her, and that she had reached for anything that would get him off her and stop the beating. The police officer asked her if Simon had ever beaten her in the past. She told

S.E.C.R.E.T.S. VOLUME II by: *Pastor Shirley*

him yes, many times; but she'd never reported the previous beatings.

Simon eventually returned to the apartment, and when the police officer asked him for his side of the story, he replied, "I don't know what got into Rita. She freaked out when I asked her a simple question and just started stabbing me. I am a preacher of God who's dedicated his life to spreading the gospel. I don't know what happened to her. She just snapped."

The officer asked Simon if he'd assaulted Rita in the past. Simon quickly said "No way. I am a man of God and preachers don't assault women." Rita was angry at Simon's bold-faced lie and without thinking of the consequences, she pulled up her shirt to show the officer her myriad bruises. He looked at Rita's torso, arms, and face and he knew that the man calling himself a preacher was beating this woman on a regular basis. He hated men who behaved in such a cowardly fashion. "If you haven't been hitting her, who has? How did her face get so bloody and swollen? Why are her face, neck, and chest filled with old and new bruises?" Simon shrugged and said, "She must've fallen when she tried to stab me."

The officer looked at Simon and then turned his gaze to Rita. "Lady, do you want to press charges against your husband for assault?" He asked?
"Her? What about me?" Simon screamed. "I'm the one who was assaulted. I"m the one who should be pressing charges!"
The discerning officer never took his gaze from Rita and he never acknowledged Simon's outburst about pressing charges.

Now Simon was afraid. He knew what happened to wife beaters in jail as he had spent a good part of his younger days in and out of prison. And there was one thing he knew beyond a shadow of a doubt—he could not endure another stint with hardened criminals. He lived in fear that he may have contracted the AIDS virus because of the many times he'd been raped by his condomless cell mates. However, he refused to take an AIDS test, preferring to believe that God would protect him. He never gave any thought to what he might have given to his wife or unborn children.

He was very afraid now and realized that he had to get his act together fast. He certainly didn't want to be arrested for beating his wife. His preaching career would be ruined; a career he had decided upon in jail. The way he saw it, he could legally rob people without pulling a gun on them. If he were persuasive enough and lively enough, he could get people to give him tax-free money. What could be better than that? When he was down to only a few months left in jail, he began working on his timing and technique. When he was released a short time later, he was ready and entered the church world with a vengeance. Then he met Rita and knew that she would be perfect as his wife and the mother of his children. She had the perfect look with an angelic face and voice to match. She was also gullible and would support him while he "tarried in the ministry and performed God's work." He had been correct. However, because of his temper, he was about to lose everything he had worked so hard to achieve. He would just have to harness his violence in the future.

The police officer interrupted Simon's thoughts and speaking to Rita said, "Since no one is pressing charges, the ambulance will be taking your husband to the hospital so that his wounds can be treated. Are you sure you don't want to go to the hospital too? You look pretty beat up?" Rita refused. She told the officer that she wanted to console her twins who were still in the corner clinging to each other in fear. As the police officer was leaving, he looked directly in Rita's eyes and said, "Lady, I do this for a living and believe me it never gets any better. As a matter of fact, it always gets worse. You'd better get out before it's too late because you might not get another chance. If you can't do it for yourself, think of your children."

After everyone left, Rita rushed to her sons and picked them both up. After kissing them, hugging them, and reassuring them that everything was going to be alright, she fed them dinner and put them to bed, praying silently as she went.

A few hours later, Simon entered the apartment glaring at Rita as he walked past her. "I better sleep with my eyes open from now on before I wake up dead." Simon said snidely. "I didn't know I was married to Jack the Knife's sister, Janice the Scissors." Simon's comment filled her with guilt and humiliation.

S.E.C.R.E.T.S. VOLUME II by: Pastor Shirley

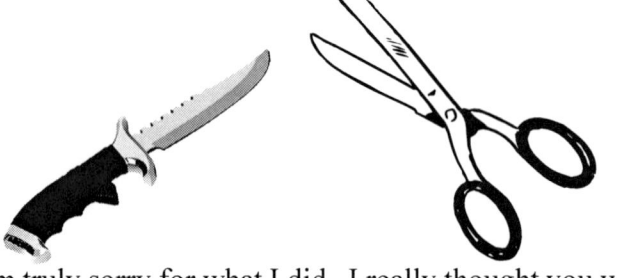

"Simon, I'm truly sorry for what I did. I really thought you were going to kill me. I was just trying to get you off me and end the vicious beating. I have repented to God and now I'm repenting to you as well. What happened shouldn't have happened and wouldn't have happened if I hadn't feared for my life."

Rita took the opportunity to talk to him about counseling as well as going to the pastor for help and advice. Simon looked at her as if she had lost her mind. "There is no way I'm going to the pastor about anything that would tarnish my carefully cultured image. As a matter of fact, I have decided to leave the church and start my own. That way I can get offerings and not have to share them with anyone else. Being a pastor is legal robbery. You can rob them in the name of the Lord and no one will be the wiser. I have always wanted to be a preacher just for that reason. They really have it made, especially if they work the system."

Rita was disgusted by Simon's admission. She left the room and went into the only other place in the small apartment that afforded her a modicum of privacy--the bathroom. She stood staring at herself in the cracked mirror over the sink. She looked much older; there were dark circles under her eyes and grey hair at her temples. When did I get so much grey hair? She thought. She looked at her skin. She'd had beautiful skin at one time, but now she needed a bit of foundation to even out her skin tone. But she couldn't wear makeup because Simon forbade it. He said that only whores wore makeup and besides, he didn't want to cut through all of that falseness to get to his wife. Yet, when they went out in public, Simon openly admired women who wore makeup.

She looked at the faded cotton dress that she was wearing. She remembered when she used to wear nice clothes, just a touch of makeup, and dine at nice restaurants. The only time she dined at a restaurant now was if her sisters or parents took her out. Simon certainly never did.

Rita thought back to when she met Simon. Why hadn't she listened to the words of the evangelist when she'd said "counterfeits will come but they are not of God." She now knew with certainty that Simon was a counterfeit in every way. Why had she settled? Why had she let go of herself and her identity? Why had she stayed with this mad man for so long? Was it really love that had kept her immobile, or was it a void within her? How was she going to reclaim her life? How was she going to save her babies and ensure they had a normal life? She didn't know what to do. She had prayed and was still waiting on an answer. She thought about all the occasions she had gone to her pastor to discuss her marital problems. He told her to stay with her husband, to pray for him, and to be patient. He quoted the scripture, "in your patience possess ye your soul." He also told her that if she left Simon she would not be in the will of God.

The person staring back at Rita in the mirror was now a stranger; someone whom she didn't recognize. She wasn't even sure if she wanted to know this person. She had been living in hell on earth since she'd been married to her husband, Satan. How in the world do you get rid of Satan?

Approximately four months later, Rita was in her bedroom when she heard Simon yelling at their three-year-old twins, Steven and Simon Jr. The negative intensity of Simon's emotions toward the twins frightened her and the boys. He acted as if he hated his own sons. Both boys were terrified of their father and cowered silently in a corner whenever he was around. Rita hated leaving the kids with Simon when she went to work, but since she could barely pay the bills, sending them to a babysitter or daycare center was out of the question.

Of the two boys, Steven was more afraid of his father. When Simon realized this, he began terrorizing the boy constantly. Interrupting her introspection, Rita suddenly heard Steven screaming hysterically. She opened the bathroom door and ran into the kitchen to see what was going on. What she saw caused the color to drain from her face. Simon had Steven by the front of his shirt and was viciously punching him in the face. The

S.E.C.R.E.T.S. VOLUME II by: *Pastor Shirley*

three year old's face and shirt were covered in blood. The entire time Simon rained punches on his son's face, he was screaming, "Stop crying like a sissy! You're gonna havta man up!"

Rita was horrified. If she didn't stop Simon, she had no doubt that her son would die at the hands of his father. She started screaming and ran toward Simon. But he'd seen her coming and anticipated her course of action. Just as she reached him, Simon flung Steven to the ground and turned to face Rita. He balled up his fist and punched her squarely in the face with all his might. The force of the blow caused Rita's head to snap back and she heard the sickening crunch of the bones in her nose and cheek. Her eyes filled with tears that blurred her vision, and blood immediately flooded her mouth gagging her. She fell to the floor clutching her face in agony. While she was on the floor, Simon savagely kicked her in the stomach and on the side of her head.

Though she was in an excruciating amount of pain, her first priority was Steven. He lay motionless on the floor near the kitchen sink. From her vantage point, she couldn't tell if he was breathing. She began to silently pray in earnest that God would save her son's life. She turned over on her stomach and began to crawl toward Steven. Simon had had his back to her when she began moving in Steven's direction but he quickly spun around at her movement. He spouted obscenities at Rita and Steven then began pacing around the adjoining living room with his arms straight up over his head in what he referred to as the "Rocky victory dance." Somehow, in his twisted, deranged mind, he considered the brutal beating he'd just bestowed on his wife and small son as some sort of a victory instead of the tragedy it truly was.

If she had any doubt in the past, Rita now knew for certain that if she stayed with this crazy man, she or her children would definitely end up dead at his hands.

Rita finally reached Steven and placed her hand over his heart. The heartbeat was faint, but it was there. She was trying to ascertain the severity of his other wounds when Simon began yelling her name and advancing menacingly toward her. The look in his eyes could only be described as maniacal. She knew beyond a shadow of a doubt that he was going to kill her, and that's when she saw him, the devil himself, staring back at her.

Rita scooted backward slowly, looking for something, anything, to defend herself against Simon. She didn't have the strength to stand up and reach the drawer where her cutlery was kept. She felt behind her back and opened the cabinet below the sink. She fumbled for anything hard, heavy, or pointed to use to somehow protect herself against the fatal assault that she knew was coming. Simon was getting closer and screaming even more loudly. He was at the point of no return. At last, she closed her hand around the Joy dish washing detergent bottle, intending to squeeze a good amount into his eyes, thereby, giving her the chance to call 911. She clumsily tried to unscrew the cap behind her back, but because she couldn't see what she was doing, it was taking too long to accomplish this simple task. Her heart was pounding and she was afraid that she wouldn't have it open by the time Simon reached her. After what felt like an eternity, the cap finally fell off as Simon came to a stop in front of her. As he reached for her, she mustered her last bit of strength, threw the dish washing detergent into Simon's face, and dropped the container on the floor. Simon immediately began screaming like a mad man while hopping up and down. He then dropped to the floor like a sack of potatoes. *Good,* she thought, t*hat dish soap really did the job. He'll be rubbing his eyes long enough for me to get help.* That's when she looked over to where she had thrown the discarded bottle. It wasn't liquid dish soap as she'd originally thought. To her utter horror, it was drain clog remover. She had thrown a poisonous, lethal substance containing acid into Simon's face. Looking at Simon she saw that it had already caused instant burns on his face, eyes, and mouth. His eyes were rolling to the back of his head, pink foam was coming out his mouth, blood was coming out of his nose, and he began flailing about like a fish out of water.

But Rita couldn't think about Simon now because it looked as if Steven had stopped breathing. She began screaming for Simon Jr. He slowly crawled from under the table, his face stained with tears and his eyes as big as saucers. "Mommy, are we going to die? Is Stevie going to die?"

S.E.C.R.E.T.S. VOLUME II by: *Pastor Shirley*

Rita tried to calm her voice so she wouldn't alarm Simon Jr. any further. "Baby, we gonna be alright and so is Stevie. No one is gonna die. Baby, I need you to do something for me, OK?" But Simon Jr. wasn't listening to her. He was too busy watching his father flailing around and screaming. He didn't want to be caught out in the open if his father got up.

"SIMON JR.!" Rita yelled in a stern voice. "Look at me now!" "Look this way baby. Over here." When he turned his head to look directly at her, Rita mustered a faint smile. "That's a good boy. Listen real good to Mommy, OK? I need your help. Go and get the cordless phone in the bedroom and bring it to Mommy so I can call someone to come and help us. OK?" Rita again smiled, but the effort sent shards of excruciating pain shooting through her head.

Simon Jr. silently nodded and backed out of the kitchen, his eyes still riveted on his father. He darted around the corner and was back in a flash with the phone. As he handed it to his mother, Rita said, "You did real good, baby. Real good."

Rita dialed 911 and told the operator, "Hurry please. I need your help. My husband beat me and my little son real bad and I don't think he is breathing. I hope we can hold on until you get here. Hurry!"

After Rita hung up the phone, all the strength she'd been using to protect Steven and herself seemed to evaporate as she slunk to the floor. She felt as if she were barely holding on to consciousness. Her last few thoughts she used to pray for her son. Lord please don't let my son die because I wasn't strong enough to leave his father. Please spare his little life. He has done nothing wrong. Protect us all…

As Rita edged closer to unconsciousness, she thought she heard the faint sound of an ambulance in the distance. At least she hoped she did.

To find out what happened to Rita and Simon Morgan, be sure to read S.E.C.R.E.T.S. of the First Ladies, Trilogy. Available soon in a bookstore near you.

Chapter 20

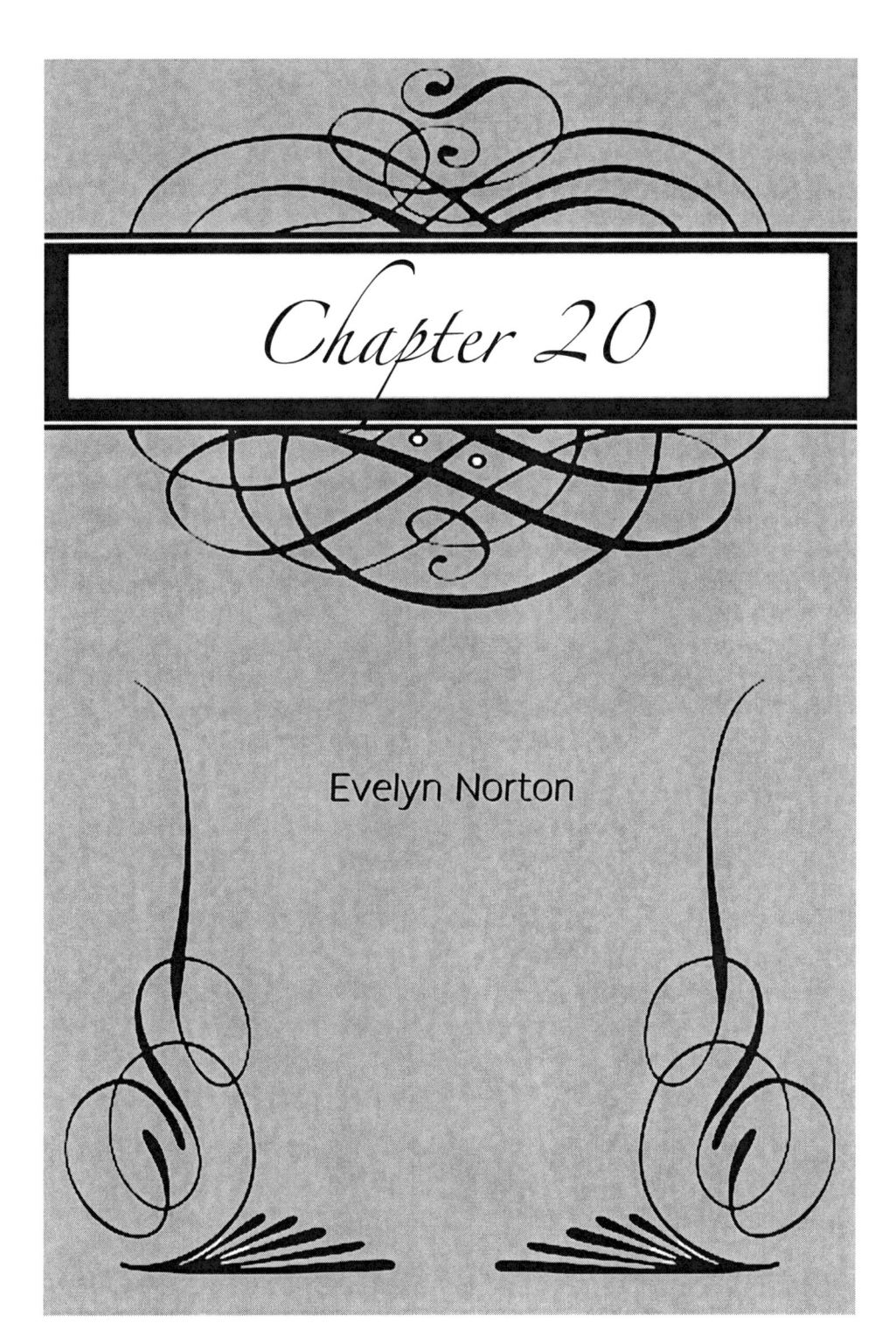

Evelyn Norton

S.E.C.R.E.T.S. VOLUME II by: *Pastor Shirley*

Evelyn Norton
7216 Sheffield Avenue

Evelyn Norton

Evelyn Norton

Evelyn...
Such a huge weight
for her fragile shoulders
Using perseverance
and determination
To move huge boulders

She has a very large
household to support
Since failure is not an option,
That will not be her report

Her uncaring husband
only wants to complain and take
But she stands strong
and relies on her faith.

Lack of support and cruelty
are her daily bread
As she searches desperately
for ways to keep her family fed

As she contemplates what to do
She knows the choices are minimal
and the options are few...

S.E.C.R.E.T.S. VOLUME II by: *Pastor Shirley*

First Lady Evelyn Norton, also known as Missionary Norton, is married to Pastor Johnny Norton, who is 20 years her senior. Johnny married Evelyn when he was 35 and she was 15. He is a Bible scholar, preacher, and pastor. They have been married for 28 years and have eight children.

Johnny was mean and cruel to both Evelyn and their children. He treated Evelyn as his personal servant and sex partner, not as his equal or beloved spouse. He forbade her to use any type of birth control and, as a result, she was pregnant every 11 or 12 months. Evelyn tried talking to her pastor and the mothers of the church about the boorish behavior being inflicted on her by her 'preacher' husband. They all told her the same thing—stay with your husband, be an obedient wife, and let God deliver you. Wanting to be saved more than anything else, she adhered to their instruction.

In those early years, Evelyn and Johnny's only source of income was to work in the cotton fields. Johnny expected all of his kids to work in the fields beginning at approximately six years of age. He even expected Evelyn to work late into her pregnancies. Unfortunately, she was extremely sick with each pregnancy and could not handle the hot sun and heavy cotton sacks. However, Johnny didn't care. He required her to pick cotton right up until the babies were born. If he was in a good mood, maybe, just maybe, he would allow her to rest for four or five days after the babies were born before returning to the fields. But that was not the case when her second son died suddenly when he was only six weeks old. Evelyn took his death extremely hard. She'd adored him, as he was such a beautiful, happy baby. Johnny only permitted her to mourn the death of their child for two days before he forced her back to the fields.

As a little girl, Evelyn was abandoned by her mother and haphazardly raised by her grandmother. She was 10 years old when she first visited a Pentecostal church. Though she didn't return until some years later, she never forgot the experience and the way it made her feel. Over the years, she had a longing for God that she could not explain. When she married Johnny, he was the pastor of a Pentecostal church. It was there that she was saved and received the gift of the Holy Spirit. Evelyn sought God with a vengeance on a daily basis. Her children often heard her praying throughout the house, especially when she prepared the family meals. They were usually awakened in the morning by her singing and praising the Lord. She said that God was first in her life above all else, and it showed in her dedication to the church and the favor that God bestowed upon her.

Her obvious anointing and her ability to explain even the most complex of Bible passages awed the members of the church. She could bring a message whereby the Spirit of the Lord reigned as well as any preacher. Because she was so on fire for the Lord, the church members always requested that she be included in teaching or praying. Johnny was extremely jealous and he hated it when the members asked for Evelyn to speak or lead the prayer service. He also hated it when the Spirit of the Lord came down in the service and the members were blessed. As Evelyn went forth in the church services, he sat silently in his seat, glaring, not saying a word; not even an 'Amen.' On one occasion when she finished, he stood up and disputed everything Evelyn had just said. The members were astonished at his blatantly vindictive actions, but none had the nerve to question the pastor of the church. These were country people and they believed in the total dominance of the pastor.

On Sunday mornings, Johnny got up and heartily devoured the breakfast that Evelyn had both paid for and prepared. He never prepared breakfast, or any other meal for that matter. He never helped with the dishes or helped with the dressing of the children; he simply ate, dressed, and left. Since they only had one vehicle, Evelyn and the kids had to either walk to church or get a ride from someone. Rides were few and far between because very few people had enough room for nine extra people. As a result, Evelyn and her eight children made it to church but were always approximately 30 minutes late. After church, Johnny drove home by himself or gave a church member a ride home, leaving Evelyn and the children to walk back home, a distance of several miles.

****

Johnny was a self-taught master builder by trade. There was nothing he

S.E.C.R.E.T.S. VOLUME II by: *Pastor Shirley*

couldn't build or fix. The houses he built were extraordinary. However, none of his carpentry mastery could be seen in his own home. He refused to fix anything and their home was in a terrible state of disrepair as a result. During the winter, his children could not only see the outside through the large cracks in the walls but could feel the cold wind whipping through them as well. The effect was absolutely bone chilling. Johnny was aware of this but still refused to repair the walls or do any work to improve the house. He just huddled closer to the wood-burning stove. He would take the warmest place in the front nearest to the stove and spread out his huge frame to cover its entire length, effectively blocking the heat and preventing it from permeating the rest of the house. Johnny was cruel and self-centered, never caring that his children were cold and relegated to getting what little warmth they could behind his large body.

Evelyn began stuffing cotton and rags into the holes in an attempt to prevent the air from coming in. When it came to the holes that were just too large to stuff, she and her two young sons bundled up and went outside in the snow with hammer and nails, and did their best to patch up the holes and decrease the amount of cold air coming into the house. Johnny watched all of this from his seat in front of the stove. He never got out of his seat to assist and he never offered to help.

After being chilled to the bone winter after winter with the only heat source being a pot-bellied wood-burning stove, Evelyn saved the money she and the kids made from the fields and paid to have a gas line installed in their house. This allowed them to get a gas heater, which provided a wonderful and readily available heat source. This also eliminated the smoky atmosphere that normally accompanied wood-burning stoves, the necessary large amounts of chopped wood, and the long wait for the stove to heat.

****

Johnny was extremely intelligent and had a head for business and numbers. From a young age, he thought like an entrepreneur. He always worked for himself and always made a great deal of money. However, he never used the money that he made to support his large family. It was

Evelyn's responsibility to support their household. Had Johnny treated Evelyn as a partner and listened to her ideas, they could have been very well off, even with eight children. In all actuality, with his building and entrepreneurial skills and Evelyn's money management and eye for future endeavors, they could have been better than well off; they could have been wealthy.

Evelyn was young in age, but God gave her wisdom. She always kept a watchful eye out for land being sold at an inexpensive price or any other investment that she thought would yield a great return. She was ecstatic when she learned that the plot of land right next to their home was going to be sold. Evelyn figured their large family could use the extra space for a large vegetable garden and as extra room for her children to play. She scrimped and saved from her job and the money that the children made in the fields. Then, to make up the final amount, she sold her cow. She was bubbling with joy as she told Johnny about the beautiful vegetables she was going to grow for their family. Johnny listened intently but never uttered a word, his mind working feverishly.

One week before Evelyn was to purchase the land, Johnny came to her and asked to borrow the money she had saved. He said that their vehicle needed to be repaired. When Evelyn objected, he promised to return the money to her in plenty of time for her to purchase the plot of land. Though she was uncomfortable giving him the money, she complied. When the day of the land sale came, Johnny told her that they weren't going to buy the land and that he had stopped her from making a huge mistake. He told her that she was young, green, and ignorant and that she needed to know her place, which was at home having babies, and that she was to leave the family decisions and investments to him.

Evelyn was horrified and hurt by his statement. He had lied to her just to get her to give him the money. He had promised to return her money, money she and the kids had worked hard to save. She had even sold *her* cow! Then he called her green and ignorant because she was thinking of ways to support *their* family, something *he* should've done as the man and head of the house. That land would've allowed her to provide her family with food all year long thanks to her knowledge of canning, freez-

S.E.C.R.E.T.S. VOLUME II by: *Pastor Shirley*

ing, and preserving food. Johnny didn't provide anything for them and now he had blocked what she knew would have been one of the greatest investments they could have ever made. It would have also helped to ease the heavy burden of providing food for her family--a burden which she shouldered alone. As Evelyn cried herself to sleep that night, she swore she would never trust him again.

In the days when people picked cotton for a living, it occurred to Johnny that there was a need for someone to locate workers and ensure that they got to the fields each day. Johnny bought a large, oversized truck and transported the workers to the fields daily. The owner of the field paid him a fee for each worker he brought and at the end the day, he was given an additional percentage of the cotton each worker picked. Johnny, therefore, made two separate fees on each worker and was well paid by the owner of the cotton field for his efforts. In those days, it was unheard of for a black man to make that type of money. Johnny made in a day what it took most others a month to make. This didn't even include the money that Johnny made selling ice-cold sodas at lunchtime to the exhausted, hot workers and field hands. After a particularly hot day, 10-year-old Leslie, one of Johnny's daughters, stood in line with the workers buying sodas. When she got to the front of the line, she said, "Daddy, can I have a soda?"

Johnny looked at his daughter angrily. "I *sell* sodas, I don't give them away. You have to buy one just like everyone else. Do you have any money?"

Leslie shook her head in the negative. *He knows I don't have any money,* she thought.

"Then get out of here, girl. Stop wasting my time. Go on, GIT!" Johnny shouted, totally humiliating Leslie in the process. The other kids in the field found this exchange particularly hilarious and laughed uproariously as they pointed at Leslie. They called her stupid and told her that her father hated her. Leslie ran over to where her siblings stood. Her older brother embraced her and told her it would be ok. Johnny looked at the kids laughing at his daughter and, uncaring, turned away to take care of his next customer, ignoring his kids completely.

****

Evelyn was young and pretty, but Johnny never ever had a kind word for her and never complimented her on anything from her looks to the delicious food she prepared. Evelyn realized early in their marriage that she would have to work if she and her kids were going to eat. She had the heavy weight of taking care of her entire family on her shoulders and it was a heavy burden to bear on her own. She worked as a domestic helper in the affluent White households in the area and the children worked in the cotton fields all summer long. God gave Evelyn favor with the people for whom she worked and they often gave her clothes and food for her family, both of which she greatly needed and appreciated.

The children worked in the cotton fields through the entire month of September. Evelyn was not happy that her children had to miss the first month of school; however, it couldn't be helped. Because Johnny did not contribute to the household finances, they needed the money for the brutal upcoming winter months. But the children hated missing the first month of school for different reasons. First, all yearbook pictures were taken during the month of September; but because they worked during this time, their photographs never appeared in any of their high school yearbooks. Second, seating assignments were given in September. Because all the choice seating had been assigned by the time they began to attend, Evelyn's children were always relegated to the back of the classroom. Evelyn's more mischievous children loved sitting in the back and had no problem with the arrangement; but her more studious children hated being 'miles' from the chalkboard. Last, and most importantly, the lunchroom helpers were selected in September. They were the lucky children who were allowed to help serve the school lunches each day. As payment for their assistance, they received a hot lunch free of charge. Evelyn's children were never selected to help in the cafeteria because they were never there when the selections were being made.

Due to lack of money for food, Evelyn was especially creative in the kitchen. During a particularly lean time, she created a dessert out of flour,

S.E.C.R.E.T.S. VOLUME II by: Pastor Shirley

butter, sugar, milk, and nutmeg. The dessert baked up golden brown and tasted like a cobbler without the fruit.

Evelyn gave each child a heaping portion, put aside a double portion for Johnny, and told the kids not to eat what was left of the dessert because there was just enough for dessert the next day.

However, the next morning, Evelyn rose to find the baking dish empty on the counter. She taught her children to be respectful and obedient; she did not tolerate disobedience. She called the children into the kitchen to question them about the dessert. All were present except Ann Marie, who was in the bathroom. Johnny was also present staring at the children with a sneer on his face while mumbling under his breath. Evelyn asked who had eaten the leftover dessert. The children looked from one to the other with blank expressions on their faces. All of them denied eating the missing dessert. When no one admitted to eating it, she said, "Well since no one will tell the truth, I'll just have to whup everyone. If I whup all of you, I'll get the right one. That dessert didn't just disappear and someone knows what happened to it. Bring me a belt."

Before anyone moved to do her bidding, Ann Marie walked into the room. "What's going on?" She asked. Evelyn told her about the missing dessert and asked her if she had eaten it. "Oh, no, I didn't eat that dessert," Ann Marie said. "Daddy ate it." She had blurted out the answer to her mother's question before she'd even thought about it. Though she had a healthy fear of her father, she was even more afraid of getting a whuppin, especially for something she didn't do.

Every head in the room whipped in Johnny's direction and nine pairs of eyes turned to gape at him. His face had gone from condemnation to shock personified. Though the other children remained silent, they thought there was no way their father had eaten the dessert. The previous night at dinner, the kids had been raving about how good it was; James, the eldest son, had said, "Mmm mmm, this dessert sure is good. Ain't it, Daddy?" Johnny had just grunted and said, "It's alright." Because his response had been short and unenthusiastic, they had all assumed that he hadn't liked it.

Before Johnny could answer, Ann Marie continued, "Last night I got up to use the bathroom and on my way back to bed I saw Daddy sitting on the little red iron stool eating the dessert and warming himself by the pilot light on the gas stove. He had on a t-shirt, which looked like it was too small because it was way up his back and he didn't have no bottoms on. I ran back to bed and hid under the covers hoping that he didn't see me because I didn't want to get in trouble."

At this point, every jaw dropped as they openly gawked at the man before them. Before Ann Marie's statement, he'd sat there looking meanly at the kids, seeming to enjoy the fact that they were about to get into trouble. He'd had no intention of informing Evelyn that he'd eaten the dessert; he was going to allow them to be punished for something he knew he had done. Evelyn and the kids stood motionless and silent with disbelief.

To break the silence, he forced a fake laugh, "Ha ha ha ha." He did not apologize for remaining silent and causing them to almost get into trouble. As a matter of fact, he didn't apologize for anything. Ever.

****

Evelyn had to pay all the household bills; buy food, which Johnny always ate heartily; and buy clothes for the children out of the money that she and the children were able to earn. Though Johnny's pockets were always full, he never contributed. Sometimes when she thought the situation was dire, she would beg him for money. It would take several days of constant arguments before he gave her any financial support and even then it was minimal. When Evelyn asked Johnny for money to buy food,

S.E.C.R.E.T.S. VOLUME II by: *Pastor Shirley*

his favorite answer was, "Woman, I'm not got no money!" Which meant he had no money and that even if he did, he wasn't giving any to her. It truly amazed Evelyn because he never stopped preaching, shouting, or teaching in church, but he absolutely refused to take care of his family.

God had given Evelyn favor. He was her Jehovah Jireh, her provider. She was well known at the utility companies, as she often had to ask them not to turn off her electricity and gas for non-payment. She made payment arrangements and God always blessed her to make the payments. When she tried to talk to Johnny about the large stack of unpaid bills, he completely ignored her and acted as if she was invisible. He continued his demeaning behavior until he wanted sex. After the act was over, Evelyn was just another woman; not his beloved wife and the mother of his children. Because of Johnny's callous attitude, Evelyn derived no pleasure from these numerous couplings. In fact, she hated every time she and Johnny engaged in sex. She certainly couldn't refer to it as lovemaking as there was no type of emotion involved except the need for Johnny's physical release.

Though Johnny rarely gave Evelyn any money for the upkeep of the household, he was quite generous with his brothers and sisters and the members of the church. Johnny always put other people's needs and desires before those of his family. This heartless practice both shamed and hurt Evelyn deeply. Johnny's brother came over at least twice a month for a monetary loan, which Johnny was only too happy to provide. If someone in the church needed money to keep his or her heat on, he readily paid. But, if his wife asked him for money, he said he didn't have any. Yet he was constantly preaching in church about the importance of family while completely ignoring the scripture in I Timothy 5:8, *"But if any provide not for his own, and especially for those of his own house, he hath denied the faith, and is worse than an infidel."*

Johnny knew that his children needed either money to buy lunch at school or food to take for lunch. Though he could have provided either, it seemed he took some type of perverted pleasure in providing neither. As a result, his daughters were so humiliated that they hid in the bathroom stalls at lunchtime, only coming out when it was time for classes to resume. They didn't want the other children to know that they didn't have money to buy lunch, nor had they brought lunch with them.

Evelyn knew that the children had not eaten all day and would be incredibly hungry as a result. Therefore, she came home every day in time to have a hot meal waiting for them when they arrived home from school. They were so hungry that they devoured the food greedily. Evelyn always rushed to feed the kids before Johnny got home. When the children ate with their father, the table was not a happy place and was always full of tension. If the children talked happily or reached for a second helping, Johnny rolled his eyes at, scowled, or yelled at them. Therefore, they were afraid to talk or to ask for a second helping. Johnny loved to eat and he had no problem eating third or even fourth helpings of the food that Evelyn and the kids had worked hard to provide.

****

Johnny was very cruel to his children. He didn't care how they suffered or who saw his treatment of them. He never told them he loved them. He never hugged them or had a kind or encouraging word for them. Kind words were reserved for others, certainly not for his family.

One day after church service, the ice cream man was outside selling his wares. Ann Marie saw her father and excitedly ran up to him. "Daddy, can I have a nickel to buy an ice cream cone?" She asked hopefully.

Johnny looked irritably at his daughter. "Girl, I'm not got no money." Feeling hurt, Ann Marie hung her head and walked away. Once she reached the bottom step, she turned back around hoping that her father might have changed his mind. She then saw her cousin, Jamie, running toward her father. She asked excitedly, "Uncle Johnny, Uncle Johnny, can I have a nickel to buy an ice cream cone?"

To Ann Marie's dismay, her father smiled fondly at Jamie, patted her on the head, and replied, "Sure you can have money for an ice cream cone." He then reached into his pocket and instead of giving her a nickel, which bought a single scoop; he gave her a dime, which bought two scoops. Jamie beamed and squealed. "A dime?! Oh, thank you Uncle Johnny!"

S.E.C.R.E.T.S. VOLUME II by: Pastor Shirley

She ran off passing Ann Marie, screaming how her uncle had given her a whole dime to herself. Johnny saw Ann Marie looking at him, hurt clearly registered on her face. He turned away ignoring her.

Later that week, Leslie overheard her parents discussing an upcoming trip into town in which her father was going to purchase a part for their car and her mother was going to buy food for Sunday dinner. The entire family did not go on these trips into town. Her two older brothers always went because they helped to carry the bags. After that, only one or two girls were permitted to go. Leslie hurried to ask her mother to accompany them before her other siblings found out.

As usual, her father walked way ahead of the family even though they were all going to the same place. It was as if he didn't want to be seen with his family. Leslie studied her one pair of shoes noting that her bare feet were showing through the worn-out soles. She went to her mom and showed her the dilapidated state of her shoes. Evelyn looked at them and sighed. She told her to go ask her father for the money to buy a new pair. When she ran up to where her father was and asked for money to buy a new pair of shoes, he roared, "Girl, I'm not got no money!"

Leslie turned from her father and ran back to her mother. She repeated what her father had said. Evelyn masked her anger and said, "Your father has money. Go ask him again." Leslie didn't want to face her father again, but she did as she was told. He again shouted his famous response about not having any money. Leslie ran back to her mother again. This went on and on with Leslie running back and forth the entire way to town. Finally Evelyn told her daughter, "Your father has money. You keep asking him until he buys you a new pair of shoes." Leslie kept asking her father and showing him the ramshackle state of her current shoes. He finally got sick of her pestering and agreed to buy her a new pair of shoes. He bought her a beautiful pair of white socks and new white sandals. As Leslie admired her beautiful new sandals, she didn't even realize that a Biblical principle had worked on her behalf.

Luke 18:1-78 (KJV), The Parable of the Persistent Widow

"And he spake a parable unto them to this end, that men ought always to pray, and not to faint; Saying, There was in a city a judge, which feared not God, neither regarded man: And there was a widow in that city; and she came unto him, saying, Avenge me of mine adversary. And he would not for a while: but afterward he said within himself, Though I fear not God, nor regard man; **Yet because this widow troubleth me, I will avenge her, lest by her continual coming she weary me**. *And the Lord said, hear what the unjust judge saith. And shall not God avenge his own elect, which cry day and night unto him, though he bear long with them? I tell you that he will avenge them speedily."*

On the way home, Leslie thought about all the begging she'd had to do to get the shoes. She also thought of all the times her father had lied saying he didn't have any money. She was so confused because she had been taught that it was wrong to tell lies and she and her siblings got into big trouble if they lied to their parents. But her father had lied about having money and he was supposed to be saved. She had always been taught that you didn't tell lies if you were saved. Though Leslie was but a child, she wanted to talk to someone about the confusion running amok in her mind. However, she dared not utter a word.

****

Johnny was well liked in the church district and was given another church to oversee, which was approximately 45 minutes away from their home. Sadly, Evelyn had the hardest time getting him to go to the second church and be a pastor to the flock of members. Often, he just wouldn't go, and would end up seeing the members of the second church once a month if

S.E.C.R.E.T.S. VOLUME II by: *Pastor Shirley*

they were lucky. Eventually, Johnny lost the second church because he did not tend the flock. The members were dedicated and just could not continue without a devoted shepherd. This bothered Evelyn greatly. The church members were such sweet people and Johnny had simply deserted them.

Shortly thereafter, when their youngest child was just 5 years old, Johnny walked out on his wife and eight children. He said that he was tired of working and having the responsibility of a large family. This was odd because he'd never supported his wife or family. He went north and was gone for six months. During that time, he preached at any church that would have him, and he sent a grand total of $40.00 to support his large family. Evelyn had been able to feed her family because of the help she received from a caring older couple in the neighborhood. They helped her to plant and tend to a large garden.

While her husband was away, Evelyn was horrified to discover that she was pregnant again. *Oh God no!* She thought. *I don't want another baby by this man. He's left me and his other eight children and he doesn't take care of them when he is home. Oh, Lord what am I going to do?* When Evelyn arrived for work the next day, she was a bit distracted. Noticing that she wasn't her usual bubbly self, her boss asked her what was wrong. Evelyn broke down crying and told her that she was expecting another child. Seeing that this wasn't a happy occasion, her boss offered to pay for an abortion at her family doctor. Evelyn realized that her boss was just trying to help her, but this advice bothered her immensely. Though the last thing she wanted was another child, she had been taught that abortion was wrong. She was saved and she just couldn't bring herself to kill her baby.

That night, Evelyn fell on her knees and poured her heart out to God. She told Him that she didn't want another child by Johnny. She begged God to allow the baby to pass through her body, to close her womb, and to not open it again unless she asked Him to do so. She then left her situation in the hands of God and fell asleep. The next morning, she awoke at daybreak with stomach cramps and an overwhelming need to go to the bathroom. She went to the bathroom and began relieving her bladder.

While doing so, she heard a loud splash and she knew beyond a shadow of a doubt that the baby had passed through her body.

The Holy Spirit told her that her prayers had been answered and He instructed her to read Isaiah 66:7-9: *"Before she was in labor, she gave birth; before her pain came, She delivered a male child. Who has heard such a thing? Who has seen such things? Shall the earth be made to give birth in one day? Or shall a nation be born at once? For as soon as Zion was in labor, She gave birth to her children. 'Shall I bring to the time of birth, and not cause delivery?' Says the LORD"* (KJV).

Evelyn never knew that these scriptures were in the Bible. She praised God for answering her prayer and shutting her womb. She never got pregnant again, nor did she ask God to open her womb.

When Johnny returned home, he was more cruel and insensitive than when he'd left. He promptly told Evelyn that she was not making enough money and that she would have to find another way to bring in more. Evelyn already worked two jobs, did all the household and maintenance chores, paid all the bills for the household, and supported the children. What more could she possibly do? Then Johnny shocked her with his most demeaning comment yet. He said, "You ain't making enough money. Why don't you sell your body to someone else, at least you would be bringing in more money. I don't care and I'll never miss what you sell. There's enough to go around and there'll always be enough for me."

Evelyn whirled around to look at her husband to see if he was joking. There was a hard glint in his eyes and a merciless set to his mouth that conveyed to her in no uncertain terms that, sadly, he wasn't. She looked at him incredulously. She couldn't believe her ears. This was a preacher and her husband telling her to sell her body like a common prostitute to make more money! Of course, *he* didn't consider getting a job. Money was more important to him than his wife or his family.

Evelyn had had enough but she didn't know what to do. She didn't have an education or skills and she had eight children to feed. But, she also had God. She knew one thing—she was not selling her body and she was

S.E.C.R.E.T.S. VOLUME II by: _Pastor Shirley_

never going to backslide for Johnny or anyone else. She also knew that she would no longer continue to subject herself or her children to this man's callous and uncaring attitude. She was sick and tired of this impoverished way of life. They deserved better. They deserved to be loved.

Bewildered and heartbroken, Evelyn was determined to find a way out of this hopeless and destitute situation.

To find out what happened to Evelyn and Johnny Norton, be sure to read S.E.C.R.E.T.S. of the First Ladies, Trilogy. Available soon in a bookstore near you.

Chapter 21

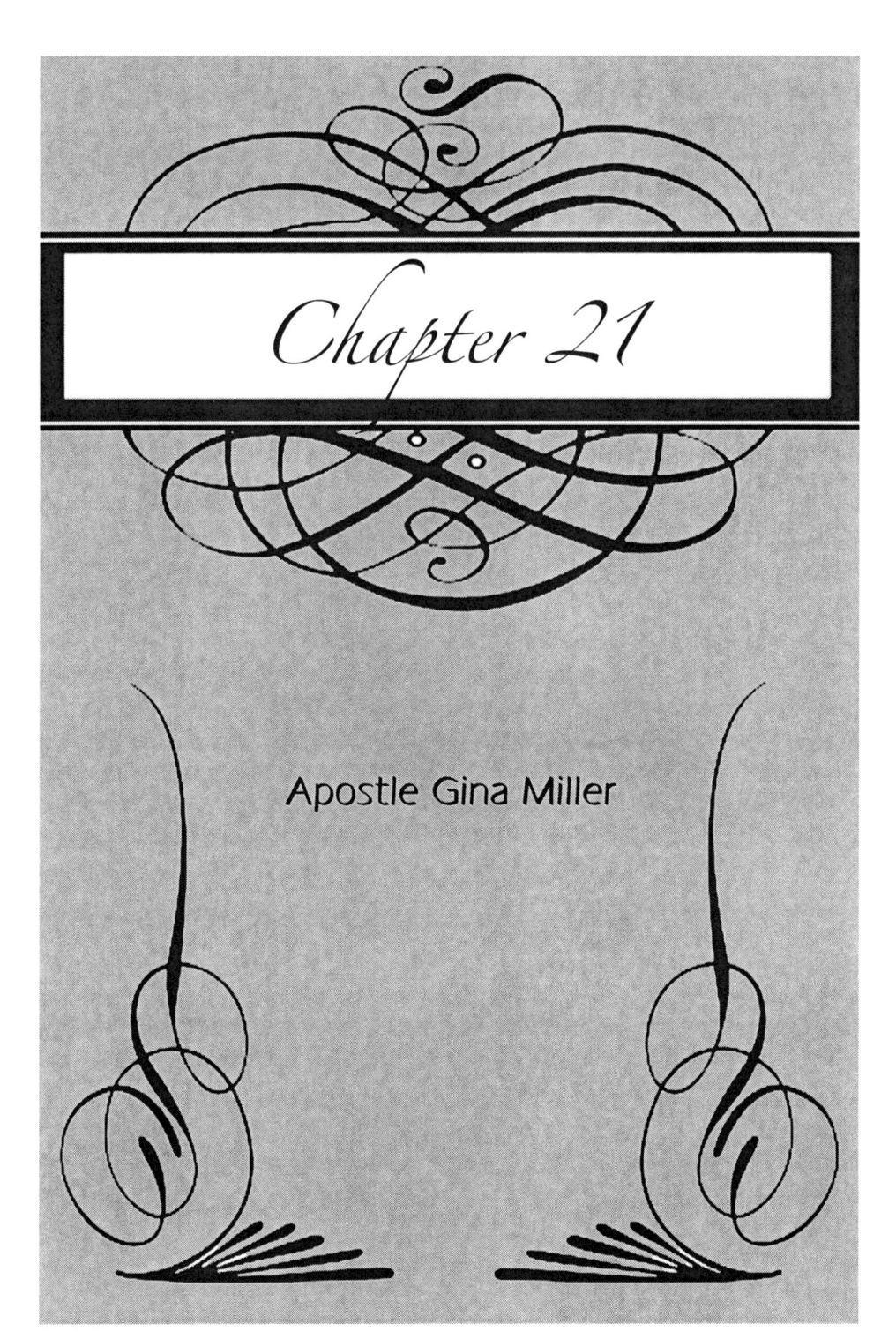

Apostle Gina Miller

S.E.C.R.E.T.S. VOLUME II by: *Pastor Shirley*

Apostle Gina Miller
264 Scenic View Lane

Apostle Gina Miller

Gina…

We've all watched
The reports about cults on the news
Not realizing we may be in jeopardy
As we sit in our very own pews…

What starts off enjoyable
And gives us a warm feeling
Turns ugly, twisted, and even grotesque
And sends our minds reeling

The grip is tight
And hard to break
The sticky, clingy cobweb
Is too dangerous and smothering to take

Caught willingly
Within the binds
But sickening reality hits
And you are out of time!

S.E.C.R.E.T.S. VOLUME II by: _Pastor Shirley_

*A*postle Gina Miller is the pastor and founder of a small ministry. She has been described as a dynamic speaker, an energetic orator, a great prophetess, and a woman of God. The size and growth of her church do not adequately reflect the many years that Apostle Gina, as she is called by her family, friends, and church members, has labored in her ministry.

Apostle Gina is a tall, large-boned, overweight woman. Though she dresses extravagantly, wearing only designer clothes, shoes, and hats, she doesn't dress to flatter her large size. She seems totally unaware of this fashion faux pas and continues to squeeze her large frame into ill-fitting suits and dresses.

Apostle Gina exudes authority and revels in her ability to control and manipulate others. She can be extremely charming if so inclined, but viciously cruel when crossed or angered. She is the lawmaker, the judge, and the jury, and any member who does not abide by her rules—rules which can, and often do, change at a moment's notice—will find him/herself the recipient of her unbridled fury. She thinks nothing of cursing her members, publicly berating them, or doing anything within her power to make their lives a living hell.

Initially, most people are overwhelmed by her engaging personality. She appears to be sweet, loving, and kind, and her demeanor is warm and friendly. But this friendly behavior is a total façade and has been rehearsed and fine-tuned until it unerringly produces the desired results. Apostle Gina's initial behavior is captivating and welcoming. Like a spider spinning her web, she flings the sticky, almost invisible tendrils wide. Unsuspecting victims fall unknowingly into the clinging entanglement, charmed by her friendliness and engaging smile. She allows you to become her best friend. She calls you regularly to check on you and to pray for you. She invites you to lunch and takes you to dinner after service on Sundays. She showers you with gifts and allows you to sit in her special pew at church. If Apostle Gina hasn't deemed anyone deserving of sitting in her special pew, it remains empty regardless of whether the church is crowded to standing room only. She then uses flattery as the icing on the cake, globbing it on until it's dripping off the top and running down the sides. She tells you how wonderful you are and how much God wants to use you. She openly brags about you from the pulpit, esteeming you highly in front of the entire congregation.

And then… And then… And then… IT HAPPENS!

But by then, it's too late, because you're already caught in her web. You struggle to get away, but you soon learn that struggling is futile as the sticky strands of her web envelope you like quicksand; the more you struggle, the deeper you sink. You try to figure out how you got into this mess in the first place; but, to your horror, you learn that your mind is no longer your own. You soon realize that the only action left is total surrender. You succumb, feeling as if you are caught up in a cult.

You are now one of the official church zombies. You smile, pray, and sing when told as you march faithfully to the Apostle's drum. You are told when to come to church, when to go home, when to have an opinion, when and where you are permitted to work, where to shop, what to eat and drink, when to fast, and for how long. You are told *if* you are permitted to have an opinion. You are told if you will be permitted to take a vacation and, if so, where you may go and for how long. To go on vacation without checking with Apostle Gina is unheard of. No one is even permitted to purchase a vehicle or a home without her consent. Her famous line is, "If you can buy luxury items for yourself, you can give more to God's house!"

If you're married, you are told when you are permitted to make love, for how long, and the permissible positions. You are not permitted to make any major decisions concerning your family without first consulting Apostle Gina. If your child needs to be disciplined, you must bring him/her to Apostle Gina's office to discuss the matter. She then decides the correct course of action, and if corporal punishment is required, she is the only person permitted to administer it. The parents must stand to the side and watch helplessly, not permitting a word or sound to escape their mouths for fear of being reprimanded in front of their child. If Apostle Gina is out of town on a speaking engagement, as is often the case, the matter is not permitted to be addressed until her return.

S.E.C.R.E.T.S. VOLUME II by: _Pastor Shirley_

Excommunication is the absolute worst form of punishment because no one in the congregation is permitted to communicate with you in any way until Apostle Gina gives the ok. Depending on how angry she is, this could be a matter of days or even a matter of months! During this time, you are required to come to church, pay your tithes and offering, and be ignored by everyone in the process. It's like being invisible to the entire congregation. You are not permitted to speak, show any emotion, or even participate in the service. You are only allowed to sit and observe in silence until Apostle Gina allows you back into the fold.

If, for any reason, you're absent from a church service during your time of excommunication, Apostle Gina adds two additional weeks for each service missed. Once a member, Sister Claudia, missed a service during her excommunication period due to the death of her mother. Unmoved, Apostle Gina coldly stated that this was no excuse as the church was now her family and was where her loyalty must be focused. She then subjected Sister Claudia to three additional weeks of excommunication.

****

Apostle Gina is extremely moody and volatile. No one knows what type of mood she is going to be in until she mounts the pulpit to preach. If it is to be a good day, the Spirit of the Lord reigns. If it is to be a bad day, she verbally belittles members of the church before her morning message. Everyone breathes a sigh of relief if she doesn't use her sharp tongue to cut someone to shreds. While she preaches, there is no such thing as not getting involved in the service. You are trained to say "Amen!" And "Preach!" And to jump to your feet in support. You must act as if you are having a spiritual conniption or risk the wrath of Apostle Gina. And since no one wants her wrath directed at them, all of her members spend the entire sermon jumping to their feet and screaming, regardless of whether they feel compelled to do so at the urging of the Lord.

Once, during a weekly prayer meeting, the members sat in their seats terrified. Literally. Even the few men who make up the congregation. Apostle Gina ascended the pulpit and it was apparent to everyone that she was angry. The members' hearts sank. This was not going to be a good service for them. She ordered everyone down on his/her knees to pray and began pacing back and forth behind them as they obeyed her command. However, her pacing made the members nervous and their focus was torn between trying to pray and watching Apostle Gina's whereabouts, as she was known to have physically assaulted members in the past. The more she paced back and forth, the more agitated she became. She began to yell at the members.

"Pray! I said pray! STOP WATCHING ME AND PRAY! You better Pray! Don't let me tell you again to stop watching me and pray! Sister Marlene, I better not see the whites of your eyes again! Keep your mind on the Lord! I DON'T HEAR THE REST OF YOU PRAYING! YOU BETTER PRAY AND YOU BETTER PRAY LOUD! I CAN'T HEAR YOU AND GOD CAN'T HEAR YOU!"

The members' voices escalated more out of fear than the moving of the Spirit of the Lord. But this was not good enough. The louder the members prayed, the louder Apostle Gina yelled. "You are not praying! I SAID PRAY! You better keep praying! PRAY LOUD!" And then she finished in a singsong voice, "I CAN'T HEAR YOU!"

This yell/scream/prayerfest went on for over two hours.

It looked and felt like something out of a cult movie classic. The presence of the Lord was nowhere in sight and when Apostle Gina allowed the members to finally end the prayer; they were all hoarse for the next two weeks.

****

S.E.C.R.E.T.S. VOLUME II by: *Pastor Shirley*

Apostle Gina had no qualms about using her members' credit cards for her personal purchases. Though she promised to pay the bills in the beginning, she never paid them in the end. Whenever new members joined the church, she made it a point to spend time with them to determine their worth. When Sister Emily Graystone joined the church, she had AAA credit, numerous credit cards, and she and her husband owned a home with over $30,000 in equity. Apostle Gina immediately took Emily under her wing and invited her everywhere. Over a period of time, Apostle Gina gained her trust and began using Sister Emily's credit cards, promising to pay any charges when the bills arrived. When Apostle Gina brought in a visiting evangelist to run a revival at her church, she flew him in first class, put the evangelist up in an expensive five-star hotel, and hosted elaborate dinners at expensive restaurants, all of which she paid for with Emily's credit cards.

During a casual conversation, Apostle Gina learned that Emily had her husband's full power of attorney while he was serving in the Armed Forces overseas. After deciding how this new information could benefit her, she convinced Emily to mortgage her house, take out the equity, and put the $30,000 into a separate account requiring both Emily's and Apostle Gina's signatures to withdraw funds. Emily was so happy to be a part of Apostle Gina's inner circle that she did this without telling her husband. Though Emily felt a prickle of unease regarding the equity account, she calmed herself by saying that the account required both of their signatures, and that she could, therefore, keep tabs on it.

Apostle Gina never mentioned the credit cards or her intent to pay them. When it came time to pay the credit card bills, Emily was uncomfortable broaching the subject. She decided to pay the minimum amounts due from her household account so that her outstanding credit rating would not be negatively impacted and her husband would remain unaware of the large purchases. When the payment came around the second time, the minimum amounts due were so large that she realized that she would be unable to pay them from her household account as she had done the previous month. She paced back and forth in her kitchen searching for a solution that did not involve Apostle Gina or explaining to her husband that she had loaned their credit cards. Emily finally decided to pay the cards from the equity account. She was so relieved when she came up with this idea that she wanted to whoop with joy.

She called the bank to confirm the balance and was stunned when the teller told her the balance was only $102.36. She told the teller that she must be mistaken and that the account had $30,000 in it. The teller said that the account *once* had a balance of $30,000, but that there had been several sizable withdrawals over the past two months bringing the balance down to $102.36. Emily thanked the teller and hung up the phone. She sat at her kitchen table in shocked disbelief. Had Apostle Gina forged her name to withdraw the funds? Emily just couldn't believe that Apostle Gina had done such a thing, and she concluded that someone else must have stolen the money from the account.

Emily called Apostle Gina and asked to see her immediately as it was extremely important. In one hour, she was granted an audience at her home office. As Emily drove to Apostle Gina's house, she mentally calculated the total of Apostle Gina's expenditures. She was shocked and very uncomfortable at the large sum. At this point, Apostle Gina had charged over $22,000 in goods and services in addition to the $30,000 in the equity account.

Apostle Gina listened to Emily go on and on about the credit card charges and the money that was missing from the equity account. She was annoyed that Emily had the nerve to ask her about payment. Apostle Gina held up hand up to Emily thereby signaling that she wished her to stop talking. She sat quietly for a moment and then decided to keep Emily waiting a bit longer, knowing that the silence was working on her composure. She picked up a letter on her desk and began reading it, seemingly completely unaware of Emily's presence. When she had finished reading the letter and jotting down a few notes across the top, she fixed Emily with an intense stare. When she spoke, her voice was cold, clipped, and had a definite edge.

"First of all I am surprised that you would take time out of my busy schedule to question me about paying some stupid credit cards bills." Emily

S.E.C.R.E.T.S. VOLUME II by: *Pastor Shirley*

gasped loudly and her eyes widened in shock and surprise. Apostle Gina continued. "Regarding the equity account, no one mistakenly took money from the account. I used the funds to the glory and honor of God. You were never around when I needed the money so I just signed your name. I wasn't aware I needed your permission to use the funds since you put them into the account for my use. The cards will be taken care of and we will talk further about the equity account, although I don't have the time to do so now. I have an appointment."

Apostle Gina rose to her feet; clearly signaling that the meeting was over. Emily stood, excused herself, and walked dumbfounded to her car. Apostle Gina had told her that the cards would be taken care of. However, she never said when and never brought the subject up again.

When the third month rolled around, Apostle Gina had charged an additional $14,000 in goods and services and had not made one single payment. The bill collectors had begun calling about the credit card payments. To Emily's utter horror, her husband, Jacob, had returned and intercepted a call. After speaking with the rude customer service rep, he hung up and began asking questions about the extremely large purchases. A huge fight ensued when Emily told him how much had been charged and by whom. Jacob forbade any further charges and told Emily to talk to the pastor about getting the bills paid immediately. Emily agreed, but was secretly scared by the prospect of facing Apostle Gina again. She hadn't told Jacob that she didn't even have the cards in her possession. Apostle Gina had asked her for them months ago, saying it would be easier for her to make travel arrangements if she had the cards on hand. Emily had felt uneasy about that, but had turned them over nonetheless.

The following Sunday, Emily waited nervously outside the pastor's office. Apostle Gina saw her waiting and knew that she had come about the credit card payments. After a ridiculously lengthy wait, during which time she changed her clothes and ate a leisurely three-course dinner, she finally called Emily in. Avoiding eye contact, Emily quickly blurted out what she'd come to tell Apostle Gina before she lost her nerve. She told her about the fight she'd had with Jacob and how upset he'd become. She explained that she needed the cards returned to her and that they had to be paid in full immediately.

Apostle Gina was outraged. She jumped up from behind the desk and began yelling. "How dare you!" She grabbed a beautiful glass angel paperweight off her desk and threw it against the wall above Emily's head, smashing it into what seemed like a million pieces. Emily's eyes were as big as dinner plates and she was visibly shaking in her seat. "How dare you waste my time with these…these…trivial matters! I NEVER said I would pay those bills and I don't even understand your presence in my office taking up my extremely valuable time when I need to be consecrating before God and gettin' a word for my evening sermon."

Emily paled and gasped loudly, gaining Apostle Gina's further anger. "Paying those bills are YOUR job. You hear me, YOUR JOB!" Apostle Gina punctuated each word with a finger in Emily's face.

Apostle Gina's face was twisted in rage. "You ought to be jumping up and down to help your pastor who is doin' the work of the Lord night and day. There is no other pastor in this city who works like I do. No other pastor who gives as much to her congregation. All that money was used to further God's message of deliverance to the masses. None of it was used for personal items." Emily knew that this was untrue, as she had viewed the numerous statements that included hair appointments, spa treatments, clothes, a vacation, and even Apostle Gina's household food and utilities. However, she dared not bring that up.

Suddenly, Apostle Gina strode to the office door and flung it open with such force that the doorknob made a hole in the opposite wall. She screamed for her secretary, Betty, to clean up the glass in her office. Shortly thereafter, Betty shyly entered with a hand broom and dustpan and hurried over to sweep up the annihilated paperweight. Apostle Gina never broke her stride or paused in her verbal tirade. After another few minutes, she flopped down in her office chair and snatched up her purse. She rifled through her purse, retrieved the credit cards, and flung them in Emily's face

"Get the hell out of my office!" Apostle Gina screamed. Completely humiliated, Emily stooped to pick the cards up and then ran from the pas-

S.E.C.R.E.T.S. VOLUME II by: Pastor Shirley

tor's office in tears.

Sadly, Apostle Gina never paid Emily's credit cards even after repeated requests. Emily not only lost her credit cards, but also her home, her AAA credit, and her husband. To add further insult to injury, Emily was excommunicated and forbidden to attend Apostle Gina's church. The congregation was forbidden to associate with her in any way, and was told that she was a troublemaker and a worker of witchcraft. Because Apostle Gina had carefully cultivated an almost cult-like fear of witchcraft and anyone associated with it, the members were literally afraid to even look at Emily.

It was a very low time for Emily. She hit rock bottom and, for the first time in her life, had thoughts of suicide. After much therapy, Emily realized that while attending Apostle Gina's church, she'd lived her life like some kind of drugged-out robot, a cog in the wheel of an outlandish cult masquerading as a church. She had lived in fear of a woman who maintained tightfisted control over her members, and who blatantly brandished and abused her authority. The one thing she couldn't understand was why she had been unable to see the church for what it was and what it wasn't at the time.

****

Apostle Gina's members catered to her every need and waited on her hand and foot. They:

>   Cleaned her house
>   Cooked her meals
>   Drove her back and forth to church and local appointments
>   Drove her to speaking engagements all over the country
>   Washed her car twice a week
>   Bathed, walked, and cleaned up after her three dogs
>   Cut her grass and weeded her flower beds
>   Pruned her trees and kept her yard leaf free
>   Ran her errands
>   Shopped for her groceries
>   Double washed her clothes
>   Changed the linen on her bed daily

Painted the inside and outside of her house every two years
Drew her bathwater
Dressed and undressed her

She felt that it was the least they could do since she shouldered the burden of leading the church and shepherding the flock.

Her cook, Sister Lola, arrived at Apostle Gina's home every day at 4am to begin baking fresh bread, rolls, and dessert items. Everything had to be made from scratch. Apostle Gina permitted nothing coming from a box or a can to be served on her table. Vegetables had to be fresh or, as a very last resort, frozen. Breads and desserts had to be homemade.

Sister Lola had worked hard all day in order to have the meal ready by Apostle Gina's specified dinner hour, which changed according to her mood. She proudly entered Apostle Gina's bedroom, barely managing to shoulder the weight of the serving tray. She proceeded to unload the items onto her dining table. She had made a mix of collards and cabbage with seasoned ham hocks; sweet potatoes brimming with butter, brown sugar, and Madagascar vanilla; creamy four-cheese macaroni and cheese with a crunchy topping of bread crumbs, herbs, and bacon; a steaming plate of crunchy fried okra; a delectable bowl of chicken and dumplings; two types of cornbread—regular and spicy southwestern; light, fluffy rolls (she never knew whether Apostle Gina would want rolls or cornbread); chess pie; red velvet cake; coconut cake; peach tea; and raspberry tea. As she unloaded the items, the smell of the perfectly prepared food permeated the room. When she was finished, she assisted Apostle Gina with her chair, spread the napkin over her lap, and stood off to the side, desperately hoping for a word of praise for her hard work. Sadly, it was not forthcoming.

Apostle Gina said nothing as she studied the food intently with a critical eye. She gave a barely perceptible nod to Sister Lola, indicating that she was ready to approve the preparation of the food and that she could serve her a small helping of each item. She picked her fork up and tasted the macaroni and cheese. Her blood-curdling scream rent the air as she

S.E.C.R.E.T.S. VOLUME II by: Pastor Shirley

jumped out of her chair, sending the entire table of food crashing to floor. It splattered all over the floor, even hitting the wall and draperies.

With eyes blazing she yelled, "I am not a heathen and I do not eat my food LUKEWARM! My food must be hot or cold just as God requires us to be in Revelations 3:15 and 16. Now you have 30 minutes to prepare my food correctly and present it to me in a manner befitting a woman of God."

With those words, she sailed out of the room screaming as she went. Sister Lola's eyes filled with tears and she began sobbing as soon as Apostle Gina cleared the doorway. Her beautiful meal was all over the walls and the floor. She headed for the kitchen not knowing if she could prepare the food in only 30 minutes and was utterly terrified as a result. On her way to the kitchen, she stopped in the living room to tell the two maids, also church members, that Apostle Gina's room needed to be cleaned up immediately. They nodded silently and tried to give her what they hoped were looks of encouragement. They'd heard Apostle Gina's tirade and though they felt sorry for her, they were glad that they weren't the targets of her anger—this time.

****

Many of Apostle Gina's members are uneducated and have few, if any, marketable employment skills. Therefore, 90% of her congregation supports their families on earnings equivalent to minimum wage. They reek of poverty, lack, and destitution.

Since the members who spend seven days per week tending to Apostle Gina's every need don't have outside jobs, she gives them just enough money to pay their rent, utilities, and to buy food. She sees no reason to give them extra funds for clothing and other personal needs, making the members totally dependent upon her for their survival. Apostle Gina never allows them to forget that she is the one who pays their rent and supports them. Because they live in constant fear of losing her favor and financial support, they strive to please her in every way.

Apostle Gina's secretary monitors all members' bank accounts to ensure that they pay their tithes to the church *first*. It doesn't matter to Apostle

Gina that their rent is due or that their children need shoes and clothes. Tithe paying comes first. Period. Apostle Gina teaches her members to prioritize the church over their family's financial needs.

When Apostle Gina's anniversary celebration rolls around, each adult member is expected to pay a $1,000 love token. Husbands and wives are required to pay $1,000 each and it doesn't matter to Apostle Gina how they get it, even if they have to work an extra job in order to meet the financial obligation. Of course, they must pay their tithes on the additional income. However, absence from church to raise the anniversary pledge is always approved. Woe be to those who do not pay! Apostle Gina has thrown members out of the church for failing to meet the anniversary obligation.

Concerned about his ability to meet the anniversary pledge, Brother Olson scheduled an appointment with Apostle Gina to request a reduced pledge. When he arrived at his scheduled time, Sister Betty was at her desk typing a letter. As he walked in, she glanced up and said, "The pastor is busy."

Brother Olson smiled and said, "Well good aft'noon, Sis Betty, how you been?" Sister Betty had the decency to look sheepish as she paused in her typing to respond, "I'm fine Brother Olson. Jus' fine."

"I have an appointment with the past—"

"The pastor is busy. What's your problem?"

Brother Olson looked around uncomfortably to see who else was waiting in the outer office. As usual, there were several other people milling around. He cleared his throat, leaned closer to the desk, and dropped the volume of his voice as he explained, "I feel a little funny talkin' to you 'bout this, 'specially out here around ev'body, but here goes. I been out of work for six whole months and I jus' got me another job. I'm jus' now beginning to get back on my feet. I'm already four months behind on my mortgage payment and if I don't make a payment soon, the mortgage company will foreclose on my house. If that happen then me, my wife, and my five kids will be put out on the street. I don't have no $2,000 for the anniversary pledge. I can't pay that, put food on my table, and keep

S.E.C.R.E.T.S. VOLUME II by: *Pastor Shirley*

my family from living on the street. I dun borrowed from ev'body I know and I been able to get a total of $500. I'll cheerfully give that to the pastor and work on havin' my pledge for next year." Brother Olson finished his explanation and looked at the secretary hopefully.

Sister Betty turned from her computer and looked Brother Olson directly in the eye. "Although I'm sorry to hear about your financial problems, it really doesn't change anything. You have to pay the $2,000 anniversary pledge and trust God to supply your needs."

This explanation just didn't seem reasonable, especially since Sister Betty was not the pastor. He was aware that she had quite a bit of power where church issues were concerned, but he needed to speak to someone who had the authority to reduce the pledge, and the only person he knew who could do that was the pastor. He cleared his throat again and asked to speak directly to Apostle Gina. Sister Betty's eyebrows raised in surprise. She got up from her desk, knocked on the office door, and waited to be asked to enter the pastor's private domain. After disappearing for about five minutes, Sister Betty returned bearing a message from Apostle Gina. "I explained your situation to Apostle Gina and she told me to tell you that your personal problems are not her problem or concern. She said you'd better come up with the $2,000 anniversary pledge even if you have to sell some personal items to do it."

Brother Olson nodded, hung his head, and left the office. He paid his mortgage to keep a roof over his family's head and took out a loan using his truck as collateral to pay his anniversary pledge. He was still paying the loan back and prayed that he didn't get laid off again in the meantime. However, Brother Olson had no idea how he was going to pay next year's anniversary pledge.

****

Bridget Mallory's sister, Mia, was a member of Apostle Gina's church. For months, Mia had been asking her sister to attend church with her. Each time Mia asked her, she declined. After months of friendly pestering, Bridget felt her sister would nag her to death if she didn't agree, so she finally said yes. Mia was thrilled that her sister had finally accepted her invitation. She even offered to pick Bridget up. On the way to church, Mia chatted excitedly about the church, the members, and, most importantly, Apostle Gina.

It was a lively service, the choir was outstanding, and Apostle Gina delivered the sermon in top oratorical form. Bridget was so inspired by all that she had seen and heard that she decided to join Apostle Gina's church. However, she decided to wait a couple of weeks before doing so. Bridget treated Mia to dinner after the service to catch up on "sister talk" and so that she could tell Mia of her decision to join the church. Mia momentarily forgot where she was and squealed with joy, drawing the startled stares of several diners. Bridget asked if she could attend the evening service with Mia and if they could return a little early so that she could meet Apostle Gina. Mia was ecstatic and grinned like a simpleton throughout the remainder of their dinner.

When they entered Apostle Gina's outer office, her secretary was nowhere in sight. *That's odd,* thought Mia, *Sister Betty is always on her job.* Apostle Gina's office door was open and Mia and Bridget heard yelling and screaming coming from within. To her utter horror and embarrassment, Mia realized it was Apostle Gina's distinctive voice doing all the yelling and that her tirade included a plethora of profanity. She could also hear loud, heart-wrenching sobs. Mia cringed at the crude words coming from the office. Then she heard Apostle Gina scream, "If you EVER embarrass me again, I will kill you! YOU. GO. STRAIGHT. TO. HELL!"

Then they heard the unmistakable ring of flesh against flesh. Someone screamed and a second later, Sister Betty bolted out of the pastor's office crying loudly and holding her left cheek. She looked utterly terrified and there was a large handprint on her face. It was obvious that Apostle Gina had slapped her quite hard judging by the dark shading of the bruise. Apostle Gina screeched from the office, "Shut that loud cryin' up and git yourself together. People will start arriving soon for the evening service!"

As Sister Betty reached for her purse, she noticed Mia and her sister staring at her in absolute shock. She was so embarrassed that she ran past

S.E.C.R.E.T.S. VOLUME II by: _Pastor Shirley_

them to the bathroom and slammed the door behind her. Upon hearing the door slam, Apostle Gina stormed to her office door, presumably to continue yelling, when she saw Mia and Bridget now staring at her. No one moved or uttered a single word for what seemed like an eternity.

"What the hell are you doing sneaking around my office, Mia? And who is that with you?"

Mia was completely mortified. She was certain that a higher level of humiliation and shame did not exist. Not only was her pastor cursing and physically assaulting church members, but to her utter shame, her sister had witnessed it all. She could barely draw air into her lungs, let alone carry on a conversation. Apostle Gina stood, hands on ample hips, awaiting an answer.

"Well?" She demanded, her voice dripping with venom and her eyes filled with fury.

"Uh…Apostle Gina… I um…was…um…bringing my sister, Bridget, to meet you," Mia said gesturing to her sister. "I have been trying to get her to visit the church for some time and she finally said yes. She was impressed with the service and asked to meet you."

Apostle Gina threw Bridget the same withering stare that had intimidated many a person—men and women alike—and had even caused them to cower. She looked her up and down and folded her hands over her generous chest. As she spoke, she never looked at Mia, but continued glowering at Bridget. "Even an idiot can see this is not a good time for any meetings. If you want me to meet your sister, make an appointment." She then turned her scowl to Mia. "And next time, don't be sneaking around in the shadows tryin' to eavesdrop on confidential church matters. What I say in my office is none of your business." With that, Apostle Gina unfolded her arms, stepped back, and slammed the door in their faces.

Mia hurriedly ushered Bridget out of the outer office and into the sanctuary. However, Bridget kept on walking through the sanctuary, out the front door, and into the parking lot. The entire time, Mia walked behind her trying in vain to explain to Bridget that Apostle Gina was a good person and that she was just having a bad day. Bridget turned to her sister and told Mia that she would never attend her church again and that any pastor who could curse her members and put her hands on them was certainly not a pastor she could respect nor one whose church she would join. As they got into the car, Bridget kept a running dialog about all that she had just witnessed. But as Mia pulled out of the church parking lot, she was engrossed in her own thoughts. Although she'd told Bridget that the pastor was having a bad day, she had heard Apostle Gina curse out more members than she cared to admit. She had even been cursed out once for not paying her tithes on time and she had never done that again. Mia dropped her sister off and returned to the church for evening service. Though Bridget told her she was crazy for returning to the church, Mia didn't have the courage to admit that she was afraid *not* to attend.

When it was time for the evening sermon, Apostle Gina mounted the pulpit, took over the service, and preached one of the liveliest sermons the church had ever heard.

****

Apostle Gina never traveled alone. Six to eight women from the church accompanied her at all times. Apostle Gina's travel companions were always clothed in a dowdy and homely manner, while Apostle Gina was adorned like a lavishly ill-fitted queen. Apostle Gina purposefully orchestrated this drastic contrast in apparel as she absolutely refused to be upstaged by her traveling companions. The focus must be on her. Her suits and hats were flamboyant and filled with feathers, rhinestones, fur, or sequins.

Her travel companions were not married. They lived in Apostle Gina's house, and were at her beck and call 24 hours a day. They carried her luggage, unpacked and ironed her clothes, drew her bath water, bathed her, dried her, dressed her, styled her hair, carried her Bible, acted as her armor bearers, and attended to any other need that she may have had.

One day, while attending a state conference, Bishop Zinc looked up as Apostle Gina and her entourage entered. He leaned over and whispered

S.E.C.R.E.T.S. VOLUME II by: Pastor Shirley

to Bishop Reynolds, "Here comes Apostle Gina Miller and her band of lesbians." Bishop Reynolds stopped reading his program and looked at Apostle Gina. His gaze swung back to Bishop Zinc and he asked, "What did you say?"

"You heard me, Reynolds," Bishop Zinc responded, "Apostle Gina Miller is a lesbian and that's why she always travels with all those unmarried women. She doesn't allow them to date or have male companionship in any way. I know all of this for a fact because one of those young ladies is my niece." Bishop Reynolds looked positively scandalized. He stared as Apostle Gina's travel companions placed a pillow on the bench on which she would sit and a small stool on the floor on which she would rest her feet.

Bishop Zinc continued. "My sister called begging me to help her get my niece out of the clutches of that woman. I drove my sister down there and we picked her up, practically kidnapping her in the process. We prayed for her night and day and even got her into counseling to help her get free of her experiences during her time with Apostle Miller. She did pretty well for a while and told us everything that went on in that retched house.

"She said Apostle Miller took her in and offered her a place to stay. Then she turned her into a lesbian. She said that each of the women take turns sleeping with Apostle Gina and the others patiently await their opportunity. It's almost like the Mormons who believe in having five or six wives. All the women get along well and work together, each competing for the attention of the Queen Bee. The women are happy to be in her presence and overjoyed to receive the pittance she calls a weekly allowance. No one objects or complains about the amount. They all want to please her and live in constant fear of disappointing her."

"What happened to your niece? How is she doing now?" Bishop Reynolds whispered conspiratorially. Bishop Zinc snorted disgustedly, causing others sitting closer to them to look at him questioningly. Not wanting to draw further attention to himself, he leaned closer to Bishop Reynolds to continue his story. Bishop Zinc's breath was so revolting that Bishop Reynolds felt the hair in his nostrils curl and his eyes begin to water. But what the man was saying was so intriguing that he leaned in closer and tried not to flinch as Bishop Zinc continued to speak.

"My niece, Katie, is back with Apostle Miller. Somehow she found out where Katie was and began calling her behind our backs. Before we knew what was happening, Katie snuck out one night and never came back. She called my sister after arriving at Apostle Miller's house and told her to stay away from her and stay out of her business. We can't even talk to her to make sure she is ok. Whenever we call, whoever answers the phone says Katie refuses to talk with us. I don't think Katie has received any of our many messages. But, what can we do? Katie is 21 and she has made her choice. The only reason Katie isn't here today is because they knew I'd be here." Bishop Zinc hung his head, obviously worried about his niece. His anger returned and he said, "I know what I'm talking about and I don't want to hear anything she has to say. I certainly don't want to hear her preach."

Bishop Reynolds scrutinized Apostle Gina closely. She didn't look like a lesbian to him, but then he didn't know what lesbians looked like. He made a mental note to watch her closely and to tell his wife this unbelievable tale the first chance he got.

****

One hot summer Sunday, a new member, Brother Steven Price, joined the church, much to the delight of the single women. Brother Steven was rare because he was a **HESTD** (pronounced hee-stud)—**H**andsome, **E**mployed, **S**ingle, **T**all, and **D**ark.

The single women in the church never had a chance with Brother Steven because Apostle Gina had plans for him. She swooped down and plucked him into her inner circle before anyone else had a chance to get to know him. True to her charming and beguiling ways, Brother Steven was unprepared for the sheer force of Apostle Gina's magnetism. He was charmed immediately, not realizing that her actions had been solely designed with a purpose in mind.

S.E.C.R.E.T.S. VOLUME II by: *Pastor Shirley*

Apostle Gina had decided long ago that she wanted a baby to call her own. However, the thought of allowing a man to touch her in any way both appalled and nauseated her, and she knew that she would never let that happen no matter how badly she wanted a baby. But now that Brother Steven had come along…

She had waited until she had just the right woman. Katie, Bishop Zinc's niece, was just the woman she was looking for. Katie was young; drug and disease free (she'd sent Katie to have a battery of tests done to prove it); and had no history of debilitating family illnesses. Katie was also extremely beautiful, graceful, and easy to manipulate. All were necessary to put her plan into action.

Katie had no problem catching Brother Steven's attention. She was, after all, quite beautiful. Apostle Gina openly pushed the pair together every chance she got. However, unbeknownst to Steven, Katie had been instructed by Apostle Gina to have sex with him as often as possible until she became pregnant.

When Katie was first given this directive, she gasped and her eyes widened in shock. Apostle Gina knew all her women well and had accurately predicted Katie's response. She smiled, patted Katie's hand reassuringly and said, "You have my blessing to do this and it will please me immensely. Just like in the Bible when Naomi showed Ruth how to get her man, I am showing you how to get me a baby. I want you to have sex with Brother Steven as often as possible until you get pregnant. I want it understood between you and me that this is the first and last time you will ever have sex with a man. You are not to enjoy your sexual encounters with him in any way, though I want you to make him think you are having the time of your life." Seeing Katie's look of confusion, Apostle Gina explained in a voice more suited to addressing a six year old. "If he thinks you're having a good time, he'll continue having sex with you until you get pregnant instead of avoiding you like the plague because he can't satisfy you. This is your duty and you must perform it for me. It will make me happy and I know you want to please your pastor, don't you?"

Upon hearing that having sex with Brother Steven would please Apostle

Gina, Katie agreed without a moment's hesitation. "I'll do whatever you want me to do, Apostle Gina. I love you. And more than anything else, I want to please you."

Apostle Gina hugged Katie and kissed her on the lips. "Go grab your purse, Katie. I'm going to take you shopping for some sexy new lingerie and new clothes. After you get pregnant, you can wear all your new stuff for me." Katie scampered off with a big smile on her face like a kid whose parent was about to take her to McDonald's.

Three months later, Katie was proud to inform Apostle Gina that she was indeed pregnant. Apostle Gina jumped out of the bed and enfolded Katie in a huge bear hug. She motioned Katie off her feet, into her special recliner, and tilted the chair back so that the footrest extended under Katie's feet. She then excitedly called the other inhabitants of her house into her room and proudly announced that she was going to have a baby of her own and that all of Katie's duties from now until after the baby was born were to be equally divided among the other ladies. Katie was to be pampered and catered to during this time.

The other ladies were outwardly happy for Katie, but inwardly envious of Katie's good luck. Though they were excited about the prospect of having a child in the house, they knew that whoever was lucky enough to give Apostle Gina a child would always have a special place in the household. As the "first wife," Katie would also have a special position in Apostle Gina's heart.

After dismissing everyone, she climbed back into her oversized four-poster bed and beamed at Katie. Then she turned serious. "I want you to understand that this is my baby, not yours. You will have no dealings whatsoever with this child. Do you understand that?" Katie nodded her agreement. Apostle Gina pulled out some papers for Katie to sign legally relinquishing all parental rights to the baby. Katie fully understood the situation before she became pregnant and signed the papers with no hesitation and without reading them. Apostle Gina's face split into a loving grin. She folded the papers, put them into her safe, and called everyone back in to discuss the location and decoration of the nursery.

S.E.C.R.E.T.S. VOLUME II by: *Pastor Shirley*

The following Sunday, Apostle Gina mounted the pulpit clearly angry. She stood quietly for a few moments making everyone uncomfortable. She began talking. "The enemy has crept into our camp and I'm going to expose that devil today." Her gaze swept over the congregation. The members cringed, hoping that her gaze did not land on them.

Apostle Gina then pointed to Brother Steven and Katie. "Stand up you two!" she ordered thunderously. They stood to their feet and eyed each other nervously. "Come up to the front of the church and let everyone look at you." As if their attention would be anywhere else at that moment. "These two people have sinned against God and against me. They have been engaging in lewwwwdddd sexual acts." Apostle Gina put a great deal of emphasis on the word lewd, drawing it out unnecessarily. "Yes, they have been committing fornication on a continual basis. They have broken God's law. FALL ON YOUR KNEES AND REPENT NOW, YOU SINNERS!" Brother Steven and Katie eagerly fell to their knees in front of the church with their heads bowed. Apostle Gina paced back and forth, continuing her rampage.

"As a result of their lewd activities, Katie is pregnant." The church gasped in shock and Brother Steven raised his head to look at Katie in surprise. When it was apparent that Katie wasn't going to look at him, he lowered his head again. "Katie came to me and confessed and she has repented to God for her sin and as a result I am not going to put her out of the church. However, Brother Steven never came to me and he never admitted his wrongdoing. Therefore, I am going to put him out of the church." Apostle Gina stopped pacing and pointed her index finger at Brother Steven. "You are never permitted to come back here ever again. Is that understood?"

Brother Steven looked up from his place on the floor and nodded his agreement. There were tears in his eyes. He had fallen head over heels in love with Katie and had been totally unaware that she was pregnant. Whenever he'd offered to use protection, Katie had persuaded him not to do so saying that she had been on the pill. He'd realized a few days prior that Katie was the one for him and that he wanted to marry her and make her his wife. But under the current circumstances, he doubted he would ever get the chance to be alone with Katie again, much less talk to her privately.

Katie listened and inwardly cringed. She had never expected to fall in love with Brother Steven, but she had. And, though she had been instructed not to enjoy her sexual liaisons with him, she had indeed done so. She had been a virgin and knew nothing of lovemaking. But, Brother Steven had proved to be an accomplished, caring, and generous lover. That's why she waited an extra month before she told Apostle Gina that she was pregnant. Even now, being this close to him, she could feel her body burning for him. She felt so sorry for the humiliation being heaped on him that she thought her heart would surely break into a million pieces. Apostle Gina had said nothing about embarrassing the man to death in front of the whole church when she'd instructed her to have sex with him. She wished she could save him from this public humiliation, but she dared not say a word. She was literally afraid of Apostle Gina and didn't want to upset her in any way. So she kept her head down, her eyes tightly closed, and prayed that the persecution of Brother Steven would end soon.

Apostle Gina's loud voice boomed from the pulpit. "LEAVE NOW, SINNER! YOU ARE NOT WELCOME HERE!" Brother Steven stumbled to his feet and went back to where he'd been sitting to retrieve his Bible and car keys. As he walked down the aisle toward the door, mortified shame infiltrating every pore of his being, Apostle Gina led the church in a chant.

"Go Sinner Go, Go!"
"Go Sinner Go, Go!"
"Go Sinner Go, Go!"

To find out what happened to Apostle Gina Miller, be sure to read S.E.C.R.E.T.S. of the First Ladies, Trilogy. Available soon in a bookstore near you.

Chapter 22

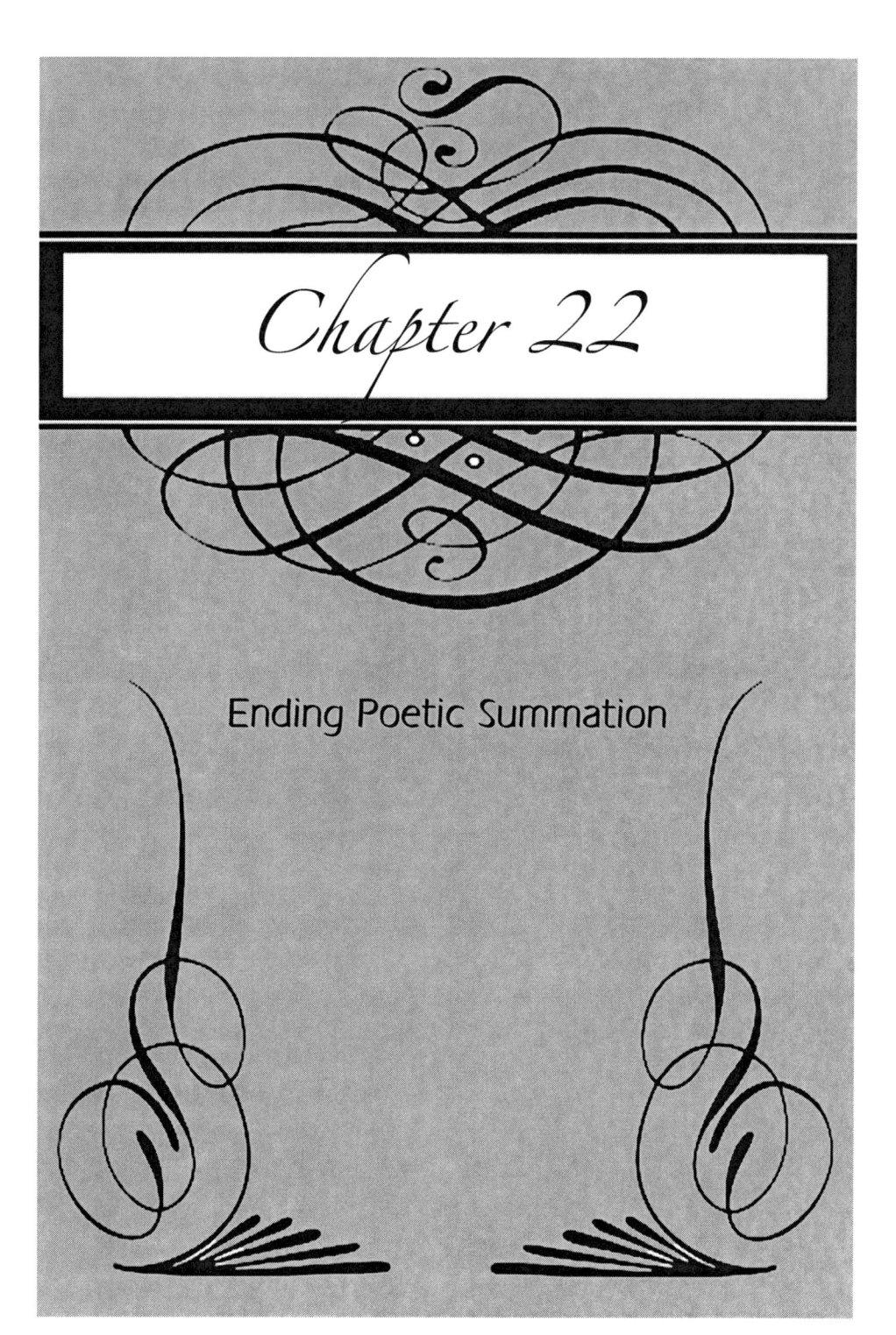

Ending Poetic Summation

S.E.C.R.E.T.S. VOLUME II by: *Pastor Shirley*

Ending Poetic Summation

So now the stories have been told,
tales of brazen behavior,
so big, so bold,
Volume 1 and Volume 2 closes
and now we await Volume 3!
To discover the outcome
of the Ladies of this Trilogy…

We watched Maritza
simmer, snap, then lay in wait
wondering while in her shooting spree,
who's life she will take

We gasped when Ashley
rocked Sarah's world,
explaining things big and small,
almost keeled over
when Sarah heard Xavier's obscene tryst
within her own bedroom walls.

Ending Poetic Summation

Many a teary eye was dabbed
concerning Eileen,
pondering if Roy, when confronted,
would pass out or come clean

Viola is a cut-throat beast,
and truly a mess!
Sharon… please deal
with Viola wisely,
this is *not* merely a test.

We witnessed Trudy
go into shock,
losing her mind while losing her poise,
after discovering Robert
is a pedophile and had a thing for little boys

S.E.C.R.E.T.S. VOLUME II by: _Pastor Shirley_

Anita's story
set it off
and is one you can't ignore,
Tell us!
With one fell swoop of her knife,
what body part is going to hit the floor?!

Stephanie knows she is one of twelve
and has an action plan of what to do
But Benson was informed
and now makes plans
to pull off the ultimate coup

Maggie's fury blazed
as she lunged and
called the mistress a guttersnipe,
Provoked beyond rational thought
as she wielded a deadly rusty pipe

Ending Poetic Summation

Now we've read it all,
but what's their fate?
The suspense is more
than any of us can take
but we know that when
it's all said and done….
We look to God and we must say…
"Thy Kingdom come,
Thy will be done"…

So now I lay me down to sleep
Awaiting Volume 3 to see
what S.E.C.R.E.T.S. they will reveal or keep…
Bring on S.E.C.R.E.T.S. TRILOGY!

To find out what happened to all the First Ladies,
be sure to read
S.E.C.R.E.T.S. of the First Ladies, TRILOGY
coming in 2012!

Section 3

Reference

Forgiveness

S.E.C.R.E.T.S. VOLUME II by: *Pastor Shirley*

FORGIVENESS

*For if ye forgive
men their trespasses,
your heavenly Father will
also forgive you…*

Matthew 6:14

"The strongest poison to the human spirit is the inability to forgive oneself or another person. Forgiveness is then no longer an option but a necessity for healing." —Caroline Myss

*I*f you live long enough, someone whom you trust will eventually hurt you. When the pain begins to feel unbearable, it changes you, how you interact with other people, and, if left unchecked, will ultimately consume your entire life.

The singular characteristic that distinguishes human beings from all other species is that we knowingly, and often without legitimate reason, cause each other to suffer (Flanigan, 1992). We lie, cheat, rape, pummel, betray, humiliate, and abandon each other (Flanigan, 1992). What is even more peculiar is that we most often do these things not to our enemies, but to the people whom we love and who are closest to us (Flanigan, 1992).

Surprisingly, the worst kinds of unforgivable physical and emotional wounds occur not on a battlefield of war, but are perpetrated by those whom we know and deem to be important. As a result, what usually follows is utter destruction. Hearts are broken, trust is betrayed, and relationship intimacy is destroyed—sometimes irrevocably.

Superficial slights are not important or deep enough to necessitate the process of forgiveness. Hurt that is deep enough to require forgiveness always includes the following three components:

1. It is personal,
2. It is unfair, and
3. It is deep (Smedes, 1984).

No matter how hard you try, you cannot shake the memory of how much you were hurt, and you certainly do not wish the perpetrator well. This is the hurt that requires forgiveness.

Forgiveness and Your Physical Health

As the hurt and anger grow, they turn into bitterness. Bitterness can prove to be more detrimental than the original wound, as it destroys your soul and wreaks havoc on your physical body as well. It is not uncommon for bitterness and emotional anguish to manifest themselves in physical ailments. The greater the severity of the psychological pain, the more dangerous and the longer the physical maladies seem to last.

Dr. Guy Petitt has been teaching and working with individuals in Europe and the United States on the application of the forgiveness process. His website details the following connection between unforgiveness and your physical body:

"Physically the body responds as it does to stress. Muscles tighten, causing imbalances or pain in your neck, back and limbs. Blood flow to the joints is decreased, making it more difficult for the blood to remove wastes

S.E.C.R.E.T.S. VOLUME II by: *Pastor Shirley*

from the tissues and reducing the supply of oxygen and nutrients to the cells. Normal processes of repair and recovery from injury or arthritis are impaired. Clenching of the jaws contributes to problems with teeth and jaw joints."

"Headaches are probable. Chronic pain may be worsened. Blood flow to the heart is constricted. Digestion is impaired. Breathing is restricted. The immune system functions less well, increasing vulnerability to infections. Injuries and accidents through inattention are more likely."

Most likely, the person who hurt you isn't racked with physical maladies, so why should you allow physical ailments to disrupt your life? The following is a list of ailments that could result from stubbornly holding onto anger, bitterness, and hate:

- Menstrual irregularities/difficulties
- Reduced immunity to infection: increased occurrences of cold and flu
- Poor concentration, forgetfulness
- Fatigue
- Feelings of worthlessness
- Stress headaches
- Increased allergies
- Indigestion, colitis, irritable bowel syndrome
- Hair loss
- Weight fluctuations
- Migraine headaches
- High blood pressure
- Peptic ulcers
- Heart palpitations
- Loss of sleep
- Irritability
- Mood swings, bursts of anger
- Spontaneous crying
- Indecisiveness
- Panic attacks, anxiety
- Clinical depression, suicidal thoughts
- Feelings of insecurity, being out of control

- Nightmares and obsessive thinking about the offender
- Shame, embarrassment, and guilt
- Self-destructive habits such as substance and alcohol abuse

Willfully holding a grudge against another person also has disastrous effects on your soul. It opens the door to evil and leaves you vulnerable to thoughts of murder (Arnold, 1997). More importantly, it also renders your prayers *powerless*. You can pray all day, but if you harbor a grudge, the door to God will remain closed. Jesus knew that the result of bitterness and unforgiveness is nothing short of the utter erosion of your soul, which is why He commands us in St. Matthew to settle our differences with others before we pray.

St. Matthew 5:23-24 (KJV): *"Therefore if thou bring thy gift to the altar, and there rememberest that thy brother hath ought against thee; leave there thy gift before the altar, and go thy way; first be reconciled to thy brother, and then come and offer thy gift."*

What Is Forgiveness?

If you look up the word "forgiveness" in the dictionary or on the Internet, you will most likely find a basic definition similar to the following: "To grant a pardon, cease to feel resentment against or to refrain from imposing judgment or punishment" (Dictionary.com). However, this definition tells only a part of the story. Forgiveness is much more complex and involves much more than refraining from imposing judgment. Forgiveness is a commitment to a process of change. It can be extremely difficult and timely. Per Beverly Flanigan, author of *Forgiving the Unforgivable*, true forgiveness includes the following three choices:

1. Making the choice to excuse a person for a fault or an offense

2. Making the choice to sever the emotional bonds connecting you to the person who hurt you

3. Making the choice to look ahead, not back; to embrace your future and not hold on to the hurts of your past.

S.E.C.R.E.T.S. VOLUME II by: _Pastor Shirley_

It is important to understand that **forgiving is not forgetting!** Remembering is why you need to be healed in the first place. Once we have forgiven, however, we get a new freedom to forget. Even if it is easier to forget after we forgive, we should not make forgetting a test of our forgiving. The test of forgiving lies with healing the lingering pain of the past, not with forgetting that the past ever occurred. Forgetting after you have forgiven your offender is now a sign of emotional and spiritual health, not an excuse to avoid forgiveness.

Forgiveness is a journey. A journey is a process, and all too often, a rocky one. The process involved in the journey of forgiveness is seldom clear. Sometimes the destination seems obscure and the best way to get there seems impossible to determine. For many people, forgiveness is one of the hardest steps in emotional healing. Yet it is absolutely imperative!

It is amazing the vast number of people who are satisfied to go on resenting and hating people who wronged them. They stew in their own inner poisons and even contaminate those around them. Forgivers, on the other hand, are not content to be stuck in a dead-end, painful situation. They reject the possibility that the rest of their lives will be determined by the unjust, heinous acts of another person. Instead, people who forgive take action to reshape their lives into something free of past hurt and pain.

Unfortunately, most of us have not been taught specifically *how* to forgive. Often parents did not understand the process of forgiveness well enough to teach the concept to their children. Thus, we have generation after generation living in complete ignorance of the wonderful gift of forgiveness and how mastering it can change our lives forever (Flanigan, 1992).

But, *how* do you forgive? And, most importantly, **why is it necessary?** The act of forgiving, by itself, is a simple act; but since it generally takes place within a sea of tortuous emotions, it sometimes seems much more difficult than it really is. Before the process of forgiveness is explained, you must first understand *what forgiveness **is**, what it **isn't**, and **why it is so important** to your emotional and spiritual health.*

Understanding Forgiveness: What it is and What it is Not.

• You must *choose* to forgive. Forgiveness does *not* happen on its own.

• When you choose to forgive, you are utilizing the best mechanism for righting wrongs.

• Forgiveness does not mean you agree with the behavior, that the behavior is acceptable, or that you are giving your permission for the behavior to continue.

• Forgiveness does not deny responsibility or excuse bad behavior. You have simply removed the curse you've imposed upon yourself to punish the guilty party and you have removed your personal reaction to it.

• Forgiveness is not forgetting. You cannot forgive someone for something about which you have forgotten. This is not to say you don't recall events of the past; rather, you just choose not to dwell on them.

• Forgiveness does not allow or condone abuse in any form. You forgive the doer, not the action/behavior.

• Forgiveness is not something you do for someone else; rather, it is to *free yourself* from ongoing, relentless pain and anger. **It is for you!**

• Forgiveness is a gift to your peace of mind, your self-esteem, your relationship with God, your relationship with others, and your future.

• Forgiveness may not eliminate all your emotional pain. One can forgive and still grieve a loss or feel pain from an emotional wound.

• Forgiveness does not mean you can change or erase what happened. What's done is done.

• No matter how things appear, the person who wronged you is not "getting away." He/she will be accountable for his/her actions with or without your misery and suffering.

S.E.C.R.E.T.S. VOLUME II by: *Pastor Shirley*

• Forgiveness brings peace to your mind and spirit, which helps you to move forward in your life. The maltreatment no longer occupies your every waking thought, nor does it prompt obsessive behavior. You will finally be able to let go of your destructive feelings of resentment, bitterness, anger, pain, discouragement, etc.

Benefits of Forgiveness: Why it is so Important.

• You release yourself from the burdens and shackles of the past—hate, pain, anger, and loneliness, etc.—and in the process, you give yourself priceless gifts—peace of mind, mental stability, sefl-confidence, etc.

• You make the conscious decision to re-enter the flow of life and not to allow the wrongs done by others to control your feelings or actions.

• You begin to heal and effectively prevent the poison of unforgiveness from spreading its contagious tentacles to all areas of your life.

• You give the person whom you forgive the freedom to live in peace—even if that person is you.

• You choose to live in the present, look forward to the future, and put the past firmly behind you.

• You understand who is hurt by your refusal or inability to forgive. Does the other person burn with anger? Does he/she feel a knot in his/her stomach as he/she relives the hurtful events over and over again? Does he/she rehearse exactly what to say to hurt you? Does he/she plan mental scenarios involving burning your house to the ground? The answer is a RESOUNDING NO! The painful burden you carry around is all yours and rests squarely on your shoulders.

• You are performing a miracle that has no equal. Nothing else within the realm of human relationships can compare to forgiveness.

• You are being obedient to the word of God. St. Matthew 6:14-15, TNIV says, *"For if you forgive men when they sin against you, your heavenly Father will also forgive you. But if you do not forgive men their sins, your*

Father will not forgive your sins" Since no one is perfect, we all need forgiveness from God.

Goal of Forgiveness

The goal of forgiveness is to let go of hurt and move forward with your life. As long as you are unable to forgive, you voluntarily keep yourself chained to the person who hurt you. You give him/her rent-free space in your mind, emotional shackles on your heart, and the right to torment you in the wee hours of the night.

Think of it this way: Imagine the person who wronged you as having a fishing pole and you are snagged on his/her hook. His/her attention is captured by something else so he/she lays the pole down. Instead of swimming away and moving on with your life, you are still floundering in the dismal waters of the past and remain snagged on the hook. As long as you devote precious energy to resentment, hate, anger, and reliving the events over and over in your mind, you will be unable to get away and swim freely. You will be unable to live in the present and look forward to the future. FREE YOURSELF! Gently remove the hook that has kept you buried in the past and swim free. Move forward with your life.

In lieu of forgiveness, some people try positive thinking techniques. This discipline maintains that thinking more positively about yourself and your experiences will result in improving your relationships with others. This may help at first and it may even decrease your emotional pain. However, the underlying effects of your pain will continue to poison all areas of your life. Like a bad dream, the pain keeps resurfacing at the most inopportune times. Sometimes, it appears in disguise, i.e., in the form of misplaced anger or mistrust of others. Years after the incident occurred, some people fly into fits of anger and rage at the mere mention of the guilty party's name. Clearly, wrongs righted in the self do not right wrongs between others. They remain in silent places, waiting for the transaction of forgiveness and the tremendous relief that only forgiveness can bring.

The only person you can change is you, and it is foolish to believe that you can change another person. Once you change, others will change.

S.E.C.R.E.T.S. VOLUME II by: *Pastor Shirley*

change and grow. Forgiveness changes all areas of your life.

Taming Your Thoughts

This is perhaps the most important step in your quest for forgiveness. You cannot get to your ultimate goal of forgiveness unless you first master this step. One of the reasons you are tormented by your experience is because you relive the injury over and over in your mind. You cannot continually focus on horrible experiences and expect to move forward. The Bible says in Proverbs 23:7, **"For as he thinketh in his heart, so is he."** In other words, the things you focus on and think about the most, are the things that manifest and become a reality in your life. That's why Paul said in Philippians 4:8, **"Finally, brethren, whatsoever things are true, honest, just, pure, lovely, of good report; think on these things."**

In order for your life to be filled with love and light, you must focus on these things, not hurtful encounters. But how do you do this? How do you keep from focusing on the pain that is overwhelming your heart?

There is a technique I call "Flipping the Switch" that I have found to be extremely effective. When negative, hurtful thoughts threaten to overcome your mind, FLIP THE SWITCH and immediately begin thinking about something else. Do *not* dwell on the negativity threatening to invade your mind. Say, "No! I will not go down this road again!"

To make flipping the switch even more effective, have what I refer to as a "happy thought" on standby to be used at a moments notice. A happy thought is something that puts a smile on your face whenever you think about it. It can be the thought of your children, grandchildren, your pet, a relaxing walk on the beach, etc. Just make sure the thought works for you.

So when negative thoughts threaten to invade our mind, FLIP THE SWITCH and immediately think of your happy thought. You will have successfully kept yourself from dwelling on a negative encounter. You will have saved yourself from mental anguish. You will have save yourself from depressing moods and hate-filled wishes of harm.

Forgiveness

In the beginning, you may have to do this many times a day. But keep doing it! It works! The number of times you have to engage in this activity will decrease over time.

Question: *"I understand why I should forgive and all the great things that will happen in my life as a result. However, the offense hurt me so deeply and on so many levels, I just don't know how to forgive."*

Solution: Confess forgiveness daily using God's words, flip the switch, and use your happy thought when negativity threatens to invade your mental and emotional peace.

The following forgiveness verses are adapted from *The Weapons of Our Warfare: A Believer's Prayer Handbook, Volume Two* by Kenneth Scott. This wonderful book is comprised of prayers for specific situations USING THE WORDS OF GOD! For the entire prayer, please refer to page 106 of Scott's book:

"Father,
I come before Your throne of grace lifting up (insert offender name) _____ and asking for Your forgiveness for him. As Jesus hung on the cross, He had been unjustly beaten and abused by men; but yet He asked You to forgive them for what they had done. Father, I now walk in the way of Christ, and I also ask that You forgive (insert offender name) _____ for (insert offense) _____ and release him from this transgression against me. I pray for (insert offender name)_____ and ask that You show him the error of his ways concerning this offense."

The preceding prayer is filled with the words of God. His words cannot go out and return unless they have accomplished that which they were sent to do! If your bitterness is extreme, confess forgiveness five to six times a day. Confess forgiveness every morning and the last thing before you go to bed at night. Put a note on your bathroom mirror, your front door, and your car to remind you to forgive. Keep confessing it until your confession becomes reality. According to Romans 4:17, you are in essence confessing those things that are not (you are confessing forgiveness that you certainly do not feel) as though they are (as though the forgive-

S.E.C.R.E.T.S. VOLUME II by: *Pastor Shirley*

ness has already occurred).

The Bible says in St. Matthew 6:12, 14, 15 (KJV), *"And forgive us our debts, as we forgive our debtors. For if ye forgive men their trespasses, your heavenly Father will also forgive you: But if ye forgive not men their trespasses, neither will your Father forgive your trespasses."*

When you choose to hold on to unforgiveness, you hurt yourself, not the person who hurt you. Since it is also one of the major causes of illness today, forgiveness is a wonderful gift you give to yourself.

The New Forgiving You

A person who has succeeded in forgiving the unforgivable has undergone several transformations. Your outlook on life has changed. The person who hurt you no longer occupies your mind or poisons your heart.

You have changed:
From: A person who trusted someone
To: A person who trusts no one
Finally to: A person who may choose to trust again in the future if he/   she so desires

You have changed
From: A person who loves
To: A person who hates
Finally to: A person whose thoughts are no longer occupied by the person who hurt them.

You have changed
From: A person who does not want to change
To: A person who accepts he/she must change
Finally to: A person who depends on and consults God on the course of his/her change. In **Proverbs 3:6, *"In all thy ways, acknowledge Him, and He shall direct thy paths."*** You just cannot go wrong when God is the captain of your vessel!

You have changed
From: A person who focuses on the past, sometimes to the exclusion of everything else
To: A person lives in the present
Finally to: A person who looks to the future

Finally, you have changed
From: A person who feels equal in power
To: A person who feels powerless
Finally to: A person who feels empowered again

Some years ago, I read an interesting plaque on my professor's wall. It read, "It's not what you're eating, but what's eating you." Don't allow the actions of others to cause you to remain in a world filled with hatred, revenge, bitterness, and darkness.

People who've struggled to forgive and accomplished it realize no one enjoys pain, but they can experience it and overcome it. Once you realize this, you don't have to be caught in the clutches of unforgiveness ever again. Forgiveness means you've developed a whole new philosophy about people and nothing will be worth the hating ever again.

Move toward the light of forgiveness and regain your energy, vitality, health, and happiness. There is absolutely nothing too hard for Him. Unforgiveness will cause you to miss out on God's blessings and it can cause you to lose your soul.

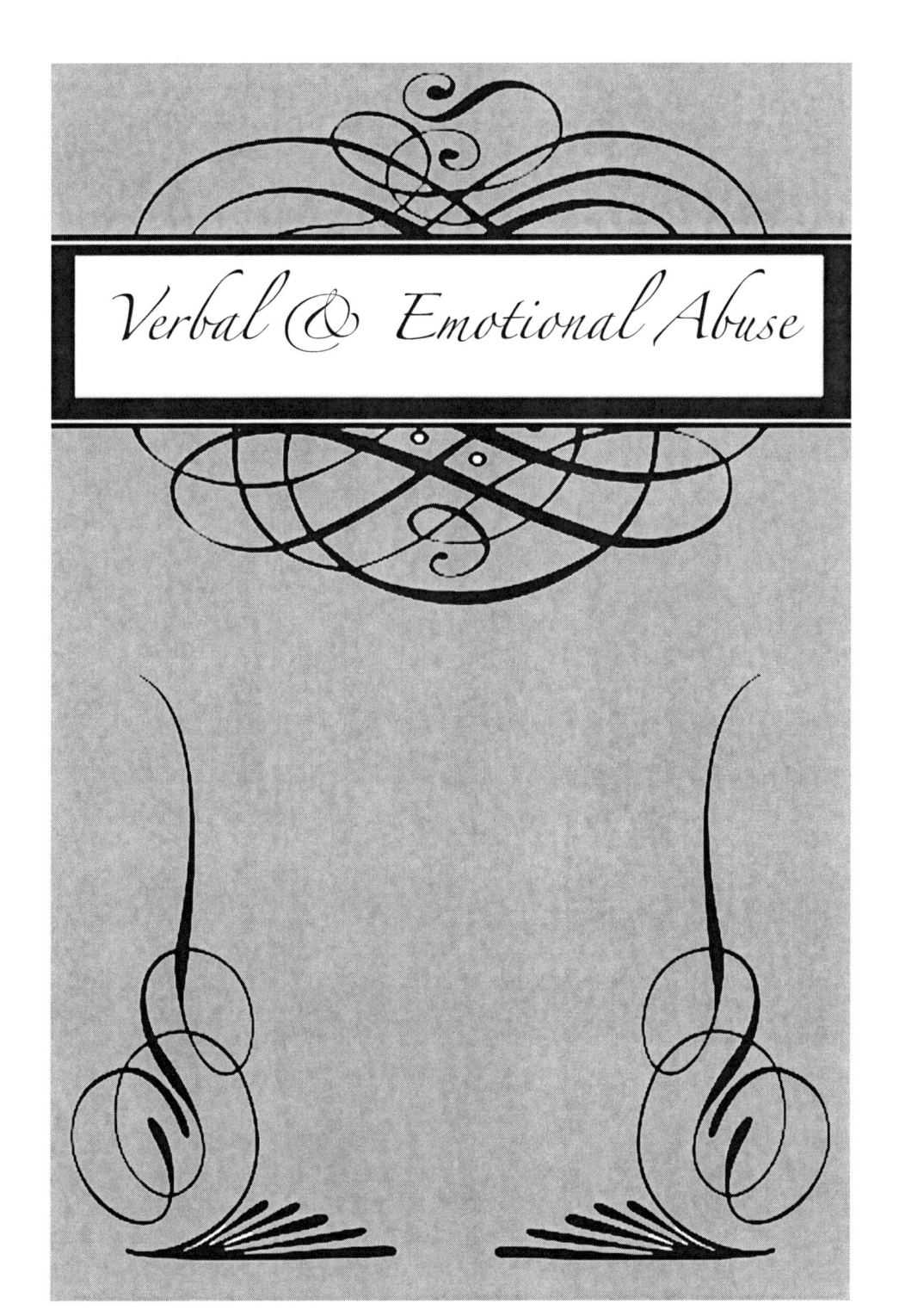

Verbal & Emotional Abuse

S.E.C.R.E.T.S. VOLUME II by: *Pastor Shirley*

VERBAL & EMOTIONAL ABUSE

*T*he family home is most often thought of as a haven, a place of safety from a brutal, frightening world. Unfortunately, this peaceful, comforting image is not a reality in many households. For many, home has become a private world of horror in which they are subjected to verbal and emotional abuse heaped on them by their family members. However, few persons in relationships experience as much persistent or varied abuse as married couples (Ketterman, 1992).

There are so many forms and nuances of verbal and emotional abuse, from the most cunningly clandestine to the blatantly direct, it is no wonder victims often have a difficult time recognizing and understanding what is really occurring in their relationships. Verbal and emotional abuse slowly destroys its victims day-by-day and word-by-word. It eats away at the very fabric of who he/she is. It is important to realize that a master at inflicting verbal/emotional abuse can damage your self-esteem while, at the same time, appear to care deeply for you.

Abuse within the confines of the familial unit is so rampant that most dismiss it as normal, having repeatedly witnessed it in their own homes as children. This sad fact perpetuates the vicious cycle of abuse and ushers it from one generation to the next.

Verbal and Emotional Abuse

There is a distinct difference between verbal and emotional abuse. However, since one usually accompanies the other, most people fail to realize that they are two different types of abuse and that both are extremely detrimental. Most people recognize name-calling as verbal abuse, but name-calling is just one of more than a dozen categories of verbal abuse. Uslegal.com defines verbal abuse is the use of words to cause harm to the person being spoken to. It is difficult to define and may take many forms. Similarly, the harm caused is often difficult to measure. The most commonly understood form is name-calling.

In the October 2011 issue of Ebony Magazine, Dr. Joyce Morley wrote an excellent article about emotional abuse entitled, "Walking on Eggshells." She describes emotional abuse as, *"A steady drizzle of cutting words, sharp tones, caustic criticisms or callous indifference that can erode the mind, body and soul as surely as tiny "insignificant" raindrops can carve a riverbed into a canyon. The little dig. The put-down. The ugly mood. The poisonous look. The cold shoulder. The nasty name uttered in the heat of anger. But when these come from a person we care about, we are unlikely to acknowledge—even to ourselves--that they are forms of abuse."*

Patricia Evans, author of *The Verbally Abusive Relationship*, writes, "How many times have you heard children gleefully recite the following lyrical rhyme? 'Sticks and stones may break my bones, but names will never hurt me!' This is simply not true! Cruel names and demeaning labels can hurt us — profoundly!" Verbal and emotional abuse victims know that words do hurt and can be as damaging as physical blows are to the body.

Most people are aware that abuse takes place in the form of physical attacks, e.g., hitting, punching, kicking, slapping, twisting limbs, etc. However, just because an abuser does not physically hurt his/her victim does not mean that the behavior is not abusive nor does it mean the behavior is harmless. Verbal/emotional abuse most often accompanies physical abuse, which is easily identifiable. Discolored bruises and black eyes are difficult to hide and graphically illustrate the physical damage inflicted by the abuser. However, the injuries resulting from verbal and emotional

S.E.C.R.E.T.S. VOLUME II by: _Pastor Shirley_

abuse do not leave such easily recognizable physical evidence, making it much more difficult to detect. The psychological scars from verbal assaults can last for years and leave their victims unsure of themselves, unable to recognize their true value, their talents and sometimes unable to adapt to life's many challenges.

Victims of verbal/emotional abuse may experience physical ailments such as anxiety, stress, disrupted sleep and nightmares, heart palpitations, exhaustion, depression, skin breakouts, suicidal thoughts, violent thoughts, migraine headaches, irritable bowel syndrome, chest pains, hair loss, and high blood pressure.

At a crucial moment in one's life, and/or coming from an important, loved, or respected person, malicious words result in emotional damage and have the power to completely cripple a person for the rest of his/her life. The victim's self-esteem is severely impaired, often without him/her recognizing it. If the abuser constantly tells the victim that he/she is crazy, the victim begins to believe this and no longer trusts his/her own feelings, judgment, and perception. This effectively kills the victim from the inside out and results in enormous damage to his/her spirit, self-esteem, and soul.

According to Steve Hein's website, www.eqi.org, emotional abuse is defined as: "any abuse that is emotional rather than physical and is designed to control and subjugate another human being through the use of fear, humiliation, intimidation, guilt, coercion, manipulation, etc."

Emotional abuse is like brainwashing in that it systematically wears away the victim's self-confidence, sense of self-worth, and trust in his/her own perceptions, resulting in the loss of all sense of self and personal value (Hein, 2008). Emotional abuse can include anything from verbal attacks and constant criticism to more subtle tactics, such as repeated disapproval or even the refusal to ever be pleased.

Emotional abuse is so covert that many spouses don't even realize that they are being abused (Meyer, 2008). Most emotional abusers are so adept at using highly camouflaged techniques that you have to actually live

Verbal and Emotional Abuse

with one in order to witness the maltreatment. Emotional abuse cuts to the very core of the victim, creating scars that may be far deeper and more lasting than physical ones (Hein, 2008).

Whether it is done by constant berating and belittling, by intimidation, or under the guise of "guidance," "suggestions," or "advice," the results of emotional abuse are highly detrimental to the victim. The constant insults, insinuations, criticism, and accusations slowly eat away at the victim's self-esteem until he/she is incapable of judging the situation realistically (Hein, 2008). She has become so beaten down emotionally that she is convinced that she is worthless and blames herself for the abuse. Her self-esteem is so low that she clings to the abuser. She believes that she has nowhere else to go because the abuser has made her feel as if no one else could possibly want her. The victim constantly changes her behavior in order to keep her partner happy, naively assuming that the happier her partner, the less abuse (physical, emotional, verbal, etc.) she will have to endure (Meyer, 2008).

Whether violent actions occur physically, verbally, or emotionally, the cycle of violence is the same. According to Dr. Lenore Walker, author of The Battered Woman, the cycle of violence has three phases:

1. Tension Building

As "real life" sets in, tensions start to build. These tensions may be anything from a bad day to major life changes such as pregnancies or job loss. It's important to note that all relationships have periods of tension. Even in healthy relationships, the couple may disagree or argue, but both have equal power in the relationship. In abusive relationships, the abusers' need for power and control underlie anger. The tension continues to escalate. Survivors often describe feeling like they're "walking on eggshells" during this time.

2. Explosion

Ultimately, there is an explosion or battering incident. Abusers may hit, attack, verbally assault, threaten, or scream at their partners. Many people feel that battering incidents occur because the abusers are so angry or

S.E.C.R.E.T.S. VOLUME II by: _Pastor Shirley_

so drunk that they lose control of themselves. We hear comments such as, "If she'd had my dinner ready on time, I wouldn't have lost my temper," or "I was so out of it, I didn't know what I was doing." Actually, abusers take control when they batter; they take immediate control of the situation, their partner, their physical space, and usually the outcome of the situation. Domestic violence is a crime of power, domination, and manipulation—it is not a result of out-of-control passion!

3. Loving and Contrite

After the explosion comes the honeymoon, or loving and contrite stage. The batterer is frequently sorry, feels guilty, and is willing to do anything to make up. There may be flowers, gifts, dates, and romance as in the beginning of the relationship. The couple may even make love in an attempt to reestablish intimacy. The batterer will minimize the abuse and blame the victim for "making him/her become violent." The victim will be upset, hurt, and will feel guilty that somehow his/her actions may have caused the explosive incident. In most cases, the victim loves the abuser and wants to believe the confessions of love and that the abuse won't happen again. After a while, the loving and contrite stage fades, and the couple begins the cycle once more. The victim convinces him/herself that each incident is isolated and unrelated to the next.

However, this is untrue. There are only two facts of which the victim can be certain:

1. Without intervention, this cycle does not get better; it gets worse and becomes more frequent.

2. Without intervention, the abuse gets worse and the loving and contrite stage begins to change as the abuser becomes less apologetic. Eventually, the loving and contrite stage disappears entirely.

Verbal/emotional abuse has many forms and clandestine levels. The following list has been adapted from the article "All Abuse Hurts" by Brenda Branson of marriagemissions.com. If you are experiencing more than two or three of the following, you are most likely a victim of verbal/emotional abuse and should take a closer look at your relationship.

Verbal and Emotional Abuse

Types of Verbal/Emotional Abuse

- **Name Calling** – Mind games, belittling, shaming, extreme manipulation, coercion.

- **Economic Abuse** – Withholding money as punishment and making your partner beg for necessities; demanding that your partner relinquish rights to his/her own paycheck; requiring your partner to account for all money spent, down to the exact penny.

- **Spiritual Abuse** – Misuses scripture to keep partner "in line"; warped interpretation of submission and lack of understanding about husband's role in the home; using scripture to justify abusive and oppressive behavior.

- **Isolation** – Limits phone calls or visits to or from friends or family; listens in or "bugs" phone calls; restricts access to telephone, mail, car, and/or other people; monitors all incoming and outgoing mail; forbids partner to leave the house without permission.

- **Sexual Abuse** – Forces partner to have sex at any time or place the abuser desires; demands sexual acts that are uncomfortable or distasteful to the partner; physically abuses the partner's sexual organs; subjects the partner to pornography or bizarre sexual activities; degrades the partner's body.

- **Threats** – A classic form of verbal abuse in which the abuser manipulates his/her partner by bringing up the very thing of which he/she is most fearful. The abuser threatens his/her partner, stating that he/she will leave or end the relationship, commit suicide or harm someone else, take the children, spread lies about the partner, hurt or kill the partner or the partner's family/friends, ruin the partner financially, destroy personal property, kill family pets, and/or reveal secrets or confidential conversations.

- **Intimidation and Humiliation** – Suggesting that the partner is inferior or "less than"; cruel remarks about the partner's looks; ridiculing the partner's ideas; using gestures, angry looks, a loud voice, or cursing to control or cause fear; yelling and screaming. It can also include inappropriate humor masquerading as harmless banter designed to put the partner down. The "humorous" comments are not spoken in jest and serve to cut the victim to his/her very soul. This entails public criticism of appearance, parenting skills, housekeeping or cooking skills; pushing the partner's face into a bowl of food (or worse); forcing food or other objects into his/her mouth; and public showing of embarrassing photos, video clips, email, or personal correspondence. These condescending comments are often delivered with craftiness and skill. However, they all have the same effect of diminishing and demeaning the victim.

- **Violence to Pets or Property** - Throwing things, punching holes in walls, stomping on things thrown on the floor, pounding fists on doors or tables to generate fear, breaking doors or windows to get to the partner, destroying the partner's personal property or keepsakes, injuring or killing family pets.

- **Silent Treatment** - Refusing to communicate, using silence as a weapon to manipulate and increase fear. The abuser effectively denies the victim the opportunity to know his/her innermost feelings and to discuss and resolve relationship issues, in essence shutting the victim out completely.

- **Using the Children** - Manipulating children to get or give information, misuse or disrespect of visitation time, withholding child support, bribing children with gifts or activities to undermine the other parent's authority, blaming or putting down the other parent in front of the children, and using subtle manipulation to brainwash the child into believing that one parent is trying to prevent him/her from seeing the other.

- **Irrational Blaming** - Holding the victim responsible for everything that goes wrong, including problems with children, financial difficulties, car breakdowns, holiday stress, loss of promotion, loss of job, weight loss or gain, losing his/her temper, violent behavior, etc.

Verbal and Emotional Abuse

- **Macho Male Privilege** - Treating the children and spouse like property that can be easily disposed of; punishing the spouse when he/she disappoints; dictating orders and making all decisions; expecting everyone in the home to cater to his/her needs; threatening anyone who defies or questions his/her authority.

- **Power and Control** - Not allowing anyone to make decisions without the abuser's approval; monitoring food consumed, money spent, utilities used (heat, air, water), phone calls, mail, time spent outside the home; governing activities inside the home; ruling TV choices and volume; restricting right to decorate or organize home without permission, refusing to allow repairs or replacement of broken appliances/items; controlling clothing choices, hairstyles, the amount of makeup worn, if any; not allowing the spouse to express opinions or develop friendships; denying the spouse any free time to relax or recover from illness; leaving a daily list of demands with a warning attached for if they are not accomplished.

- **Blocking and Diverting** - This category of verbal abuse specifically controls interpersonal communication (communication between two or more people). The verbal abuser refuses to communicate and/or establishes what will and will not be discussed; withholds information; prevents any possibility of resolving conflicts; and decides when the conversation is finished. A marriage requires intimacy, and intimacy requires that both partners identify and try to understand the other's feelings. If one partner withholds information, finances, and feelings, etc., the marital bond weakens. The abuser who refuses to listen to his/her partner and denies his/her feelings and experiences leaves the victim isolated.

- **Stalking** - Following the victim to work, church, appointments, etc.; calling multiple times a day to check up on the spouse; spying, leaving messages on the car or under the door to let the victim know that he/she always has access to him/her; finding out about appointments with doctors, lawyers, or counselors and contacting them before the victim arrives to confirm the victim's appointment.

- **Countering** - This is very destructive to a relationship because it prevents the victim from knowing the abuser's innermost feelings. This is the preferred response of the verbal abuser who views the victim as an adversary. The verbal abuser will cut off the discussion in mid-sentence before the victim can finish his/her thought, thereby discounting and denying the reality and experiences of the victim. By doing so, the abuser not only withholds emotional support, but also thoroughly erodes the victim's confidence and determination.

Please remember that there is nothing that you can say or do to change another person. The other person must want to change and not everyone will be willing to do so. Also, you will most likely be met with intense denial. The abusers are not suffering in the way that their partners are and, therefore, are not as motivated to make changes to the relationship. It is important to understand that unless the abuser is willing to give up his/her denial, he/she cannot begin to change. If the abuser denies everything, is unwilling to discuss the relationship, and remains hostile, HE/SHE DOES NOT WANT TO CHANGE! If your mate is unable or unwilling to change, perhaps you should entertain the thought of ending the relationship.

Whatever you decide to do, get help. Professional therapy and support groups offer valuable information and advice. They can be extremely helpful in assisting you in the articulation of your limits and boundaries and more importantly, recognizing and cherishing your self-worth.

Selecting a Verbal/Emotional Abuse Therapist

Regarding selecting a therapist, Dr. Irene Matiatos, PhD, who is an abuse therapist, states the following on her website, drirene.com:

"When looking for a therapist, try to find one who is trained in abuse and battery, as this is a very specialized area. During the initial interview, ask the counselor if they have specific training or experience treating verbal abuse victims. Sometimes a well-intentioned therapist who has little or no familiarity with the field may think they can handle your case. They cannot! Verbal abuse issues are radically different from any in which they

Verbal and Emotional Abuse

have been trained. Ask this test question: Who is Patricia Evans? If they cannot tell you about her work, they do not understand verbal/emotional abuse."

Patricia Evans, author of The Verbally Abusive Relationship and several other books, was one of the first therapists to recognize verbal battery as a form of abuse. In her book, she outlines in detail verbal abuse in all its many forms and how best to respond to it. A therapist trained in verbal/emotional abuse would have studied her work and should, therefore, understand the many nuances of this type of abuse.

Your best referral for a verbal/emotional abuse counselor is through your local battered women's program. These groups can refer you to knowledgeable counselors who treat victims and abusers. You can also call your local police department or family court. Many localities have battery programs in place and may have good referral suggestions.

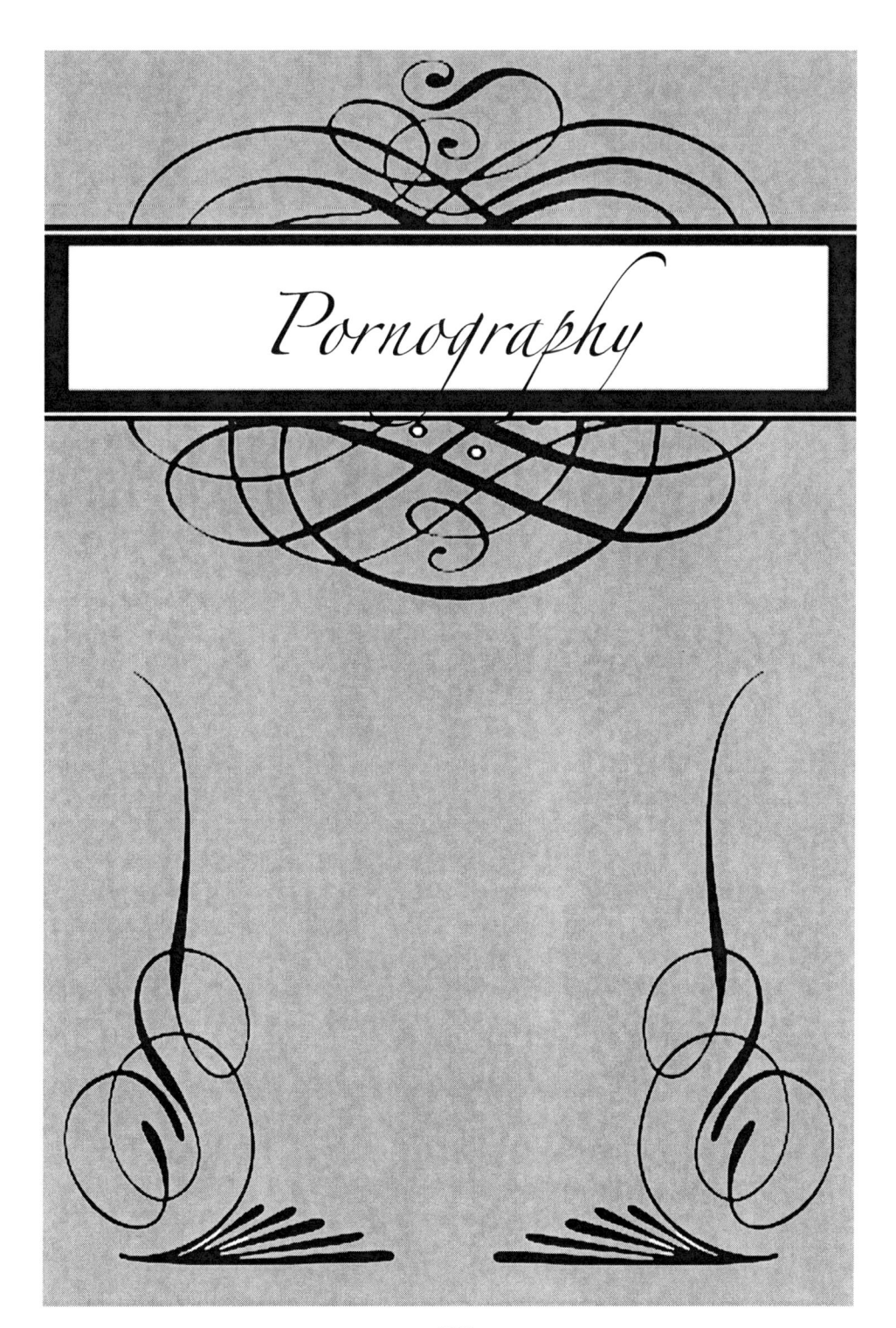

Pornography

S.E.C.R.E.T.S. VOLUME II by: *Pastor Shirley*

PORNOGRAPHY

*P*ornography has torn apart the very fabric of our society. Yet many people, especially Christians, are often uneducated about the dire consequences of engaging in pornography and the need to control it.

Pornography, once thought of as photos of nude women in seductive poses, has gone way beyond mere photographs. **Pornography**, the explicit representation of the human body with the goal of sexual arousal and/or sexual relief, includes explicit photographs, short stories, literature, sculptures, drawings, animation, cybersex, phone sex, sound recordings, film, video, and video games (Wikipedia, 2007). Therefore, **pornography addiction** can be described as a psychological compulsion and/or dependence that causes one to engage in a specific activity, despite harmful consequences to the person's health, mental state, professional responsibilities, or social life (Wikipedia, 2007). Pornography addiction is usually characterized by obsessive viewing, reading, and thinking about pornography to the detriment of other areas of one's life (Wikipedia, 2007).

Pornography

Online pornography addiction involves pornography obtained from the Internet.

Psychologists argue that online addiction is much stronger and much more addictive than ordinary pornography addiction because the Internet is widely available, customizable to the viewer's preferences, and provides privacy and anonymity that pornography obtained through other channels does not (Wikipedia, 2007).

The popularity of the Internet has brought many good things to our lives. But along with those good things, the Internet has also brought easy access to a thriving underworld that is seemingly filled with sexual gratification. Additionally, the emergence of the VCR and DVD has also drastically increased production, purchase, and access to pornographic material (Wikipedia, 2007). The wages of sin are astronomical when pornography is involved. Adult bookstores outnumber McDonald's restaurants in the United States by a margin of three to one (US Senate Judiciary Committee, 1984). Cyber/Internet porn, "900" phone sex lines, adult magazines, adult movies, and sex/strip clubs generate 12 billion in revenue a year in the United States and 57 billion worldwide (Ropelato, 2006).

What was once on the fringes of our society is now very much in the mainstream. No longer is it necessary to don a disguise, drive to the seediest section of town, circle the adult bookstore to ensure that you do not recognize anyone or any of the cars in the parking lot, and then dash inside to carefully select the pornographic images you desire while hoping that your car will not be stolen while you are making your purchase. The Internet has made such clandestine missions a thing of the past. It offers anonymity and easy, affordable access to porn within the privacy of your own home.

The Internet also offers specialized access allowing you to download only those images that are of interest to you rather than purchasing an entire DVD or magazine. Those who engage in downloading pornographic images say that the Internet is a less dangerous outlet for exploring different aspects of their sexuality as it protects them from rejection and diseases while allowing them to be sexually fulfilled without the encumbrances of maintaining a physical relationship. Though this reasoning may sound logical to some, sexual gratification via the use of pornography is an unfulfilling substitute for the real thing and the rationalization for refraining from building a healthy, meaningful relationship with a real, flesh-and-blood person is poor.

Anyone who must pursue sexual gratification under the veil of secrecy is a person who is in conflict. Such persons have been taught to believe one thing to be true, and yet their actions do not match up to this standard. Pornography addiction is a secret, and addiction to Internet pornography is an *extremely* dangerous secret. It usually begins innocently by viewing sites that may contain sexy images, but nothing that could be classified as pornography; such sites include personal home pages, sites that show models in lingerie, etc. Very quickly, however, these pictures no longer excite them and they begin to **crave** more extreme images. The need continues to grow at an alarming rate, requiring more and more images to provide stimulation.

Most people understand drug addiction or alcohol addiction, both of which involve the use of a behavior-altering substance. However, when the addiction does not involve such substances, as is the case with addiction to pornography, and is driven by internal thoughts, fantasies, or actions, many people doubt if an addiction really exists. Unfortunately, the addiction is real, has adverse effects on the user's life and relationships, and is difficult, though not impossible, to control. A study by Stanford and Duquesne Universities revealed that at least 200,000 Americans are hopelessly addicted to Internet pornography (Koerner, 2000). This number is grossly understated as many people suffer their addiction in silence and shame.

Pornography addiction triggers some of the same bodily reactions as substance/alcohol abuse. According to psychologist, J. L. McGaugh,

"The human body is a fascinating specimen. In anticipation of certain events, it prepares itself in a number of ways. The stomach secretes gastric juices in anticipation of a meal and it feeds the muscles adrenalin

Pornography

in anticipation of an athletic event or in the case of nervousness. In the same way the body secrets hormones, pornography stimulates the body to release powerful stimulants, hormones, and chemicals into the bloodstream. Emotional/sexual arousal causes the release of epinephrine in the brain that chemically burns the pictures into your permanent memory. This enables those airbrushed and digitally enhanced pictures to remain with you through adolescence and adulthood, and emerge at the most inopportune times.

The use of pornography causes stimulants to rush through the bloodstream like a rushing wind. In its wake, it leaves a great feeling of excitement, power, sexual arousal, etc. Please understand, **by merely thinking about pornography**, *the body begins gearing up for the event by flooding the bloodstream with hormonal stimulants which produce compelling, chemically-driven urges."*

The use of pornography causes stimulants to rush through the bloodstream like a raging fire. In its wake, it leaves a great feeling of excitement, power, sexual arousal, etc. Please understand, by **merely thinking about pornography,** the body begins gearing up for the event by flooding the bloodstream with hormonal stimulants which produce compelling, chemically-driven urges."

Christ said in St. Matthew 5:27-28 NIV, *"You have heard that it was said, you shall not commit adultery. But I tell you that anyone who looks at a woman lustfully has already committed adultery with her in his heart."*

When the pleasurable, stimulant-induced feelings become linked to the use of pornography, what began as a pleasurable experience immediately becomes a full-out addiction. The use of pornography elicits some of the same addictive internal surges as cocaine and is, in fact, sometimes referred to as the "crack cocaine of the internet." Sexual arousal is considerably intensified when viewing pornography and like any "high," your body will crave another "hit." The result is a harrowing cycle of addiction, escalation, and shame. Pictures of women in lingerie will soon become uninteresting, full nudity follows, and then photos of sexual acts. When

S.E.C.R.E.T.S. VOLUME II by: *Pastor Shirley*

these are no longer of any interest, intense photos that once sickened the user become stimulating. Dr. Victor Cline of the University of Utah describes the stages and pattern of pornography addiction as follows:

> **Addiction** - You keep coming back to pornography. It becomes a regular part of your life. You're hooked and can't quit, though in most cases you don't admit it yet.
>
> **Escalation** - You start to look for more graphic pornography. You start viewing pornography that disgusted you earlier, but is now enticing to you.
>
> **Desensitization** - You begin feeling numb towards the images you see. Even the most graphic pornography is no longer arousing. You become desperate to feel the same thrill again, but you can't find it. Your physical relationships suffer greatly.
>
> **Acting out sexually** - You make a critical jump and start acting out the images you have seen and rehearsed in your mind.

Are You Engaging in Addictive Behaviors?

Steve Earll is a licensed professional counselor as well as a licensed addictions counselor who runs a private practice in Colorado Springs, Colorado. He has conducted training with therapists, educators, and churches regarding addictions and family trauma in the United States, Canada, Europe, and the Middle East.

According to Earll, all addictions have common elements. The following steps have been adapted from his article entitled, "Signs of Trouble."_

1. Fantasy

All addictions and compulsive behaviors involve fantasy. If the addiction does not provide relief and escape from life's everyday pressures, it's not worth doing. We have already discussed how a mere thought (fantasizing) causes stimulating hormones to course through the body in anticipa-

Pornography

tion of an event. This feeling creates excitement, which, in turn, often triggers an addictive episode.

St. James 1:13-15 (TNIV), *"When tempted, no one should say, 'God is tempting me.' For God cannot be tempted by evil, nor does he tempt anyone; but each of you is tempted when you are dragged away by your own evil desire and enticed. Then, after desire has conceived, it gives birth to sin; and sin, when it is full-grown, gives birth to death."*

People are trapped by their own desires and fantasies, which stimulate the need to act out the addictive behavior. When the fantasy is encouraged, it soon takes on a life of its own. What people focus on or constantly think about, their mind and body begin to treat as real. The power of fantasy is the enduring power of addiction!

2. Euphoric Feelings
When a person engages in an addictive behavior, his or her feelings are altered. Life's stresses are temporarily relieved and the user feels happy, euphoric feelings. For a time, life actually feels better. This change in reality is guaranteed for as long as the user engages in the addictive behavior. It can be counted on to provide relief, unlike other friendships and relationships. Quickly, the addiction becomes the strongest relationship in the user's life.

3. Progressive Involvement
Undoubtedly, addictive behaviors are progressive. What initially provided euphoric feelings quickly ceases to do so. The user must use increased quantities, harder substances, or seek more intense images in order to experience the initial high. What ensues is the constant manipulation of amounts of substances and behaviors in order to achieve new levels of euphoria. If one hour of Internet pornography is relaxing, then perhaps an all-night binge may provide more stress relief. The user is drawn into a vicious cycle of intense addictive behavior with less to show for it.

4. False Sense of Control
When normal, everyday stresses overwhelm persons who are engaged

S.E.C.R.E.T.S. VOLUME II by: *Pastor Shirley*

in addictive behaviors, they are fooled into believing that its continued use allows them to regain control over their lives. Addressing the cause of the stress isn't considered, nor is it an option. The users turn first and foremost to the addictive behavior for stress relief, euphoric feelings, and to regain control of a situation, feeling that nothing else can provide this solace.

Unfortunately, nothing could be further from the truth! The actuality of the matter is that addictive behaviors do NOT provide control for life stress. Instead, they are the primary cause of increased stress and chaos. Addictive behaviors are all encompassing. The degree to which the behavior negatively affects the other areas of the user's life indicates the depth of this individual's trouble with that addiction. Over time, it is clearly evident how the user's false hope of control spirals into a progressively out-of-control lifestyle.

Selecting a Therapist

S.E.C.R.E.T.S. VOLUME II by: *Pastor Shirley*

How To Select A Therapist

Dr. Karen Ellington, PSY.D
Family Therapist

*F*irst, it is critical to understand that seeing a therapist has nothing to do with being crazy. If you had a toothache, wouldn't you go to a dentist—a doctor trained in the care and maintenance of your teeth? If you were going to have a baby, would you not consult an OB/GYN doctor? *Of course you would!* Then why would going to someone trained to deal with the mind and behavioral changes be any different? Everyone has problems, and therapy is one avenue that can be used to deal with them. It involves talking privately to someone who has gone to school for many years to learn how to deal with psychological problems and provide successful treatment.

If you needed child care, you would interview numerous possible candidates, questioning each thoroughly in order to find the right person. You would want to find out as much as possible about the individual's skills, background, and references, as well as his/her character. You would also want someone with whom you feel comfortable; after all, this person will be taking care of your children.

Why would you do any less when looking for a competent therapist to assist you? Often, people spend little, if any, time shopping around for a qualified therapist. Assessing the competency of a professional therapist is difficult when you are in pain and emotionally vulnerable. However, it is imperative that you do so.

Keep in mind that it is highly important to find a therapist who meets your specific personal requirements for the job. Therapy is a *collaborative* process, and it only works if you are comfortable telling your therapist everything that he/she needs to know to help you. Positive outcomes in counseling and psychotherapy can be substantial. But they are the result of informed decision-making and the selection of a counselor or therapist who best meets your needs.

Therapy (Also Known as Psychotherapy): What Is It Really?

Psychologists are not just people who give you advice. They are highly trained professionals with expertise in the areas of human behavior, mental health assessment, diagnosis and treatment, and behavior change. Psychotherapists work with patients to change their feelings and attitudes and to help them to develop healthier, more effective patterns of behavior (Ainsworth, 2007).

Psychotherapy is a specialized technique, which is highly effective in helping you to cope with a wide range of difficulties and can produce lasting changes in your life (Ainsworth, 2007). Psychotherapists apply scientifically validated procedures to help people to change their thoughts, emotions, and behaviors. Psychotherapy is a collaborative effort between an individual and a psychotherapist. It provides a supportive environment in which to talk openly and confidentially about concerns and feelings.

Again, the foundation of psychotherapy is the *relationship* that you establish with the therapist. During your sessions, you will intentionally make yourself deeply vulnerable to another human being, which can be extremely frightening. But you must realize that it is this process of self-revelation and trust building that puts you on the journey to recovery and

S.E.C.R.E.T.S. VOLUME II by: _Pastor Shirley_

healing. As therapy progresses and trust is established, you will actually use the relationship between you and your therapist as a workspace to resolve problems in your life. At the end of this frightening and difficult path lies inner peace, healing, and wholeness (American Psychological Association, 2007).

Where Do I Find a Good Therapist?
Finding a good, qualified therapist may take a little bit of digging. If you're not at all sure where to begin, there are a number of places from which you can obtain referrals. A referral is when someone recommends a specific therapist, and this recommendation is usually based on personal experience. Some of the most common places from which you can obtain referrals include: Your primary care doctor

- Local clergy
- State psychological organizations
- Friends / Family members
- Local police station
- College/university clinics
- Hospitals
- The Internet
- Community mental health centers

What Type of Credentials/Licenses Should I Look For?
Many people mistakenly assume that if a person has several letters behind his/her name, an advanced degree, and a license, he/she is qualified (Fishbein, 2007). This is not the case. Anyone who wants to call him/herself a therapist or counselor may do so without training or licensure. However, psychiatrist and psychologist are titles protected by state law and these individuals require a license and several years of graduate education.

Also, the letters after a therapist's name cannot reliably be used as a rating system to distinguish between a good therapist and an incompetent one as some are licensed, some are certified, and still others are registered, with each group believing its credentials to be the best (Fishbein, 2007). But an academic degree and even a government license are no guarantee that a particular therapist is qualified and will be successful in assisting you.

Selecting a Therapist

Therapy is as much about expertise as it is about scientific methods and, as a result, a degree of talent is required. Additionally, you want a therapist who possesses human qualities such as compassion, empathy, character, and a non-judgmental attitude (Fishbein, 2004).

There are, however, several basic types of mental health professionals about which you should be aware. They are as follows:

- **Psychiatrists** are medical doctors who have completed medical school and a residency in psychiatry. The distinguishing characteristic of psychiatrists is that they can prescribe medication and have M.D. after their name.

- **Psychologists** have a doctorate in psychology, are licensed to practice in their state, and they have Ph.D., Psy.D., or Ed.D. after their name. They cannot write prescriptions but they can explain why you may need particular medication and they work with you to address the issues in your life. Per the American Psychological Association, psychologists have an average of 7.2 years of education and training beyond their undergraduate education. After graduation from college, psychologists spend an average of seven years in graduate education training and research before receiving a doctoral degree. As part of their professional training, they must complete a supervised clinical internship in a hospital or organized health setting and at least one year of post-doctoral supervised experience before they can practice independently in any health care arena. It's this combination of doctoral-level training and a clinical internship that distinguishes psychologists from many other mental health care providers. Because of their doctorate in psychology, they get to be called doctors. However, the big difference between them and psychiatrists is that psychiatrists went to medical school, while psychologists went to graduate school and received a degree in psychology.

- **Licensed clinical social workers** have generally completed a two-year Master's degree in social work, have some amount of supervised clinical training, and are licensed in their state. Social workers tend to work with family problems such as domestic abuse or kids in foster care. They are given titles such as L.C.S.W., A.C.S.W., or C.S.W.

S.E.C.R.E.T.S. VOLUME II by: *Pastor Shirley*

- **Family therapists and psychiatric nurses** are other types of mental health professionals who may be specifically licensed to practice therapy.

According to John Fishbein, a competent therapist will have the following three qualifications. If you are contemplating a therapist who does not have all three, cross him/her off your list and find someone who does.

Competent therapists should have the following three qualifications:

1. Academic Study in the Mental Health Field

Talent and human characteristics are important; however, they are not enough. Specialized knowledge in the mental health field is essential!

2. Supervised Clinical Experience

A good therapist has completed an extensive training program. It may have been part of his/her academic degree or it may have been a separate postgraduate program. This is a very important step because some therapists have academic knowledge only and have never had actual training or practice in therapy. You cannot simply learn psychotherapy in a classroom or out of a book. You need the education to build a solid foundation; however, it is during a supervised residency that a therapist learns his/her trade. Think of it as on-the-job training.

3. Certification, Licensure, or Registration

After completion of a supervised residency, the therapist will be pronounced competent to practice by an authority to which he/she will be accountable. This authority could be a government licensing board or some other credentialing organization. Some of the common designations include: LCSW, CSW, MFT, LMFT, MFCC, AAPC, LPC, NCC, and NCPsyA.

After you have found a therapist who has the above-listed surface qualifications, you now need to go a little deeper. How well your counselor answers the following questions and how you feel in the process will help you to make the best decision. You must be satisfied with the goals and feel comfortable with the therapist.

The following is a list of questions that will help you to select the best counselor or psychotherapist. Before doing so, make sure you are comfortable with their answers and that you can trust them. If you do not feel this way, thank them for their time, and go to the next name on your list.

Education, Background, and Training

1. What is your education, training, and experience?
2. Are you licensed? What is your license?
3. Have you completed a supervised clinical residency? When? Where?
4. Who is your supervisor?
5. Are you a member of any professional organization(s)?
6. What are your qualifications to work with this type of problem?
7. When was the last time you successfully resolved a similar case? What was the resolution?
8. Have you ever had an ethical complaint filed by your state licensing board?
9. Do you consult with other professionals? Who are they and what is their specialty?

Method and Length of Therapy

1. What method of therapy do you practice?
2. Who will be involved in the sessions? Me alone? My family? Group sessions?
3. Do you prescribe medication for mental conditions?
4. How many weeks/months should counseling sessions for this issue take?
5. How will I know if I am benefiting from counseling? What do I do if I am not?

S.E.C.R.E.T.S. VOLUME II by: *Pastor Shirley*

   6. How will I know when it is time to end my counseling sessions?
   7. How will I know if you are the right person to work with me?

Availability

1. How often do you recommend seeing me initially? (Does this fit into your schedule?)
2. What hours are you available to see me?
3. What is your availability should I need to reschedule an appointment?
4. Are you reachable in the event of an emergency?
5. Does another licensed doctor cover for you when you are not available? If so, who is he/she and what are his/her qualifications?
6. How do you feel about phone contact between scheduled sessions should the need arise?

Fees

1. What is the cost per session? What is the estimated overall cost?
2. If I cannot attend a session, will I be billed for it?
3. Are you a qualified provider for third-party payment purposes (i.e., insurance reimbursement)?
4. Are you willing to wait for payment from my insurance company or must sessions be paid for immediately?
5. Is there a risk that my insurance company will restrict my treatment or terminate payment before my therapy is completed?

Miscellaneous

1. Can you provide me with a client reference? (Some clients offer to act as a reference following successful completion of treatment. Ethical therapists will not give your name as a reference without your permission.)
2. Do you have an informational handout or website that describes your services?

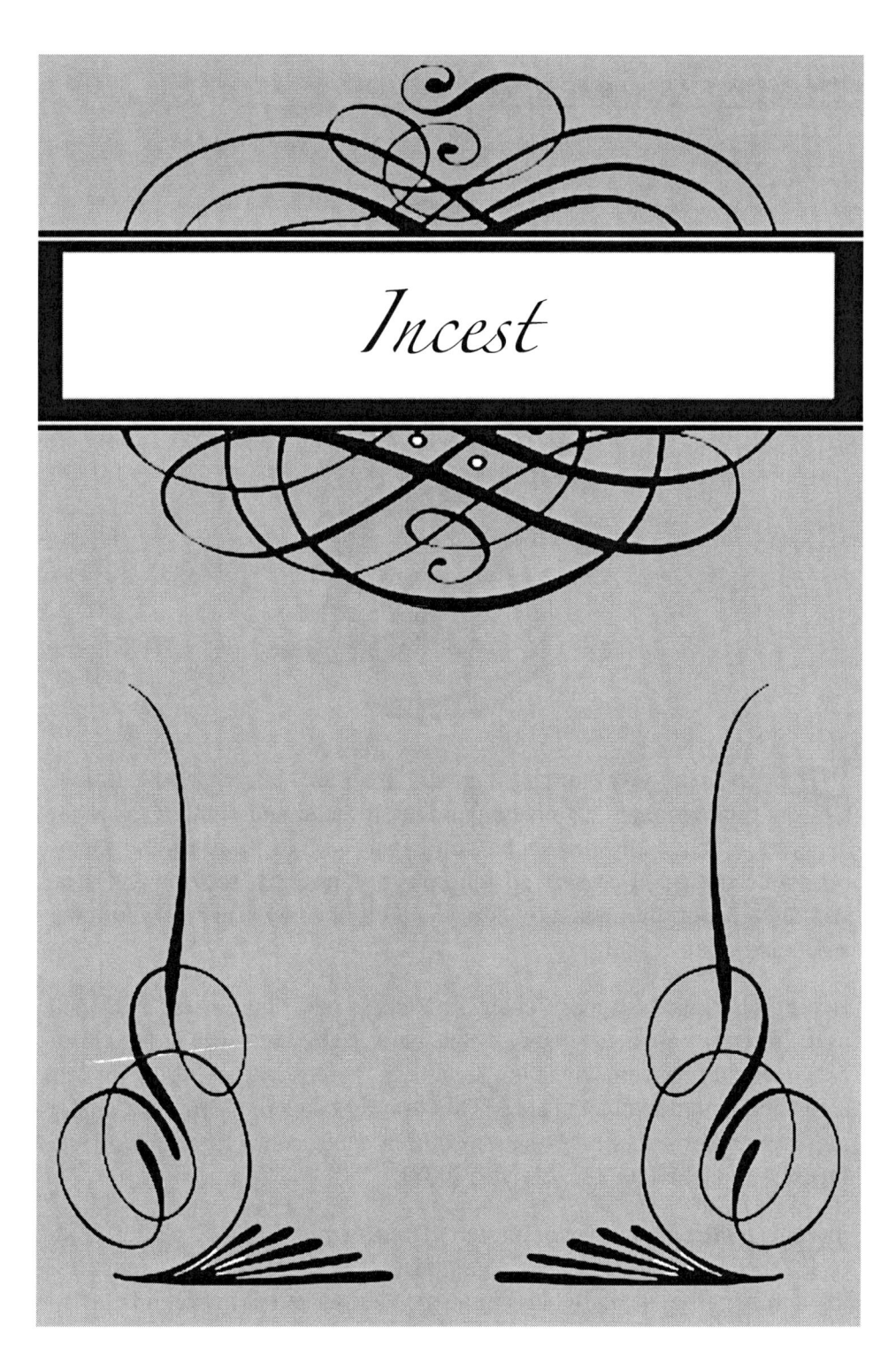

Incest

S.E.C.R.E.T.S. VOLUME II by: _Pastor Shirley_

INCEST

*T*he sad reality is that incest exists. It's real. It's common. It does not discriminate. It occurs among all racial and ethnic groups. It happens in financially privileged families as well as those of low socio-economic status. It crosses all religious and political sectors, and it is, without a doubt, devastatingly detrimental to the physical and emotional wellbeing of any child.

According to the National Center for Victims of Crime, incest is defined as the forced or coerced sexual contact between persons who are so closely related that their marriage is illegal (e.g., parents and children, uncles/aunts and nieces/nephews, etc.) This usually takes the form of an older family member sexually abusing a child or adolescent. (Rape, Abuse and Incest National Network, RAINN, 2008).

Incest can include, but is not limited to, oral-genital contact, genital, and/or anal penetration, "accidental" genital and bodily touching, sexual kissing and hugging, sexually staring at the victim, verbal invitations to en-

Incest

gage in sexual activity, reading of sexually explicit material to the victim (Caruso, 1987). It also includes exposure to inappropriate sexual activity, acts of seduction, implied or direct sexual threats, physical violence, sexual assaults and other forms of sexual victimization such as voyeurism, exhibitionism, and exposure to pornography (Vanderbilt, 1992). Unfortunately, the abuse of children is rarely limited to only one of these manifestations; rather, it often appears in varying combinations, durations, and intensities. What all forms have in common, however, is their devastating, long-term effects on the child (Lew, 1991).

Contrary to popular belief, victims of incest are not only female; they are boys and girls, infants and adolescents. Incest occurs between fathers and daughters, fathers and sons, mothers and daughters, and mothers and sons. Perpetrators of incest can also be aunts, uncles, cousins, nieces, nephews, stepparents, stepchildren, grandparents, and grandchildren. In addition, incest offenders can be persons without a direct blood or legal relationship to the victim, such as a parent's lover or housekeeper, etc., as this abuse takes place within the confines of the family and the home environment (Vanderbilt, 1992).

World-renowned psychologist Anna Salter has been studying sexual offenders and their victims for more than 20 years. Her extensive research and resulting book shocked America as it dispelled the myths surrounding sexual offenders, how they think, how they deceive their victims, and how they evade the law. Salter contends that molestation is seldom an unplanned crime of impulse; rather, predators use careful premeditation, meticulous planning, and sophisticated deception techniques to gain our trust and the trust of our children (Salter, 2003). Additionally, Salter maintains that one in four girls and one in six boys will have sexual contact with an adult. Even more alarming is the fact that fewer than 5% of sex offenders are ever apprehended. One man interviewed by Salter admitted to victimizing more than 1,000 children before he was incarcerated.

The statistics related to the sexual abuse of children are staggering. It is estimated that over 10 million Americans have been victims of incest.

S.E.C.R.E.T.S. VOLUME II by: *Pastor Shirley*

In 2000, the Child Welfare Information Gateway, formerly known as the National Clearinghouse on Child Abuse and Neglect, reported 879,000 substantiated cases of sexual abuse and maltreatment of children. Many more go unsubstantiated and unreported.

The Child Help website states that:

- 90% of all perpetrators are known to the victim.
- 1/3 of all abused children will later abuse their own children, continuing the horrible cycle of abuse.
- The rate of child abuse is estimated to be three times greater than is reported.
- In over 85% of the cases, the perpetrator is often a victim's parent or relative.
- The closer the relationship of the offender to the child, the less likely it is that the child will report the incidents of abuse.
- According to the Child Molestation and Prevention Institute, it is estimated that at least two out of every ten girls and one out of every ten boys are sexually abused by the end of their 13th year.

Incest remains an extremely under reported crime. Because the child experiences such an appalling existence, one wonders why he/she doesn't immediately tell someone of the abuse. There are many reasons that incest victims are afraid to disclose their harrowing experiences. Boys are extremely hesitant to disclose incest victimization because of the sexual details and their fear that it may indicate homosexuality and/or weakness, which would result in negative social stigmatization (Vanderbilt, 1992).

All too often, incest victims fear that they will not be believed and or will be blamed if they report the abuse. Unfortunately, this fear is supported by the deeply ingrained cultural belief that children lie about sexual abuse. Therefore, children who gather the large amount of courage it takes to report their abuse will most likely have their allegations dismissed as childish fantasies or outright prevarication. Others will be blamed for the abuse.

Incest

Male and female victims of incest are extremely reluctant to divulge sexual abuse because their abuser is usually a person in a position of trust and authority. Pressure from family members and threats or pressure from the abuser result in extreme reluctance to reveal abuse and to subsequently obtain help (Matsakis, 1991). Sometimes the incest victim does not understand—or denies—that anything is wrong with the behavior that he/she is encountering (Vanderbilt, 1992). Additionally, recent research indicates that some victims of incest may suffer from a form of trauma-induced amnesia. This condition is triggered by a severe traumatic situation, such as a sexual assault, which causes the body to undergo a number of complex neurological changes resulting in complete or partial amnesia. Thus, any immediate and/or latent memory of the incident(s) is repressed (Matsakis, 1991).

We foolishly continue to believe that abusive behavior by those closest to the child is less severe than that which is perpetrated by strangers. Without a doubt, the reverse is true (Lew, 1991). In the face of absolute parental authority, a child loses all "adult" rights—to privacy, independence, and even control over his/her body. When, however, the very individual who should be crucial to the healing process commits the injuries, where can the child turn? Theoretically, a child molested by a stranger can turn to his/her parents for comfort and assistance. A victim of incest does not have this option. The world as the child knows it is destroyed, leaving him/her trapped and isolated in the abuse.

Father-daughter incest is the most commonly reported sexual abuse among children. The success of incest perpetrators relies on the fact that parents have more power than children, who are completely dependent on their parents or guardians for survival. It is no accident that incest commonly occurs in a relationship in which the victims are most powerless.

It is understood that children need the unconditional love and protection of their parents for healthy emotional development and a happy, fulfilling childhood. Parents should not expect their children to fulfill their own needs for food, clothing, shelter, or sex. When a parent compels a child

S.E.C.R.E.T.S. VOLUME II by: *Pastor Shirley*

to work to support the family, that is exploitation of child labor (Herman 1981). When a parent compels a child to fulfill his/her sexual needs, that is incest (Herman 1981). When a parent forces his/her child to pay with his/her body for affection and care, which should be freely given, he/she destroys the protective bond between parent and child and initiates the child into prostitution (Herman 1981).

Contrary to popular belief, incest affects the entire family; even those members who may not be aware of the abuse. This is especially true considering that incest is a relationship between at least three persons—the two active participants and the other parent (Kosof, 1985).

The reality of the abuse and the stress of keeping a horrible secret alters the relationship that the abused child has with his/her family. It also violates the normal parental relationship between the child and *both* parents. The relationships between the abused child, the perpetrator, and the other family members become a source of anxiety and confusion. If a female child is involved in an incestuous relationship with her father, she no longer has an ordinary parent-child relationship with him. She has, in effect, become "his woman", his lover.

The child's relationship with her mother also suffers, as her mother becomes the wife of the man with whom she is having a sexual relationship—or the "other" woman, the rival. The child is forced into a role that any normal adult would find it difficult to navigate effectively. She is thrown into a bizarre love triangle without the support of the people who are closest to her—her parents. Because incest is secretive by nature, incest victims are forced to keep a heinous secret that most other children are not required to keep. Aside from the emotional devastation that the child is experiencing, she often realizes that her father would go to prison, the family would be split up, and their lives would change forever. The burden of this secret is so massive that even adults could not bear its oppressive weight without proper support.

Not surprisingly, most incest victims believe that their mother has betrayed them. After all, how could their mother know when they hadn't done their homework or sneaked a cookie from the pantry, yet not know that her husband was regularly having sex with her child under her own roof? The child becomes angry knowing that her mother did not shield her from her father, thus, making it easier for the father to intimidate and threaten her into silence and repeated sexual episodes (Kosof, 1985).

Incest victims' feelings of betrayal most often begin when their mother refuses to believe their account of the sexual abuse. Most people wonder why a mother chooses to believe her husband and not her child when the secret is finally broken. The truth of the matter is actually quite simple, though extremely sad; the mother has nothing to gain and everything to lose by siding with her child. Most mothers in this situation are dependent on and subservient to their husbands. They may also have a physical or emotional disability, which makes the prospect of supporting themselves and their children practically impossible.

Rather than risk her home and financial support, the mother in this situation chooses to defend her husband and keep her home intact. If this also includes the sexual sacrifice of her child, then so be it. The mother feels trapped and that she has no other choice but to agree by avidly defending her husband. Thoughts of supporting herself and her family, as well as images of social workers and lawyers suddenly fill her waking hours, resulting in the mother experiencing feelings of hate and anger toward both her husband and her child.

The first step in helping victims of incest is learning to recognize the symptoms of sexual abuse. Parents, grandparents, guardians, you should be aware of the signs noted below as these could indicate that your child is being or has been sexually molested. You should note that some of these behavioral changes may have other explanations; they may be due to causes other than sexual exploitation. These include medical, family, or school-related problems. Nevertheless, if you observe any of these behaviors, talk to your child about the causes.

Per the American Academy of Child and Adolescent Psychiatry, there are

S.E.C.R.E.T.S. VOLUME II by: *Pastor Shirley*

many signs of sexual abuse. Consider the possibility of sexual abuse if you notice any of the following:

Signs of Sexual Abuse:

- Difficulty walking or sitting

- A child forced to perform oral sex will complain of a persistent sore throat, unexplained gagging, and or have trouble swallowing.

- Recurrent urinary tract infections or yeast infections

- Blood in urine or stools

- Regression: an older child behaving like a younger child, such as bed-wetting, thumb sucking, baby talk, or clinging

- Sexual activities with toys, other children, or pets, such as simulating sex with dolls or asking other children or siblings to behave sexually

- Inserting objects into the vagina or rectum

- Demonstrating bizarre, sophisticated, or unusual sexual knowledge, behavior, or language far beyond the developmentally normal level

- Complaining of pain or itching while urinating or having a bowel movement

- Exhibiting symptoms of genital trauma or infections such as offensive odors emanating from genitalia; vaginal or penile bleeding or discharge; unexplained bruises; lacerations, redness, swelling, or symptoms of a sexually transmitted disease

Incest

- Torn, stained, or bloody underclothing

- Stomach illness with no identifiable reason

- Loss of appetite or trouble eating

- Sudden fear of a certain place or particular area of the house, like the babysitter's house, or the upstairs attic

- Sudden fearfulness or continuous protests by a child not wanting to be left alone with a specific person, whether parent, friend, relative, babysitter, or another child.

- Not wanting someone, including a parent, to change his/her diaper or give him/her a bath

- Waking up during the night screaming, sweating, hysterical, shaking with nightmares, trouble sleeping, fear of the dark, sleepwalking, and/or other sleep disturbances

- Drawing pictures depicting sexual activity

- Refusing to go to the house of a relative or friend for no apparent reason

- Preoccupation with sex in conversations and showing exaggerated interest in people's bodies

- Making unusual comments that only make sense in a sexual context

Duties

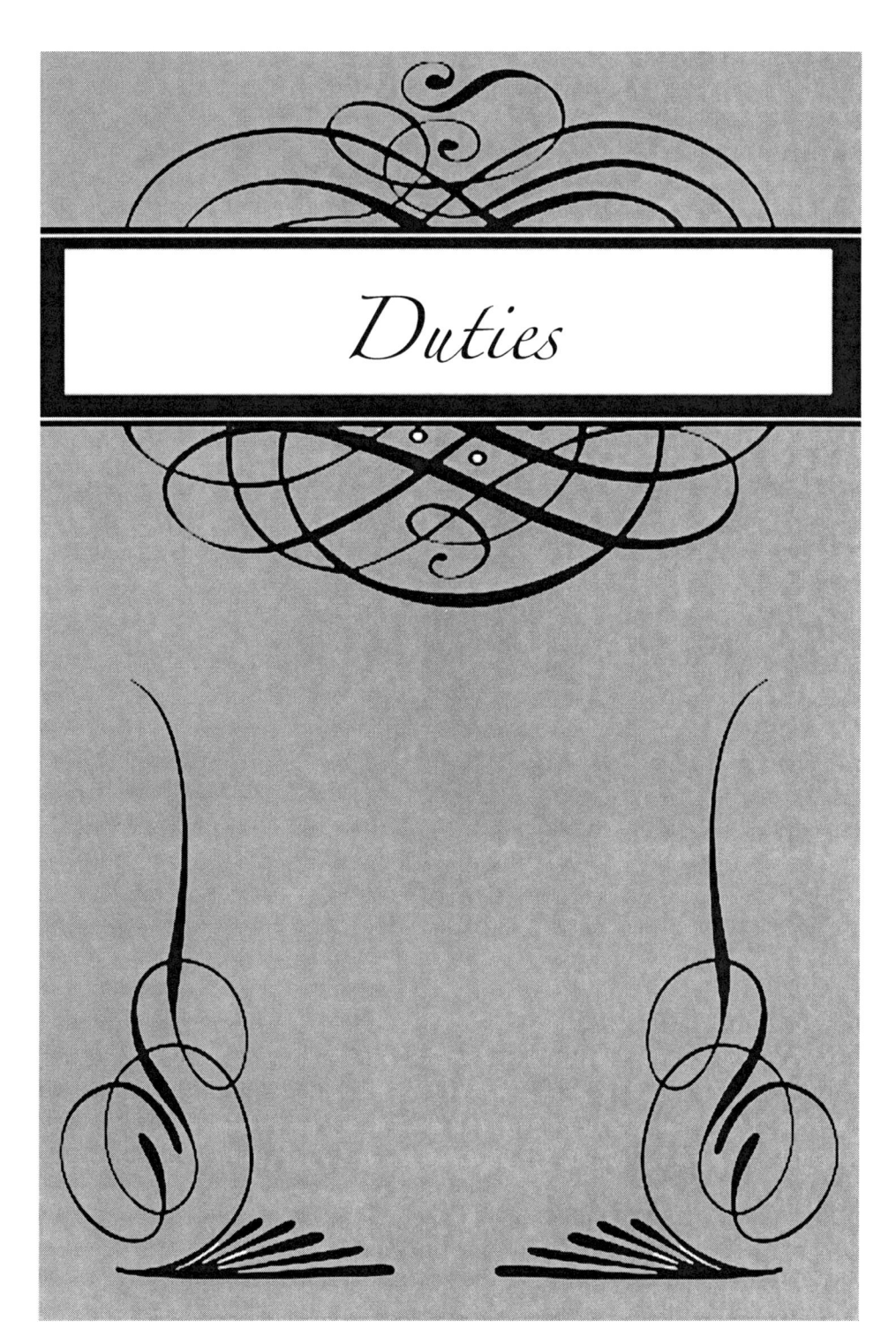

S.E.C.R.E.T.S. VOLUME II by: *Pastor Shirley*

Duties of a Wife

"Wives, submit yourselves unto your own husbands, as unto the Lord. For the husband is the head of the wife, even as Christ is the head of the church: and he is the saviour of the body. Therefore as the church is subject unto Christ, so let the wives be to their own husbands in every thing."

-Ephesians 5: 22-24, KJV

"The aged women likewise, that they be in behaviour as becometh holiness, not false accusers, not given to much wine, teachers of good things; That they may teach the young women to be sober, to love their husbands, to love their children, To be discreet, chaste, keepers at home, good, obedient to their own husbands, that the word of God be not blasphemed."

-Titus 5: 3-5, KJV

Duties of a Husband

"Therefore shall a man leave his father and his mother, and shall cleave unto his wife: and they shall be one flesh."
                              -Genesis 2: 24

"Husbands, in the same way be considerate as you live with your wives, and treat them with respect as the weaker partner and as heirs with you of the gracious gift of life, so that nothing will hinder your prayers."
                              -I Peter 3: 7 (NIV)

"Husbands, love your wives, even as Christ also loved the church, and gave himself for it;"
                              -Ephesians 5: 25

"So ought men to love their wives as their own bodies. He that loveth his wife loveth himself. For no man ever yet hated his own flesh; but nourisheth and cherisheth it, even as the Lord the church:"
                              -Ephesians 5: 28,29

S.E.C.R.E.T.S. VOLUME II by: _Pastor Shirley_

(Duties of a Husband, Continued)

"For this cause shall a man leave his father and mother, and shall be joined unto his wife, and they two shall be one flesh."
-Ephesians 5: 31

"Nevertheless let every one of you in particular so love his wife even as himself; and the wife see that she reverence her husband."
-Ephesians 5: 33

"Husbands, love your wives, and be not bitter against them."
-Colossians 3: 19

Duties of a Bishop, Pastor, Elder, Preacher, Apostle, and Deacon

"A bishop then must be blameless, the husband of one wife, vigilant, sober, of good behaviour, given to hospitality, apt to teach; Not given to wine, no striker, not greedy of filthy lucre; but patient, not a brawler, not covetous; One that ruleth well his own house, having his children in subjection with all gravity;"

"Likewise must the deacons be grave, not doubletongued, not given to much wine, not greedy of filthy lucre;"

-I Peter 5: 2-3

"Let the deacons be the husbands of one wife, ruling their children and their own houses well. For they that have used the office of a deacon well purchase to themselves a good degree, and great boldness in the faith which is in Christ Jesus."

-I Timothy 3: 2-4,8,12-13

S.E.C.R.E.T.S. VOLUME II by: _Pastor Shirley_

(Duties of a bishop, pastor, elder, preacher, apostle, deacon, Continued)

"Let the elders that rule well be counted worthy of double honour, especially they who labour in the word and doctrine."

I Timothy 5:17

"If any be blameless, the husband of one wife, having faithful children not accused of riot or unruly."

Titus 1:6

"Feed the flock of God which is among you, taking the oversight thereof, not by constraint, but willingly; not for filthy lucre, but of a ready mind; Neither as being lords over God's heritage, but being examples to the flock."

-I Peter 5: 2-3

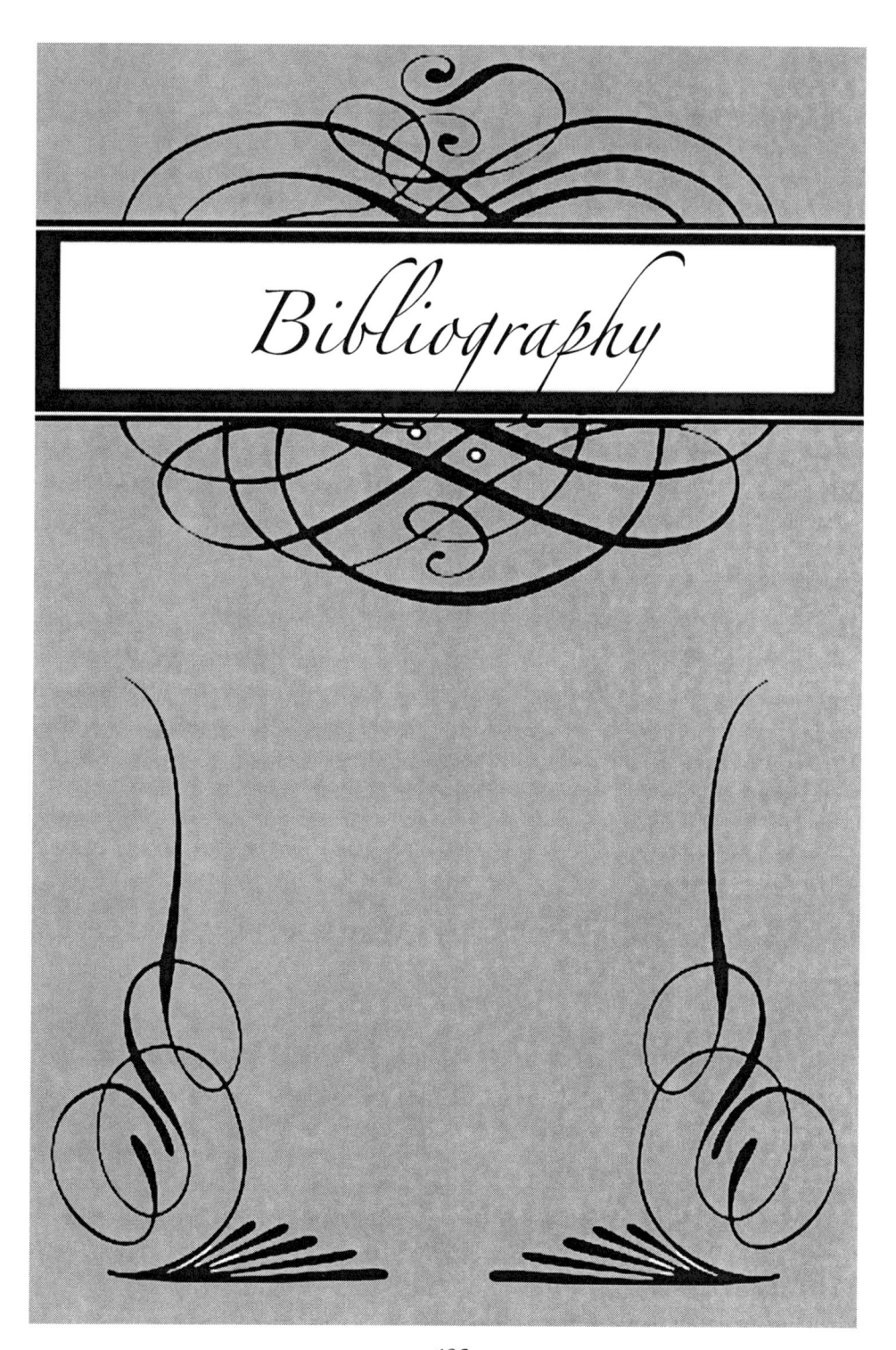

Bibliography

S.E.C.R.E.T.S. VOLUME II by: *Pastor Shirley*

Bibliography

Ainsworth, Maritza. "What is Psychotherapy?" www.metanoia.com. 30 Jan. 2007 <www.metanoia.com>.

Alcorn, Randy. "Finding Forgiveness for Your Sin." Eternal Perspective Ministries. <www.epm.org>.

Anderson, Kerby. "Responding to Verbal Abuse." 2001. Probe Ministries International. 07 Jan. 2008 <www.probe.org>.

"Are You Emotionally Abused?" 08 Jan. 2008 <www.womanabuseprevention.com>.

Arnold, Johann Christoph. Seventy Times Seven the Power of Forgiveness. Farmington, PA, USA: Plough Pub. House, 1997.

Bach, George Robert, and Ronald M. Deutsch. Stop! You're Driving Me Crazy. New York: Putnam, 1979.

Bancroft, Lundy. When Dad Hurts Mom Helping Your Children Heal the Wounds of Witnessing Abuse. New York: G.P. Putnam & Apos's Sons, 2004.

Bancroft, Lundy. Why Does He Do That? Inside the Minds of Angry and Controlling Men. New York: Putnam & Apos's Sons, 2002.

Bergan, Jacqueline Syrup, and Marie Schwan. Forgiveness a Guide for Prayer. Winona, MN: Saint Mary &Apos's P, 1985.

"Breaking Pornography Addition: a Plan for Personal Success." <http://www.no-porn.com/>.

Brody, Jane. "Cybersex Gives Birth to a Psychological Disorder." New York Times 16 May 2000.

Branson, Brenda. "All Abuse Hurts." Marriage Missions. 2004. <http://www.marriagemissions.com/troubled/abuse_hurts.php>.

Carnes, Patrick. In the Shadows of the Net Breaking Free of Compulsive Online Sexual Behavior. Center City, MN: Hazelden, 2001.

Caruso, Beverly. The Impact of Incest. Center City: Hazelden Education-

Bibliography

al Materials, 1987.

"Child Sexual Abuse." National Network for Child Care. 2003. American Academy of Child and Adolescent Psychiatry. 28 Jan. 2008 <www.nncc.org>.

Children's Bureau. U. S. Department of Health and Human Services. Child Maltreatment 2002. Washington, DC: U. S. Government Printing Office, 2004.

Cline, Dr. Victor B. "Pornography's Effect on Adults and Children." <www.moralityinmedia.org/pronsEffects/clineart.htm>.

De Young, Mary. The Sexual Victimization of Children. Jefferson, N.C: McFarland, 1982.

Dictionary .com, <www.dictionary.com>.

Earll, Steven. "Signs of Trouble: Five Criteria for Addiction Assessment." Pure Intimacy Ministries. <http://www.pureintimacy.org/gr/intimacy/understanding/a0000132.cfm>.

"Early Diagnosis and Effective Treatment." Child Molestation and Prevention Institute. Winter 2007 <http://www.childmolestationprevention.org/index.html>.

Effect of Pornography on Women and Children. U. S. Senate Judiciary Committee. Sub-committee on Juvenile Justice, 98th Congress, 2nd Session, 1984.

Elgin, Suzette Haden. You Can't Say That to Me! Stopping the Pain of Verbal Abuse : an 8-Step Program. New York: Wiley, 1995.

Ellis, Albert, and Marcia Grad Powers. The Secret of Overcoming Verbal Abuse: Getting Off the Emotional Roller Coaster and Regaining Control of Your Life. Hollywood, CA: Melvin Powers/Wilshire Book Co., 2000.

Ellis, Robert. "The Chemical Science of Pornography Addiction." American Family Association. <http://www.afa.net/pornography/addiction.asp>.

Engel, Beverly. Encouragements for the Emotionally Abused Woman. Chicago: Contemporary Books, 1993.

S.E.C.R.E.T.S. VOLUME II by: *Pastor Shirley*

Engel, Beverly. Healing Your Emotional Self a Powerful Program to Help You Raise Your Self-Esteem, Quiet Your Inner Critic, and Overcome Your Shame. Hoboken, N.J: J. Wiley, 2006.

Engel, Beverly. Loving Him Without Losing You How to Stop Disappearing and Start Being Yourself. New York: John Wiley, 2000.

Engel, Beverly. The Emotionally Abusive Relationship How to Stop Being Abused and How to Stop Abusing. Hoboken, N.J: John Wiley & Sons, 2002.

Evans, Patricia. Controlling People How to Recognize, Understand, and Deal with People Who Try to Control You. Avon, Mass: Adams Media Corp., 2002.

Evans, Patricia. The Verbally Abusive Relationship How to Recognize It and How to Respond. Expanded 2nd Ed. ed. Holbrook, Mass: Adams Media Corporation, 1996.

Evans, Patricia. Verbal Abuse Survivors Speak Out on Relationship and Recovery. Holbrook, Mass: Bob Adams, 1993.

Fishbein, John. "How to Select a Therapist." 30 Jan. 2007 <www.johnfishbein.com>.

Flanigan, Beverly. Forgiving the Unforgivable. New York: Maxwell Macmillan International, 1992.

Flowers, Ronald B. The Victimization and Exploitation of Women and Children a Study of Physical, Mental, and Sexual Maltreatment in the United States. Jefferson, N.C: McFarland & Co., 1994.

Forward, Susan. Men Who Hate Women & the Women Who Love Them. New York, NY: Bantam Audio, 1987.

Forward, Susan, and Donna Frazier. Emotional Blackmail When the People in Your Life Use Fear, Obligation, and Guilt to Manipulate You. 1st Ed. ed. New York, NY: HarperCollins, 1997.

Giarretto, Henry. Integrated Treatment of Child Sexual Abuse a Treatment and Training Manual. Palo Alto, CA: Science and Behavior Books, 1982.

Bibliography

Grosshandler, Janet. <u>Coping with Verbal Abuse</u>. New York, N.Y: Rosen Pub. Group, 1989

Hall, Laurie. <u>An Affair of the Mind One Woman's Courageous Battle to Salvage Her Family From the Devastation of Pornography</u>. Colorado Springs, CO: Focus on the Family, 1996.

Hein, Steve. "What is Emotional Abuse?", 15 Jan. 2008 <www.stevehein.com>.

Herman, Judith Lewis, and Lisa Hirschman. <u>Father-Daughter Incest</u>. Cambridge, Mass: Harvard UP, 1981.

"How to Choose a Psychotherapist." <u>American Psychological Association</u>. 30 Jan. 2008 <www.apa.org>.

"How Pornography Harms Children" Protect Kids. <wwww.protectkids.com/effects/harms.htm>.

"How to Select a Therapist." <u>www.psychohealthservices.com</u>. 30 Jan. 2008 <www.pscohealthservices.com>.

Howitt, Dennis. <u>Pedophiles and Sexual Offences Against Children</u>. New York: Wiley, 1995.

Hunter, Mic. <u>Abused Boys: The Neglected Victims of Sexual Abuse</u>. Lexington, Mass: Lexington Books, 1990.

James, Larry. "Forgiveness.. What's It for?" <u>Celebrate Love</u>. <www.celebratelove.com>.

Ketterman, Grace H. <u>Marriage First Things First</u>. Kansas City, Mo: Beacon Hill of Kansas City, 1995.

Ketterman, Grace H. <u>Real Solutions for Abuse-Proofing Your Child</u>. Ann Arbor, MI: Vine Books, 2001.

Ketterman, Grace H. <u>Verbal Abuse</u>. Ann Arbor, MI: Servant Publications, 1992.

Koerner, Brendan I. "A Lust for Profits." <u>U. S. News and World Report</u> 27 Mar. 2000.

Kosof, Anna. <u>Incest Families in Crisis</u>. New York: F. Watts, 1985.

S.E.C.R.E.T.S. VOLUME II by: *Pastor Shirley*

Layton, Julia. "How Brainwashing Works." How Stuff Works. 11 Feb. 2008 <www.howstuffworks.com>.

Lew, Mike. Victims No Longer: Men Recovering From Incest and Other Sexual Child Abuse. 1st Perennial Library Ed. ed. New York: Perennial Library, 1991.

Loring, Marti Tamm. Emotional Abuse. New York: Maxwell Macmillan International, 1994.

Matiatos, Irene. www.drirene.com. 07 Jan. 2008 <www.drirene.com>.

Matsakis, Aphrodite. When the Bough Breaks. Oakland, CA: New Harbinger Publications, 1991.

Mayer, Adele. Sexual Abuse: Causes, Consequences, and Treatment of Incestuous and Pedophilic Acts. Holmes Beach, FL: Learning Publications, 1985.

Means, Marsha. Living with Your Husband's Secret Wars. Grand Rapids, MI: F.H. Revell, 1999.

Meninger, William. The Process of Forgiveness. New York: Continuum, 1996.

Meyer, Cathy. "Are You a Victim of Emotional Abuse?" About.Com. 04 Jan. 2008 <www.about.com>.

McGaugh, J. L. "Preserving the Presence of the Past." American Psychologist Feb. 1983.

Morley, Joyce, Ed.D. "Walking on Eggshells." Ebony magazine, Oct. 2011

Mills, Linda G. Insult to Injury: Rethinking Our Responses to Intimate Abuse. Princeton, N.J: Princeton UP, 2003.

"National Child Abuse Statistics." Childhelp.Org. Fall 2007 <www.Childhelp.org/resources/statistics>.

Perkins, Bill. Fatal Attractions: Overcoming Our Secret Addictions. Eugene, Or: Harvest House, 1991.

"Pornography Addiction." <http://www.pureonline.com/porn-addiction-

Bibliography

information.cfm>.

Position Report on Drug Policy. Physician Leadership on National Drug Policy (PLNDP). Brown University Center for Alcohol and Addiction Studies, 2000.

Possible Signs of Sexual Abuse." Survivors and Friends. <www.survivors-and-friends.org>.

Pryor, Arly, Rev. "You Can Choose to Love." Black Women's Health. <www.blackwomenshealth.com>.

Pryor, Rev., Arly. "The Power of Forgiveness." Black Women's Health. <www.blackwomenshealth.com>.

Reimer, Kristi. "An Invaluable Journey." Science and Spirit. <www.science-spirit.org>.

Reinert, Dale Robert. Sexual Abuse and Incest. Springfield, NJ, USA: Enslow, 1997.

Ropelato, Jerry. "Internet Pornography Statistics." Top Ten Reviews. <http://internet-filter-review.toptenreviews.com/internet-pornography-statistics.html>., 2006.

Robinson, Diana. "The Top Ten Steps to Forgiveness." Coachville Training. <http://topten.org/content/tt.BE1.htm>.

Salter, Anna C. Predators Pedophiles, Rapists, and Other Sex Offenders : Who They are, How They Operate, and How We Can Protect Ourselves and Our Children. New York: Basic Books, 2003.

Salter, Anna C., Transforming Trauma: A Guide to Understanding and Treating Adult Survivors of Child Sexual Abuse. Thousand Oaks, CA: Sage, 1995.

Schell, David W. Daily Meditations to Open Your Heart to Forgiveness. St. Meinrad, IN: One Caring Place, 2000.

Scott, Kenneth. The Weapons of Our Warfare: a Believer's Prayer Handbook. Vol. 2. Birmingham: Spiritual Warfare Ministries, Inc, 2001.

Shank, Arlene Spoto. Pedophilia and Sex Behaviors Index of New Infor-

S.E.C.R.E.T.S. VOLUME II by: *Pastor Shirley*

mation. Washington, D.C: Abbe Association, 1995.

Smedes, Lewis B. Forgive and Forget: Healing the Hurts We Don't Deserve. 1st Ed. ed. San Francisco: Harper & Row, 1984.

Smedley, Kathy. "Signs of Sexual Abuse." Protect Kids. <www.protectkids.com>.

"Steps to Forgiveness." Worldwide Forgiveness Alliance. <www.forgivenessday.org>.

Steve Watters &, Ryan Hosley. "The Dangers and Disappointments of Pornography." Pure Intimacy Ministries. <http://www.pureintimacy.org/gr/intimacy/understanding/a0000133.cfm>.

Substance Abuse: the Nation's Number One Health Problem. Institute for Health Policy. 1993, 2000, & 2001: Brandeis University.

"Treatment Programs." The Watershed Addiction Treatment Programs. <http://www.thewatershed.com>.

"Treatment Works!" Ohio Dept. of Alcohol and Drug Addiction Services,. 1994. Comprehensive Assessment Treatment Outcomes Registry Data. Winter 2007 <http://www.daacinfo.org/treatment_works.html>.

"Treatment Works!" www.familydoctor.org. 1999. National Institute on Drug Abuse. Winter 2007 <http://www.daacinfo.org/treatment_works.html>.

Trimble, John F. Pedophilia. Torrance, Calif.: Monogram Publications, 1968.

Trimpey, Jack. Rational Recovery the New Cure for Substance Addiction. New York: Pocket Books, 1996

"Toxic Porn, Toxic Sex: a Real Look At Pornography." <http://everystudent.com/wires/toxic.html>.

unknown. "Symptoms of Emotional Abuse." Lilac Lane. <http://www.lilaclane.com/relationships/emotional-abuse>.

Vaknin, Sam. "The Gradations of Abuse." 01 Sept. 2003.

Vanderbilt, Heidi. "Incest: A Chilling Report." National Center for Victims of Crime and Crime Victims Research and Treatment Center. Arlington, 1992.

Walker, Lenore E. The Battered Woman. 1st Ed. ed. New York: Harper & Row, 1979

Ward, Elizabeth. Father-Daughter Rape. London: Women&Apos's P, 1984.

"Warning Signs About Child Sexual Abuse." Stop It Now. 03 Apr. 2005. <www.stopitnow.com>.

"The War Against Pornography." Newsweek 18 Mar. 1985.

Watters, Steve. "I Know What You Did Last Night." American Family Association. <http://www.afa.net/journal/march/pornd.asp>.

Wikipedia, <www.wikipedia.com>.

Wildmon-White, Lynn. "A Journey to Peace." www.afa.net/pornography/lw121202.asp

Wilson, Heather P. <www.forgivenessweb.com>.

Section 4

Book Club

Book Club Discussion Guide

S.E.C.R.E.T.S. VOLUME II by: _Pastor Shirley_

GENERAL QUESTIONS

1. When you hear the term "First Lady" what comes to mind?

2. With whom can a First Lady discuss her personal problems in confidence?

3. Which characters have religious beliefs that resonate with yours? In what way?

4. Are there any circumstances in the book to which you can personally relate? How so?

5. Is there any advice or ideas you can take and apply to your own life? How so?

6. Have you ever suspected someone was a victim of abuse, but did not address it? Why?

7. Regarding the forgiveness reference chapter, were you aware unforgiveness played such a major role in your physical and mental health?

8. What is your church's stance on homosexuality?

9. Would you remain a member of a church in which the pastor commits adultery and fathers children outside his marriage?

10. How do you feel about pastors that require their members to furnish their W-2 forms to ensure proper payment of tithes?

Book Club Discussion Guide

CHARACTER QUESTIONS

Viola Lucas and Sharon Baker-Lucas

11. At what point, if ever, did you suspect Viola might not be as passive as everyone thought?

12. Why was the ministry so important to Viola and her son, Richard Jr.?

13. Was Sharon's physical violence justified? Why?

14. Do you think Pastor Lucas knew the truth about Richard Jr? Why?

Rita Morgan

15. Why do you think Rita remained in such an abusive marriage?

16. Why didn't she stay with her sister and her husband or her parents?

Apostle Gina Miller

17. Before the story revealed Apostle Gina was a lesbian, were there any prior indications or hints in the story? If so, when?

18. How do you feel about loaning your pastor money or allowing him/her to use your credit cards?

Leta Byron and Mei Li Byron

19. When Leta slaps Mei Li, was this Christian behavior? Would you have done the same? Why?

20.

S.E.C.R.E.T.S. VOLUME II by: *Pastor Shirley*

21. When Leta refused to have anything to do with her husband's children with his mistress, is she penalizing the children for her husband's betrayal? How so?

Nettie Proctor

22. Do you consider it a sin for Christians to gamble? Why?

Sarah Wells

23. At what point should Sarah have suspected the sexual relationship between her husband and her adopted daughter?

24. Why do you think she did not confront the issue?

Summer Hamilton

25. Look at the facial expression on her sketch. What emotion does it convey to you?

26. Near the end of the story, Summer's husband misinterpreted her response of *"I wasn't looking at nothing"* to mean she was calling him nothing. Because her husband became angrier, she did not explain the mistake. Do you think she could have handled the situation differently? How?

Frances Murdock-Washington

27. Do you consider it a sin if Christians drink alcohol or smoke cigarettes? Why?

28. At what point should Frances have insisted her husband get help with his alcohol addiction?

29. What do you think will happen to their ministry?

Book Club Discussion Guide

Discussion Notes

S.E.C.R.E.T.S. VOLUME II by: _Pastor Shirley_

Discussion Notes

Book Club Discussion Guide

Discussion Notes

S.E.C.R.E.T.S. VOLUME II by: _Pastor Shirley_

Discussion Notes

Section 5

Contact

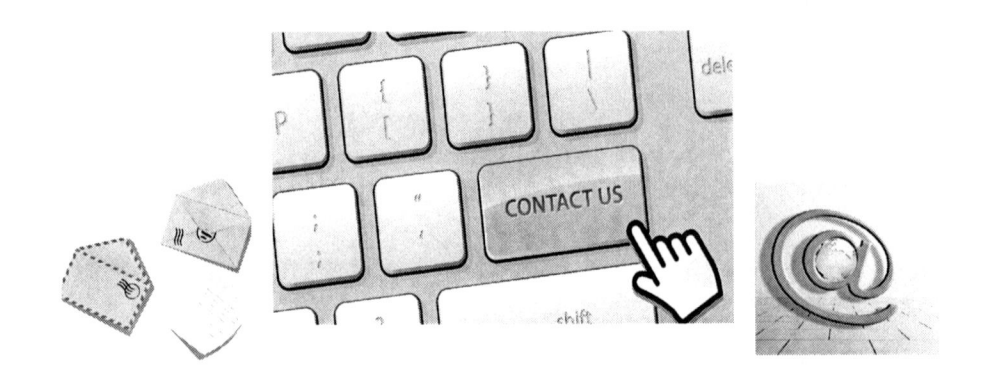

* To learn more about Pastor Shirley and the outreach ministries with which she is involved, please visit her website at:
www.pastorshirley.com

* To learn more about the amazing First Ladies and the S.E.C.R.E.T.S. they keep, please visit: *www.secretsofthefirstladies.com or www.sotfl.com*

* To send Pastor Shirley confidential prayer requests, please email to:
prayer@pastorshirley.com

* Follow us on twitter at: allthefirstladies
* Like us on Facebook at: SECRETS of the First Ladies
* To view video interviews for S.E.C.R.E.T.S. of The First Ladies, Volume I, visit us on Facebook.

* COMING SOON - Video Trailers for Volume I & II, See your favorite character story in all its video glory. Check Facebook regularly for details.

* To obtain volume discounts for purchasing multiple copies of Volume I, Volume II, or preordering Trilogy, please contact Von Gordon at (609) 877-0222 or via email at onlineorders@pastorshirley.com

* Availability: Nationwide by arrangement and via telephone.
For more information, please contact Von Gordon at (609) 877-0222

CPSIA information can be obtained at www.ICGtesting.com
Printed in the USA
BVOW072358261211

279086BV00002B/3/P